Jud. v Hobr.
P. v0

# A SOCIAL AND RELIGIOUS
# HISTORY OF THE JEWS

*Late Middle Ages and Era of European Expansion,*
*1200–1650*

## VOLUME IX
### UNDER CHURCH AND EMPIRE

# A SOCIAL
# AND RELIGIOUS
# HISTORY OF
# THE JEWS

By SALO WITTMAYER BARON

*Second Edition, Revised and Enlarged*

*Late Middle Ages and Era of European Expansion,*
*1200–1650*

VOLUME IX

UNDER CHURCH AND EMPIRE

Columbia University Press
*New York and London   1965*

The Jewish Publication Society of America
*Philadelphia   5726*

# PREFACE

I N CHOOSING THE PERIOD of 1200 to 1650 for the forthcoming
volumes, I am fully aware of the unorthodox nature of this
chronological division. All divisions of history into periods are
more or less arbitrary. Certainly Jewish life was not markedly
different in 1201 than it had been in 1199. However, in the
Preface to Volume III (where the methods of transliteration and
citing bibliographical references also are briefly discussed) I have
tried to explain how, because of the fateful shift of the center
of gravity of Jewish life and thought from Muslim to Christian
lands, the thirteenth century marked the beginning of a new
epoch in Jewish history. The leadership of Western Jewry has,
in fact, remained uncontested to the present day.

Equally clear, it seems to me, is the *terminus ad quem*. The
Jewish Emancipation era has often been dated from the formal
pronunciamentos of Jewish equality of rights by the French Revolution, or, somewhat more obliquely, by the American Constitution. However, departing from this purely legalistic approach, I
have long felt that the underlying more decisive socioeconomic
and cultural transformations accompanying the rise of modern
capitalism, the rapid growth of Western populations, the international migrations, the aftereffects of Humanism, the Reformation, and the progress of modern science, long antedated these
formal constitutional fiats. While such developments can never be
so precisely dated as legal enactments, treaties, wars, or biographies
of leading personalities, the mid-seventeenth century may indeed
be considered a major turning point in both world and Jewish
history. For our purposes it certainly may serve as the most con-
venient dividing line between the pre-Emancipation and the
Emancipation eras.

The Treaty of Westphalia of 1648, which terminated the Thirty
Years' War, proclaimed, on an international scale, the general
principle of liberty of conscience, however hazy and ill-defined.

Because the war had been fought to a deadlock, the statesmen assembled at Osnabrück and Münster came to the conclusion that no peace would endure in Central Europe unless Protestant states tolerated Catholics in their midst and Catholic states extended freedom of worship to Protestant subjects. Although not directly referring to Jews, this new approach toward mutual toleration of religious diversity opened up new vistas for equal treatment of Jewish subjects, too. Simultaneously, a new era was beginning for the Jewish people by its resettlement in Western Europe and the latter's colonial possessions. The small and struggling Jewish community in Holland now assumed international importance, and its major center in Amsterdam was not unjustly styled the "New Jerusalem." Foundations were also laid for the rise of new Jewish communities in France, England, and the Western Hemisphere.

At the same time the great eastern centers of Jewish life in Poland-Lithuania and the Ottoman Empire suffered sharp reverses. Decimated by Cossack and Ukrainian rebels, Polish Jewry never regained its former glory, in part because of the general decline of the Polish-Lithuanian "Republic." Similarly, the formerly expanding Ottoman Empire was gradually disintegrating; its decline would have affected Ottoman Jewry even if the latter had not been thrown into a state of confusion by the Shabbetian movement. While in the preceding several centuries the general Jewish migratory movements went from west to east, from England, France, and Spain to the Holy Roman Empire and Italy, and from there to Poland and the Middle East, these trends were now reversed. The years 1648–56 may indeed be considered the starting point for the large westward trek of Jewish migrants which was to culminate in the great East-European exodus overseas in the decades preceding the First World War.

Intellectually, too, the period of 1200–1650 represented the completion of the medieval Jewish codification and its final fruition in the *Shulḥan 'Arukh,* the Karo-Isserles Code, together with its major commentaries. The Kabbalah likewise celebrated its greatest victories in the thirteenth-century compilation of the *Zohar* and in the sixteenth-century school of Lurianic mysticism. By the mid-seventeenth century, on the other hand, the burgeoning new forces of Enlightenment and intellectual rapprochement with the Christian world produced not only a Spinoza and a Uriel da Costa but also the more intrinsically Jewish manifestations of the Italian, Dutch, and Berlin Haskalah. The period around 1650, which undoubtedly represented the nadir of Jewish population strength and to superficial observers seemed to presage an inevitable eclipse of Jewry, yet carried in itself the seeds of a new evolution which led to a vigorous rebirth of the ancient people.

In the forthcoming volumes I shall attempt first to analyze the general developments in Western Jewry during the Late Middle Ages. The description of the basic attitudes shaped by the combined traditions of the Catholic Church and the Carolingian Empire will be followed by that of the gradual evolution of Jewish life in the respective countries. Beginning with the Holy Roman Empire, where the imperial regime was soon rivaled by those of powerful electors, ecclesiastical and lay, other princes and bishops, as well as by cities, the narrative will sketch the diverse lines of evolution in the neighboring territories of Switzerland, the Low Countries, Hungary, and Poland, and the great transformations which took place in France (both in the royal domain and in the areas under the rule of the Crown's powerful vassals in the east and south) and England down to the final elimination of Jews from both regions. Even fuller treatment will be accorded to the marvelous expansion and later contraction and final elimination of Iberian Jewry, as well as to the enormous differences characterizing the evolution of the Italian communities from the Kingdom of the Two Sicilies through the Papal States to the glorious republics and principalities of Northern Italy.

This topographical-chronological treatment will be supplemented by a systematic analysis of the legal status in different countries of late medieval Jewry, the manifold similarities and dissimilarities of which often transcended the geographic and chronological boundaries. Apart from the attitudes of Church and state, moreover, cognizance will be taken of the deeper roots of anti-Jewish feelings derived from medieval folklore and the popular suspicions of Jewish "blasphemies" and magic arts, and the attribution to Jews of such hostile acts as ritual murders, poisoning of wells, and desecration of hosts. If these popular animosities culminated in the conception of the Jew as an eternal wanderer, his presence was doubly resented during the rising tide of European nationalism which, at least semiconsciously, strove to achieve national homogeneity within each country. These forces of nationalism, combined with religious animosities, popular suspicions, and economic rivalries, were finally responsible for the recurrent waves of massacres and expulsions during the last medieval centuries. The general economic evolution, in its affirmative as well as negative aspects, will likewise be treated here at some length, particularly since Georg Caro's standard work in this field is no longer up to date and leaves us completely in the dark concerning the crucial developments after 1350. To avoid excessive repetition many facts and interpretations which might have been treated under the respective countries (for instance, the story of massacres and expulsions) were analyzed in the systematic sections or vice versa. The reader is urgently advised to view the picture presented in Volumes IX–XII as integral parts of the same treatment.

Although sixteenth-century Jewish life continued to evolve under the shadow of the Spanish-Portuguese Inquisition and the Marrano problem—both medieval excrescences—the unhappy vicissitudes of the vast Marrano diaspora were largely responsible for opening up both Western Europe and the Western Hemisphere to Jewish settlement. Simultaneously, the Old World was undergoing radical transformations under the impact of Humanism, the Protestant Reformation, the Catholic Restoration, and the prolonged Wars of Religion. All these movements left a deep imprint on Jewish life, too. The ensuing vital changes in the century and a half from 1500 to 1650 in both the old and the new centers of Jewish life have been a source of great fascination to me, and I hope to be able to communicate some of this excitement to the reader.

This Western evolution will be rounded out by a more succinct analysis of the position of Jews within the Byzantine sphere of interest and under late medieval Islam, in both of which it essentially continued along the lines described in Volumes III–

VIII. Only the emergence of the Ottoman Empire, which largely displaced both the Byzantine and the Middle-Eastern regimes, and soon extended from Budapest to Cairo and beyond, injected a new powerful ingredient into the perennial conflict between East and West, deeply affecting the life of world Jewry.

Subsequent volumes will deal with the internal evolution of the Jewish community, the development of its older and newer institutions, the rich and variegated life within the ghetto walls, and the novel religious movements. Additional chapters will be devoted to the newer manifestations of the ever creative adjustments of Jewish law to life, the flowering of mysticism, the continued cultivation of Jewish philosophy and science, and the manifold intellectual endeavors in the fields of Hebrew homiletics, linguistics, poetry, and Bible learning. Special attention will also be paid to the rise of new Jewish dialects and such new languages as Yiddish and Ladino, as well as to the early modern Jewish historiography which far transcended in both quality and quantity anything known in Jewish letters since the days of Josephus.

As in the earlier volumes, an effort has been made to cite the most recent literature on the subjects under review. Though working without any outside research assistants, I have endeavored to verify every quotation from the primary sources, both printed and unpublished, as well as from the vast secondary literature. However, a small residuum of bibliographical entries still remains unchecked because of the unavailability of these works in the American, European, or Israeli libraries. Like their predecessors in the previous volumes, these entries, if unverified at the time of publication of the ultimate Bibliography (scheduled to appear after the completion of the whole series), will be marked by a dagger.

It is a pleasure to express thanks to the various institutions and their personnel whose kind cooperation alone made possible the extended research needed for the preparation of these volumes. First and foremost I must mention Columbia University Library, of which I have been practically a daily visitor. Other major New York libraries including those of the Jewish Theological Seminary, the New York Public Library with its excellent Jewish division, the Hebrew Union College-Jewish Institute of Religion, and Union Theological Seminary, have likewise proved extremely helpful. Abroad I have made particularly good use—to cite them in chronological order—of the University Library with its Rosenthaliana Collection in Amsterdam; the Paris Bibliothèque Nationale and Archives Nationales; the Frankfort Stadtarchiv and the University Library; the State Library in Munich; the State Archives and the National and University Libraries in Vienna; the Hebrew University Library, with its microfilm collection, and the Israel Historical Society, both in Jerusalem; the National and University Libraries in Rome; the State Archives and the Marciana Library in Venice; and the National Libraries and National Archives in both Madrid and Lisbon. To the directors of these institutions and their associates, as well as to the American cultural attachés who graciously offered their assistance whenever needed, go my deep thanks.

I am also extremely grateful to Columbia University, especially its School of International Affairs under Dean Andrew Cordier and its History Department under the chairmanship of Professor Henry F. Graff, who were able to secure for me a substantial research grant which greatly facilitated my journey to the aforementioned libraries and archives abroad. All along I have enjoyed the cordial cooperation of the officials of Columbia University Press and the Jewish Publication Society.

My gratitude is also due to my secretary, Mrs. Rebecca Fischer, who during the last couple of years has, with great competence and much devotion, helped to take care of many technical problems connected with the preparation of the present manuscript. Above all, I owe much more than I can express in words to my wife, Jeannette M. Baron, who has untiringly worked with me from the initial stages of research and writing through the protracted processes of checking and editing the manuscript down to the final proofreading. Without her cooperation the completion of this work would have been delayed by years.

SALO W. BARON

*Yifat Shalom*
*Canaan, Conn.*
*August 19, 1965*

# CONTENTS

# A SOCIAL AND RELIGIOUS HISTORY
# OF THE JEWS

## PUBLISHED VOLUMES

### *Ancient Times*

### I. TO THE BEGINNING OF THE CHRISTIAN ERA

### II. CHRISTIAN ERA: THE FIRST FIVE CENTURIES

### *High Middle Ages*

### III. HEIRS OF ROME AND PERSIA

### IV. MEETING OF EAST AND WEST

### V. RELIGIOUS CONTROLS AND DISSENSIONS

### VI. LAWS, HOMILIES, AND THE BIBLE

### VII. HEBREW LANGUAGE AND LETTERS

### VIII. PHILOSOPHY AND SCIENCE

### INDEX TO VOLUMES I–VIII

### *Late Middle Ages and Era of European Expansion*

### IX. UNDER CHURCH AND EMPIRE

### X. ON THE EMPIRE'S PERIPHERY

# UNDER CHURCH AND EMPIRE

# XXXVII

# INFIDEL

EXPANSION and contraction of West-European Jewry coincided with the great rise and decline in the temporal power of the Roman Church. The same thirteenth century which witnessed the climactic prestige of the Papacy from Innocent III to Boniface VIII and ultimately resulted in the latter's well-known bull of 1302, *Unam Sanctam,* in which the pope claimed both spiritual and temporal supremacy over all of Christendom, also marked the high point of prosperity and sociopolitical influence of the Spanish, French, and English Jewries. Beginning with the expulsion from England in 1290 and culminating in the expulsion from Spain in 1492, the forced conversion in Portugal in 1496, and lesser acts of intolerance in other regions during the following decades, West-European Jewry reached the nadir of its numbers and affluence in the middle of the sixteenth century. Simultaneously the Papacy, too, suffered serious reversals; it soon faced the sharp revolt of various reform movements which ultimately led to the total separation of the Protestant churches.

This was no mere coincidence. The Jewish people and the Church universal were victimized by essentially the same factors. We shall see how destructive of the entire Jewish position was the rising tide of medieval nationalism. Less conscious and, in many respects, less virulent than modern nationalism, the medieval drives toward national unity, most clearly exemplified in the struggle of the French Crown with its feudal vassals, operated in the direction of ethnic exclusivity and national sovereignty. The former played an enormous role, as will become clear in a later chapter, in underscoring the "alien" character of the Jewish minority and in the ultimate quest for its total elimination via expulsion, conversion, or extermination. The aspiration toward national sovereignty, on the other hand, undermined that very spiritual and cultural universality which had lent a semblance of realism to the ecumenical leadership of the Church. In this way,

the destinies of medieval Jewry and those of the medieval Church
became subtly intertwined beyond the ken and wishes of the leaders of either party.[1]

Partly because of the ascendancy of the Church, which tried to
regulate almost all walks of public life, and partly because of the
increase in the Jewish population and economic activity, nearly
every pope reigning during the last three centuries of the
medieval era had something to say on the Jewish question, which
was then being debated with increasing acerbity in both lay and
ecclesiastical circles. Among the more articulate occupants of the
papal see on this score were the powerful popes, Innocent III
(1198–1216), Gregory IX (1227–41), Innocent IV (1243–54), Nicholas III (1277–80), Nicholas IV (1288–92), Boniface VIII (1294–
1303), John XXII (1316–34), Benedict XII (1334–42), Benedict
XIII (1394–1417; died 1423), Martin V (1417–31), Eugenius IV
(1431–47), Nicholas V (1447–55), Paul II (1464–71), and Alexander VI (1492–1503).

The most important Councils to take a stand were the Fourth
Lateran (1215), the Vienne (1311–12), and the two great Reform Councils of Constance (1414–18) and Basel (1431–48).
Many papal bulls and conciliar canons found their way into the
Decretals of Pope Gregory IX or their supplements, known as the
*Extravagantes communes.* They thus received the additional sanction of being part of the *Corpus juris canonici,* the chief code of
canon law, which was to retain its validity until the promulgation
of a new code in 1918. Even many epistles written by popes on
specific occasions were later quoted as authoritative interpretations of the law or as precedent-setting judicial decisions. Significant discussions were also contributed by influential bishops and
other churchmen, especially members of the new preaching orders
of Dominicans and Franciscans, as well as by several leading canon
jurists and scholastic philosophers. From this maze of utterances,
often quite vague and of studied obscurity, if not altogether contradictory, it is not always possible to draw safe generalizations.
Nonetheless, certain basic principles and attitudes emerge as the
fairly constant *leitmotif* of Church policies toward Jews and
Judaism.[2]

Although the Church as such had little executive power outside the Pontifical States and the feudal lordships of individual bishops, these principles and attitudes deeply colored the entire Christian-Jewish symbiosis. There were, needless to say, many local and regional differences, determined by different national heritages and socioeconomic needs. At times, the Church itself responded to such local influences and modified its own stand. As a result there were great variations on the same basic themes in various countries and periods, which will become manifest in later chapters dealing with the attitudes of the respective states and peoples and systematically reviewing the position of medieval Jewry in its diverse environments. It is hoped that the ensuing unavoidable repetitions will be held to a minimum.

## TOLERATION

As a matter of principle, the Church continued its traditional policy of extending to Jews general sufferance with severe qualifications. The innovations of the later Middle Ages consisted chiefly in more detailed exposition and clarification of these relationships. With the Jewish question looming ever larger in the minds of churchmen and with the Church arrogating to itself ever increasing authority in guiding the Christian peoples, particularly in their relations with infidels and heretics, such clarification became imperative. The growth of scholastic philosophy, too, led to more comprehensive analyses of all major issues.

The quandary facing most thinkers of the time was not so much why Jewish toleration should be subjected to severe limitations but rather why Jews should be tolerated at all. Combining in itself the heritage of Jewish monotheistic exclusivity with that of implacable Roman imperialism, the Church sought complete control over the souls of the faithful and the suppression of all heterogeneous currents. Islam was not tolerated at all, except on a temporary basis in those Spanish and southern Italian areas where the former Muslim regimes had left behind powerful segments of the population that were numerically important and economically and culturally self-assertive. The thirteenth century witnessed the bloody suppression of the Albigensian and other heresies. Ultimately, the struggle between Catholic intolerance and the rising tides of Reform embroiled Europe in a century and a half of sanguinary Wars of Religion, in which the Jews often appeared as the only neutrals. Under these circumstances the very principle of tolerating Jewish "infidels" within Christian society required a rationale.

Among the great thirteenth-century scholastics it was first Alexander of Hales, called by his contemporaries the *doctor irrefragabilis et theologorum monarcha,* who devoted several paragraphs to a detailed consideration of the arguments for and against toleration of Jews. "On the face of it," he contended, "it appears that they should not be tolerated." They were known to blaspheme against both Christ and the Virgin, persecute the Christian faith, and cause injury to ecclesiastical sacraments. Referring to the Decretals of Gregory IX, he argued that according to Old Testament law Jews were guilty of a capital crime if they committed blasphemy against their own religion. How much more should they thus be punished for offending the Christian faith! Moreover, they considered the Talmud and its teachings as their official law, although that work (as was reiterated by its contemporary Christian accusers) included much blasphemous material against Christ and the Virgin. Finally, echoing the contemporary call to the Crusades, Alexander argued that Christians fought the Muslims to death merely because the latter were in possession of the Holy Land. How much greater was the injury to the Christian faith arising from the Jewish contumely against the Redeemer! Hence it would appear that Christians ought to fight to death also the perpetrators of that contumely.

In answer to these arguments, the distinguished schoolman pointed out that Scripture had warned against the total elimination of Jews and that Jesus himself had prayed for them. Moreover, the Jews were necessary as a testimony for the Christian faith, for such "testimony is the stronger as it is offered by enemies, the Catholic Church receiving such testimony from the Old Law which the Jews observe." Their blasphemies, too, could be excused on subjective grounds, since they believed that the Messiah had not yet come, although, of course, the Church must not tolerate such blasphemies to be committed in public and must urge the secular princes to suppress them and to burn the books containing them. Finally, Jews were not quite comparable to those heathens occupying the Holy Land, for "we have accepted the Old Law from them, Christ issued from their seed, and the promise was given of their ultimate salvation." After further deliberation Alexander also reached the conclusion that Jewish rites could by no means be equated with idolatry and that the Jews were to be allowed to observe them freely.[3]

Alexander's reasoning is fairly typical of contemporary papal and scholastic opinion. Some of the twelfth-century popes, to be sure, tried to present their toleration of Jews as a wholly disinterested matter. It was done, asserted Alexander III, "out of mildness of Christian piety" or, as Clement II phrased it, "from pure grace and pity." Yet most of them, as well as the majority of the medieval schoolmen, unhesitatingly subscribed to the doctrine of the ancient Church Fathers that, although no longer Israel in the spirit, Jews still were Israel in the flesh. As such they had a great function to perform. Thomas Aquinas wrote:

Thus, from the fact that the Jews observe their rites which, of old, foreshadowed the truth of the faith which we hold, there follows this good—that our very enemies bear witness to our faith, and that our faith is represented in a figure so to speak [quasi in figura]. For this reason they are tolerated in the observance of their rites.

In contrast, rites of other "unbelievers" were not to be tolerated at all except in order to avoid some scandal or for other extraordinary reasons. Jews were indeed to be tolerated until the end of days, when all of them would be converted to the Christian faith and thereby help usher in the second coming of Christ.[4]

The need for Jewish testimony, to be sure, must have had a slightly archaic sound in the thirteenth century. Very important during the early missionary struggles of the Church which had tried through Old Testament "testimonies" to convince the heathen nations of the genuineness of the Gospels, this argument must have lost much of its force when Christianity was firmly established among the European nations and the divine origin of the Gospels was no longer disputed even by heretics. Nevertheless, some doubts may still have lingered among persons familiar with the then extensive practice of conveniently forging documents in order to prove contentions, legal or theological.[5] While until the

Renaissance age few doubted the authenticity of the *Donatio Constantini,* most contemporaries must have suspected the genuineness of many other famous documents. Hence only testimony unwittingly offered by the Church's hereditary "enemies" was considered truly incontrovertible. The upshot of all these debates was that the old ecclesiastical policy inherited from the patristic age was substantially maintained despite all the new storms and stresses.

Need of Jewish testimony did not completely tie the hands of Christian rulers, however, with respect to keeping or admitting Jews. New vistas on the entire problem were opened by the frequent contention of ecclesiastical writers that Jews were to be tolerated in Christian lands out of feelings of Christian charity. We find an interesting discussion of this notion in the comprehensive tractate on Jews, written by the generally unfriendly sixteenth-century jurist, Marquardus de Susannis. The author first presents the reasons advanced by protagonists of the idea of untrammeled state rights over Jews and the freedom of rulers to expel them at will. "While no private person is entitled to molest them, a prince is allowed to do so, because since the death of Christ they have become our slaves. . . . If he is entitled to sell them, how much more should he be able to expel them!" Other jurists, however, including Oldradus, had held that a prince could not expel Jews "without legitimate cause," for such an act would "run counter to the precepts of charity." Marquardus himself was inclined to subscribe to the latter point of view, although his tractate appeared in 1558 with the approval of the otherwise strongly anti-Jewish Pope Paul IV.[6]

The first and foremost implication of toleration was protection for Jewish life and limb. This is indeed the tenor of the recurrent papal *Constitutio pro Judaeis* which, ever since Calixtus II, was granted to the Jews of Rome by most of the succeeding popes. "Without the judgment of the authority of the land," that decree provided, "no Christian shall presume to wound their persons, or kill them, or deprive them of their money or alter the good customs under which they have lived in their respective regions." It became quite customary for the Jews not only of Rome but of France, Germany, and other countries to secure copies of that decree for home use. To be sure, with the general deterioration of Jewish status in the age of the Crusades such protection became both more urgent and less effective. Ultimately, the insecurity of Jewish life found expression in the diminishing penalties inflicted on murderers of Jews. For one example, in 1285 Honorius IV, in his renewal of a provision first enacted by Emperor Frederick II for the Kingdom of Sicily and Naples, provided that communities where an undetected murder had been committed were to be fined 100 augustals if the victim was a Christian, but only 50 augustals if he was a Jew or a Saracen.[7]

Special protection was needed in the frenzied periods of preparation for the successive Crusades. It often took several years between the original call to a Crusade and the actual expedition. In the meantime any man who took the Cross fell immediately under the jurisdiction of the Church. Apart from the financial losses sustained by Jewish businessmen from moratoria on all pending debts granted to Crusaders, all Jews were exposed to frequent attacks by a populace aroused to religious frenzy by local preachers urging enlistment in the armies which were to fight the infidels in the Holy Land. Popes found themselves, therefore, obliged to issue special bulls protecting the Jews against assaults by fanatics or profiteers. Referring to a "lachrymose" petition received from the Jews of France, Gregory IX, on September 5 (or 9), 1236, wrote to the archbishop of Bordeaux and several French bishops censuring the Crusaders who, instead of being filled with fear and love of God,

steep themselves in their obnoxious desires, thereby provoking divine displeasure against themselves. . . . [They] plot impious designs against the Jews and . . . try to wipe them almost completely off the face of the earth. . . . In order to cover such an inhuman crime under the cloak of virtue, and in some way to justify their unholy cause, they pretend to have done the above and threaten to do worse on the ground that they [the Jews] refuse to be baptized. . . . Therefore, lest such great temerity, if not repressed, be turned into abuse toward other persons as well, We order that each one of you force the inhabitants of your dioceses who commit such excesses, to bring proper satisfaction for the crimes perpetrated against the Jews and for the property stolen from them. After giving due warning you may use ecclesiastical punishment without appeal.

In the face of even more serious persecutions by the so-called Pastoureaux, Pope John XXII on June 29, 1320, asked secular authorities as well as French bishops to protect Jews.[8]

Another basic implication of this protective legislation was the freedom of Jewish worship. It meant little to medieval Jews to be allowed to live as individuals without simultaneously being given the right to cultivate their religion. From time immemorial, therefore, special regulations extended safeguards to Jewish houses of worship and cemeteries. Curiously, while under the ancient Roman Empire the controversy over illicit appropriations of synagogues by mobs, often led by priests, engaged the attention of secular and ecclesiastical authorities and, on one occasion, led to a serious conflict between Saint Ambrose and Emperor Theodosius, now such expropriations became very infrequent, except when occasioned by a general or local expulsion of Jews. The main difficulty, likewise inherited from ancient legislation, now lay in the prohibition against the erection of new or the enlargement of old synagogues. Such laws, understandable when applied to the contracting population of the ancient Roman Empire, became quite pointless during the medieval expansion of both Christianity and the areas of Jewish settlement. Certainly, wherever Jews founded a new community they wished to build a house of worship. This was often done with the concurrence of the local ecclesiastical authorities, while the Papacy and general Councils closed their eyes.

Sometimes, however, the issue was raised and the old laws were invoked. In Cordova, for instance, the bishop and the secular authorities seem to have acquiesced in the building of a new synagogue, but the archdeacon and the episcopal chapter objected and appealed to the pope. Innocent IV promptly responded on April 13, 1250, enjoining the bishop "to execute against the Jews the duties of your office." In the tense atmosphere of thirteenth-century England, the provincial synods of Oxford (canon 39, 1222) and Chichester (*De Judaeis,* 1246) insisted on unrelenting adherence to the prohibition. This was a period of general contraction of Anglo-Jewish settlements, with several cities securing the privilege *de non tolerandis Judaeis.* Undoubtedly there was less need for the erection of new Jewish houses of worship, yet the ecclesiastics assembled at the two synods must have felt that a reit-

eration of the ancient prohibition could still serve a useful purpose. As late as July 30, 1281, Archbishop John Peckham of
Canterbury ordered the bishop of London to investigate the
rumor that Jews were erecting a new house of worship in the English capital and, if true, to stop all further work under the threat of
excommunication and interdict of any cooperating Christian officials or workmen, "in which endeavor we are prepared to assist
you with all our strength." Pope Boniface VIII, on August 31,
1295, ordered a canon of Treves (Trier) to cause the Jews of
Wetzlar to desist from building their new synagogue under the
threat of a church-sponsored boycott by their Christian neighbors.
At times the issue was complicated by conflicting fiscal interests. A
French parlement, held by the king in Paris in 1278, condemned
the bishop of Béziers for having allowed local Jews to move from
the Jewish quarter in the royal section to that under his jurisdiction and for having constructed a new synagogue for them. The
meeting demanded the return of the Jews to their former habitation, their renewed payment of taxes to the king, and the destruction of the new synagogue.[9]

In the case of Jewish cemeteries, the main issue was not whether
Jews were to be allowed to bury their dead in ground consecrated
by them. (That issue was to loom large in modern times both in
the Old and New Worlds.) Jewish corpses were rarely accepted for
burial in general cemeteries, although this happened in Barrois
during the years 1321–23. As a rule, Jews were allowed to maintain their own "houses of eternity," so the real question was
whether their burial places would be left undisturbed by rowdies
and grave robbers. The papal bull, Sicut Judaeis, carried such a
protective provision, which was repeated and somewhat amplified
in its subsequent renewals. The reiteration of these and other laws
testify to the frequency of their violation and to the inefficacy of
both ecclesiastical and secular authorities to stem abuses nurtured
by both sadism and greed. Sometimes priests themselves seem to
have been involved in such desecrations. In 1278 Pedro III censured the clergy of Gerona for its part in the despoliation of the
local Jewish cemetery and threatened it with severe penalties if
violations continued. But no one ever interfered with the rulers'
legalized vandalism on cemeteries of banished Jews.[10]

## CONVERSION

Toleration by the Church did not mean, of course, that the ecclesiastical authorities were to spare efforts to persuade Jews to join the dominant faith voluntarily. Yet while, according to many jurists, pagans and Muslims were to be Christianized at the point of the sword, Jews were not to be baptized forcibly. This principle had been fully established under the ancient Christian Empire and frequently reiterated thereafter by popes and teachers of the Church, including Gregory the Great. Thomas Aquinas merely restated that old doctrine (clearly formulated by Augustine) when he taught that Jews should not be "forced to the faith so that they might believe, for belief is a matter of will [*quia credere voluntatis est*]." It was later expanded by one of Thomas' chief commentators, Tommaso de Vio, better known as Cardinal Cajetan, who, as general of the Dominican order and papal legate, was to play a considerable role in combating the reformatory trends of the early sixteenth century. In his commentary on that Thomistic passage Cajetan deduced therefrom that

threats and terror wherewith the princes force their subjects to embrace the faith result only in their servile, rather than voluntary, conversion, and hence in sacrilege. . . . For to receive the sacraments under force is to bring contumely upon them. . . . It certainly is a greater evil to live secretly as an unbeliever after having received the sacraments of the faith, than to live freely as an infidel, for thus one avoids [at least] the contumely to the sacraments.

He did not even accept the argument that the offspring of such forced converts in the third and fourth generations would become true Christians. Taught by experience with the Spanish *conversos,* he contended that such fictitious Christians "nurture their children in a faith similar to theirs." Even Vicente Ferrer, whose violent sermons were the source of great tribulation for Spanish Jewry, publicly protested against the bloodshed of Jews as a means of propagating Christianity. He merely insisted that they regularly attend his missionary sermons. In 1414 he rejoiced when he was informed by Ferdinand I of Aragon that, as a result of such a sermon delivered by another Franciscan monk reinforced by a miracle the nature of which Ferrer subsequently explained to the king,

122 Jews of Guadalajara adopted Christianity. Gregory I, on the other hand, in his interpretation of voluntary conversion, had allowed the use of all sorts of inducements. This method was constantly refined and used extensively in the later Middle Ages. Baptism by persuasion was so highly appreciated that Thomas Aquinas himself must have greatly rejoiced when an opportunity offered itself to him to convert two Jews.[11]

The concept of forcible conversion itself, however, was open to widely divergent interpretations. According to medieval students of both canon and civil law, one had to draw the old Roman distinction between absolute enforcement (*vis absoluta*) and more indirect compulsion (*vis compulsiva*), or as Alexander of Hales styled it "conditional enforcement" (*coactio conditionalis*). Unlike his predecessors, Innocent III endeavored to define the different categories of force, but his distinctions leave much to be desired in legal clarity. In a letter to the Archbishop of Arles of September or October of 1201, he reiterated the prohibition of forcing the adoption of Christianity upon a person who is "steadily unwilling and openly contradicting." But he added: "For this reason some [jurists] distinguish not without merit between one kind of unwillingness and another, one kind of compulsion and another." In the pope's opinion only one who had never consented but staunchly opposed conversion and never submitted to the substance or the character of the sacrament could claim that he had been violently baptized. More sweepingly, some canon jurists taught that baptism to be considered truly enforced had to result from direct physical constraint. Quoting medieval glossators, Marquardus de Susannis argued that the prohibited violent form of baptism "is to be understood only in the case of direct compulsion [*coactio praecisa*], such as when one is brought to the baptismal font with his hands and feet tied, and forcibly immersed over his protests." Everyone admitted that such a ceremony was null and void. But the extent to which baptism performed under serious threats other than immediate loss of life was to be invalidated became the subject of controversy. According to most canon jurists, Jews threatened with expulsion and thus faced with the alternatives of either embracing Christianity or else relinquishing their homes, suffering the extremely serious discomforts of migration, and sustaining severe economic losses, were not classified as acting under legal duress if they chose to be baptized. Had not Pope Leo VII once advised the Archbishop of Mayence (Mainz) that he could expel the Jews from his states with papal permission, "for we ought not to associate with the Lord's enemies"? Indeed, all the medieval expulsions were based on the assumption, explicit or implicit, that if they wished to embrace Christianity, Jews would automatically secure the right to remain. Among the occasional objections raised to the banishment of Jews from any particular region one rarely, if ever, heard the argument that such exclusion was tantamount to forcible conversion. [12]

Other differences of opinion arose from the question of the legal validity of accomplished facts. Granted that a Jew should not have been forcibly baptized, how was he to be treated thereafter? Was the act to be invalidated, and the convert allowed to return to his ancestral faith? Were the perpetrators of that transgression to be severely punished? In practice, punishment was hardly ever meted out for such excess of missionary zeal unless it was combined with actual bloodshed. Even then, the prosecution was for murder or assault and battery, not for the crime of forcible conversion.

Few churchmen were prepared to nullify an accomplished act of baptism. When, after the massacres of 1096, Emperor Henry IV of Germany and William II of England and Normandy allowed the pitiful remnants of the Jewish communities destroyed by the Crusaders to return to their former faith, Antipope Clement III vigorously protested. More circumspectly, the Fourth Lateran Council of 1215 (canon 70) censured only those who, although they "had voluntarily approached the baptismal font, had not completely driven out the old self in order the more perfectly to bring in the new." It ordered the prelates of the churches to use "salutary compulsion" to prevent such new converts from observing their old rites, "that they may be saved." More broadly, the jurist Durandus of San Porciano (d. 1334), after a lengthy discussion of the issues involved in the conversion of both children and adults, including the prohibited use of "threats and temporal penalties," intimated that such forced converts were entitled to relapse. Durandus himself may have been suspected of heretical leanings, but his opinion was shared by some later Dominican theologians. The majority of more zealous jurists, however, insisted upon the indelible character of the sacrament of baptism which, they taught, must remain inviolate if performed without direct physical compulsion. "He who is violently drawn," stated Innocent III in his aforementioned letter to the archbishop of Arles of 1201, "through threats and entreaties, and in order to avoid damages accepts the sacrament of baptism, such a one . . . , so to say conditionally willing, although absolutely not willing, is to be compelled to observe the Christian faith." Innocent also taught that anyone receiving baptism while asleep or in a demented state must remain Christian to the end of his life, since his "association with the divine sacrament had already been established and the grace of baptism had been received." Even more outspokenly Clement IV in his bull, *Turbato corde* (of July 26, 1267, repeated by Gregory X in 1274 and Nicholas IV in 1289), decided that a relapsed convert, even if he had been baptized under a threat to his life, was to be treated as an outright heretic, that is, subject to the extreme penalty.[13]

Equally puzzling was the problem of conversion of children. Presumably they had no will of their own and hence could consciously neither accept nor resist baptism. Once again Thomas Aquinas restated the prevailing doctrine when he asserted, though somewhat too broadly, that "it was never the custom of the Church to baptize Jewish children against the will of their parents. . . . There are two reasons for this custom: One is on account of the danger to the faith [of these children when they come of age. The other because] it is against natural justice." Similarly, Innocent IV enjoined the king of Navarre in 1246 to "outlaw to the extent of your power any violence being committed in baptizing their [the Jews'] children since this ought to be a voluntary, not a forced, offering." But even he would not have controverted the doctrine enunciated by his predecessor, Innocent III, in 1201 (subsequently incorporated in the Gregorian Decretals) that once baptized, even without their and their parents' consent, such children must remain Christian even more staunchly than adults. Although too young either to understand what was going on or to believe in the new faith, they must consider the act valid, for it redeemed them from the original sin which had likewise come to them without their knowledge. For purposes of conversion, Martin V and other popes and jurists declared any minor of twelve or over as in full possession of the necessary discernment. Otherwise canon law drew a distinction between children below and above seven years of age. The absent will of the younger children could be substituted by that of parents. Some doctors of the Church went further and declared that the positive desire of one grandparent sufficed for the performance of baptism even if both parents objected. Allegedly only children between seven and twelve were not subject to conversion by either their own will which was considered insufficiently developed, or the parental will which no longer served as a full-fledged substitute.[14]

Whatever the theory, many a jurist sharpened his legal acumen to find subterfuges even for the wholesale conversion of Jewish children. Vincent of Beauvais (d. 1264) wished to see this right limited to the monarch who, as overlord of the Jews, was master over all their belongings including their offspring. On the other hand, living in the overheated atmosphere of widespread Jew-baiting in England or France before and after the expulsions of 1290 and 1306, John Duns Scotus eloquently pleaded for the princes' moral obligation to promote the indiscriminate Christianization of all Jewish minors. Insisting that God's rights precede those of parents, this leading schoolman merely warned that such conversions should be performed with the necessary care (*cum bona cautela*)—a phrase frequently repeated in the subsequent literature. He had in mind that newly baptized children be immediately removed from their parental homes and handed over to Christians for religious education, thus forestalling the danger of relapse stressed by Thomas Aquinas. If there is any truth at all in a Continental Jewish record, Scotus' doctrine was given wholesale application during the expulsion from England when many Jewish children were refused permission to leave the country and were forced to grow up as Christians.[15]

This matter continued to be heatedly debated by churchmen and jurists for generations thereafter. In the fifteenth century Antonine of Florence, while himself siding with the more lenient Thomistic view, nevertheless cited a number of authorities expounding the opposing Scotist doctrine. Not surprisingly, the latter found wide acceptance also during the tense period of Judeo-Christian relations in pre-Reformation Germany, whose annals were filled with regional and local expulsions of Jewish communities. Stimulated by a widely debated incident in Freiburg im Breisgau (which will be described in a later chapter), the prominent jurist, Ulrich Zasius, quoted with approval the following "conclusions" formulated by one Georg Nothöfer:

The first conclusion is . . . : The prince or anyone else in authority over Jews not only may, but he ought to cause, Jewish children to be baptized *cum cautela bona.*—The second conclusion is: Not only a prince and the like, but any good Christian may, and ought to, under circumstances, baptize a child of a Jew or heathen without parental consent.—The third conclusion is: Although adults must not be simply forced to accept baptism, they may be induced to do so by threats and terror, that is by conditional force [*coactione conditionata*].

Here, too, Zasius followed in the footsteps of Duns Scotus who regarded the forcible conversion of Jewish adults as a lesser evil than permitting them to practice their illicit faith. Moreover, Scotus declared, the offspring of such forcible converts would, "if properly educated, become genuine believers in the third and fourth generation." To square his demand with the traditional view that Jews ought to be maintained until the second coming of Christ, he suggested, far from humorously, that these prophetic enunciations could be met by the settlement of a limited number of Jews on some distant island where they might be maintained at Christendom's expense to the end of days. Perhaps echoing his English fellow Franciscan, John Capistrano allegedly offered Pope Eugenius IV a fleet to transport all Roman Jews to some distant locality.[16]

When it came to action, the more tolerant legal maxims of the majority were often discarded. If a child had been removed from the custody of its parents and brought into a monastery, or even if someone illegally performed on it the ritual of baptism, the Christian authorities were particularly reluctant to give it up. Such cases occurred rather frequently down to modern times, as in the celebrated Mortara Affair of 1858 which assumed an international character and even led to the pro-Jewish intercessions by the Catholic emperors, Francis Joseph I and Napoleon III—all without avail.

## INDUCEMENTS

Probably far more effective in the long run were the tangible benefits which accrued to the new converts. Immediately after baptism, however, many of them found themselves without means of support. Even prospective converts required some assistance, especially if one took seriously the canonical regulations concerning their preparatory instruction in the fundamentals of the Christain faith. As early as 506, the Council of Agde had decreed that converts be subjected to intensive training in the principles and observances of the new faith over a period of eight months. This period was reduced by Gregory the Great to forty days in 598. Despite their inherent contradiction, both provisions were incorporated in the *Decretum Gratiani*. To be sure, few medieval priests who were engaged in the conversion of Jews adhered strictly to such lengthy waiting periods and, particularly during popular commotions, many Jews were baptized immediately. Yet the legal theory persisted that preliminary training of some duration was required. Arguing the two sides of the question, Alexander of Hales decided that only in ancient times when the Holy Spirit was manifest had it been possible speedily to impress prospective converts, but that later it had to be left to the discretion of the baptizing priest whether he considered the candidate sufficiently well trained. However, no matter how conscientiously the catechumens applied themselves to the acquisition of the required knowledge, usually they were deprived of their accustomed financial support by relatives or the Jewish community, and they had to look for assistance to Christian benefactors. The *Domus Conversorum,* established in London in 1232 and continuing to function there long after the expulsion of 1290, as well as the similar house of catechumens founded in Rome in 1543, provided food and shelter for candidates for baptism during that preparatory period. True, many a hard-pressed Jew made fraudulent use of these opportunities, only to escape shortly before the final act of baptism. But many others became and remained Christian. The baptismal ceremony itself was often turned into an impressive pageant, with a dignitary of Church or state serving as god-father.[17]

Utilizing its increased power and prestige, the Church also tried to protect the economic status of the new converts who, to cite a privilege of Emperor Charles IV recorded in a fourteenth-century German formulary, "brought with them nothing from their Jewish past except their nude bodies." The Third Lateran Council of 1179 adopted a resolution demanding that converts not be deprived of their property, for they ought to "enjoy a better status than the one they had before accepting the faith" (canon 26). More picturesquely, in 1213 Innocent III enunciated the policy that "a new plant of this kind should not only be reinforced by the dew of doctrine but also be nurtured by temporal benefits so that God may grant it an increase." This rhetoric did not conceal, however, the Church's serious difficulties in enforcing the policy against rulers who viewed with jaundiced eyes the ensuing loss of taxable Jewish property. Innocent III's letter of 1213, therefore, addressed to the archbishop of Sens, urged him to assume financial responsibility for the maintenance of neophytes. Similar letters were addressed by the pope and his successors (including Honorius III, Gregory IX, Innocent IV) to other ecclesiastical dignitaries. In a collection of epistles by Innocent IV recently made available from a manuscript in the Bibliotheca Antoniniana of Padua, no less than three are devoted to such urgings of the Church's duty to take care of converts, "in order that all of Israel be thus saved." But the response to such appeals often left much to be desired. A *cause célèbre* of a baptized family arose in Mayence during the very pontificate of Innocent III and continued for some eighteen years until Gregory IX persuaded the Church of Fulda to extend financial aid to some of its members. The Council of Valladolid of 1322 went further and recommended the appointment of all capable men among the converts to some clerical office. They were to be allowed to preach if they passed an appropriate examination (canon 21). More broadly, in 1434 the Council of Basel appealed to all clergy and laymen to support new converts. Even earlier they were partly subsidized by private citizens, as well as by secular rulers such as Louis IX in France and

Edward I in England. But the main obligation still rested with the bishops. It is not surprising, therefore, that these new financial burdens often tempered the missionary zeal of influential ecclesiastics.[18]

The interests of the state often were more directly involved. To influence the Christian governments of ancient Rome and its early medieval successor states to protect baptized Jews against disinheritance by enraged parents was a relatively easy task, for it cost the state very little. Even the loss of special taxpayers wherever Jews were subject to a capitation tax could at least in part be made up by additional taxes on professing Jews as was done in Visigothic Spain under King Egica. With the development of Jewish serfdom, however, many later medieval rulers felt that, through the act of conversion, a person theretofore classified as a royal serf escaped the king's overlordship. Through most of the period of Jewish settlement in medieval England, therefore, the king insisted that a convert's property be escheat to the royal Treasury. Only a short time before the expulsion, in 1280, the Exchequer was ready to accept only half the estate, which it promised to use for the support of the *Domus Conversorum*. Most other European countries allowed the Jewish families, even the community at large, to retain the property of apostasizing members. According to the main privileges of German Jewry since the days of Henry IV, "Just as they have relinquished the law of their forefathers, so did they abandon also their possessions." Understandably, the Church combated this position which threatened to undermine its missionary efforts. In his bull addressed in 1171 to the Spanish episcopate, Alexander III expressed his amazement and pain over reports that all movable property of converts was confiscated by the state, while their immovables were being taken over by Jewish relatives. Eight years later he induced the Third Lateran Council to adopt the aforementioned canon (26) which stated, "We enjoin the princes and authorities . . . under pain of excommunication to cause the full restoration [to these converts] of their hereditary portion and their possessions." Repeated in the Decretals of Gregory IX, these provisions became part of recognized canon law.[19]

In their practical application, however, these regulations were frequently observed in the breach, despite their repetition by many subsequent popes including Gregory IX himself (1236) and John XXII (1320). John XXII's bull is remarkable in so far as it clearly reveals that at the beginning of the fourteenth century the postulates were completely disregarded in the pope's own hereditary possessions. The pope wrote:

It is both unbecoming and senseless that those who while living as infidels enjoyed abundance should, upon turning believers, be forced to beg. We forbid, therefore, all our rectors and other officials in the County of Venaissin and in the other counties and territories subject to the Apostolic See to cause such converted Jews, or those to be converted in the future, to suffer damage in their property and possessions for whatever cause or allow others to injure them. They [the officials] ought rather to show themselves favorably disposed toward them, protect them against insults and molestations, so that they realize that they had left bondage for freedom, and would not be forced ignominiously to beg and to relapse.

Among interested secular rulers the reception of the canonical demands was mixed. On the one hand, James I of Aragon in 1242 expressly permitted a baptized Jew or Muslim to retain all his property, for which the king received appropriate praise from Innocent IV. Alphonso X of Castile, too, provided in his Code (*Las Siete Partidas*) that converts be treated as regular heirs. When, after some preparatory work at the Council of Siena, the universal Council of Basel began discussing the Jewish question at some length, John of Segovia, speaking in behalf of the king of Castile, actually boasted of the good treatment received by new converts in his country. As a result in particular of the effective preachment by Vicente Ferrer, the authorities had freed the neophytes from all taxes and the public had showered gifts on them "so that many became rich." Yet at the Basel Council session of September 3, 1434, the envoy of King Louis of Sicily, though claiming that his country had left all converts in the possession of their goods, nevertheless argued against the adoption of a sharp canon to this effect. He suggested that the Council limit itself to a mere exhortation to the authorities without the threat of excommunication. He was overruled and in its strongly worded and unanimously adopted resolution the Council not only demanded generous support for the neophytes, but resolved another knotty problem in their favor. It decided that if converts had accumulated fortunes from usury they should restore such unlawful gains only to clearly identifiable owners; otherwise they might use such funds for charitable purposes or even for themselves since they were proper objects of Christian charity.[20]

Notwithstanding this show of determination and persuasive rhetoric, the threat of either expropriation or the disinheritance of converts by enraged parents served as a serious deterrent to missionary efforts. In the perennial conflict between economic self-interest on the part of rulers and churchmen, and the ideal quest for spreading the Gospel, the former often prevailed. Did not many a Muslim governor, during the expansion of Islam, also prefer to leave their subjects in their state of "infidelity," rather than lose a productive source of revenue?

A host of other social problems often arose from the severance of family ties. Invariably, the Church tried to humor converts by modifying some well-established principles of canon law. For example, if Jewish marriage laws allowed an uncle to marry a niece, or a levir to wed his former sister-in-law, papal decrees gave such neophyte couples special dispensations to continue their marital ties. On the other hand, if one mate refused to be baptized, the marriage was considered automatically dissolved, the baptized partner being forbidden to cohabit with the Jewish mate but allowed to marry a Christian. The custody of the children was, sometimes by strained juridical arguments, handed over to the baptized parent. The Church also went out of its way to protect converts against insults. In his aforementioned decree of 1242, James I of Aragon provided "that no one shall dare taunt with his condition, any convert . . . by saying or calling him 'renegade' or 'jornadiz,' or any similar name." This provision shared in the praise extended to that decree by Innocent IV.[21]

How effective was the Christian mission? Of course, statistical data, even those for individual countries and periods, are extremely sketchy. Bishop Stephen of Tournai was not guilty of understatement when, in asking the almoner of Philip Augustus for a subsidy for a recent convert from Leon, he wrote: "It rarely happens that a member of the stubborn uncircumcised [sic] people converts himself faithfully and is reborn in the new Church." Nonetheless, at times the number of baptized Jews, particularly in

Mediterranean countries, was far from inconsiderable. In southern Italy, for example, we have records of some 1,300 Jewish converts during the thirteenth century. Of this number 310 lived in the city of Trani alone. The disputation of Tortosa of 1413–14, as we shall see, left in its wake a large number of voluntary converts. This process continued on the Iberian Peninsula during the remainder of the century. The Jewish community of Saragossa, for instance, in drawing up its budget always had to reckon with the possibility of diminishing revenue on account of desertion. Even among steadfast German Jewry, apostates are mentioned from time to time, particularly in the "Book of the Pious." Whatever the cumulative effects of voluntary baptisms may have been, they were indubitably far surpassed numerically by those of mass Catholicization under duress, especially during massacres and expulsions.[22]

This was not a one-way street, however. Although medieval Jewry had long given up any missionary aspirations, the number of Jewish proselytes was by no means insignificant. Honorius IV doubtless exaggerated when in 1286 he accused the Jews of France and England of attracting Christians to their faith by inviting them to their homes and synagogues on Sabbaths. He may have been more nearly correct in stating that they had made special efforts to induce baptized Jews to revert to Judaism. In all such cases Jews had to behave with utmost caution. The "Book of the Pious," which quite accurately reflects the conditions in the northern Jewish communities in the twelfth and thirteenth centuries, rarely refers to proselytes. But it graphically describes the fear of one Jewish community to circumcise a prospective German newcomer who had accepted the full burden of Jewish commandments, and that of another community which refrained from antagonizing a convert to Christianity lest he turn informer. Returnees to Judaism were welcomed back and immediately treated as full-fledged Jews. They were not even supposed to be reminded of their temporary apostasy. Yet one could never be too sure of their honesty, since many a relapsed convert sought other than spiritual solace. Moreover, any aid to such relapsers often ran afoul of the watchful eyes of inquisitors. Nevertheless, the occasional Jewish acts of public proselyting were dramatized in those years by the unstable mystic and self-styled "prophet" Abraham

Abulafia, who, in August 1280, set out for Rome in order to convert the pope to Judaism! [23]

In contrast to Jewish converts to Christianity, Christian proselytes to Judaism seem to have been recruited almost exclusively from the lower classes. The occasional converts from the ranks of the Christian clergy, like Bodo and Vecelin during the High Middle Ages, and like the two unnamed Cistercian monks, an Oxford deacon, and a Dominican monk in England shortly before and after 1200, caused a great sensation and were invariably recorded by contemporary chroniclers. Less distinguished people, however, who were either in the service of Jews or lived in the immediate vicinity of a Jewish quarter and were thus subjected to direct Jewish influences, doubtless entered Judaism surreptitiously, without leaving any overt traces in the sources. Many undoubtedly moved to another locality where they started life afresh, perhaps unbeknown even to their new Jewish neighbors.

Matters are further complicated by the fact that, as in ancient times, conversion to Judaism, or even the relapse of former converts, need not have involved total acceptance of the Jewish faith. Like the ancient "God-fearing" semiproselytes, these half-Jews observed only certain rituals without joining the community as such. Speaking particularly of the relapsed converts, we recall, the Fourth Lateran Council specifically condemned those who had "voluntarily approached the baptismal font but have not completely driven out the old self" (canon 70). Comparing that type of syncretism with the Old Testament prohibition of mixing linen and wool, the Council decreed that the converts should be forced to observe the Christian faith fully. Several later popes also roundly condemned the compromisers. Nicholas IV in 1290 went into some detail in describing such "aberrations" as kindling candles in the synagogues and the offering there of gifts and protracted prayers so that some relative might recover from a grave illness or sterility or be saved from shipwreck.[24]

## SEGREGATION

In general, conversionist efforts should have run counter to the Church's old policy of segregation. More justified from the

Church's viewpoint at a time when the Christian mission concentrated on converting entire pagan nations rather than individuals, this policy should have been modified, if not altogether abandoned, after the successful Christianization of almost all of Europe in the late Middle Ages. Furthermore, the originally superior social status of the Jews, which had inspired fear that they might exercise undue influence on Christians, had steadily deteriorated under the impact of mass hostility and discriminatory legislation. Now the ecclesiastical leaders could legitimately expect to bring more Jews into the Christian fold by intensifying their social intercourse with those of their Christian neighbors who were their equals or superiors in affluence and cultural amenities. Nonetheless, the force of tradition was so powerful that, rather than weakening the ancient provisions aimed at segregating the two groups, popes, councils, and canon jurists united in advocating ever stricter measures for keeping them apart, particularly in those areas where their social intercourse was relatively amicable, as in the Mediterranean countries. At the same time the rabbinic leaders, who were less interested in gaining souls for their faith than they were fearful of losing them, more realistically saw in segregation an eminent means for the survival of their much-harassed minority people.

Consequently, the old segregationist regulations inherited from the Roman Empire and the High Middle Ages were now expanded and elaborated in minutest detail. There was constant reiteration of the ancient prohibition against the ownership of Christian slaves by Jews, although with the progressive decline of slavery in Europe this regulation lost much of its significance. Innocent III, in trying to promote the conversion of pagan and Muslim slaves owned by Jews, insisted that indemnification to Jewish owners be held to a nominal sum. At that time Jewish slaveholding and slave trade were of some importance only in the eastern Mediterranean, especially in the Black Sea region, where as late as the fifteenth century Jews were reputed to be exporting human merchandise to the Islamic lands. Even the generally friendly Pope Martin V, horrified in 1425 by reports of the ensuing alienation of Christian slaves, tried to stem this practice by a sharply worded bull.[25]

Of more relevance in practice was the increasingly stringent prohibition against the employment by Jews of Christian servants and nurses. With his usual rhetoric, Innocent III exclaimed, "It is not seemly that those who, through baptism, were reborn in Christ and adopted as children of the true light, should live together with those whose stone-heartedness has blinded them to the recognition of the true light, lest those whom the true faith had introduced into light be led into the darkness of the latter's error." Additional arguments were advanced, for instance by the Council of Oxford of 1222, which maintained that "it is absurd that children of the free woman [the Church] should be subservient to the children of the bondswoman [the Synagogue]," and stressed the possible scandal of illicit sexual relations. In Spain where concubinage was still widely and openly practiced, the Church tried to prevent Christians from maintaining illicit relations with "unbelieving" women. The Council of Valladolid tersely decreed in 1322 that any married Christian keeping a concubine of whatever faith, and any unmarried man keeping an infidel, should consider themselves excommunicated *ipso facto,* that is without a trial and judgment by a court. This provision was repeated by the Council of Palencia sixty-six years later. The clergy also lent a willing ear to rumors about the anti-Christian bias of Jewish employers of Christian nurses. Echoing Innocent III's intimation of 1205, incorporated in the Gregorian Decretals, the synod of the newly organized archdiocese of Prague, held in 1346, condemned the alleged practice—"awful not only to mention but even to contemplate"—of withholding from infants for three days the milk of Christian nurses who had taken communion and throwing it into privies. The Council decided to renew the old prohibition against the employment by Jews of Christian midwives, nurses, and male or female servants.[26]

Other categories were gradually added. Harking back to the oldest segregationist decrees of the early church councils of Spain and Merovingian France, but spelling them out in a more contemporary vein, the Council of Basel in 1434 forbade Christians to participate in Jewish festivities, to attend their weddings and parties, to bathe with them, and generally to maintain close social relations with them. Although following therein in the footsteps of

Antipope Benedict XIII, the Council omitted the additional prohibitions against Christians' preparing food or kindling lights for
Jews on the Sabbath. Neither did it specifically forbid Jews to offer
unleavened bread and other Jewish holiday dishes to their Christian neighbors or to sell them meat prohibited by Jewish law. Such
regulations were not infrequent, however, in local and regional
laws.

In a typical sermon, ironically devoted to the "love of God,"
Bernardino da Siena (1380–1444), whose reputation for extraordinary saintliness was to earn him canonization within six years
after his death, declared:

I hear that there are many Jews here in Padua; hence I wish to state
several truths about them and about our relations with them. The first
truth is that you commit a cardinal sin if you eat or drink with them;
for just as they are forbidden to eat with us, so we must not consume
food with them. The second truth is that a sick man seeking to regain
his health must not repair to a Jew; for this, too, is a cardinal sin. The
third truth is that one must not bathe together with a Jew. The fourth
truth is that Jews must not enlarge their synagogues nor build new
ones, although I know that in this very city the opposite has been the
case.

Exhortations of this type impressed even relatively liberal
Palermo, for two of its Christian burghers were fined for partici-
pating in a Jewish circumcision ceremony.[27]

Most far-reaching was the formal introduction under Church
auspices of the Jewish badge during the thirteenth century. In
Muslim countries, to be sure, distinguishing marks or even different colors of the whole attire worn by members of various denominations had been practiced for many centuries and had been the
subject of much detailed legislation since the so-called Covenant of
'Umar. In countries adjacent to Muslim possessions some such distinctions in clothing began making their appearance during the
age of the Crusades. Perhaps stimulated by such examples, Innocent III, as early as 1204, expressed the desire to single out Jews by
some special marks. But it was not until the Fourth Lateran Council in 1215 that a general resolution to this effect was adopted by
the 412 bishops, 71 archbishops, and more than 800 abbots and
priors, as well as the numerous ambassadors of the leading Christian states who attended that momentous gathering. Presided over

by Innocent III, who saw in it a means of accomplishing his two greatest tasks of organizing a new Crusade to the Holy Land and of instituting a general reform of the Church, the Council considered various aspects of the Jewish question. One canon specifically dealt with the defense of Christianity against the Jews' "blasphemies" and their alleged ridicule of the Christians' grief over the holy passion. It further provided:

In some provinces of the Church a diversity in clothing distinguishes Jews or Saracens from the Christians, but in certain others there has insinuated itself such confusion that no difference is noticeable. Hence it sometimes happens that by error Christians have intercourse with Jewish or Saracen women, and Jews or Saracens with Christian women. Lest, therefore, these [transgressors] advance the excuse of such error to cloak the sin of that condemned relationship, We decree that such persons of either sex be distinguished from other peoples by the kind of clothes worn in public in every Christian province and at all times.

This resolution set in motion a long chain of detailed regulations which varied from place to place and from generation to generation. The social impact of that outward symbol of separation and the various forms it took in law and practice will be discussed in later chapters. Here we need but concern ourselves with the frequent resistance of the Jewish communities, often abetted by the governments, and on the other hand, with the unrelenting drive of the various Church organs to see this regulation implemented. Before long the badge lost all connection with the original purpose of preventing illicit sex relations between members of the three denominations and became an intended symbol of Jewish degradation on a par with the distinguishing marks ordered by law for heretics, lepers, vagrants and prostitutes, or the various kinds of ignominious attire prescribed for different classes of criminals. It assumed the character of a real "badge of shame," as it came to be called in later Jewish literature.[28]

For this reason the institution came to be resented even by those Jews who, for the sake of preserving their own religious identity and way of life, welcomed the principle of segregation. At times the wearing of a distinguishing sign increased the insecurity of the bearer, particularly during journeys. As an exception, when Jews lived under the protection of a special treaty of peace (*treuga dei*) such as that initiated by Henry IV in 1102, some outward identification might have been considered an additional safeguard. Usually, however, the insecurity of highways was so great and Jewish defenselessness so widely known that wearing a badge was a direct invitation to attack. That is why Innocent III himself, probably heeding Jewish protests, in a letter to the bishops of France (the full text is unfortunately lost), ordered them, somewhat ambiguously, "to permit Jews to wear clothes whereby they might be distinguished among Christians, but not to compel them to wear garments through which they might sustain loss of life." Subsequently many canonical ordinances, provincial and local, beginning with those adopted by the two Councils of Arles in 1234 and 1236, perhaps on papal initiative, specifically exempted Jews from wearing their badges on journeys.[29]

It took a century and more before this institution became firmly rooted. We shall see in other contexts how deeply intertwined it quickly became with the varying regional and local political interests and popular prejudices. Although, under the influence of its recognized temporal overlord, Innocent III, England introduced the badge in 1217 and France (where sporadic cases of distinguishing marks are recorded even before 1215) speedily followed in 1219, the pertinent laws were often observed in their breach until the expulsion of Jews from those countries. In Spain, Italy and Germany its progress was even slower. In 1219, Castilian Jews threatened to leave the country unless King Ferdinand revoked the law, which he did with the concurrence of the ecclesiastical authorities. Half a century later, in 1269, Mordecai ben Joseph of Avignon, author of a significant apologetic treatise, and Solomon de Salon were arrested by the Inquisition for indignantly opposing the badge. They were freed by Charles I of Anjou, ruler of the Provence and the two Sicilies, who decided in 1270 that Jews must "not be forced to wear any new signs, but only those they have worn in the past." Even in Rome itself the badge made but slow progress, and influential Jews, especially financiers, scholars and physicians, often secured individual exemptions for themselves and their families.[30]

Like almost everything else of this kind, the Jewish badge was soon converted into a source of state revenue. In some regions special administrators were appointed to collect the fines from transgressors. Such a *custos rotellae rubeae* is recorded, for example, in Sicily from 1369. Occasionally Christian municipalities, for instance those of Trapani in 1423 and of Palermo in 1425–26, secured for themselves the right of supervising the Jewish badge, and by implication obtained that additional source of revenue. Moreover, the dispensations frequently granted by rulers to individual Jews or Jewish communities had a substantial monetary value. In 1273, Charles I of Anjou, in return for an annual payment of two augustals for every person of more than ten years of age, and one augustal for children, liberated the Jewries of his various provinces from the badge. The precarious nature of such exemptions is, however, well illustrated by the sweeping revocation of all pertinent privileges in the arbitration agreement between the weak King Henry IV and the estates of Castile concluded in 1465 under the chairmanship of Alphonso de Oropesa, general of the Hieronymite order.[31]

Perhaps precisely because Judeo-Christian relations became more intimate during the Renaissance in Italy and Spain, the Church became ever more insistent upon the distinguishing marks. Under its prompting, the Venetian Republic reenacted this requirement on nine successive occasions. Gradually, the ecclesiastical will prevailed and in the fifteenth century the badge won fairly general acceptance. At that time it was particularly championed by the great philosopher and papal legate, Nicolaus Cusanus, and the fanatical preacher, John Capistrano.

The vicissitudes of many Jewish communities on this score are illustrated by the happenings in Frankfort in the 1450s. From time immemorial, it appears, Jews in that city had been in the habit of wearing the same garb as their Christian neighbors. Upon his arrival there, Nicolaus Cusanus complained to the city's Senate about this public neglect of a canonical regulation of old standing and demanded that Jews be made to wear distinguishing marks of the kind worn in Rome (a yellow wheel a digit wide for men, and blue-striped veils for women). Complying with the papal legate's orders, somewhat belatedly, Archbishop Diether of Mayence issued two harsh ordinances in 1457 censuring the Frankfort Jews for their ingratitude toward Christains and demanding that "just as they are alien to our faith, so shall they also be distinguished by their clothes." He prescribed that thenceforth all Jewish males should wear a gray wheel the size of a large apple on their coats, while women should display gray stripes the size of a stole. After Jewish protestations about the vagueness of these sizes, possibly supported by douceurs for the then very impoverished arch-episcopal treasury, as well as an appeal by the city council to the pope, Diether reversed himself and restored the previous *status quo.* Elsewhere, too, Cusanus overreached himself. He succeeded in pushing such resolutions through the synods of Bamberg, Eichstädt, and Constance, and in securing pertinent ordinances from the bishops of Mayence, Cologne, Würzburg, Augsburg, and Minden, and from the city council of Erfurt. But he also elicited many protests from local rulers, both secular and ecclesiastical. At the request of Emperor Frederick III, on May 1, 1452 Pope Nicholas V revoked the ordinances issued by his legate at the Council of Bamberg. In 1453, the pope similarly annulled Cusanus' orders relating to Jewish attire as well as to moneylending, on petitions from the bishop of Bamberg and the archbishop of Salzburg.[32]

Nevertheless, the badge made steady progress also in the lands of the Holy Roman Empire, where the more intensive self-imposed Jewish isolation seems to have made such outward signs of segregation of greater theoretical than practical import. On the other hand, during the fifteenth century, probably unaware that it was adopting an idea of the deranged Caliph Al-Ḥakim, the Council of Salzburg of 1418, going beyond the postulates of the Council of Vienna of 1267 which it generally followed, suggested that Jewish women wear small bells as well as badges. Most prevalent, however, was the use of a yellow wheel as recorded, for instance, in the city of Augsburg in 1434. Other local ordinances like that of Cologne of 1404 stressed the limitations on the shape, size, or costliness of the various Jewish garments so that their wearers "be distinguished as Jews." Typical of the methods of enforcement was a decree issued by Ferdinand I in 1551 for his Austrian hereditary provinces, which threatened any Jew found without his badge with the forfeit of his wearing apparel and everything found upon him. Half the fine was promised to the informer as a reward. A third offender was threatened with exile, together with his family, from all the Habsburg hereditary lands.[33]

## JEWISH QUARTERS

Probably because it aroused less Jewish and governmental opposition and because it had deep roots in immemorial habits, the institution of separate Jewish quarters, though intrinsically far more significant than requirements for distinguishing forms of dress, aroused less controversy and was the subject of fewer regulations. Even in ancient times and under Islam Jews often settled in close proximity to one another, in order the better to utilize the communal facilities in their synagogues, schools, and other institutions. In the Christian Middle Ages they derived an additional incentive from the growing one-sidedness of their economic endeavor and corporate separation. Like many other corporations, especially those of tailors, shoemakers or bakers, Jews preferred to settle in streets of their own. During the Crusades, when assaults on Jewish habitations began to multiply, they were often formally permitted to establish separate quarters surrounded by walls for more effective defense. Such a privilege had been enacted, even before the tragedy of 1096, by Bishop Huozmann-Rüdiger of Spires when he wished to attract Jews to his city in 1084. In time, however, the Church began demanding more and more insistently that Christians not live among Jews, and ultimately, also that the latter be formally separated in a quarter of their own. Expanding old segregationist demands of provincial synods, the universal Third Lateran Council of 1179 resolved that, throughout the whole Western world, Christians "who will presume to live with them [the Jews] be excommunicated." Because the provincial Council of Breslau of 1267 believed that it particularly had to protect the archdiocese of Gniezno with its relatively recent Christianized population against religious influences of Jews, it adopted the following canon (xii):

Since the Polish country still is a young plant in the body of Christendom, the Christian people might the more easily be infected by the superstitions and the depraved mores of the Jews living with them. In order that the Christian faith be more easily and quickly implanted in the heart of the faithful in these regions, we strictly prescribe that the Jews inhabiting this province of Gniezno should not indiscriminately dwell among the Christians, but should possess contiguous or adjoining houses in a segregated location of each city or village. This should be so arranged that the Jewish quarter be separated from the common habitation of the Christians by a fence, a wall or a ditch.[34]

Such segregationist tendencies on the part of the Church had their counterparts in similar Jewish efforts, both rabbinic and sectarian. If the ancient Damascus sect had forbidden its adherents to live on a Saturday "in a place close to Gentiles," the Talmud, too, wished to discourage the sojourn of Gentiles among Jews in Palestine, and of Jews among Gentiles in other lands, on that day of rest. Sectarians, such as the Samaritans and Karaites, wished to see an even more total exclusion of Gentiles from close settlement with Jews. We must differentiate, therefore, between the ghetto in the technical sense, in which according to law all Jews were bound to live and from which all Gentiles were excluded, and the non-technical ghetto, that is a Jewish quarter growing up freely without any legal constraint. In a sense, the technical ghetto was the less effective of the two. Neither the shape of the Jewish quarter nor of its houses was of particular concern to the Church and secular powers, although it was to those local authorities who had to assign new habitations to Jews. Here topography and other matters of expediency, rather than principle, played the decisive role. Only the erection of synagogues came within the purview of the Church, inasmuch as it tried to outlaw the building of new Jewish houses of worship and, for prestige reasons, endeavored to prevent their height from exceeding that of the local churches. In its perennial losing battle against new synagogues, it often had to compromise, as when in 1405, the Abbot of Oña, Castile, permitted the building of a new synagogue provided it would in no way be distinguished from the neighboring houses. Beginning with the fourteenth century, however, and especially after the "holy war" proclaimed against the Jews of Spain by Ferrant Martinez in 1391, technical ghettos became ever more common.[35]

Remarkably, the Church as such played only a secondary role in that evolution. Not until the days of the Counter Reformation, as we shall see, did the popes and their officials take an active hand in establishing formal ghettos in the Papal States, although a few had earlier advocated separate districts in other lands. Upon receiving the homage of Pedro IV of Aragon in 1339, Benedict XII reminded him sharply of the practice of requiring Jews and Saracens to live in separate quarters so that they would be removed "from excessive and perilous familiarity" with Christians. This usage, the pope complained, had been neglected in recent years, when unbelievers were even allowed to build synagogues and mosques in the midst of Christian populations, and in their daily contacts with Christians "to commit many indecent, unspeakable and horrible" acts. To reinforce his injunction the pope repeated it in the following year, and appealed over the king's head to the archbishops of Tarragona and Saragossa, as well as to the lords of the realm and the citizens of Saragossa, to see that it be implemented. A century later (1442), Eugenius IV sweepingly declared, "Jews shall not live among Christians, but rather they ought to dwell among themselves, separated and segregated from Christians within a certain district or place, outside of which they should by no means be allowed to own houses." Even more insistently, several provincial councils and individual churchmen agitated for the territorial segregation of Jewry. Some synods, as far apart as France, Italy, and Spain, made somewhat different proposals. That of Bourges demanded in 1276 that Jews be allowed to live only in cities and other major localities, lest they seduce simple villagers and impress upon them their own errors (canon 14). The Council of Ravenna decreed in 1311 that Jews be permitted to settle only in places where synagogues existed (canon 23). More narrowly, in 1335 the Council of Salamanca forbade Jews to live in houses belonging to a church or adjacent to a Christian cemetery (canon 12). Other synods provided that Christians of either sex not live in Jewish houses. Here the argument of the possible impairment of the morals of Christian women played a lesser role than the general postulate of segregation.[36]

For the most part, however, the records mainly mention the secular authorities who took the initiative in establishing separate Jewish quarters. For example, in 1312 Frederick III of the Two Sicilies suddenly removed the Jews of Palermo outside the city walls so as to assure their segregated living. But he reconsidered, and soon the Jews were allowed to return to their ancient habitat, which had been known as a Jewish quarter ever since the Muslim domination. Similarly, the harsh penalty imposed upon Jews who violated the segregation laws, included in the Castilian arbitration agreement of 1465, betrays its origin from the secular lords. Although the arbiters had been headed by the monk Alphonso de Oropesa, who seems to have greatly influenced the other provisions, the penalty that all Jewish transgressors become slaves of the lords on whose territories they happened to be apprehended was probably inserted by representatives of the interested parties. In general, it appears that, except perhaps in such outlying Catholic territories as Poland, the recency of whose Christianization accounted for the Church's feeling of insecurity, the ecclesiastical organs rarely took the initiative but often merely followed the lead of Christian rulers or masses reinforced by the wishes of the Jews themselves. Not surprisingly, because in this area the Church failed to supply its accustomed active and uniform guidance, the technical ghetto grew rather chaotically throughout the various provinces.[37]

Of course, secular and religious motivations were often indistinguishably blended. Gregory I had been annoyed by the *vox psallentium* reaching him from a neighboring synagogue. Since Jewish settlements dated back to the beginnings of many cities, it was natural for the synagogue to be located not far from the cathedral or some other major church. Apparently the officiating clergy grew accustomed to the synagogue's liturgical sounds, but pious laymen often felt that such an intermingling of prayers was a disgrace to the dominant faith. Hence, in 1470 the Sicilian viceroy ordered the transfer of the synagogue of Savoca from its "central and favored location" to a less desirable place, because the Jews "chant loudly their prayers particularly on the day of Sabbath" and thus disturb the occupants of the neighboring houses and churches. Better known is the incident of such a liturgical "disturbance" which led to the establishment of the new Jewish quarter in Frankfort, one of the most famous ghettos of all time. Although efforts to displace Jews from their commercially advantageous location in the center of town and close to the Main River

had been made under the driving force of the Jews' main commercial competitors, nothing was accomplished until 1442, when
Emperor Frederick III intervened. Generally rather friendly to
Jews, Frederick was irked by their presence in the heart of the city
and in the vicinity of its most aristocratic quarters. He was particularly aroused by the noises emanating from their dwellings during
prayers at the main church, because of which "the service is often
disturbed and insulted." His order, however, to the city council to
put an end to that "nuisance" was long disobeyed, the council
making but perfunctory motions. The local clergy, too, remained
rather passive. It required another sharp imperial command in
1458, reinforced by Pope Pius II's order of 1462, to set the stage
finally for the transfer of the synagogue and the rest of the Jewish
quarter to an outlying district, where in subsequent centuries it
became one of the major centers of German Jewish life.[38]

Although the Church did not always appear in the forefront,
the underlying idea of the separation of Jews from Christians in
different locations was in no way alien to its general intent of
closely supervising all Jewish contacts with the Christian world.
On the contrary, the ghetto idea was so closely related to the
Church's segregationist program that it, too, must be counted as a
major feature in the relations between Church and Synagogue.
The relative restraint of popes and universal councils doubtless
stemmed mainly from the realization that the Jews themselves
generally preferred living in quarters of their own, and that little
direct pressure had to be applied to achieve this result, except
perhaps in areas of close Jewish-Christian symbiosis such as medieval Spain, Poland, or early modern Italy.

## DISCRIMINATION

Segregation often led to economic and social discrimination. On
grounds of both prestige and self-defense, Jewish inferiority had
long become another pivot of Church policies toward Jews. Time
and again popes and councils echoed the patristic postulate that
the Synagogue, as the Church's handmaiden, should not be allowed to appear more prosperous and powerful than her mis-
tress. Typical of the contemporary rhetoric is Innocent III's letter

to Philip Augustus of January 16, 1204. Complaining of the favoritism extended to Jews by various Christian princes, the pope wrote that all "who preferred the sons of crucifiers, against whom His blood still cries out to the ears of the Father, to the heirs of Christ crucified are extremely offensive to the sight of the Divine Majesty. They prefer Jewish bondage to the freedom of the latter whom the Son had liberated, as if the son of the slave girl could and should be an heir together with the son of the free woman." In graphic arts this theme was often represented by the Church victorious contrasted to a subdued Synagogue. For example, the beautiful statuary in front of the Cathedral of Strasbourg represents the Church and the Synagogue as two good-looking women, one of whom stands erect and proudly displays her scepter; the other looks down, head bowed, with a broken scepter in her arms.[39]

A first conclusion, already drawn by ancient Christian teachers and emperors, was to forbid Jews to exercise any kind of dominion over Christians. This was an additional reason for prohibiting them from owning Christian slaves or employing Christian servants. The Christian Roman emperors removed Jews from the *honos militiae et administrationis,* but this restriction was frequently observed in its breach and canon law sought to reinforce it by additional arguments. Its official code warned that "our mores and those of the Jews do not agree in anything. Hence they might be able easily to make simple souls incline toward their superstition and unbelief through their continuous contact and assiduous familiarity," a statement repeated by many churchmen including Alexander of Hales. Papal shafts were aimed particularly at the Iberian kingdoms and the Provence, whose large Jewish populations maintained relatively close contacts with other religious groups, and at such recently missionized countries as Hungary where Christianity was still rather weak. In such areas kings made frequent use of Jewish officials. In 1209 the papal legate Milo made Count Raymond VI of Toulouse and the barons, as well as the city elders of Argentière and Montpellier, take the following oath:

We shall altogether remove Jews from all public or private administrative offices and never at any time entrust the same or any other Jews with the same or any other posts. Nor shall we take their advice against Christians, or allow Christian men or women to perform services in their houses. Should they hold such [servants] in defiance of that prohibition, we shall confiscate all the property of both the Jews and the Christians living with them.

Twenty-two years later, Gregory IX, after receiving from Archbishop Robert of Gran the "horrifying news" that the position of Jews and Saracens in Hungary was in many ways superior to that of the Christian masses, insisted in a lengthy, sharply worded letter that it is "thoroughly out of keeping that a blasphemer of Christ should exercise any authority over Christians." Understandably, the pope was irked most by the report that Jewish and Saracen officials often dared to impose outrageous burdens upon the churches.[40]

Warnings against the employment of Jewish physicians and apothecaries likewise had discriminatory, as well as segregationist, features. To frighten prospective Christian patients, the Church helped circulate popular rumors that Jewish doctors so indiscriminately hated Christians that they wilfully undermined their Christian patients' health. The Synod of Valladolid of 1322 lent that prejudice the prestige of a deliberate conciliar judgment (canon 21 or 22). Realizing the potential damage to the sick, however, some councils permitted the use of Jewish doctors in emergencies. Sometimes the popes themselves sought the best available medical help. As early as the thirteenth century one Maestro Gaio (Isaac ben Mordecai) allegedly served as papal court physician. Following him, as we shall see, many of his coreligionists officiated at the courts of Renaissance popes. Nor may we completely discount the sweeping assertion of Arnaldo de Vilanova, Christian apologist and competing physician though he was, when he wrote to Frederick III of Sicily that, notwithstanding the canonical prohibition, the general custom in Spain was "for no other physician to enter cloisters than a Jew; this is the case not only of cloisters for men, but also for women." [41]

A number of discriminatory provisions arose in reaction to Jewish ritualistic requirements. It was perfectly natural, then as today, for Jewish butchers to sell to Christian consumers carcasses which, upon closer examination by Jewish slaughterers, had turned out to be ritually unsatisfactory. Canon legislation often saw this practice as a humiliation for those Christians who purchased meat that was not considered good enough for Jews. Hence numerous councils (for instance that of Albi in 1254, in canon 66) forbade Jews to sell such meat in public markets or even through Christian butcher shops. Apparently little was done, however, about private sales to individual Christian households. Similarly, wine became the subject of controversy, because of the Jewish repudiation of the so-called "wine of libation," that is, wine touched by Gentile hands. To be sure, medieval rabbis often tried to tone down that regulation, which had originated in ages when wine was put to idolatrous use. Nonetheless, because of the prestige factor, many pious Christians were disturbed by such one-way sales of Jewish wine, especially if it was to be used in connection with church services. To these objections, which were reinforced by popular prejudice, Innocent III lent the sanction of his name when in his letter to Count Hervé of Nevers of January 17, 1208, he censured a number of "detestable" practices in that county. "At the vintage season," the pope wrote, "the Jew, shod in linen boots, treads the wine, and having extracted the purer wine according to the Jewish ritual he retains some for his own pleasure while leaving the rest, rejected by him, to faithful Christians." We need but realize the importance of wine in the general trade and consumption of the Middle Ages to understand how injurious such a prohibition, if stringently put into effect, might have become to Jewish business. With the gradual transfer of the center of gravity of the Jewish people, however, from the Latin wine-consuming countries to central and eastern Europe, the impact of that discriminatory legislation greatly diminished.[42]

Other canonical regulations, likewise originating in part from religious and folkloristic biases, were related to the competence of ecclesiastical courts and the validity of testimony rendered by Jewish or Christian witnesses. In its drive for universal power, the Church occasionally tried to arrogate to itself direct jurisdiction over Jews. There was especially great temptation for clerics to have their litigations with Jews adjudicated by courts of their own peers. But here the Church ran counter to well-rooted traditions, as well as to the pecuniary interests of states and municipalities.

On principle, it had to concede to secular rulers the right of regulating judicial administration in their lands. Yet, in theory, the clergy never formally abandoned the right to judge Jews and other "unbelievers." In a typically scholastic debate as to "whether the Church should judge infidels," Alexander of Hales cited numerous examples from the *Corpus* and reached the conclusion that the Church might indeed "impose upon them temporal penalties and even use indirect spiritual sanctions by removing Christians from any contact with them." A pertinent canon *Cum Judaei,* circulated at the universal Council of Vienne of 1311–12, must have helped to impress the attending lay statesmen with the seriousness of the Church's attempt to safeguard its judicial authority over Jews. As we shall see, however, this struggle was but one facet of the ever more tangled and conflicting jurisdictions affecting Jewish life in various lands. At no time did the Church wholly succeed in overruling the long-accepted principle that Jewish defendants should never be convicted on the sole testimony of Christian witnesses, just as, conversely, Jewish testimony alone should not suffice to convict a Christian defendant. Here, too, ecclesiastical agitation merely injected another ingredient into the existing maze of detailed regulations, which varied from place to place and from period to period.[43]

Neither was the Church itself quite consistent. Enlightened popes realized that giving free reign to Christian accusers would open the gates to a flood of unbridled denunciations, reflecting accumulated hatreds and suspicions rather than authenticated facts. In the obscure realm of folklore, particularly, one could always find witnesses ready to testify from hearsay or because of self-interest. The growing wave of Blood Accusations in the thirteenth century, especially, persuaded Pope Gregory X that the practice of condemning Jews on the basis of the testimony solely of Christians would result in frequent murders under the guise of justice. The pope, therefore, expanded the old constitution, *Sicut Judaeis,* by adding the following strongly worded provision:

We decree that the testimony of Christians against Jews not be valid unless there is some Jew among these Christians to confirm that testimony, just as Jews [alone] may not offer testimony against Christians. For it happens from time to time that Christians kill their own Christian children, and then the charge is brought against Jews by their enemies that they secretly abduct these Christian children and kill them, and offer sacrifices of their heart and blood. Then the fathers of these children or other Christians, competitors of these Jews, secretly conceal these children so that they may injure the Jews or else that, by restoring what they had taken away, they may extort a sum of money from the Jews. They assert most falsely that the Jews secretly and stealthily had kidnapped the children, killed them and offered sacrifices of their heart and blood, although their [the Jews] law expressly and absolutely forbids this. For the Jews may not sacrifice nor eat, nor drink blood, nor even eat of the flesh of animals, which have cloven hoofs. This has been corroborated in our Curia a number of times by Jewish converts to the Christian faith on occasions such as these when many Jews have often been seized and detained contrary to justice. Therefore we decree that Christians not be allowed to testify against Jews on such occasions, and we order that Jews, seized on frivolous accusations of this sort, be freed from prison, and not be again imprisoned on such frivolous charges, unless they are seized in the flagrant commission of the crime, which we do not believe to be true.

Many lesser churchmen, however, were less sympathetic to this provision, particularly in cases involving less obvious biases. At the same time they wished to see Jewish witnesses disqualified from testifying against Christians, except where they might assist in convicting persons accused of heresy. Ultimately, growing suspicion of the genuineness of fifteenth-century conversions even led to occasional prohibitions (for instance, in southern Italy) against accepting the testimony of converts in litigations between Christians and Jews.[44]

Of more permanent effect was the Church's share in the development of discriminatory ceremonies and formulas with respect to the Jewish oath. This matter assumed increasing significance, when the Church began opposing court decisions based on ordeals and made the outcome of litigations largely dependent on testimony offered by witnesses or parties under oath. Apart from secular sanctions, the main deterrent to perjury came from the religious dread of supernatural penalties which the omniscient Deity would inflict upon the perjurer even if he escaped detection. Hence it was natural for Christians, as well as for Jews and Muslims, to suspect each other's veracity. Once again, folkloristic prejudices played a far greater role than those emanating from official leaders of the Church, who at times actually tried to mitigate the widespread excesses. In 1302, for example, the archbishop of Cologne specifically provided that "Jews should present and execute oaths in the way they have been accustomed of old to present and execute them." The more universal codification of canon law by Gratian had likewise assured the Christian public that "Jews swear in the name of the true God." Yet on the whole, the official Church organs indirectly helped to nurture the underlying suspicions by their constant reference to "perfidious Jews." Although the term, *perfidia Judaeorum,* was originally intended to convey only the idea of Jewish "unbelief," it could not but conjure up in the minds of many Christians the picture of an ever unfaithful Jew ready to perjure himself either out of self-interest or because of his hatred of Christians. This ambivalence of the Church necessarily stimulated the growth, throughout the Middle Ages, of those numerous degrading formulas and ceremonies which came to be associated with the oath *more judaico.*[45]

One must bear in mind, to be sure, that parts of that awesome ceremonial arose from the Jews' own exaggerated emphasis upon the sanctity of oaths, which often induced rabbis and communal leaders to surround them with awe-inspiring features. Following geonic precedents, Abraham ben David of Posquières ruled that, in order to remind the witness of the Day of Judgment, Jewish adjurations should be administered in the synagogue with all lights extinguished and in front of a casket. The Christians went further. Apparently starting with the oath of abjuration taken by converts to Christianity, the Byzantine Empire evolved increasingly elaborate formulas for the oath of professing Jews as well. From Byzantium or its predecessor, the ancient Roman Empire, the institution spread both east and west. We find it well established in Muslim countries in the thirteenth century. In western and central Europe it was readily accepted, as the Teutonic idea of oath as an act of self-exposure to the wrath of gods for perjury had long before created a receptive mood. Entire phrases in the Jewish oath, from the brief Erfurt formula to that much amplified in the *Schwabenspiegel,* occur in early medieval references to the testimony of Teutons. In parts of Aragon, perhaps under combined Visigothic and Islamic influences, a formula containing the Ten

Commandments and the endless list of curses in Deuteronomy 28:16–68 was long recited. The Jew had to repeat "I swear" after each commandment and "Amen" after each curse. Other, more obnoxious ceremonies, such as standing on a bloody sow hide or a three-legged stool, spread rapidly throughout the northern countries. Falling off the stool was punishable by a fine; repetition often entailed loss of the law suit. Some such customs are recorded in the annals of Dortmund, Silesia, Hungary and Poland. In all these aberrations the Church was by no means the driving force, but it helped create the climate of opinion out of which they were able to emerge.[46]

More indirect were the effects of certain discriminatory laws arising from the Church's insistence upon Christian religious observance. Rather than merely complaining, as had Agobard of Lyons, that the public market day had been changed from Saturday to Sunday, several councils, beginning with the High Middle Ages, demanded that Jews not be allowed to perform any work on Sundays or Christian holidays. Such a prohibition, whether or not expressly stated, applied only to work in public. But it must have imposed a heavy additional burden, particularly on the Jewish farmer who, by observing the even stricter Jewish Sabbath laws from Friday sundown to Saturday evening, lost two important working days or more every week. Since the weather may have interfered with his work during the preceding or following weekdays, his competitive position must have suffered greatly. Fortunately for him, these regulations were often disobeyed in practice, and their repetition by successive synods merely underscored their ineffectiveness. On the other hand, it was this very ecclesiastical reiteration which may have stimulated Jewish leaders to relax the Talmud's stringent prohibition against Jews' trading in public on Gentile holidays. Such relaxation, begun in the early Middle Ages, ultimately led to a complete disregard of the talmudic injunctions, even on Christmas.[47]

As in the earlier Middle Ages, complications also arose from the religious fervor, often translated into anti-Jewish resentment, aroused by the sermons preached and the miracle plays performed during the Holy Week. Some barbarous local customs such as the slap publicly administered to a Jew in Toulouse, or the legitimized stoning of the Jewish quarter in Béziers, may have been replaced by special Jewish taxes. But many synodal regulations now forbade Jews to show themselves publicly on Good Friday, either as a preventive measure against anti-Jewish riots or in order to forestall the impression that carefree Jewish passers-by were ridiculing the sorrow of Christian congregations. The Councils of Fritzlar in 1259 (canon 8) and of Aschaffenburg in 1292 (canon 18) forbade Jews to show themselves at the windows or gates of their houses, under penalty of the rather heavy fine of one silver mark. In many areas the prohibition was extended to the entire weekend. According to the decision of the court of arbitration headed by Alphonso de Oropesa, Henry IV and the Castilian Estates pledged themselves in 1465 to prohibit Jews from leaving their houses between Thursday noon and Saturday morning.[48]

## FISCAL CONFLICTS AND USURY

The Church's fiscal interests often ran counter to Jewish economic endeavors. Wherever popes ruled as sovereigns, they, like the other monarchs, often exploited their Jewish taxpayers. Although, as in the days of Benjamin of Tudela, no regular Jewish poll taxes were collected in Rome, the revenue officials found ways of effectively covering the budgetary needs through a system of direct and indirect imposts, to which Jews, as the most defenseless group, doubtless contributed a disproportionate share.

Regrettably, available data do not allow for comprehensive reconstruction of Jewish taxation in Rome and other papal possessions. But it appears that, at least in the fourteenth century, its mainstay was a property tax (sometimes subsumed under the general heading of the ecclesiastical tithe) of $\frac{1}{2}$ ducat for property ranging up to 100 ducats in value, 1 ducat for property valued at 100 to 500 ducats, $1\frac{1}{2}$ ducats for that valued up to 1000 and for every 1000 ducats above that sum. In addition, Jews paid special imposts, contributed to the cost of public festivities (this tribute seems to have amounted in 1385 to the sizable sum of 1,130 florins), paid municipal taxes and dues to the merchant guild, and so forth. The prorating of these payments over the Italian provinces led to constant bickerings between the Roman Jewish and the local communities. In 1399 Pope Boniface IX admitted that "because of the economic depression and wars . . . the aforementioned Jewish community [of Rome] has been reduced to poverty and destitution." He therefore ordered the provincial communities to resume their accustomed share. In the French possessions, on the other hand, the popes largely maintained the earlier fiscal structure, except for the breaks in historic continuity occasioned by temporary outbursts of intolerance in 1322 and 1350. In Carpentras, for example, the Jews had to pay 3 pounds each of ginger and pepper annually for permission to bury their dead in the Jewish cemetery. They also paid a capitation tax, the total of which was established at 18 livres in 1276, drastically reduced to 4 sous in 1343 (so long as the number of Jewish families would not exceed 90), and then restored to 18 livres in 1385. Extraordinary imposts included a tax of six deniers annually, lest, it was said, the clergy insult Jews. Papal regulations were often amplified by city statutes such as that of Rome which, on the one hand, tried to protect Jewish taxpayers against illegal bureaucratic exactions, and on the other hand encouraged denunciations of delinquent taxpayers by promising informers 50 percent of the amount thus recovered. Nor did the papal capital escape that perennial plague of medieval administrations, special privileges for favored individuals. In a remarkable decree of 1405, the Roman Senate conferred upon the physician Elia di Sabbato and his progeny, Roman "citizenship," general exemption from the duty of wearing a badge, and full tax immunity. He was even assigned a lifetime pension of 20 gold florins annually from Jewish revenue.[49]

At times the papal administration, in enlightened self-interest, freed Jewish merchants from certain payments. In his remarkable decree of February 1, 1255, Alexander IV exempted five Jewish merchants (listed by name) and their associates from all road taxes throughout the Papal States and the Two Sicilies, a privilege extended several weeks later also to Christian merchants. On the other hand, the Papacy was always prepared to back the fiscal demands of ecclesiastical authorities against the opposition of secular rulers. When the struggle between Papacy and Empire reached a climax, as under Innocent IV, the papal Treasury had to be refilled by sharp exactions from both Jews and non-Jews. On other occasions, too, the popes were able to devise certain special imposts to foster their own international enterprises. As late as the fifteenth century when the idea of the Crusades had long lost its luster, the papal Treasury still imposed special taxes upon Jews to finance expeditions to the Holy Land. After the rise of the Ottoman Empire another *vigesima,* or a 5 percent property tax, was imposed on Jews to help finance the fight against the Turks. Most remarkably, reacting in 1429 to rumors that Jews in Jerusalem had been implicated in the destruction of the Franciscan monastery there, the generally friendly Pope Martin V imposed a "certain sum of money" on Jews in the Republic of Venice and the March of Ancona to help restore that sanctuary.[50]

So widely known were the Jewish financial contributions to the papal Treasury that contemporaries suspected any favorable papal action, such as the bulls against the Blood Accusation, of being obtained by Jewish bribery. The papal bureaucracy was, indeed, as open to tangible blandishments as were its opposite numbers in other lands. But, dependent as it was on voluntary donations from the whole Christian world, the papal Treasury was able to accept financial contributions publicly, even from foreign Jews made in recognition of favors conferred or in order to avert inimical acts. Possessing, moreover, the combined authority of Church and state, the papal administration avoided some of the conflicts which, as in the case of ecclesiastical tithes, plagued Jewries of other lands. Only on occasions of instability of papal authority at home, invasion by foreign monarchs, political plays by leading families of Rome, and occasional outbursts of popular discontent which, as in the case of Cola de Rienzo, led to seizure of power by the revolutionary party, was the smooth relationship between the pope's fiscal organs and the Jewish community interrupted. Most popes doubtless appreciated the steady income flowing from their Jewish subjects and the latter's financial reserve power which could readily be tapped in emergencies. Together with the ideological considerations connected with the doctrine of toleration of Jews, which made even the thirteenth-century polemicist Raymond Martini exclaim, "No enemy of the Christian faith is more familiar and more indispensable for us, than the Jew," the Church's financial self-interest accounted for the relative stability of Jewish life in the Papal States. It also helped maintain the newly acquired French possessions in Avignon and the Comtat Venaissin as an island within the raging seas of anti-Jewish hostility in the days of the Pastoureaux and the Western expulsions.[51]

Partially because of that stability, which enabled Jews to engage in more diversified pursuits in the Papal States than in lands north of the Alps, papal tax collectors seem also to have evinced little interest in the provenance of their revenue from such forbidden sources as Jewish income from usury. True, the connection between Jewish taxation and usury caused occasional soul searching in ecclesiastical circles. Following in the footsteps of Gregory IX in his correspondence with the king and leading clergy of France in 1237–38, Thomas Aquinas took pains to explain to Aleyde (or Margaret), the Duchess of Brabant, that although she would thereby become a partner in usurious practices she nevertheless was entitled to tax the Jews. While admitting that Jewish money, in so far as it was derived from usury, should be returned to those from whom it had been extorted, Thomas conveniently took for granted that the borrowers could not be located. Consequently, the duchess might devote the Jews' money to pious causes or "else the common use of the land," a category which could include practically any expense of the royal Treasury. Her son (or husband), John I, could actually authorize the city of Louvain "to keep the Jews and Cahorsins in the same status as that granted them in Brussels." On the other hand, pursuing his general economic theory based upon a fairly static social order, Thomas advised the duchess not to "exact from the Jews services which they had not been accustomed to render before." The popes neither required the comfort of the distinguished Dominican's sophistry in permitting the use of such revenue, nor felt any compunction about raising it beyond the accustomed level. In such fairly diversified and dynamically changing economies as those of Rome and Avignon, this debate must have sounded purely academic.[52]

The papal attitude on this score, it may be noted, was particularly inconsistent during the preceding quarter century. On the one hand, Gregory IX in 1237 pacified Louis IX's conscience by declaring the king's subsidy to the Latin Empire of Constantinople for its struggle against the Muslims a sufficient restitution for deriving revenue from usurers. (Louis did not rest, however, until he completely outlawed Jewish usury in 1254.) On the other hand, Innocent IV enjoined King Thibaut II of Navarre in 1247 to force Christian debtors to repay "honest loans" from Jews despite the French barons' oath not to make such repayments. This did not prevent his successor, Alexander IV, from allowing the king of Navarre nine years later to confiscate all Jewish property derived from usury and either to restore the proceeds to the legitimate owners or to use it for pious purposes. Boniface VIII doubtless also had revenue derived from Jewish usury in mind when, on September 3, 1297, he advised the queen-widow Margaret of Sicily to select a father confessor, "who would absolve her from whatever [sin she had committed through] illicit extortion of money from Jews of her lands or from any other persons whom she might not remember, so long as she would divert these extorted funds to the support of the infirm and the poor." [53]

Certain general principles guiding the Church's economic policies adversely affected Jews far beyond the confines of the Papal States. The insistence of canon jurists that, except in cases of urgent necessity, all Church property must remain inalienable led to an increase of mortmain which ultimately caused much concern to secular rulers, particularly since the Church demanded complete tax exemption for such property and its clerical beneficiaries. To Jews it meant that land sold by them, directly or indirectly, to the Church could never be regained. This was, indeed, an additional factor in the progressive alienation of the Jews from the soil, which in the northern lands reached its apogee after the twelfth century.

Some synods urged Christian laymen to refrain from selling houses to Jews. Originally conceived as a segregationist measure, this regulation often resulted in Christian ownership of houses on Jewish streets, as happened, for instance, in Rome after the establishment of the technical ghetto in 1555. As we shall see, within half a century on June 5, 1604, Pope Clement VIII felt obliged to protect Jewish tenants against exploitation by their landlords. The tenants possessed only hereditary leaseholds, as a result of rent laws known under the characteristic name of *jus di gazagà,* a derivative from the Hebrew laws of *ḥazaqah* (long-term possession). In the long run these manifold prohibitions reinforced the general economic trend toward restricting Jewish occupations to fewer and fewer branches; in some countries Jews were forbidden to own any real estate whatsoever.[54]

Among the fiscal problems of the Christian world, that of ecclesiastical tithes continued to loom large. Even before 1200, the Church's drive for imposing that tax not only on rural property but also on rents in urban houses acquired by Jews from Christians had often led it into conflict with secular authorities, who viewed all Jewish property as their special preserve. Later the drive was greatly intensified, although in the ensuing clarification Jews secured general relief from its application to personal taxes. Summarizing the existing regulations and, as was his custom, arguing their pros and cons, Alexander of Hales concluded that Jews were to be compelled to pay only the so-called *decimas praediales*, tithes from real estate, since new owners of landed property had to assume all its liabilities but not the *decimas personales*, or personal tithes. Among the grievances of the Sicilian and other clergy which Gregory IX pressed before the imperial court in 1236 were those relating to Jewish imposts owed to certain churches. On February 12, 1289 Nicholas IV confirmed a treaty with King Dinis of Portugal, obligating the latter, among other matters, not to appoint Jewish officials, to enforce the badge, and to refrain from interfering with the forcible collection of tithes due from his Jewish subjects (Art. 27).[55]

Of course, whenever secular authorities refused to cooperate, the Church could only threaten to order Christians to sever all contacts with defaulting Jewish taxpayers. As explained by the fifteenth-century jurist, Bonifatius de Vitelinis (who incidentally reiterated the duty of Jews to pay the tithe), "this is a major penalty for Jews, . . . because of such severance of relations they are so to say placed outside their [the Christians'] protection, and the law teaches that it is a great penalty to be unable to converse with other people and to lack human contacts." In practice, most Jews must have felt such threats less significant, as their human relations were largely restricted to the Jewish quarter. Similarly, outside the Papal States the withdrawal of the Church's protection was meaningful only if it was supported by the secular authorities.[56]

In one domain, however, the Church actually promoted Jewish economic endeavors. In its unending struggle against Christian usury, it often encouraged Jews to take over that economic function, the indispensability of which, under the expansive economy of the later Middle Ages, even churchmen could not wholly deny. Some aspects of the ramified canonical legislation concerning usury have been discussed in an earlier volume; its broader economic effects upon Jews will be analyzed in connection with the general economic evolution of the late medieval community. Suffice it to say here that leading scholastics such as Thomas Aquinas now added to it the weight of Aristotelian arguments, namely that "money has no children." Under the combination of an old misunderstanding of the Vulgate's translation of the verse in Luke (6:35), *mutuum date nihil inde sperantes,* with the Aristotelian teachings of the total unproductivity of money, the leading spokesmen of the Church condemned any accretion to the original capital as a sinful appropriation of the debtor's property. Of course, these arguments could be, and were at times, used also against Jewish moneylending with interest. Economic evolution, increasingly requiring credit for productive as well as consumptive purposes, was so irresistible that churchmen had to close their eyes to the frequent methods of evasion employed by Christian lenders. It was generally considered a lesser evil to allow Jews to engage in this forbidden commerce, since they were not subject to the prohibitions of canon law and were condemned to perpetual damnation in any case because of their repudiation of Christian teachings. To appease the conscience of Emperor Frederick III and other rulers, Pope Nicholas V reassured them that "it is much better that this people should perpetrate usury than that Christians should engage in it with one another." [57]

Such permissiveness did not, of course, prevent the Christian world, lay as well as clerical, from clamoring against Jewish exploitation. In view of the prevailing high rates of interest, repayment of unproductive loans made for the satisfaction of temporary wants, even whims, became ever more burdensome. Certainly no factor contributed more to the growing bitterness permeating all late medieval Judeo-Christian relations than did the increasing concentration of Jews upon this single branch of the economy.

Out of this welter of interests and desires emerged many inconsistencies, as in the postulated return of all usurious gains to legitimate owners. With respect to such gains acquired by recent converts, it was conveniently argued that, whenever the original owners were no longer identifiable, these profits could be retained by the converts under the guise of charitable subsidies for their own maintenance. The Council of Constance in 1416 attempted to compromise by allowing the newly baptized Jews to retain half their unlawful gains. Eighteen years later, on the other hand, the Council of Basel insisted that "no sin can be forgiven until after the restoration of the robbed objects." However, even that Council and subsequent synods and popes never abandoned the fiction that previous owners were as a rule unidentifiable.[58]

Other compromises had to be made with hard economic realities. In Renaissance Italy many formal invitations were extended by cities to Jews to establish themselves in their midst, "in order to provide credit for the needy population." The city elders issuing such *condottas* were, of course, aware of their violation of the Church's antiusurious teachings, and some of them sought relief for their troubled consciences by appealing for papal dispensation. The popes seem to have accommodated such petitioners without much difficulty. In 1452 Nicholas V issued a blanket permission for the city elders of Lucca to maintain "at their discretion one or many Jewish usurers." Similarly, in 1489 Innocent VIII ordered the vicar general of the archbishopric of Siena to free the local authorities from the threatened ecclesiastical penalties for admitting Jewish usurers to Siena, "which had become necessary for the benefit of the burghers and others, particularly the poor." [59]

Despite such papal forbearance, the constant growth of Jewish communities in northern Italy, combined with the erection of new synagogues and the general expansion of Jewish religious and cultural life, understandably aroused the ire of some zealous churchmen. To counteract the imperative need for Jewish lenders, Franciscans, such as Barnabas of Terni, Agostino Maccabeo of

Perugia, and especially Bernardino da Feltre, devised a program of establishing charitable loan banks (*monti di pietà*) which would provide credit at nominal rates of interest.

In Terni, to be sure, where anti-Jewish propaganda had been set in motion in 1464, that effort and one following it three years later failed. Nevertheless, under the impact of persistent petitions by Agostino da Perugia, another *monte* was founded in 1472. Ironically, its support by the municipality was cut short by ecclesiastical interference. The city had been deeply in debt; it owed money to the bishops of Terni and Manfredonia, as well as to some Roman merchants. The latter secured direct papal intervention, and the city was threatened with excommunication if it failed to meet its obligations without delay. In desperate straits, the municipal elders appealed to Jews of other localities to come to their rescue. They were forced to accept a treaty guaranteeing the rights of new Jewish settlers to lend money at maximum rates of 30 percent to local citizens and 40 percent to foreigners. Unlike the earlier Jewish residents and visitors, the new arrivals were exempted from displaying their distinguishing marks.[60]

Such reversals, however, did not discourage Agostino and the other Franciscan protagonists of charitable loan banks. The leadership was soon taken over by Bernardino da Feltre, a rabble rousing orator who often found that his appeals were most effective if he combined them with attacks on Jewish moneylending and on the Jewish people as a whole. His Jew-baiting sermons attracted vast audiences but at the same time became the source of much discord and unrest. Occasionally the mobs of listeners attacked Jewish passers-by or marched on the Jewish quarter. As a result, various Italian rulers such as the Duke of Milan for Bergamo and Ticino and the authorities of the Republic of Venice prohibited Da Feltre from preaching in their churches. However, recognizing the effectiveness of his appeals for charitable loan banks (in 1534 the Council of Ten had to issue a decree stating that "one must neither propose nor discuss any such matters pertaining to *monti di pietà* without the express permission and deliberation of this Council"), the Venetian authorities ultimately persuaded the Jewish community itself to provide Christians with cheap credit through charitable pawnbroking. This was the origin of the so-called *Banchi del Ghetto,* institutions serving not Jewish clients within the ghetto of Venice, but rather Christian compatriots outside it. Despite the opposition of Dominicans who, resentful of the success of their Franciscan rivals, had insisted that any charges however nominal by the *monti* constituted usury, the institution gained ground rapidly. Supported by the Fifth Lateran Council of 1513–17 and the Council of Trent, it became a permanent fixture in the early modern economy without, however, completely displacing conventional Jewish moneylenders.[61]

## ADJUSTABLE POLARITIES

Despite the alarms sounded on occasion by fervent preachers, Jewish moneylending rarely constituted a major preoccupation of the Church. Here, as in other areas, the lower clergy was often stimulated to anti-Jewish pronunciamentos and to actions under pressure of local economic and political conflicts, which were unrelated to the traditions of the Church universal. In that period of transition from medieval feudal economy and polity to modern capitalistic states and societies, the clergy often shared in the distress of classes ground under the wheels of the new evolution. Sometimes local animosities, especially if they also penetrated the economically rather quiescent Papal States, communicated themselves also to the popes or more directly to the universal and provincial councils. However, on the whole, the Papacy tried to pursue its traditional course with but minor adjustments to changing social demands.

In their drive for world dominion, the ambitious popes of the thirteenth century refined the papal claim to total overlordship of the Jews living under Christendom. We shall see how controversial the doctrine of Jewish "serfdom" became in the ever sharpening conflict between Papacy and Empire, with the Papacy insisting upon the ancient doctrine of the submission of Jews to the supremacy of the Church as such. With the weakening of papal power, there was a more mellow interpretation of that assertion. In fact, because Western societies were going through the travail of transition from medieval to modern systems of economics and politics, the popes' conservatory policies often proved a life buoy

to embattled Jewish communities when they were submerged by
one wave of hostility after another. In the fourteenth and fifteenth
centuries, indeed, papal voices were heard more frequently in the
defense of the right of Jews to survive in the Christian world than
in the earlier, more quiescent periods.

At the same time, the Church never abandoned its general insistence upon keeping Jews in a state of lowly submission and segregation. While constantly repeating the protective constitution,
*Sicut Judaeis,* and sharply condemning the Blood Accusation, the
popes also spelled out in much greater detail the anti-Jewish provisions of canon law. By confirming the *Decretum Gratiani* and
adding many new decretals, they placed (through the *Corpus
juris canonici*) an official reference work in the hands of clerics
and jurists for the enforcement of those provisions. Whenever they
felt that the Jews were excessively favored by Catholic monarchs,
especially by being entrusted with high public office and dominion
over Christians, they as well as the councils raised their voices in
protest. But whenever popular hostilities, nurtured by such folkloristic accusations as the blood libel, poisoning of wells, and desecration of the host, threatened widespread blood baths, popes
and other churchmen often came to the rescue. As it happened,
the fourteenth and fifteenth centuries furnished more opportunities for popes to counsel restraint than to be in the vanguard of
the accusers of Jewry.

Of course, there always were exceptions. Some popes, like Pedro
de Luna serving as Antipope Benedict XIII, caught the spirit of
popular hostility in their own countries and led the chorus of anti-
Jewish accusers. But those exceptions were, as a rule, quickly overcome by the return of the Church to its traditional "golden
mean." Benedict XIII not only faced the opposition of two rival
occupants of the Holy See, but he was followed by the universally
recognized pope, Martin V, who leaned backward in emphasizing
pro-Jewish aspects of canonical tradition. In this way the Church
served, on the whole, as the conserving force, helping to preserve
the Jewish "remnant" to the end of days.

# STUBBORN DISSENTER

ANTI-JEWISH discrimination and segregation were primarily intended for the defense of Christian doctrine and observance. By pointing up Jewish inferiority and erecting a thick wall of separation, the ecclesiastical leaders hoped to stave off the impact of influential Jewish neighbors on wavering Christians. Now that the Church found itself in an increasingly embattled position, these traditionally accepted methods were ever more emphasized. The last centuries of the Middle Ages were, indeed, a period of heated controversies with heretical and reformatory movements within the Christian body politic.

In such periods of crisis the Church, not unreasonably, feared that the presence of Jewish "infidels" might add new fuel to sectarian deviations. To the Church it seemed absolutely imperative that, at least consciously, the Jews should not strengthen deviationist forces, whether directly by influencing Christians or converted Jews to profess Judaism, or indirectly by raising doubts in the minds of Christians about the truth of their accepted doctrines and institutions. Utterances aimed at Jesus and the Virgin were considered particularly subversive, inasmuch as various heretical trends within Christianity were questioning the traditional ecclesiastical interpretation.

## HERESY HUNTING

Judaism, often invoked as a witness for Christianity because it attested the authenticity of the Bible, could also become an inimical force in an age when Scripture began to serve as an armory for heretical teachings. The Church looked askance at the mere presence of Bibles in the hands of laymen. In 1199, Innocent III, in part echoing Gregory VII, declared that Scripture contained lessons too profound to be comprehended by the laity, and therefore the faithful ought to rely wholly on the clergy for its proper interpretation. Thirty years later the Council of Toulouse went further and forbade laymen to possess Bibles in either Latin or the vernacular. In 1234, James I of Aragon at the Council of Tarragona ordered all owners of Old and New Testaments written in "Romancio" to deliver them to the authorities, or else become suspect of heretical leanings. Hebrew Bibles in the possession of Jews appeared less dangerous because of the linguistic barrier, but their oral interpretations by Jews could stimulate inquiring Christian minds to view Scripture in an unauthorized light. Hence the "most celebrated" preacher, Berthold of Ratisbon, warned Christians not to discuss biblical issues with Jews "for ye are unlearned while they are learned in Scriptures." And Berthold spoke to vast audiences coming from distant localities, exaggeratedly estimated by contemporaries as ranging between 12,000 and 200,000.[1]

New forces of rationalism, which made themselves felt during the Twelfth-Century Renaissance, likewise threatened to undermine the Church's undisputed control over the laity. The rise of a lay intelligentsia with independent access to sources of knowledge removed the major prop from under its monopolistic ideological controls. It spiritedly reacted by encouraging the Franciscan preachment of the supremacy of piety over learning and, at the other extreme, helping the Dominicans closely to regulate the literature available to the reading public, even outlawing, for a time, all Aristotelian writings. Within a few years after the formation of the Dominican order, a chronicler reported that one of the monks had been much impressed by the study of philosophy. Thereupon he was told, "You are not a friar but a philosopher." He was ordered to undress "and was flogged so hard that for fifteen days he felt as if all his limbs were fractured and he sustained most severe pains in his back." The early anti-intellectualism of the order found further expression when Abbot Macharius discovered that one of his monks kept a number of books in his cell and shared them gladly with his brethren. The abbot exclaimed, "You are doing good work, but you would do even better if you owned no books whatsoever." To such men the Jews, then in the forefront of transmitters of Eastern science and philosophy to the West, could only appear as dangerous disseminators of heterodox teachings, and of a new methodology which, in the long run, could prove even more subversive.[2]

Assuming, as Henry Charles Lea phrased it, that toleration of heretics was tantamount to persecution of Catholic Christianity, the Church also suspected Jews of aiding and abetting individual heretics. Jews often found themselves in the midst of sharp Christian ideological and ritualistic controversies, particularly in southern France where before the Anti-Albigensian Crusade a large segment of the population betrayed some sectarian leanings. Whether as outright heretics, called *perfecti,* or as *credentes* (those who believed in certain heretical doctrines without adopting all sectarian laws and observances), the heterodox were well represented in all classes with whom the affluent and culturally alert Provençal Jewish communities maintained close social relations. It was but natural that in periods of danger, when sectarianism largely went underground, individual "heretics" should seek refuge with Jewish friends. Such *receptatores hereticorum* often acted from humanitarian rather than anti-Catholic impulses. Similarly, those converts from Judaism to Christianity who found their spiritual and economic adjustments to the new life too arduous, or were otherwise disappointed, often tried to revert to their former faith with the aid of Jewish friends or relatives. Inquisitors implacably prosecuted all such accessories to apostasy or heresy. Bernard Gui of southern France and Nicholas Eymeric of Aragon even taught (to quote the latter) that "the pope may also judge Jews, if they do something against their own law as well as in matters of moral behavior in so far as their own superiors fail to punish them. The same holds true if they invent heresies against their own religion." There always existed the possibility that such internal Jewish heresies might infect the neighboring Christian communities as well.[3]

Nor were apprehensions altogether lacking that Jews might utilize existing tensions to spread their own faith. The accusations of the fourteenth-century Spanish monk, Lucas of Túy (Tudensis), in his venomous attack on the "Albigensian Errors," though vastly exaggerated, did reflect the fears entertained by many Christian clerics and laymen. He wrote:

Heretics simulate the Jewish infidelity. Some of them with deliberate malice become circumcised and, under the guise of being Jews, come to Christians and ask heretical questions as if starting a disputation. Thus as apparent Jews they sow heresies more freely, while previously they had not dared to utter a word of heresy. The secular princes and city magistrates listen to these doctrines of heresy from Jews whom they number among their acquaintances and friends. If anyone, inspired by zeal for the law of God, exasperates one of them, he is punished as if he touched the pupil of the eye of the city magistrate. They also teach other [real] Jews to utter blasphemies against Christians, in order the better to pervert the Catholic faith. All synagogues of the malignant Jews have patrons of their own; they placate the princes with innumerable gifts, and with gold seduce the magistrates to their own worship [culturam].

Lucas wound up this harangue with an attack on the Catholic clergy for passively tolerating such misdeeds. Had not Innocent III written to various French archbishops in 1198 about heretics who tried to appear "just" in order to be called "rabbis" in the market place? One of the Albigensian articles of faith (Art. 10) allegedly asserted that "the law of Jews is better than that of Christians." [4]

Ironically, such accusations were often hurled at the Catharists, many of whom had inherited the ancient gnostic-Marcionite hostility to Judaism. With their Manichaean heritage these men professed an essentially dualistic doctrine and sharply separated the good God of the New Testament from the God-Satan (inferior even to the Marcionite "demiurge") of the old dispensation. They were quoted by opponents as contending "that Lucifer who is called the devil has given the Old Testament and the Law." In his confession an accused Catharist quoted Guillaume Belibasta's saying that "the devil still visits the Jews, because he is the same who had appeared to them in the shape of a calf and gave them the law, and whom the Jews call the Messiah. . . . The souls of dying Jews are carried off to the devil; no Jewish soul has ever been, or ever will be, saved." They attributed, in particular, the deluge, the destruction of Sodom and Gomorrah, the Exodus from Egypt, the drowning of the Egyptians, as well as the animal sacrifices, to the devil pretending to be God. In short, "Jews and renegade heretics alike hold the worst of faiths." True, the Catharists had to admit that their revered New Testament frequently cited passages and facts from the Old Testament with approval.

Certainly the glorified Davidic descent of Christ could no more be denied than were the messianic predictions of the Prophets or the ethics of the Ten Commandments. Characteristic of their compromise solutions for these contradictions is the report of Raynier Sacconi concerning certain Catharist disciples who taught that:

the devil was the author of the entire Old Testament except for the following books: Job, Psalms, the Books of Solomon, Wisdom, Sirach, Isaiah, Jeremiah, Ezekiel, Daniel and the Twelve Prophets, some of which, they contend, were written in heaven, namely those which had been written before the destruction of Jerusalem which they concede had been caused by heaven.

Many Catharists, when they wanted to deliver the supreme insult, called the established Church with its priesthood, its worldly and political power, "the synagogue of Satan." Yet because some French lords evinced pro-Catharist leanings, their Jewish subjects, too, were often accused of aiding and abetting individual Catharists. Even Philip the Fair, who generally resented the encroachment of the Papacy and its inquisitorial organs upon his Jewish "serfs," nevertheless conceded in 1299 the right of inquisitors to prosecute Jews not only because of their conversionist activities, which he greatly exaggerated, but also because "they harbor refugee heretics and hide them." [5]

More pertinent seemed the imputation of close relationships between the Waldensian theology and Judaism. In their sharp opposition to image worship and their rejection of prayers for aid to Mary and the saints, the Waldenses often cited Jewish interpretations of the Old Testament. In a Waldensian treatise on the Antichrist we read that the latter "deceitfully causes them [good Christians] to serve the idols of all the world under the guise of saints and relics." The Waldenses also repudiated the existing Church and its "pharisaic" traditions and observances. According to an inquisitor's biased report, their preachers often disguised themselves as peddlers and addressed crowds in market places, gradually leading up to a denunciation of the Church in such terms as: "Your teachers are fastidious in their dress and manners; they like to occupy the places of honor at feasts and be styled, Master, Rabbi! We do not ask for such rabbis!" At the same time they considered it a matter of honor to be called Israel in the spirit.

The Passagii, in some respects but a subdivision of the Waldensian sect, went further and postulated the continued validity of most Mosaic laws, including the Jewish form of Sabbath observance and ritual food commandments, and even demanded ritual circumcision, a demand which earned them the designation of *circumcisi*. They also betrayed underground Arian survivals when, in their doctrine of the Trinity, they placed God the Son below God the Father. While not going as far as the Jewish denial of the messiahship and divine character of Jesus, the Passagii were able to borrow from Jewish apologists many an argument against the traditional Trinitarian dogma. They could thus readily appear as a Judaizing sect, and superficial observers freely assailed Jews for having inspired such deviations. Charles of Anjou probably had those rumors in mind when, in his edict of July 4, 1276, he ordered the seneschal and other officials of the Provence to extend full support to the inquisitor, Bertrand de Rocca, "against heretics and against those reprobate Christians who turn from Christianity to Judaism, their patrons, receivers, and defenders, as well as against the Jews who induce Christians [to accept] Judaism." Apparently, the main reason we hear of relatively few direct Judeo-Waldensian contacts is that that sect spread principally in northern Italy, where there were few Jewish communities at the time.[6]

Numerous minor sects, too, could by some stretch of imagination be brought into connection with Jews and Judaism. In his bull of February 1231, Gregory IX named the Poor Men of Lyons, the Patarenes, Josephinists, Arnaldists, and Speronists, though only in his letter to the archbishop of Mayence and others of June 13, 1233 did he describe the origins of the so-called Luciferians, whom he accused of the regular practice of desecrating hosts at Easter. In general, though, the Church preferred vague formulations such as that offered by Pope Lucius III at the Council of Verona of 1184, which was taken over in the *Decretales* of Gregory IX and thus became part of the *Corpus juris canonici*. The following summary is quite succinct:

A heretic who thinks ill or teaches ill about the sacraments of the Church is to be excommunicated. If convicted, unless he mends his ways and abjures the error, he is to be handed over to the secular court which is to punish both a cleric after his disrobing and a layman. The same penalty is to be inflicted on suspects of heresy if they do not mend their ways, while relapsed heretics ought to be denied all hearing. Secular princes who refuse to swear to defend the Church against heretics shall be excommunicated and their lands subjected to an interdict; their cities which resist shall be deprived of commerce with other cities and of the episcopal dignity; those exempt shall be under the discipline of the ordinary bishops in all these matters which shall be instituted against the heretics.

Vague interdicts such as these gave ecclesiastical authorities all the leeway they needed. While sometimes checked by rivalry between episcopal courts and the monastic Inquisition, the authorities usually proceeded according to self-adopted, often fairly arbitrary, rules. It is small wonder, then, that the actual relationships between Jews and sectarians are rarely recorded in sources and that even the alleged Jewish ingredients of their theology were never fully examined. In any case, the occasional Jew drawn into the dragnet of inquisitorial prosecution usually looked to his secular ruler for protection.[7]

Jews came into conflict with the rising power of the papal or monastic Inquisition chiefly as abettors of heresy. Enormous as its impact appeared to later generations, that fateful institution did not loom quite so large in the minds of contemporary popes, only a small fraction of whose correspondence dealt with the prosecution of "heretical depravity." Nor was the personnel of inquisitorial courts, for the most part supplied by the newly founded Dominican order, very large. There were at one time only two inquisitors in the Languedoc, two in the Dauphiny and the Provence, and four to six in the rest of France. However, these militant defenders of orthodoxy made up in zeal and ruthlessness for their small number. In proclaiming the Anti-Albigensian Crusade in 1208, Innocent III confirmed the principle that "according to the canons of the saintly Fathers, he who does not keep faith with God need not be kept faith with." This adumbration of the well-known doctrine of the end justifying the means left inquisitors in possession of a very flexible procedural system and opened the gates to arbitrary judgment and outright miscarriage of justice. Yet it appears that professing Jews suffered more indirectly from increased tensions than from direct prosecution by these tribunals, whose excessive zeal was curbed in France not only by their own general directives, as summarized in Gui's *Practica*, but also by the king's jealous watchfulness lest his Jewish "serfs" be subject to any other than royal jurisdiction. Though personally not a friend of Jews, Philip IV in 1288 ordered the seneschal of Carcassonne to protect them against ecclesiastical vexations. Five years later he enjoined that official to prevent inquisitorial seizure and imprisonment of even relapsed Jewish converts without a preliminary investigation by civil authorities. Frederick III (II) of Sicily, too, tried to protect converts against unjustified suspicions and in 1310 sharply forbade anyone to call them *canes renegatos* (renegade dogs). On the whole, in the entire century and a half before the expulsion of the Jews from France in 1394, perhaps only five professing Jews were burned at the stake by the southern French inquisitors.[8]

Because of these facts, it seems appropriate for us to postpone fuller consideration of the inquisitorial proceedings against Jews, overt or secret, the methods of investigation and penalties inflicted on the accused, as well as their impact on late medieval and early modern Jewish life and thought, to our general analysis of the medieval and early modern Spanish and Portuguese Inquisitions. The story of the Iberian courts is not only far better known, but they were also more intensively engaged in prosecutions for "Judaizing" than were their French forerunners.

## THOUGHT CONTROL

More immediately threatening to Jewish religious life was the Church's censorship of Jewish books. Until the Inquisition, supervision of the written word had been halfhearted and ineffectual. Since dissemination of manuscripts of any kind was both costly and time-consuming, and their market was largely limited to ecclesiastical circles, close surveillance was hardly needed. Now, however, books and pamphlets for use by the lay intelligentsia were considered highly explosive. Before the invention of printing, precensorship was not feasible but the destruction of existing copies and the threat of severe penalties for further distribution appeared as a tempting method of interfering with any large-scale

heretical propaganda. For a long time, to be sure, the general difficulty of controlling copyists dispersed over a wide area was aggravated by the absence of central organs and the bishops' exclusive
jurisdiction in this field. But with the growth of centrally administered preaching orders and the ensuing establishment of "holy
offices" to prosecute heretics, the suppression of unwelcome
publications became a distinct possibility. Reflecting the new
realities, Alexander of Hales declared tersely that "their [the
Jews'] books containing blasphemies shall be burned." These
methods were further refined after the invention of printing.[9]

Among the first Jewish books to suffer from the newly introduced inquisitorial censorship was Maimonides' *Guide for the
Perplexed*. Ironically, the objections raised against it were not
based on the Fusṭaṭ sage's occasional strictures against Christian
Trinitarianism, but rather on his general rationalistic approach to
religion which, in the accusers' opinion, threatened to subvert
both the Jewish and the Christian faiths. The initiative, too, was
taken not by Christian leaders, few of whom had access to the
Arabic or Hebrew texts, but rather by Jewish anti-Maimonists.
After issuing their own ban in 1232, Solomon ben Abraham of
Montpellier and his associates denounced the *Guide* also to the
Dominican inquisitors. At the order of the papal legate all copies
in the hands of Montpellier Jewry had to be delivered to the authorities who, in December 1233, destroyed them in a public
bonfire, thus setting a precedent for the wholesale burning of Jewish books.[10]

More serious was the denunciation of talmudic literature, because the Talmud was so much more fundamental for Jewish life
and learning, and because that voluminous compendium did
indeed contain a number of anti-Christian utterances and often
spoke disparagingly about Gentiles in general. While originally
aimed at pagans, the latter passages could be represented as reflecting the hostile feelings of Jews toward their Christian neighbors as
well.

Remarkably, despite earlier attacks on Jewish teachings and
rituals and particularly on Jewish emphasis on law by many Christian controversialists, the Talmud as such had not been subjected
to closer scrutiny by Catholic authorities. Even Agobard of Ly-

ons' strictures against Jewish "superstitions" and "blasphemies" evidently referred only to such mystical tracts as the *She'ur qomah* (The Measure of the [Divine] Stature) and such blatantly anti-Christian writings as the *Toledot Yeshu* (Biography of Jesus). Only during the Crusades, when the curiosity of churchmen about Muslim and Jewish letters was whetted by their new missionary efforts, did Peter of Cluny evince some interest in talmudic literature. Nor was the Cistercian monk, Nicholas Manjacoria, alone in becoming, as A. Wilmart states, "a student of the rabbis." Other industrious students of Hebrew letters included Herbert Bosham, and Peter Comestor who familiarized himself particularly with the findings of Jewish Bible exegetes like Rashi. Nevertheless, so little was known about the Talmud early in the thirteenth century that Pope Gregory IX, deeply impressed though he was by the new accusations, merely urged the appointment of a commission to investigate the charges while giving the Jews a chance to disprove them.[11]

As on many similar occasions, the accuser was a Jewish convert, Nicholas Donin, a native of La Rochelle (probably of La Manche). As a Jew Nicholas had betrayed heretical tendencies, perhaps inspired by some underground survivals from the Roman age reinforced by incipient Karaite antitalmudic propaganda in western Europe. His questioning of the authority of the Talmud had brought upon his head a ban to which he angrily reacted by abandoning his faith and by denouncing his fellow Jews to the authorities. Apart from recklessly alluding to rumored Jewish ritual murders, he concentrated his wrath on rabbinic writings. In 1236 he appeared before Gregory IX and submitted to him a memorandum enumerating thirty-five points against the Talmud and stressing its alleged blasphemies against Jesus and Mary and its purported hatred of all non-Jews. The accusation further stated that by placing the Oral Law on a par with the Written Law of Moses, the Talmud had also led the Jews to assign to a man-made work a rank equal to that of divine revelation. In actual practice, Donin contended, Judaism gave precedence to talmudic over biblical law, and thereby erected an almost impenetrable barrier against all efforts to convert Jews to Christianity. This intimation must have made a particularly strong impression on the pope, who in that very year was assuring two Jewish converts, Nivello and Anselm, "We embrace converts from Judaism with even greater affection [than other converts], as we hope that, if a branch of a wild olive tree when grafted, against nature, unto a good olive tree bears delicious fruits, branches broken off a sacred tree would all the more successfully be implanted upon an olive tree which corresponds to their own nature." [12]

After listening to Donin's detailed "exposure" of so dangerous a book, Gregory IX seems to have hesitated at first to add fuel to the anti-Jewish animosities which had resulted in severe attacks on Jews in Donin's French homeland, and which Gregory was trying to stem through his bull, *Lachrymabilem Judaeorum*, of September 1236. He apparently instituted a preliminary investigation, and only after three years decided to proceed with the suppression of the Talmud. Gregory may also have been guided by certain international considerations. In the perennial struggle between Papacy and Empire, the 1230s marked, as we shall see, the first clear assertion by an emperor that all Jews were serfs of the imperial Chamber. After his definitive break with Emperor Frederick II (his second excommunication of the emperor was promulgated on March 2, 1239), Gregory may have felt it opportune to reassert the universal submission of all Jews to the authority of the Church. On June 9–20, 1239, therefore, he addressed circular letters to the bishops of France and, with minor variations, to the episcopacies of England, Spain, and Portugal, but not of the Holy Roman Empire, in which he summarized Donin's accusations and declared that the Talmud contained "matters so abusive and nefarious that it becomes a shame to its speakers and a horror to its listeners." He ordered the recipients of the letter, and especially the bishop of Paris, the well-known philosopher William of Auvergne, to arrange for a sudden descent of officials upon Jews assembled in their synagogues on the first Saturday of the following Lent (March 3, 1240). The officials were to seize all books belonging to Jews and to hand them over to local Dominicans and Franciscans for careful examination. Although some nine months elapsed between the issuance of the papal epistle and the actual seizure of Jewish books, the order seems to have been a fairly well-kept secret, at least to the unsuspecting Jews. Some Christian owners of

Jewish books were forewarned, however, for the pope authorized the recipients of his letter to issue bans against all those who, "whether clergy or laity refused to deliver Hebrew books in their possession notwithstanding either the general warnings they had received in the churches or their having been especially admonished." [13]

It appears that of all the countries so addressed only France, and particularly Paris, took the expected action. As we shall presently see, this issue became the subject of a famous disputation between Nicholas Donin and Rabbi Yehiel of Paris. Despite all valiant efforts of the Jewish delegation, the inquisitorial commission condemned the Talmud. A high prelate of the Church delayed the punitive action, but in June 1242 twenty-four carloads totaling perhaps 12,000 books were handed over to the executioner for a public bonfire—not, it appears, without additional urging by the Papacy. In a letter to Louis IX of May 9, 1244, Innocent IV still insisted:

They [Jews] raise and nurture their children in traditions which they call "Talmud" in Hebrew and which is a large volume exceeding the biblical texts in size. In it are found blasphemies against God and His Christ and manifestly intricate fables about the Blessed Virgin, as well as abusive errors and unheard-of stupidities. At the same time they make their children almost wholly ignorant of the teachings of the Law and the Prophets. They fear that, after perceiving the truth contained in that Law and the Prophets and their testimony concerning the only-begotten Son of God appearing in the flesh, these children might be converted to the faith and humbly revert to their Redeemer.

While praising the action taken by the churchmen in Paris and particularly lauding the king for his support, the pope urged his correspondent to see to it that in the future such books "be burned in fire wherever they may be found throughout your kingdom." This letter did not call for immediate action, but merely wished to proclaim a permanent principle. The king followed suit, apparently by a further confiscation of Hebrew books in 1247 and 1248. While we possess no record of an actual bonfire, we learn from a report of the papal legate, Bishop Odo of Tusculum (Frascati), dated May 1247, that a number of Hebrew books had been delivered to ecclesiastical authorities. After careful examination he and forty-four other churchmen, including Albertus

Magnus, agreed that "these books ought not to be tolerated, nor returned to the Jewish masters. We condemn them in judgment."[14]

King Louis IX and his successors likewise insisted on the permanent outlawry of the Talmud. In his ordinance of December 1254, dedicated to the general reform of French *mores* (cap. 32), Louis referred to an earlier decree in which he had ordered the Jews to observe "in perpetuity" the following regulations: "They are to abstain from usuries and blasphemies, sorcery and magic signs [*characteribus*], while the Talmud and other books in which blasphemies are found are to be burned. Jews refusing to observe this decree shall be expelled and [other] transgressors shall be punished according to law." This ordinance was confirmed by Philip III in 1284 and by Philip IV in 1290 and 1299. On readmitting Jews to France in 1315, Louis X provided that the previously confiscated, but still unsold, books of Jewish law should be restored to the returning exiles, "except the condemned *Talameus* [Talmuds]." But only one large bonfire of two carloads of books is reliably recorded in the fourteenth century—that ordered by Inquisitor Bernard Gui in Toulouse in 1319.[15]

Other countries very slowly followed the French lead. Neither England nor the Iberian kingdoms seem to have reacted in any way to Gregory IX's circular letter. Even the generally docile Henry III of England, great admirer of Louis IX though he was, seems to have limited himself to a perfunctory seizure of rabbinic books. His action made so slight an impression on the English public that it is hardly referred to by the ever loquacious contemporary chroniclers. There is a brief reference in the *Close Rolls* to a royal order of 1245 to the justices of the Jews "to sell the books of Judaism on the Old Testament which are in their custody." Most of the books were doubtless sold back to Jews. Evidently Henry's greed and impecuniousness exceeded his zeal for religious persecution. Similarly, Honorius IV's anti-Jewish bull of 1286, though widely discussed in the tense preexpulsion atmosphere, remained without any visible effect on Jewish books. In Spain, too, James I of Aragon, in his privilege of 1257, exempted the community of Lérida from the obligation to reply to accusers of Hebrew books except in cases of overt blasphemies against Jesus and Mary. Even after the memorable disputation of Barcelona in 1263, the king merely ordered the expurgation of incriminated passages. He repeated that order in 1264, although with a more pronounced anti-Jewish bias. This basic policy continued until the accession of the Jew-baiting antipope, Benedict XIII, who instituted a new search for Jewish writings. After his deposition by the Council of Constance, however, Alphonso V ordered all Jewish books returned to their owners, provided only that "the aforementioned errors are separated and expunged . . . whereupon they [the Jews] shall be able to read, study and teach those as they wish." In Castile, Alphonso the Wise limited himself to a general provision that the Jews be allowed to live in the country, "observing their law and not speaking evil of the faith of our Lord Jesus Christ which the Christians observe." [16]

Before long the Church began interfering also with other rabbinic writings considered "glosses" on the Talmud. Rashi's commentaries on the Talmud were condemned, sometimes by the very ecclesiastics who made excellent use of his commentaries on the Bible. Nicholas de Lyra, for example, whose *Postilla,* a classic of Latin exegetical literature, was deeply indebted to the sage of Troyes, nevertheless consistently attacked all such rabbinic writings in his anti-Jewish pamphlets. A similar fate befell David Qimḥi, whose grammatical works were likewise to influence many Christian Hebraists. Summarizing in his manual for inquisitors the prohibitions enacted in the preceding decades, Bernard Gui condemned not only the works of Rashi and David Qimḥi but also "the gloss of Moses the Egyptian [Maimonides]," which treated Christians as heretics and contended that Christ had erred more grievously than Mohammed. Such wholesale repudiation elicited occasional protests from informed Christian scholars. Reflecting the shift in the Christian position at the disputation of Barcelona, Raymond Martini, who as member of the Aragonese commission charged with the examination of thousands of confiscated Hebrew books had acquired a specialized knowledge of rabbinic letters, argued that some of them contained genuine rabbinic traditions going back to Moses and that they could actually serve to reinforce the truth of Christianity. In his *Pugio Fidei* (Poniard of the

Faith), he cited a number of rabbinic texts, otherwise no longer extant, which served that apologetic purpose.[17]

Nevertheless, the Papacy persisted in its attacks on the Talmud. In his letters to the archbishops of Bourges and Toulouse of September 4, 1320, John XXII ordered them and their suffragans to see to it that Christians "abstain from the blasphemies, errors, imprecations, and falsehoods which are contained in the books called by the Jews Talamutz [Talmud]." Similar condemnations were issued by Alexander V on August 30, 1409, Antipope Benedict XIII on May 1415, and, at least by implication, by Eugenius IV on August 8, 1442. The Church's antagonism to the Talmud was strengthened by reiterated attacks on it by Jewish converts filled with hatred of their former faith. In his *De Judaicis erroribus ex Talmut,* Geronimo de Santa Fé (formerly Joshua ibn Vives ha-Lorqi), a leading Christian spokesman at the disputation of Tortosa in 1413–14, indiscriminately repudiated that Jewish classic as consisting of "lying, foul, foolish, and abominable quibbles, contrary to the Law of God, to the Law of Nature and to the Law as written." [18]

Repeated papal accusations of this type naturally bore poisonous fruit. Soon after Gregory's circular letter of 1239, the usually moderate thinker Alexander of Hales raised the question whether Jews holding fast to the blasphemous teachings of the Talmud should not be destroyed together with it. But he answered that query by merely demanding the burning of all books containing obnoxious statements and an appropriate penalty for those who persisted in public blasphemies, adding that "it is different, however, if they blaspheme in secret." On June 4, 1474, the Sicilian viceroy ordered an investigation of the Jews in Termini Imerese who allegedly possessed books "against the Christian faith." On August 2, however, only a few weeks later, in lieu of the death penalty he accepted 5,000 florins for the royal curia from certain Palermo Jews who "presumed to affirm, say and teach some obscene, depraved and diabolical figments derived from their most erroneous dogmas and renowned books against Jesus Christ, the Saviour of the whole human kind as well as against the glorious and immaculate Virgin Mary His mother." Among the Jews, on the other hand, the conflagrations elicited widespread mourning. Poets composed dirges similar in tone to those written after major massacres of their people. The leading German Jewish scholar of the day, Meir b. Baruch of Rothenburg, modeled his poem after the famous Zionide of Yehudah Halevi, intimating that the first burning of the Talmud resembled the destruction of the ancient Temple. Connecting this event with the preceding condemnation of Maimonides' *Guide* in Montpellier, R. Jonah Gerondi dramatically recanted his attacks on that great philosophic work and promised to pay penance at the philosopher's grave in the Holy Land. When John XXII's order of 1320 threatened a renewal of the burning of the Talmud in the papal possessions of France, the affected communities not only petitioned the pope against the execution of that order but they also proclaimed a fast day for 1321. Prayers composed for recitation at services to be held on that occasion were still included in an Italian *Maḥzor* (prayer book for holidays) copied *ca.* 1420.[19]

In fact, however, no public autos-da-fé of Hebrew books were staged outside France until the period of the Counter Reformation, when the new censorship once again plunged Jewish communities, this time in Italy, into great difficulties on account of the Talmud. As a result of the sharp measures taken during 1553–55 by Pope Julius III and by Gian Pietro Caraffa both as Grand Inquisitor and as Pope Paul IV, Jews lost many literary treasures. From the outset some of them undoubtedly failed to deliver their copies. Writing under the direct impression of the persecutions of the 1550s, the historian Joseph b. Joshua ha-Kohen claimed that during Antipope Benedict XIII's attacks some Savoy Jews had hidden their manuscripts in wells in order to prevent their destruction. He himself had seen one such greatly damaged copy.[20]

Outside France and Counter Reformation Italy, however, ecclesiastical courts as a rule returned confiscated books to Jewish owners after expunging objectionable passages. Because of these deletions the first Hebrew printer to undertake the publication of the Babylonian Talmud, Gershom Soncino, found many lacunae in the Spanish manuscripts at his disposal. Some copies retained by ecclesiastical authorities were incorporated in one or another monastic library and thus were preserved for posterity. Many more must have been kept and constantly reproduced in the other focal centers of talmudic studies, particularly in the Holy Roman Empire and the Muslim lands. Probably the main causes for the disappearance of the talmudic tractates, as well as of other Hebrew books, less renowned and hence less frequently attacked, lay in their constant use by industrious students until most of them were torn to shreds, and in the frequent changes of domicile on the part of individual Jews and entire communities. The common adage among modern archivists that "moving an archive twice is worse than a fire" doubly applied to the precipitate removal of many medieval Jewish libraries. Damage by fire, flood, water, and other natural causes must also have been quite frequent, particularly in the more crowded ghettos of the late medieval and early modern periods. Consequently, the frequently held assumption that the mass destruction of talmudic texts as a result of the action initiated by Nicholas Donin was solely responsible for the nearly total disappearance of medieval Talmud manuscripts, which has so greatly hampered modern research in this field, is but another characteristic of the long-regnant "lachrymose conception of Jewish history."

## COMPULSORY SERMONS

Apart from defensive actions to forestall Jewish help to heretics and to suppress anti-Christian statements in Hebrew letters, the Church also took the offensive in trying to wean Jews away from their inherited faith. In line with its self-imposed limitation of not forcing Jews to be baptized were its attempts to bring about conversion by suasion and a variety of inducements. Next to offering new converts a variety of legal and pecuniary benefits, the simplest means of persuasion was the preaching of the Gospel wherever Jewish listeners were available. Such cases occurred throughout the centuries of Judeo-Christian symbiosis and have been mentioned in our treatment of ancient and early medieval times. But these efforts were intensified in the thirteenth century, particularly by the new preaching orders of Dominicans and Franciscans.

Curiously, at first the Papacy held aloof, leaving it to secular authorities and the provincial clergy to put "teeth" into the missionary postulates. In a decree of 1242, James I of Aragon provided that

whenever the archbishops, bishops, Dominican or Franciscan monks, visit towns or localities inhabited by Saracens or Jews and wish to espouse the word of God to those Jews or Saracens, the latter shall foregather at such calls and patiently listen to these sermons. Should they refuse to come voluntarily, Our officials shall compel them to do so without any subterfuge.

Fifteen years later the king relaxed and excused Jews from attending sermons outside their quarter. But he soon reversed himself and in 1263, at the instigation of the convert Pablo Christiani, he permitted monks to enter synagogues en masse and ordered the civil officials to force Jews and Saracens, "young and old, men and women, to convene at the will of these friars in any chosen place and at any time and to listen to their words diligently and silently." Yielding to Jewish protests, however, James again restricted the monks' privilege to sermons delivered within the confines of Jewish quarters and voluntarily attended by Jewish listeners. In 1268 he further limited it to a forcible invasion of the synagogue precincts by no more than ten monks and attendants. This procedure was imitated by Louis IX in France, who in 1263 specifically authorized Pablo Christiani to preach to Jews, Edward I who did the same in England in 1280 and other rulers. The Papacy followed suit and in 1278 Nicholas III ordered the Franciscan monks in Austria to promote the conversion of Jews by convocations and other methods. Similar orders were issued to the provincial heads of the Dominican order in Lombardy and France. On the other hand, it appears that when the Jews of Pamplona secured from the same pope a copy of his *Constitutio pro Judaeis*, they considered it an effective safeguard against the interruption of their services by invading preachers.[21]

Such compulsory attendance at sermons became an ever more regular feature, first in Spain and later especially in the Papal States and the rest of Italy. In his ardent quest to convert Jews and Moors, Raymond Lull in 1299 secured from James II of Aragon permission to preach the Gospel in all synagogues and mosques of the realm every Sunday and either Saturday or Friday. The Jews had to listen calmly to his or his associates' expositions, although

they were also given the unusual right to reply. Later Lull broad-
ened his horizons and, on his motion, the ecumenical Council of
Vienne of 1311–12 adopted a resolution demanding the universal
use of sermons as a means of converting unbelievers, for "the intellect takes greater delight in, and is more deeply impressed by, understanding than by belief." To make such preachment more effective, Lull persuaded the Council to adopt another momentous
resolution, urging the establishment of chairs for Hebrew and
Arabic at the leading universities of Bologna, Paris, Oxford, and
Salamanca (following the example set as early as 1254 by
Alphonso the Wise of Castile in his newly founded, but short-
lived, *studium generale* in Seville), to enable preachers to cite non-
Christian sources in support of their theological propositions.[22]

Spanish preachers were frequently recruited from among Jewish
converts, who were more familiar with both the Hebrew sources
and the predilections of Jewish audiences. An interesting illustration of the lengths to which many neophytes were prepared to go
is offered by the Jewish apologist, Moses Cohen of Tordesillas.
Describing the origin of his apologetic tract, *'Ezer ha-emunah*
(Aid to Faith), written in 1374–75, Moses refers to two converts
(John of Valladolid and a disciple of Abner of Burgos, about
whom more anon) who had turned itinerant preachers. Independently equipped with royal letters enjoining Jewish audiences
to listen to their sermons, each of the speakers staged public performances in many Spanish cities. In 1372 they addressed the Jews
of Avila four times in the large local church, in the presence of
many Christians and Muslims. One of them, according to Moses,
was a skilled dialectician. Since the Jews were given the opportunity to reply, the sermons turned into regular debates, our author
answering the preacher point by point. He claims that his arguments proved so effective that he was urged by his friends to circulate them in pamphlet form.

Needless to say, the performances were not always calm and dis-
passionate. In their conversionist zeal many preachers were prone
to exaggerate Thomas Aquinas' injunction that, in imitation of
Jesus' attack on the scribes and the Pharisees, "the preacher and
the teacher should not fear to offend [perverse] men, so that he
may insure the salvation of the multitude." Vicente Ferrer was, on

principle, opposed to forced conversions. In a sermon he emphatically declared, "the temporal rulers ought to convert the infidels of their lands, but without violence, whether physically injurious or juridical. What has been done to Jews some years ago [in 1391] is disgusting to the Lord." Yet he not only insisted upon the Jews' regular attendance when he preached, but sometimes delivered his addresses in so incendiary a fashion that they were followed by anti-Jewish riots. Saragossan Jews who failed to appear at his sermons were fined by him 1,000 florins, while Infante Alphonso put many of them behind prison bars (December 17, 1414). They were freed only on King Ferdinand I's personal intervention. On the other hand, several months earlier (August 21) the Infante himself had forced the local authorities of the smaller city of Aynsa to readmit Jews who had left town in anticipation of the disturbances after Ferrer's appearance. Ultimately rejoicing in the effects of the disputation of Tortosa which he had initiated, Antipope Benedict XIII wrote in his harsh decree of May 11, 1415 (repeated almost verbatim in an ordinance by Ferdinand I of Aragon):

We order that in all cities, towns and localities where, in the bishop's opinion, sufficiently large numbers of Jews reside, there should be delivered three public sermons annually by professors of sacred theology and other competent men specifically designated by the bishops. . . . We expressly order that all Jews of both sexes from the age of twelve who are able to appear in these cities or towns must unconditionally attend. Recalcitrant Jews are to be punished by the bishops by forbidding them all intercourse with Christians until they offer full satisfaction according to the bishops' judgment.[23]

From Spain the scene soon shifted to Italy. The vagaries of Church policy in this matter are well illustrated by the fits and spasms with which regulations were adopted, then abrogated, and then reintroduced, with or without modification, in various southern Italian communities. When the Jews of Marsala complained to King Martin in 1399 that they were not only forced to attend Christian services on St. Stephen's Day and on Christmas but that, on their return from church, the populace pelted them with stones, the king indignantly put an end to the entire practice. He repeated his decree in December 1405, but he was obliged to restore the forced attendance, minus the subsequent attacks, several weeks later. Special conversionist *lettori degli Ebrei* were instituted for all of Sicily in 1428. Although this ordinance was revoked three years later in response to protests by the Jewish communities represented by Moses di Bonavoglia, another such preacher is recorded in 1467. Interveningly, Pope Nicholas V permitted the Sicilian authorities to force the Jews to attend sermons under threat of confiscation of property and incarceration. Later on, as we shall see, Counter Reformation popes began regulating in increasing detail the selection of preachers, the number of Jews bound to attend, and the obligation of the Jewish community to furnish listeners. The whole area of enforcement so clearly ran counter to the professed principle of the voluntary nature of belief that scholastics had to sharpen their ingenuity to find some sort of justification. The renowned Spanish thinker, Francisco Suárez, could advance no better rationale than the right of *secular* authorities to seek greater unity for the state; for this purpose they might use persuasion to induce religious minorities to submit also to the politically desirable religious conformity.[24]

Of an entirely different nature, of course, were the far more numerous sermons delivered *against* Jews before Christian audiences. This practice, reaching back to the apostolic age, often served to heighten anti-Jewish tensions, particularly during Holy Week. Yet, in the thirteenth and fourteenth centuries we rarely hear of papal protests against incendiary sermons, such as that voiced by Martin V in his bull of February 20, 1422. Interventions of this kind by ecclesiastical and secular authorities became increasingly necessary to forestall attacks on Jews during the tense fifteenth century.[25]

## DISPUTATIONS

Some Judaizing influences doubtless emanated unwittingly from ordinary daily contacts between Jews and Christians. In a religiously enthusiastic age acquaintances of diverse creeds must often have inquired about each other's religious convictions. No less frequent must have been attempts by Christians to convert their Jewish friends, thereby eliciting replies in defense of the Jewish tradition. Such informal exchanges doubtless contributed greatly to a deeper understanding of traditional differences, but at times they must also have aroused serious questions in the interlocutors' minds.

As a permanent minority dependent on the good will of Christian rulers and churchmen, Jews generally adhered to their traditional policy of holding aloof from controversial debates. Their prevailing sentiments were well expressed by Yehudah b. Samuel the Pious and his associates in the following admonition:

When one is approached by a priest or monk, an informed and argumentative heretic, or by a learned, but ambitious and not sin-fearing Jew, while he himself is righteous but not so wise, or if he is wise but he is approached by a magician that he debate with him matters of Torah so that he be attracted to his [opponent's] way of thinking, in all such cases it is written "Answer not a fool according to his folly lest thou also be like unto him" (Prov. 26:4). That is . . . lest thou be unable to answer him and thy heart be attracted to him. "Thou also" for not only he may cause thee to sin, but because thou mayest also cause him to sin by making him more extreme in his negation. Even if thou art wiser than he, thou must not allow the unlearned to sit and listen to your disputation, for they might be misled, since they do not understand the truth.

The Christian position was less uniform. As an expansive missionary religion, Christianity had always relied on the effective preachment of the Gospel to unbelievers.

The rise of medieval heresies in the West, as well as the intensification of theological training at the great Western universities, tended vastly to increase the number of ready debaters. Nonetheless private disputations among laymen were frowned upon, as it became manifest that many Jewish and heretical spokesmen were superior to their orthodox counterparts in intellectual power and Bible learning. Thomas Aquinas tried, therefore, to draw a line of demarcation between informed Christians of staunch convictions whom one was to encourage to engage in intellectual duels, and persons insecure in their beliefs who were to refrain from exposing their weakness. The simple-minded ordinary folk ought not even to listen to such debates, particularly in truly Catholic lands where their faith was not under attack. In this connection Thomas referred to an ancient decree of Emperor Marcion of 452, incorporated in Justinian's codification, which had forbidden all public

debates with heretics. The "angelic doctor" had the more reason
to favor an exception for well-trained Christian debaters, as he
himself was said to have tasted the sweet fruit of victory in a controversy with two Jews. According to his biographers, Peter Calo
and William Tocco, he met two wealthy Italian Jews at Christmas
time in the castle of Cardinal Richard in Molara, near Rome. At
the host's instigation the two Jewish guests entered into a religious
disputation with the learned Dominican and, conceding defeat on
the second day, adopted Christianity.[26]

In his warning against unqualified debaters, however, Thomas
could also have invoked the authority of Pope Gregory IX who
had succinctly stated in 1231, "We strictly prohibit any lay person
from publicly or privately debating the Christian faith." Two
years later the pope invoked secular assistance in punishing both
Christian and Jewish participants in such disputations, "lest the
simple-minded be thus led into error." Similar prohibitions were
also repeatedly enacted by various councils (Treves, 1227; Tarragona under James I of Aragon, 1233; Vienna, 1267; Freising,
1440; and Bamberg, 1491), and were restated by Cajetan in his
*Commentary* on Aquinas' *Summa*. However, as a result of the
intervening growth of a lay intelligentsia, the sixteenth-century
commentator exempted learned laymen from the restriction.[27]

Nevertheless the medieval mind was too deeply preoccupied
with all aspects of belief and observance not to indulge in altercations about deeply cherished convictions and, occasionally, in a
genuine quest for new truths. The preaching orders, in particular,
considered it their special task to persuade unbelievers of the
unreasonableness and sinfulness of their resistance to Christianity.
Converts from Judaism were apt to rationalize their action by
publicly attacking their former faith and, if they had abandoned it
for worldly reasons, to cover up this weakness by a show of re-
doubled religious ardor.

Not surprisingly, only a few of these debates found their way
into the records. For the most part they were mentioned only in
connection with some other event. But rarely did one form part of
an autobiographical sketch, such as was left behind by one Baruch,
a Jew from Germany who happened to be present during the
bloody attack on Jews by the French Pastoureaux. He saved his life

by accepting baptism. Only later did the bishop try to persuade him that his baptism was valid, since it had not been performed by force nor by "absolute" compulsion (*non vi vel coactione absoluta*), and to show him the superiority of his new faith. This effort led to a protracted debate between the still reluctant convert and the bishop assisted by other converts. Sometimes such discussions are summarized in a controversial tract by a Jewish or Christian apologist. Here the dialogue is usually embellished with picturesque descriptions, peppered with anecdotes and humorous replies, and enriched with ingenious interpretations of the Bible —much of it doubtless representing afterthoughts or even pure inventions. Invariably the author of the account retains the upper hand. Nor is it always easy to distinguish between the reporting of an historical event and the use of a purely fictitious dialogue as a literary artifice. This is true especially of many Christian controversial tracts, but also of such works as Ibn Verga's *Shebet Yehudah*. The medium of fictionalized dialogue was also frequently used by contemporary poets. Only a few accounts are based upon actual exchanges. On the Christian side, we need mention only Gilbert Crispin, Peter de Blois, Peter of Cornwall, the convert Abner of Burgos (Alphonso of Valladolid), and Nicholas de Lyra. The main Jewish spokesmen were Jacob b. Reuben, Nathan Official and his son Joseph, Moses Kohen of Tordesillas, Shem Ṭob b. Isaac Shapruṭ of Tudela, and Abraham b. Mordecai Farissol. Most discussions were conducted in private, or at best in small incidental gatherings, and they owe their perpetuation only to their inclusion in literary works circulated for apologetic purposes.[28]

Public debates, too, which had taken place from the earliest periods of separation between the two faiths, became more frequent and better publicized after the rise of the preaching orders. Whether the latter addressed Jews forcibly convoked in churches or synagogues, preached to casually assembled groups on the street, or invited representative Jews to a discussion in a monastery, the Dominicans and Franciscans instigated many disputes paralleling contemporary sectarian controversies and debates over the reform of the Church. As a rule, Jewish discussants were aware of the danger to themselves and their communities, even in the case of a victorious argument; some must have felt handicapped by the terrifying vistas of an unsuccessful defense. Especially during the tense transition from the Middle Ages to early modern times, defeat in a disputation could serve as a pretext for banishing all Jews from a city or region. To cite one example, when a converted former rabbi, Viktor von Carben, allegedly overcame his Jewish disputants in a debate in Poppelsdorf, this event served as justification for the expulsion of Jews from Brühl, Deutz, and other communities (*ca.* 1486). On other occasions the purported defeat of Jewish debaters led to the stampede of many coreligionists to the baptismal font. John Capistrano claimed that, after one such debate in Rome in 1450, the leader of the Jewish community and fifty-two other Jews accepted baptism within a year. Quite often the dispute was simply resolved by force. Louis IX of France decided that only a well-instructed cleric should debate with Jews, but that a layman hearing one speaking ill of the Christian faith "should not defend it but by his sword, wherewith he should pierce the vitals of the reviler as far as it will go"—a phrase also used, perhaps independently, by Berthold of Ratisbon. According to Jean de Joinville, Louis' biographer, the king referred to a debate between clerics and Jews at the monastery in Cluny. After listening to the presentation of Christian dogmas, the Jewish debater had simply declared that he believed nothing of the sort. In reply one of the nobles present "raised his crutch, hit the Jew behind his ear and threw him to the floor. Whereupon the Jews were put to flight, carrying away their wounded master, and thus ended the debate." Nonetheless there were quite a few fearless or hotheaded Jews who, even without compulsion, were ready to take up the cudgel in defense of their faith.[29]

The public disputations held in Paris in 1240, in Barcelona in 1263, and in Tortosa in 1413–14 left a permanent imprint on the apologetic thinking of both parties. We possess records compiled not long after these events. Although incomplete, contradictory, and invariably biased, these reports have enabled modern scholars plausibly to reconstruct the actual proceedings.

## PARIS AND BARCELONA

The first of these public debates was staged in Paris at the order of Louis IX in response to Gregory IX's circular demanding the seizure of all available copies of the Talmud and rabbinic letters. William of Auvergne—bishop of Paris and a leading protagonist in the unfolding drama—and his associates doubtless realized that they were dealing with a matter touching the very core of the Jewish faith, the general toleration of which had long been proclaimed by Church and state. To give the Jewish leaders an opportunity to defend their treasured letters, three public sessions were held on June 25–27, 1240, presided over by the strong-willed Queen Mother Blanche of Castile. Her presence certainly exerted a calming influence. In contrast to most inquisitorial proceedings in which the defendants were kept in the dark about their accusers, the ecclesiastical case against the Talmud was advanced in the presence of a Jew by Nicholas Donin, probably the only available Christian "expert" on talmudic literature. "Even according to the Jews' testimony," the Latin *rapporteur* informs us, "he [Donin] was superlatively erudite in Hebrew, so that he could hardly find any equal with respect to the substance and grammar of the Hebrew sermon." On the other hand, though four leading rabbis had been summoned by royal order, only one at a time was admitted to the hearings. During the interval between sessions, the chief Jewish spokesman, Yeḥiel (Vivo or Vives) ben Joseph, head of the Paris academy, which had so greatly impressed Benjamin of Tudela seventy years before, was kept in "bitter" confinement, so that he could not inform his successor of the position he had taken. Yet when Yehudah ben David of Melun appeared before the assembly on June 27, his independent testimony agreed in all essentials with Rabbi Yeḥiel's assertions. The audience, which included several distinguished doctors of the University and many leading churchmen and nobles, thus gained the impression that the views they expounded were universally shared by French Jewry.[30]

Donin's original list of thirty-five accusations which the convert had submitted to Pope Gregory IX now served as the basis of disputation. These points may be summarized under the following main headings: (1) the great authority of the Talmud among Jews; (2) its immoral, particularly anti-Gentile utterances; (3) its grossly anthropomorphic teachings concerning God; (4) its blasphemies against Jesus and Mary, as well as attacks on the Church; and (5) its numerous stupidities and revolting tales. Culling passages from the large four-volume manuscript of the Talmud, probably with Rashi's commentary, which he held in front of him, Nicholas tried to show that the Jews not only believed that the Talmud, as a repository of the Oral Law, was co-ordinate with the Bible but that it was assigned a far greater role in the instruction of children. The accuser had little difficulty in finding irate anti-Gentile passages, citing tractate and chapter in an apparently too literal but otherwise fairly accurate Latin translation. All these utterances he automatically applied to Christians. To whip up Christian resentment against talmudic anthropomorphism despite the accepted doctrine of Incarnation, Donin had to prove that God was presented in the Talmud as acting unethically, failing in his omniscience and often being overruled by the will of man. Apart from containing irreverent utterances concerning the founder of Christianity, Nicholas claimed, the Talmud and Jewish liturgy were also sharply antagonistic to the pope and Christendom, teaching Jews to pray three times daily against the Church. Even bad Jews were assured that their suffering in Hell would be terminated after twelve months. Among the "stupidities" of the Talmud, Donin pointed out especially the legends concerning Adam's sexual relations with animals, Eve's with the serpent, and Ham's misconduct toward his own father.[31]

R. Yeḥiel, though not denying the existence of such passages, tried to give them a different interpretation. He admitted that the Talmud held uncontested validity among Jews, but he emphasized that it was its very canonicity which made it immune from attack. For fifteen centuries, he contended, it had guided Jewish life, and without its interpretations Jews would neither be able to understand their Scripture, nor properly adhere to their faith. The essentiality of the Talmud to the Jewish religion had been recognized by churchmen of earlier generations, including St. Jerome "who knew all of our Torah and the whole Talmud." It could not be condemned without abrogating the principle of toleration of Jews, "because for the sake of the Torah we shall die and he who touches it touches the apple of our eye." Moreover, the Talmud's outlawry by the French Church would in no way lead to its total suppression. It existed "in Babylonia and Media, in Greece and among all seventy nations, even beyond the rivers of Ethiopia. Hence only our bodies are in your hands, not our souls, for you cannot eradicate the Torah except within your own kingdom." Without denying the anti-Gentile utterances, R. Yeḥiel contrasted them with numerous other talmudic statements sympathetic to the Gentile world. He also contended that all the hostile passages there as well as in the Jewish liturgy related to ancient pagans and not to contemporary Christians. "We certainly would not return evil for good to this country or to the pope who, with all his power, acts so that we should be guarded and maintained and allowed to make a living. . . . And if an individual enemy does us wrong, shall we be angry at the whole people?" Nor did R. Yeḥiel gainsay the condemnation of Jesus and his mother by the ancient rabbis, but pointed out that the father of the Jesus of the Talmud bore a different name from the father of Jesus in the Gospels, and that he had been rejected by R. Joshua ben Peraḥiah of the second century B.C.E. Therefore, he claimed, the talmudic attacks were aimed not at the founder of Christianity but rather at another Jesus who lived some two centuries earlier. Cleverly referring to the king's name, he emphasized that "not all the Louis born are equal and some are not kings of France." Thus an argument which Abraham ibn Daud had directed against the reliability of the Gospels allegedly written two centuries after the events described in them, was now used to whitewash the Talmud from any hostile reference to the Christian messiah. As to the numerous anthropomorphic passages and other "stupidities," the best the Jewish spokesman could do was to explain that they were merely part of the Aggadah and that, if properly interpreted, even such objectionable passages offered valuable lessons. These explanations, though often at variance with the regnant opinions of Rashi and the Tosafists, were independently confirmed by the second debater, Yehudah ben David, showing that most of these issues had been anticipated by the French Jewish leaders and that they had agreed in advance on their line of defense.[32]

We may regret that the early termination of the hearings prevented the appearance of Moses of Coucy, the successful preacher and celebrated author of the *Sefer ha-Miṣvot* (Book of Commandments later called the "Great"). He probably was a better

orator than Yeḥiel. Apart from reasons of seniority and his official position in the French capital, the latter may have been chosen
as the first spokesman because of his close contacts with certain French hierarchs and court personalities, to which he seems
to allude in his "disputation." In any case, Queen Blanche, who
throughout the proceedings had tried to assuage the feelings of
Jewish witnesses, apparently felt that there was no point in pro-
longing the debate. Certainly little was to be gained by listening
to two more rabbis reiterate the same explanations. The debate
was therefore adjourned and the material turned over to the
investigating committee. The points presented by R. Yeḥiel appeared sufficiently weighty for the pro-Jewish faction to delay the
condemnation of the Talmud for about two years. The sudden
suspension of the hearings and the committee's subsequent hesita-
tion may well have persuaded the Jews that they had successfully
defended their literary treasures. This underlying conviction inspired the ultimate author of the *Viqquaḥ* to describe the events
in terms of outright victory for the Jewish pleader. As such, his
booklet became a popular apologetic treatise which helped to
strengthen the morale of the French Jewish population and aided
Yeḥiel's successors in other Judeo-Christian debates in their defense of the Talmud.[33]

When the scene shifted to Aragon in 1263, the disputation rose
to a higher level. Fra Pablo (Paul) Christiani, the Christian protagonist in the Barcelona debate, may have been a less learned
talmudist than Donin but he apparently was a more assiduous student of Christology and Christian dogma. In his debate he was
supported by no less a figure than Raymond Peñaforte, a former
general of the Dominican order and a celebrated codifier of canon
law. Though eighty-seven years old, Peñaforte still showed the
traits of an ardent and effective missionary. He could claim that,
by making his pupils study Arabic, he had brought about the conversion of 10,000 Saracens. Hebrew studies, too, he believed, were
helpful in realizing Gregory I's program that "Jews, as well as
Saracens, ought to be induced to adopt the Christian faith by [the
citing of] authorities, reasonings and blandishments, rather than
through harsh treatment. They must not be forced to do so, for
enforced worship does not please the Lord." For this purpose Peña-

forte had established, apparently with the aid of the kings of both Castile and Aragon, colleges for the study of Arabic and Hebrew, an adumbration of the policies later adopted by the Ecumenical Council of Vienne. Along the same lines one of Peñaforte's disciples, Raymond Martini, five years before the disputation, had tried in his *Explanatio symboli apostolorum* to reinterpret Christian doctrine in the light of objections raised by Jews and Muslims. On the Jewish side appeared the famous Moses b. Naḥman (abbreviated Ramban) or Naḥmanides (known among Christians as Bonastrug de Porta), then rabbi of Gerona. As an outstanding jurist, kabbalist, and Bible commentator, he was in a position to argue authoritatively about the meaning of both scriptural and rabbinic passages. Here, too, the term "disputation" is a misnomer, for, as the Latin protocol has it, "the faith of the Lord Jesus Christ cannot, because of its certainty, be placed under dispute." Hence the debate reduced itself to a discussion of certain talmudic sources selected by Christiani. When, after three days, the rabbi requested that a day be set aside for questions by him, the king refused. From the outset Naḥmanides could only stipulate that he be allowed to answer freely. Forewarned not to blaspheme against the dominant faith, he replied, "I have enough knowledge and tact to speak in the proper manner." [34]

In the Barcelona hearings, in contrast to those of Paris, the Talmud as such was not under indictment. Christiani had evinced no pro-Karaite leanings while still a Jew; his conversion to Christianity, perhaps on Peñaforte's initiative, may have been owing to a genuine belief in Christ and the Trinity. He now made an effort to prove from the Talmud itself that the messiah had come, and that he had been simultaneously God and man—that is, God Incarnate and as such a member of the Trinity. In addition to these two major points, the hearings were to demonstrate, likewise from traditional Jewish sources, the prophecy that the messiah was to suffer and die for the salvation of mankind and that, upon his arrival, Jewish ceremonial law was to be no longer binding. Understandably, no word was spoken about the alleged talmudic follies or blasphemies against Jesus and Mary, which could only weaken Christiani's endeavor to use the Talmud as evidence for the validity of the Christian tradition. Christiani thus tried to live up to Peñaforte's expectation that missionaries familiar with Hebrew would be able "to refute the Jews' malice and errors, since these could no longer audaciously deny, as they did before, the genuine text and glosses of their own ancient sages whenever they agree with our saints in matters pertaining to the Catholic faith." Nor did the discussion degenerate into denunciations of rabbinic legends. In his replies, too, Naḥmanides refrained from personal attacks and from the cruder explanations of incriminated utterances such as had been offered by R. Yeḥiel. He merely referred to Fra Pablo's previous missionary journeys through the Provençal Jewish communities, whom Christiani had tried in vain to persuade that the talmudic sages themselves had conceded the messiahship of Jesus. If that had been true, asked Naḥmanides, why would the Jews have persisted during the talmudic era, that is during four or five centuries after Jesus, in rejecting the Christian faith and remaining loyal Jews? [35]

Not surprisingly, the debate soon veered from the talmudic to the old biblical "testimonies" concerning the advent of a redeemer, which had been adduced by Christian apologists ever since ancient times. Both sides repeated many traditional arguments formulated in the patristic and talmudic age and further developed in the tricornered debates under Islam. More strongly than his predecessors Naḥmanides stressed the purely human character of the Jewish messiah and the lesser centrality of the messianic credo in the Jewish faith. He went even further than the more rationalistic Maimonides, who had counted messianism among the indispensable thirteen principles of Judaism. The subtle discussion of the Trinitarian dogma largely reflected certain philosophic approaches imported from the scholastically advanced Renaissance of Islam. The Christian side argued that three-in-oneness can be graphically demonstrated by a glass of wine whose taste, color and odor are merely three different aspects of the same entity. It also invoked the old doctrine that the three attributes of Wisdom, Will, and Power are facets of the same divine Oneness of God. In his rebuttal Naḥmanides characteristically failed to refer to the long-debated extension of the divine attributes to five, seven, or an infinite number, but merely replied that "wisdom in the Creator is not an accident but He and His wisdom are one, He and His will are one, He and His power are one. Hence wisdom, will, and power are one thing. Even if they were accidents, moreover, this would not mean that there is a triad in Godhead but only that there is one God subject to three accidents." In this somewhat equivocal phraseology the Gerona rabbi seemed to express the doctrine of negative attributes in an oversimplified manner in order to make it more comprehensible to the king and the numerous philosophically untrained nobles in the audience.[36]

Consideration for the Jewish public likewise influenced the rabbi's formulations not only in his written tract, but during the original debate. He must have been doubly aware of his delicate position during the discussion of attributes which took place at the final session in the main synagogue of Barcelona (August 4). Probably few Jews had accompanied their spokesman to the royal palace and the cathedral during the preceding sessions of July 20, 23, 26 and 27. But for the last session the king, Christiani, and many other dignitaries presented themselves at the synagogue, the king personally delivering a warm missionary address in which he offered the aforementioned homespun simile of the three characteristics of a glass of wine. The dramatic change of locale must have attracted a large Jewish audience; it was but part of the then growing effort to convert Jews by making them listen to Christian preachers. Probably to weaken the impact of the Christian addresses, Naḥmanides delivered—perhaps after the departure of the king and the Christian dignitaries—a famous sermon, "The Law of the Lord Is Perfect," expatiating on the immutability and perfection of the Law of Moses.[37]

The missionary pressures were continued after the adjournment of the disputation. Between August 26 and 30, 1263, soon after Naḥmanides' return to Gerona (about August 12), James issued five anti-Jewish decrees. They provided for the compulsory attendance of Jews at missionary sermons and the protection of the property of recent converts; the burning of the "books called *soffrim* [*shofeṭim,* the last section of the Code] composed by Moses son of Maimon, an Egyptian of Cairo, which contained blasphemies against Jesus Christ"; the appointment of Pablo Christiani as a special preacher of the word of God among Jews; and an order to all Jewish communities to expunge from their books within three months any blasphemous utterances designated as such by Christiani in cooperation with Peñaforte and Arnaldo de Segarra. The expurgation was to be supervised in each Jewish community by twenty or thirty elders especially sworn in for that purpose. At the same time the king confirmed the protocol of the Barcelona hearings, which had been written in an obviously anti-Jewish vein. All this did not satisfy the Peñaforte group. Although the rabbi had published his *Viqquah* at the prompting of the Gerona bishop, Don Pedro de Castellnou, he evoked by it the wrath of the influential ecclesiastics. In 1265 the king was persuaded to order the banishment of Nahmanides from the country for two years and the suppression of his report. Dissatisfied with the mildness of this sentence and resentful of royal laxness in executing it and enforcing the other sharp decrees (the king had speedily modified some of them), the churchmen appealed to the pope, presenting Nahmanides as an outright liar and offender of the Christian faith. In a letter written in 1266 or 1267, Clement IV urged the king to punish the rabbi severely, though not by execution or physical mutilation. Soon thereafter (July 15, 1267), apparently still unaware of the changed attitude toward the Talmud which had characterized the Barcelona hearings four years earlier, the pope reverted to the older position of Gregory IX and the Paris theologians and, through the archbishop of Tarragona, demanded that the royal officials help confiscate and destroy all copies of the Talmud and rabbinic letters containing blasphemies against Christianity. It is small wonder, then, that Nahmanides felt it the better part of wisdom to leave the country. Rather than settling in neighboring Castile, Portugal, or France, he decided to realize a lifelong dream. Like R. Yehiel of Paris he emigrated to Palestine, where he died a few years later.[38]

## TORTOSA

The Paris and Barcelona debates appeared like child's play compared with the mammoth disputation arranged by Antipope Benedict XIII in Tortosa, which lasted, with interruptions, from February 7, 1413 to November 13, 1414. The original intention apparently was to debate the issues only locally in the community of Alcañiz, the birthplace of the chief Christian spokesman, Geronimo de Santa Fé (formerly Joshua ha-Lorqi). The debate was soon enlarged to a country-wide performance, the leading Jewish communities of Aragon having been ordered to send representatives to Tortosa. Here the Jews were not expected, as in the preceding disputations, merely to testify and ultimately to "confess," but they were also supposed to receive instruction (*informatio*) about the controversial dogmas. In the tense atmosphere which had persisted throughout Spain since the massacres of 1391, such a disputation boded ill for the Jewish participants. Yet they yielded to the pressure of the antipope, whose hostility as papal legate Pedro de Luna they doubtless remembered. Now, when his own position was increasingly threatened (four years later he was to be deposed by the Ecumenical Council of Constance), Benedict may have felt that a spectacular debate ending in conversion of numerous Jews might enhance his position at least in the Spanish kingdoms and thus perhaps help to stave off his day of reckoning. He may also have been annoyed by the accusation of heterodoxy hurled at him by some opponents. In fact, the Pisa Commission, meeting in 1409 in advance of the Council of Constance, devoted fully thirteen sessions to hearings of a lengthy indictment imputing sorcery to both Benedict XIII and Gregory XII. One of the thirty-seven counts included in this strange document, still extant at the Vatican Library, alleged that Benedict had sought to secure books of magic from Saracens and a book demonstrating the magic character of Jesus' miracles from Jews. Benedict must have thought that a colorful pageant such as that ultimately staged in Tortosa could go far in disproving such denunciations.[39]

Not that Benedict had from the outset envisaged such a long-drawn-out disputation. By January 1414 he himself complained that it had grown out of bounds. Yet he gladly seized the opportunity offered him by Geronimo de Santa Fé who, soon after his conversion by Vicente Ferrer in Alcañiz in 1412, had begun debating religious issues with the local rabbi, Astruch ha-Levi, subsequently a member of the Jewish delegation. The enlarged country-wide scope may actually have originated from the quest of Alcañiz Jewry to call in experts from other communities. In Tortosa the antipope probably hoped that the Jewish delegates would be quickly silenced. To his surprise he found their defense protracted and stubborn. He accused them of long-winded arguments, forgetting that time and again they had in vain tried to stop the discussion and that they merely had to respond in kind to Geronimo's long perorations on the meaning of certain talmudic passages. In fact, perhaps more frequently than was prudent, they seem to have wished to cut off the discussion by professing inability to answer certain questions.

Unlike the preceding disputations, the controversy in Tortosa left behind no comprehensive firsthand Jewish report. Only brief, rather confused, summaries based upon personal recollections of participants were included in later compilations. On the other hand, the more extensive protocols of the sixty-nine sessions, prepared by Benedict's officials, exist in several Latin versions and have furnished modern scholars a documentary basis for a more or less comprehensive reconstruction of the debates. They have the additional advantage of including memoranda from both sides. At first the debate was conducted quite informally and was merely summarized by the official scribe. But when Geronimo's quotations from the rabbis' previous utterances were disputed by them, it was agreed after the ninth session that each party submit written statements which could then be officially cited. After the conclusion of the first series of sessions on August 30, the papal secretaries reviewed the entire record under Geronimo's personal supervision, allegedly in the presence "of eight Jews delegated for that purpose by the Jewish assembly." [40]

Geronimo was a much more learned and versatile opponent than either Donin or Christiani. While still a professing Jew he evinced deep concern about the mutual relationship between the two faiths. When his friend, Rabbi Solomon ha-Levi, accepted baptism and, as Paul of Burgos, joined the clergy and soon became bishop of Burgos and a leading anti-Jewish controversialist, Joshua ha-Lorqi addressed a letter to him in which censure for this action was mixed with curiosity about his underlying motives. Ultimately, perhaps under Paul's influence, Joshua followed his example.[41]

The Jewish representation was similarly well equipped. The leading thinker of that generation, Ḥisdai Crescas, died before the disputation, but his best pupil in philosophy, Joseph Albo, then a young man of thirty-three and later the celebrated author of the *Sefer 'Iqqarim* (Book of Principles), served through most of the proceedings. That Albo did not appear as chief spokesman may have been owing to his relative youth, his explosive temperament, and possibly to his inadequate facility in orating in Latin, the main language of the debates. As chief delegates three Saragossans alternately appeared: Don Vidal Benveniste de la Cavalleria, diplomat rather than scholar; Mattathias ha-Yishari, preacher and Bible commentator; and most importantly Zeraḥiah ha-Levi, rabbinic author. Called in Spanish Ferrer, the latter became a namesake of Vicente Ferrer, who in some respects may be considered the spiritual patron of the entire disputation. The great drama attracted Jewish visitors, among them the controversialist Profiat Duran Efodi and the poet Solomon Bonafed. From the outset the Jews were overawed by the great pomp of the proceedings. In Tortosa, reports Bonastruch Desmaestre, "we have come before the pope and found the whole large auditorium, the place of the debate, decorated in purple. There were seventy chairs for the cardinals, archbishops and bishops, all dressed in gold vestments. There also were other grandees of the Roman church as well as burghers and nobles, approximately one thousand persons. This was true throughout the disputation. Our hearts melted and turned to water." Occasionally, we are told, the audience numbered over two thousand persons. In their excessive anxiety the Jewish debaters sometimes failed to concert their answers. More often, undoubtedly, they quarreled among themselves after the adjournment of a session and, with a typical *esprit d'escalier*, blamed one another for failure to answer properly.[42]

Nor was Benedict's opening address very reassuring. To quote the Jewish reporter again, the pope stated:

You, the Jewish sages, ought to bear in mind that I am not here, nor have I sent for you to come to this place, in order to discuss which of the two religions is true. For I know that my faith is the only true one; yours had once been true but it has since been superseded. You have come here only on account of Geronimo who has promised to prove, through the very Talmud of your masters who were wiser than yourselves, that the messiah has already come. You shall debate before me this topic exclusively.

In fact, the problem of the messiah occupied all the sessions of 1413, and after the three-months' adjournment of August 30 to November 30, 1413 it was again talked about during the early sessions of 1414. However, soon the discussion shifted to other less theological issues. At the forty-eight session of January 8, 1414, which really initiated the second series of debates, Benedict announced that he wished to have further clarity concerning the following five points which evidently were intended to become the subjects of special canonical, as well as state, regulations:

First and principally, on the subject of the book commonly called *Talmut,* because of the fallacies, heresies, and abominations contained therein. Secondly, on the subject of the crime of usury which they practice in an execrable manner. Thirdly, on the subject of their synagogues, particularly those which they had recently erected without the authorization of the Apostolic See, or which they had enlarged, embellished, or enriched. Fourthly, on the subject of their [close social] relations with the Catholics. Fifthly, on the subject of public offices which Jews ought not to occupy among Christians.

The debates on these subjects were continued when, on June 15, the concluding sessions were transferred to neighboring San Mateo. Here again Geronimo concentrated his attacks on the Talmud, which he had previously assailed in a Latin pamphlet *De Judaicis erroribus ex Talmut.* But he did not overlook the economic issues, and in one of the final sessions, the sixty-fifth of September 27, 1414, he referred to a forthcoming papal constitution concerning the Jews, prompted, as he explained, by the Jews' "living very luxuriously and quietly in sensitive positions of trust and enjoying many gains extorted from the Christian people by exorbitant usury. They also maintain magnificent synagogues, hold the lives of Christian persons in their power through the professions of medicine and surgery, and control Christian property through their economic and administrative functions." [43]

Little time was left, however, to debate these problems. The great interest evinced by the public at the beginning of the disputation had been waning. The Jewish delegation, which from the outset had reluctantly presented itself for the intellectual combat, now lost all interest in continuing the hopeless struggle. Several members complained bitterly of discomforts during their stay in Tortosa, serious financial losses at home, and the deterioration of their family life during their enforced absence. One or another left Tortosa without authorization and was hailed back by papal summons. Even the scribes, who at the early sessions had kept the minutes at considerable length, got tired and recorded the concluding debates with relative brevity.

It is small wonder, therefore, that the outcome for the Jewish debaters was short of catastrophic. Unlike the disputants of 1240 and 1263, they did not depart with the feeling of a mission well accomplished. During the course of the debate, its managers, bent upon theatrical effects, succeeded in repeatedly baptizing groups of Jews in public ceremonies in front of the conference. The following claim by Geronimo in the official protocol of the sixty-second session of April 19, 1414, is typical: "At that time [August 30, 1413] under the inspiration of the Divine Grace a certain notable [or noble] Jew named Don Todros Benveniste, a physician, and with him seven other Jews, on their own initiative submitted requests to be baptized." Another official entry mentions the conversion on February 2, 1414 of seventeen members of the community of Saragossa, "the most noble Jews of the whole community, both by scientific achievement and by birth, namely those of the military race called De la Cavalleria." On still another occasion there was a mass conversion of two hundred and fifty persons. Many others proceeded to the baptismal fonts in their respective communities. Still other thousands independently decided to abandon the sinking ship of Judaism. Long weakened in their faith by the diversity of their intellectual interests, their close social relations with Gentile neighbors, and their relative economic well-being, many Spanish Jews were not mentally equipped to resist, as staunchly as had their northern coreligionists, the combination of bloody attacks and legal harassments which had bedeviled their lives during the preceding quarter century. The apparent disunity of the rabbis together with their defeat by a skilled dialectician from their own midst was the final straw which broke down their defenses—without, however, impinging upon their self-respect as would conversion under ordinary circumstances.[44]

There also was much popular pressure before, during, and after the disputation. Instigated by local agitators, the populace often attacked Jews, while the city elders harassed them with all sorts of chicaneries. The mere fact that Vicente Ferrer was scheduled to address the local church audience sufficed to put the entire Jewish community of Tamarite de Litera to flight. Although in this particular case King Ferdinand intervened and ordered the authorities to protect the returning Jews, the pressure did not diminish. In fact, a former rabbi of Tamarite, in his petition for royal support, described how together with his wife, three sons, and two daughters he had accepted baptism in Ferrer's presence. "Not satisfied," he added (referring to himself), "with his own belief and prompted by very great devotion and charity, he wished to instruct others in the precious possession he had received and began to preach the Catholic faith." He claimed that, as a result of his preachment, "a very great multitude" of Jews had given up their ancient errors and joined Christianity. It appears that the Treasury did not turn a deaf ear to this pathetic plea. In another petition, dated in 1418, a priest of Fraga contended that the entire Jewish community, once quite important in Spanish history, had adopted Christianity and asked that he be allotted the former synagogue, interveningly converted into a church, with all its appurtenances and rights. On November 20, 1413, the king himself asked Ferrer for the second time to proceed to Tortosa and subsequently to Saragossa, since in both places there were many Jews awaiting conversion. An extensive report submitted to Ferdinand by Infante Alphonso on October 31, 1414, shortly before the adjournment of the disputation, graphically describes the enormous pressures exerted on Jews by the secular as well as ecclesiastical authorities of Daroca, Joseph Albo's home town. This description is probably typical of what happened in many other parts of Aragon as well.[45]

As a result, a wave of hysteria swept over the Jewish communities of Aragon and, to a lesser extent, of the other Iberian kingdoms. There was no end of personal tragedies when husbands separated from wives, children from parents, some choosing to join Christianity, while others retained their loyalty to their ancestral creed. A final blow was struck by Benedict in his aforementioned lengthy bull, *Et si doctoris*, of May 10, 1415, which had been adumbrated in the discussions at San Mateo. Here the antipope boasted that, as a result of the disputation, nearly 3,000 Jews had accepted baptism. As early as July 27, 1414 Benedict allowed the synagogue in Tamarite de Litera to be converted into a Benedictine chapel, for after the conversion of most local Jews it had remained unoccupied. Several more such rescripts were recorded in the following twelve months, showing the total dissolution of many old Aragonese communities. If anything, the number of 3,000 converts is conservative and relates only to Aragon. The years 1413–15 represented, moreover, but the culmination of tremendous pressures over a period of a quarter of a century. The claim that, owing to Vicente Ferrer's efforts alone, 25,000 Jews and 8,000 Saracens found their way to the baptismal font appears quite reasonable. The staggering psychological impression these events made upon the Spanish Jews and the ensuing chain reaction are well illustrated in the subsequent tradition recorded by the chronicler Abraham b. Solomon of Torrutiel. Referring to the period around 1412, this apologetic writer asserted that "more than two hundred thousand Jews" had deserted their faith in those years. The storm blew over only when Pedro de Luna was discharged by the Council of Constance and when Ferdinand I's death in 1416 placed upon the throne of Aragon the much friendlier ruler, Alphonso V.[46]

## UNEASY COEXISTENCE

The Judeo-Christian symbiosis in the later Middle Ages thus reveals many inherent contradictions. One could indeed view the large spectrum of medieval relations between the two faiths in terms of such a polarity of traditions, drives, and needs.

Historically originating as a sectarian minority within Judaism, Christianity saw its role completely reversed from the days of Constantine. By the thirteenth century the Jewish minority was but a tiny fraction of the total European population under the sway of Christendom. From this initial transformation, as well as the subsequent historic realities, there emerged the perennial polarity of the Church's policies: toleration of Jews as the only legitimate religious minority in the Christian world, combined with ever sharper segregation and discrimination, even degradation. Yet, having accepted the principle of allowing Jewish dissidence, the Roman Church dreaded the spread of Christian dissidence nurtured on Jewish sources. Constantly invoking the need of Jews and their Old Testament as "testimonies" for the Christian faith, it resented the use of that very Testament by heretics rebellious against its established doctrine and social order. Many churchmen realized that they could benefit from Jewish help in unraveling the mysteries of the Hebrew Bible. Yet they increasingly distrusted their own masses to fathom those mysteries by the reading of Scripture, and tried to discourage its spread in vernacular translations.

Unable to repudiate the Old Testament as such, many ecclesiastical spokesmen, particularly from among recent converts, blamed the Jews for their stubbornness in refusing to see the light on alleged misinterpretations by the Jewish Oral Law. The rabbinic literature and particularly the Talmud were now denounced not only as anti-Christian and full of "blasphemies," but also as replete with "stupidities" and barbarisms intolerable to any right-thinking person. Yet some of the accusing churchmen personally knew many intelligent and high-minded Jewish devotees of rabbinic lore. Out of sheer embarrassment Willam of Auvergne, personally coresponsible for the first burning of the Talmud, could only state that the Jew "had turned to incredible fables and given himself over totally to them with the exception of a very few who, by mixing with the Saracen people, have engaged in philosophizing." It did not take long, however, before other churchmen invoked that very Talmud as convincing testimony that the messiah had come and that, hence, Jesus was the real Christ.[47]

Other discrepancies emerged when in their drive toward conformity the ecclesiastical leaders sought to convert as many Jews as possible without violating the principle of basic toleration. They were ready, through the use of various syllogisms, to stretch the assumption of "voluntary" conversion to illogical extremes. This drive was often slowed down because of the simple practical difficulty that newly converted Jews, even prospective converts, would become public charges and have to be maintained from episcopal treasuries. Perhaps an even greater antithesis manifested itself when many ecclesiastical champions of "natural rights" were prepared to deny the most basic natural right, namely that of parents to bring up their offspring in their own homes in consonance with their ancestral mores.

Such inconsistencies were not only the results of trying to adhere to a basic theory in the midst of ever changing socioeconomic, political, and cultural conditions, but were rather inherent in the very relationship between the two denominations. They are the more remarkable as they ran counter to the general stability of the Church's outlook on life and its canon law. Understandably, they generated many areas of perennial conflict, but they also opened new vistas and furnished novel opportunities for the adjustment of the rigid requirements of the law to existing conditions in various lands and periods. Most directly, they stimulated a constant process of rethinking of one's own ideological position and generated an unending flow of polemical writings destined to persuade the opponent as well as to reaffirm and strengthen one's own faith and to elaborate it with ever finer discrimination.

# XXXIX

# SPIRITED APOLOGIST

ORAL disputations were, by their very nature, of a fugitive character. Unless their substance was recorded in written form and incorporated, with whatever variations the compiler deemed fit, in a pamphlet intended for distribution among readers, such discussions were quickly forgotten, sometimes by the very participants. Even the famous disputations of Paris, Barcelona, and Tortosa might have remained without permanent ideological results, were it not for the burning of the Talmud, which the Paris debate was unable to prevent but for which it was not really responsible.

On the Christian side the records of those disputations seem not to have been intended for wide dissemination. The disputation of Tortosa, despite its extreme length and its numerous highly dramatic incidents, was recorded by its managers only in dry-as-dust protocols. Clearly, the writers did not intend to circulate the minutes very widely and only three copies, somewhat divergent from one another, have been preserved in Spanish and Vatican libraries.

If the Jewish point of view, as presented by R. Yehiel and Nahmanides, was not only recorded for posterity but also circulated among the Jewish communities, this was done in Yehiel's case by an outsider some seven years after the event. Nahmanides waited two years before publishing a statement of his own. Both men were evidently prompted by rumors of the victory of the Christian side, which they felt obliged to deny and thus to help build up the morale of the Jewish public. After the lost battles of Tortosa, the Jewish leaders apparently failed to distribute widely any semi-official report of the stand they had taken. At best one or another participant privately wrote a few notes for his personal remembrance. It is small wonder, then, that the innumerable lesser disputations, private as well as public, have left few traces in the extant records.

In contrast, written polemics often had an enduring quality. In the absence of a daily press, pamphlets distributed in numerous copies increasingly served as potent weapons in partisan struggles. At the same time large compendia containing extensive quotations from sources and detailed arguments served as armories from which pamphleteers as well as preachers could select the weapons suitable for their particular purposes. True, the traditional literature *Adversus Judeaos,* which had become fashionable as early as the patristic age and continued throughout the High Middle Ages, was no longer needed to serve its original aims of helping to convert pagans or of strengthening the faith of wavering Christians. Now Christianity was firmly rooted. But because the official Church had become deeply embroiled in its struggle with the numerous heretical movements and because the Jewish question had assumed a much more serious character in Western society, the polemists had to take a more direct stand on certain vital issues, both doctrinal and sociopolitical.

On the other hand, it no longer sufficed to repeat the ancient denunciations without reference to the actual position taken by opponents. In this respect the disputations were serving the useful purpose of direct confrontation. Effective polemics could now be conducted only on the basis of some familiarity with the major sources of the opposing dogma. Martin de León's exclamation foreshadowed the new approach: "I wish with God's help to vanquish you with your own weapons, that is with the revelations of your law and prophets. For no adversary is more effectively overcome than when he is fought with his own arms." Here De León referred primarily to the traditional Old Testament "testimonies," but one more step sufficed for the Christian polemists to try to convince the Jews of the fallacy of their repudiation of Christ on the basis of their own talmudic and rabbinic sources. For this purpose many of them became students of Hebrew and, at least superficially, of rabbinic literature, encouraged therein by their own leaders assembled at the Ecumenical Council of Vienne. Informed converts from Judaism, who in their youth had acquired some knowledge of rabbinics, now easily became the protagonists in that polemical drama. Even the scientifically minded King Alphonso X probably pursued primarily missionary aims when he induced Jewish scholars to translate for him "the whole

Jewish law," the Talmud and certain kabbalistic works. At least his grandnephew, Don Juan, to whom we owe this information, explained that "he [Alphonso] did it because it is manifest that their [the Jews'] entire law had been but an adumbration [figura] of the law which we Christians hold." [1]

On their part some Jewish spokesmen, too, felt that an effective answer could not limit itself to a defense of what they considered the correct interpretation of biblical and rabbinic sources, but that they also ought occasionally to undermine the Christian position by assailing certain New Testament passages. For this reason the rabbis, especially in the more exposed Mediterranean lands, had to relax their old policy of ignoring non-Jewish religious literatures; they had to allow at least some disciples to familiarize themselves with the Gospels and other revered Christian letters. The result was a considerably greater depth and penetration in the mutual argumentation, even if the basic issues were substantially the same as those which had been so repetitively aired over the preceding millennium.

## LITERARY POLEMICS

With the vast accumulation of polemical writings at his disposal, Antipope Benedict XIII, for one, could quite well prepare himself when as cardinal-legate he debated the merits of the two faiths with Shem Ṭob b. Isaac Shapruṭ in Pamplona. His deep interest in Christian apologetical literature is evidenced by the inventory of his library examined by modern scholars. No less than eighteen numbers (156–73) of his collection dealt with "heresies," ten consisting of anti-Jewish polemics by Benedict's Spanish predecessors, St. Isidore of Seville, Petrus Alphonsi, Bernardo Oliver, Raymond Martini, and Abner of Burgos. He kept some of these works, especially Martini's compendium, in more than one manuscript version. It was perhaps a mere accident that he failed to formulate his anti-Jewish views in a special pamphlet of his own.[2]

In substance, the distinction between oral disputation and literary polemic was quite tenuous. The occasional published accounts of the former essentially served the same purposes as other writings composed in dialogue form, where the disputation was partially or wholly imaginary. Both these categories also bore close resemblance to the equally fictitious dialogues in popular dramas, where they were imbedded in some sort of plot, mostly of a religious nature. The main difference was that, even if written, such plays were primarily intended for production on the medieval stage, which was indeed greatly indebted to the dramatization of biblical events, for the most part in an anti-Jewish vein. Hence they were aimed at the broader masses of the population, whereas the strictly literary dialogues addressed themselves as a rule to educated readers, both ecclesiastical and lay. Only the latter represented the considered opinion of the Church's intellectual elite, while the dramas belong to the realm of folklore as much as to that of literature. On the borderline between the two literary genres were the frequent anti-Jewish polemics incorporated into the Christian liturgy. In the Byzantine world, we recall, many ornate church pageants, like the great dramas by Romanos, included pointedly anti-Jewish messages. In the West, too, some liturgical poems written by such outstanding churchmen as St. Bernard of Clairvaux sought to demonstrate the supremacy of the Church by deprecating the Synagogue. On the other hand, the prayer, *Pro perfidis Judaeis,* continued to take some of the edge off the Church's Jew-baiting preachment. However, even in the liturgical area the depth and novelty of argumentation and its impact upon intellectual opinion were less significant than their influence on the mass of worshipers. All these facets must be relegated, therefore, to our general analysis of the varying popular attitudes toward Jews and Judaism.[3]

Quantitatively, too, polemical treatises now increased by leaps and bounds, reaching a climax in the tense fifteenth century. The output of that one century probably exceeded in bulk that of all the preceding fourteen centuries combined. A contributing factor was the generally greater articulateness of late medieval Western writers and the larger circulation and better preservation of their output, especially after the introduction of printing, but primarily it was attributable to the "burning" issues created by the widespread anti-Jewish hostility ever since 1290 characterized by massacres and expulsions. At least some of the writers tried to justify the acts of violence and legal intolerance by the Jews' own stubbornness and misdeeds. More significantly, the new literature more vigorously pursued avowed missionary aims. In the Roman and Byzantine empires, and even in western Europe before the age of the Crusades, the numerous tracts "Against the Jews" primarily had Christian audiences in mind. Now, on the contrary, the Church viewed the apologetic literature as but another weapon in its march toward world domination. The new offensive, seized particularly by the preaching orders, also infused new vigor and introduced novel facets into the polemics which, together with the vastly expanding missionary sermons and oral disputations, tried to persuade the Jews of the "foolishness" of their stubborn perseverance.

Understandably, the controversy raged most violently in Spain and the Provence where the large number, affluence, and intellectual acumen of the Jewish population had long irritated expansionist Christian leaders. Here the heritage of the Crusades, which had led to the reconquest of practically the whole Iberian Peninsula, was reinforced by heated internal political clashes and a high level of literary culture. Next to Spain pre-expulsion England and France and later Germany and Italy were the main battle grounds. Some of the greatest minds of Western Christendom joined the ranks of the anti-Jewish controversialists. Whether they wrote on the subject in a moderate vein as did Robert Grosseteste, Vincent of Beauvais, Thomas Aquinas, or later Marsilio Ficino, or whether they contributed more or less sharply worded anti-Jewish pamphlets, they naturally argued from a more refined dialectical level. Certainly a philosopher of history like Joachim of Floris, a polyhistor like Raymond Lull, a thinker and scientist like Arnaldo de Vilanova, and such informed Christian Hebraists as Raymond Martini and Nicholas de Lyra—all necessarily placed the imprint of their remarkable personalities and thoughts on their polemical writings.[4]

In contrast to most writers who closely adhered to the traditional line and merely offered variations on the old themes, the fascinating personality of Joachim of Floris and his attitude to the Jews have often puzzled investigators. On the one hand, he has much in common with ancient gnosticism, which may help explain some of his anti-Jewish formulations, particularly those involving the Old Testament. On the other hand, in his anti-Jewish tract he insisted that Jesus was the true messiah predicted in the Old Testament and not another redeemer expected by Jews, and he adduced the well-known chronological "proof" from the prophecy of Daniel. But he added, "If the prophet was mistaken in regard to the number of years, he could be equally deceived with respect to the other matters he predicted. . . . In this case it would be appropriate for us, together with the Patarene heretics, to refute the entire Old Testament in which the faith is rooted." He also often followed the lead of Petrus Alphonsi. Yet Geoffrey of Auxerre may have had this original fellow Cistercian in mind when he spoke of a prophet Joachim as a descendant of Jews. More significantly, Joachim's penetrating view on historical cycles, in which he adumbrated much of the cyclical conception of history of Gianbattista Vico, may have been at least indirectly influenced by a Jewish doctrine often discussed in the apologetic literature of both faiths. Here the history of the world was divided into three 2000-year cycles of Tohu, Torah, and the messianic age, corresponding to the six days of creation, each day of God representing a thousand years (according to Ps. 90:4). But such contradictions are the less amazing in the case of this creative mystic, as in his polemics against Jews he could even less afford to espouse an avowedly Marcionite doctrine than in his other writings. His own views were, in fact, sufficiently non-committal for Honorius IV and the Church as a whole to condone his teachings while condemning the exaggerated interpretations of them by some of his followers.[5]

At the same time a number of Jewish converts to Catholicism injected into the polemical literature not only their zest as neophytes but also their intimate knowledge of Judaism and Jewish ways of life. Some also brought with them a considerable amount of Jewish learning. The convert as an anti-Jewish controversialist had been an old phenomenon in Jewish history, but apart from Petrus Alphonsi Western Christendom had not previously gained any high-level intellectual spokesmen through conversion. Now, however, in addition to the neo-Christian protagonists at the three great disputations, there appeared such thinkers as Abner of Burgos (Alphonso of Valladolid) and Solomon ha-Levi (Paul of Burgos). In fact, rumor had it that even Joachim of Floris and Raymond Martini were either converts or sons of converts.[6]

On the Jewish side, too, there appeared far more articulate, informed, and well-trained debaters. While none of them reached the intellectual stature of Naḥmanides, many were steeped in theological studies, were much more familiar than their predecessors with the New Testament and Church doctrines, and wielded their pens with greater facility. One outstanding controversialist was Isaac b. Moses Efodi, known in Spanish as Profiat Duran, who for a while was swayed by the wave of conversions in 1391 but subsequently returned to Judaism and became one of its chief defenders. Characteristic of the new dimensions of Jewish polemics are the subjects discussed in his major tract, entitled the *Kelimat hagoyim* (The Shame of Gentiles), all documented from the New Testament and other authoritative Christian sources. Its twelve chapters intended:

I. To prove . . . that neither the alleged messiah nor his disciples claimed that he was God. . . . II. To analyze their [the Christians'] belief in Trinity and the passages supporting it. . . . III. To analyze their belief in Incarnation and its main purpose in connection with the "original" sin. . . . IV. To show that Jesus never thought of opposing the divine Torah, but wished to maintain it for ever, and that even his disciples considered it eternal for the people which had been ordered to observe it. V. To show the reasons adduced by the later followers of Jesus in their opposition to the Torah and their erroneous and shameful belief in its abrogation. . . . VI. To analyze the problem of the divine bread and wine [Eucharist] which they believe lose their forms and turn into the body of Christ. . . . VII. To analyze the problem of baptism which they consider one of the fundamentals of their faith. . . . VIII. To analyze the problem of the pope, whom they call *papa* in charge of their Church, which they likewise consider one of the fundamentals of their faith. . . . IX. To analyze the problem of Mary, Jesus' mother and other matters relating to the fundamentals of their faith and their ramifications. . . . X. To analyze the mistakes, errors and wrong interpretations given by Jesus, his disciples and later apostles concerning biblical verses contrary to the words of the living God, whereby they have shown their lack of understanding. XI. Concerning their error with respect to chronology which they style the *era del nacimiento* from the birth of Jesus. . . . XII. To analyze the errors of Jerome, the faulty translator of Scripture from Hebrew into Latin, and to prove that the scriptural text in our possession is precisely true and nothing must ever be added to it or subtracted from it.

Other leading apologists for Judaism before and after Duran were Jacob b. Reuben, Jacob b. Elijah of Valencia, Nathan Official and his son Joseph, Isaac Pollegar, Shem Ṭob b. Isaac Shapruṭ, Joshua ha-Lorqi (before he turned Geronimo de Santa Fé and leading participant in the disputation of Tortosa), Yom Ṭob Lipmann-Mühlhausen, the distinguished halakhist Simon b. Ṣemaḥ Duran, his son Solomon, Joseph ibn Shem Ṭob, and Ḥayyim b. Yehudah ibn Musa.[7]

Although principally a book of history, the *Shebeṭ Yehudah* by Solomon ibn Verga is filled with dialogues on Jews and Judaism, both historical and fictitious, so that it may also be classified as an apologetic tract. Oral disputants like Yeḥiel of Paris, Meir b. Simon of Narbonne, Naḥmanides of Gerona, Moses Kohen of Tordesillas, and Abraham b. Mordecai Farissol of Ferrara left records of their debates. Many of their works enjoyed wide circulation and lent comfort to their coreligionists. So deeply concerned had the Jewish intelligentsia become over the constant attacks on their faith that apologetics colored their writings more than ever, especially in the fields of philosophy and poetry. We have noted the impact of religious controversies on the works of Solomon b. Moses of Salerno and Joseph Albo. It was no less evident in those of Albo's teacher, Ḥisdai b. Yehudah Crescas, who felt impelled to publish (*ca.* 1400) a special polemical *Tratado* in Spanish, which was later translated into Hebrew. Popular preachers of the type of Israel b. Joseph al-Naqawa or Isaac b. Moses 'Arama reacted even more vigorously, though not with quite the same venom as their opposite numbers among Christian homilists. Poets not only expatiated on traditional themes of Jewish suffering, pointing an accusing finger at their persecutors, but also indulged in direct ideological polemics which often differed more in form than in substance from their prose counterparts. The Hebrew liturgical poem, *Yigdal* (May the Living God be Magnified), included in the daily recitations of many Jewish congregations, lent itself particularly well to biting parodies. Couched in philosophic terms which strongly emphasized the unity of God, it could easily be rephrased so as to ridicule Christianity's unity within trinity. Alexander Marx identified four such parodies, including one each by the apologists David Nasi of Candia and Elijah Ḥayyim of Genezzano.[8]

## NEW APPROACHES

Expansive missionary polemics against Jews required new methods of attack. So long as Christian apologias had primarily a Christian or pagan audience in mind, it was enough to adduce "testimonies" from the Old Testament to prove that the Gospel narratives bore out ancient prophetic predictions. This line of persuasion was applied to Jews as well, but it now became far more important to convince them that their own traditional sources, contemporaneous with or subsequent to the rise of Christianity, demonstrated that the messiah had arrived and that his characteristic features were recognizable in the person of Jesus. The new approach came to the fore at the disputation of Barcelona, and continued in that of Tortosa and in much of the apologetic literature from the thirteenth century on. It was not quite consistent, however, inasmuch as Christian authors, particularly those of Jewish descent, were still trying to prove that the Talmud and other rabbinic writings contained many anti-Christian references and were generally immoral and stupid.

Linguistically, too, there was evidence of the change in aims. For the first time some Christian controversial tracts (for instance, Abner's several essays and Paul of Burgos' somewhat heavy but understandable reply to Joshua ha-Lorqi's letter) appeared in Hebrew, clearly indicating that the authors wished to reach Jewish audiences. Jews reciprocated and from time to time wrote polemical tracts in Spanish, though not in Latin. Perhaps only few knew how to employ Latin effectively; perhaps they suspected that Latin pamphlets would reach only the clergy and a few Catholic intellectuals on whom they would make little impression. But many doubtless still regarded that language as an instrument of ecclesiastical control, almost as the "holy tongue" of Catholicism. This view, perfectly justified almost to the end of the Middle Ages, was abandoned only after the secularization of Latin letters during the Italian Renaissance when, indeed, Elijah Delmedigo of Candia (1460–97) wrote several philosophic essays in Latin. But those writings did not deal with denominationally controversial subjects.

A classic Christian apologia utilizing rabbinic sources, in many respects the fountainhead of all subsequent treatments of this kind, was Raymond Martini's *Pugio Fidei* written in 1278. Although documentary evidence dates only from the fifteenth century, there is no reason to doubt Martini's Jewish ancestry. Apart from his possible early rabbinic training, he received instruction in Oriental languages at Peñaforte's special college. In 1263 he may have attended the disputation of Barcelona as an interested observer, and in the following year served on the committee of five charged with reviewing all Hebrew books forcibly assembled from various parts of Aragon. Among those thousands of manuscripts he undoubtedly found many old Provençal Jewish writings from the school of Moses ha-Darshan and others, some of which have since completely disappeared.

Out of these vast materials Martini compiled a large volume (its printed edition covers more than 700 folio pages), trying to buttress the fundamental teachings of Christianity not only through Old Testament passages but also through "certain traditions which I found in the Talmud, the Midrashim, and the sayings of ancient Jews, and which I picked out like pearls from a dung heap, to my great joy." He also decided, following Apostle Paul's example, to quote the Hebrew Bible, rather than its Greek or Latin versions, thus evidently trying to forestall Jewish criticism that both the Septuagint and the Vulgate had incorrectly reproduced the Hebrew text by frequently giving it a messianic twist where no such meaning was intended by the prophets. On the other hand, like most of his colleagues, Martini ignored the objections raised by Naḥmanides and other Jewish apologists that, if the talmudic sages had borne witness to the truth of Christianity, they would not have repudiated the new faith. He and his successors also preferred to choose passages fitting their purpose and totally to disregard all contradictory evidence. "Let him who wishes to defend the faith," he declared, "and to attack the Jews' error . . . carefully distinguish what fits the first and the second coming of Christ, and whether any prophecy belongs to His human or to His divine nature. Let him also note what Scripture says about the good and the bad Israel and Jacob." Naturally enough, Jewish readers were not at all impressed by such selectivity and rejected some passages as altogether spurious. At the disputation of Tortosa in particular, they often pointed to the authentic versions current in Jewish communities and repudiated many readings quoted by Geronimo de Santa Fé from Martini's collection.[9]

The obscure nature of Martini's sources and his rather arbitrary use of them gave rise to doubts about their authenticity. The accusation that most of them were outright forgeries, first indirectly leveled against him by Don Isaac Abravanel in 1497, has since been repeated by modern scholars. However, this thirteenth-century Christian apologist also found erudite defenders among Jewish experts in the midrashic literature.[10]

Without entering here into the details of this complicated debate, one may state that the weight of evidence favors the assumption that neither Martini, nor any of his Christian predecessors whose works he may have used, was guilty of outright forgeries. Of course, none of them was a critical scholar, not even by the standards soon thereafter developed by the Italian Renaissance. Nor were they unbiased. Martini pursued overt missionary aims and doubtless did not mind quoting passages out of context or with omissions. At times abridgments were necessitated by the length and discursiveness of the original sources, but on other occasions the deletions doubtless served to underscore certain points in the debate. The same is admittedly true of his whole selection of sources.

All this was a fairly normal procedure at that time, particularly in an apologetic work composed from the outset *ad majorem Dei gloriam*. But direct forgeries of nonexistent texts would actually have defeated the entire purpose of Martini's weighty volume directed against pagans and philosophers as well as Jews. Certainly, in order to persuade Jewish students that their cherished rabbis, if properly understood, bore witness to the truth of Christianity, one had to present them with texts the interpretation of which could be debatable but the existence of which could not simply be rejected out of hand.

Among the thousands of volumes scrutinized by Martini and his fellow commissioners in 1264 there undoubtedly appeared some texts which, reflecting homiletic and folkloristic traditions of the obscure first millennium in the history of West-European Jewish communities, no longer agreed with the accepted teachings of rabbinic schools by the time of Alfasi, Gershom, and Rashi. Many such texts, destroyed by the Christian inquisitors of the thirteenth century, were never reproduced by the following generations of Jews, and their spokesmen at Tortosa, as we recall, could truthfully assert that a number of passages cited by Geronimo (in part from Martini's *Pugio fidei*) were not found in any books current in their communities. Needless to say, even if authentic these passages did not have the christological implications attributed to them by Martini; otherwise, as the Jewish apologists rightly claimed, their authors would have turned Christian. But in their general lack of sophistication and particularly when speaking in an age when these issues had not yet become the subjects of heated controversy, the early Jewish sages could indulge in speculations the doctrinal ambiguity of which escaped them entirely. Their statements could now be paraded as authenic "proofs" for the Christian tradition from the mouths of its enemies.

Martini's book was speedily adopted as a treasure trove of anti-Jewish polemics. Only fourteen years after the publication of the *Pugio,* Arnaldo de Vilanova expressed his firm belief that the book had been written under divine inspiration. It was extensively used even by such rabbinically trained converts as Geronimo and Paul of Burgos who, having independent knowledge of rabbinic sources, lent new meaning to passages quoted from it. Most independent was Abner of Burgos. After his conversion at the age of sixty (according to his admirer Paul of Burgos, who called him "a great Bible scholar, philosopher and metaphysician"), he joined the ranks of anti-Jewish controversialists. Like many of his fellow polemists, he endeavored to convert "the Jews by showing them the truth of Christianity from the Talmud and the Midrashim without appealing to the Bible," but his arguments were more learned and penetrating. Abner therefore exerted considerable influence on both contemporaries and successors, and affected many a doctrine espoused even by such orthodox Jewish thinkers as Ḥisdai Crescas and Joseph Albo. He sensed, in particular, the growing reaction among both Jews and Christians against Aristotelian rationalism and the widespread escape into mysticism. He effectively attacked the friend of his youth, Isaac Pollegar, whose rationalist world outlook, particularly concerning the doctrine of free will, he roundly condemned as typical of the entire Spanish-Jewish intelligentsia.[11]

Yet Abner had too original a mind, even if permeated with rabbinic modes of thinking, and he was too independent of any tradition, Christian or Jewish, to be fully accepted by the orthodox of either faith. Apart from being quite erudite in the then current rabbinic and Christian texts, he had apparently familiarized himself with Karaite writings, was a devotee of the Kabbalah, and studied also some works by Muslims and pagans accessible to him in Hebrew or Spanish, though he seems never to have mastered Latin. As a result of his early heterodox leanings, reminding one of the career of Nicholas Donin, he concentrated some of his attacks on Jewish liturgy. A 1336 edict by Alphonso XI of Castile prohibiting Jews from reciting the old antiheretical prayer is often attributed to Abner's contention in a debate with Jewish scholars of Valladolid that this prayer revealed a specific anti-Christian animus.[12]

In these vigorous intellectual debates, voices denouncing the Old Testament as such were not altogether absent. Despite the repudiation of Marcionism by the Church Fathers and of the Catharist schism by the medieval Church, some thoughtful Christians raised that issue anew. Joseph Albo thus recorded his interesting discussion with a Christian scholar who had attacked the Torah of Moses as defective and inferior to the New Testament with respect to the four fundamental criteria—the material, the efficient, the final, and the formal:

It is defective [he contended] in respect to its matter, for it contains stories and other matters which are not Torah, i.e. teaching and guidance; whereas the teaching of Jesus has nothing but instruction. It is defective in respect to the efficient cause, because it expresses the divine mysteries alluding to the Trinity in a very obscure manner, so that it is not possible to understand from it the perfection of the Maker and His attributes; while it is very clear in the teaching of Jesus the Nazarene that God is father, son and holy ghost, and that they are all one. It is defective in respect to the final cause, for it says nothing about spiritual happiness, which is the purpose of man, but speaks only of material happiness. The teaching of Jesus, on the other hand, promises spiritual happiness and not material successes. It is defective in respect to the formal cause for . . . it is defective in the duties of man to God, i.e. in the ceremonial part, which prescribes the manner of divine worship. For it commands the slaughter of animals, the burning of the flesh and the fat, the sprinkling of the blood, all of which are unclean forms of worship; whereas the manner of worship prescribed in the law of Jesus is clean, consisting of bread and wine. It is defective also in the social and judicial precepts, which concern human relations, for it permits interest saying: "Unto a foreigner thou mayest lend upon interest" [Deut. 23:21]; whereas interest is destructive of social life. . . . It is defective in the matter of a man's duty to himself, for the law of Moses commands only right action, and says nothing about purity of heart; whereas the law of Jesus commands purity of heart, and thus saves man from the judgment of gehenna.

Albo's answer, likewise couched in philosophic terms and citing other passages from the Hebrew Bible and rabbinic letters, denied these allegations as "due to a lack of understanding or insight or knowledge of the ideas of the Torah." This reply not only satisfied most of Albo's coreligionists but it may, in part, also have evoked a responsive echo among staunch Catholic defenders of the Old Testament.[13]

As a rule, Jewish apologists adjusted their strategy to the new lines of attack. Utilizing their greater familiarity with rabbinic letters, they repudiated as spurious many passages quoted by their opponents or else rejected the latter's interpretations as doing injustice to the authors' original intent. In regard to the Bible, they adhered to its more literal interpretation rather than the more allegorical presentation still common among churchmen, although critical study of the Bible had made sufficient advances for most Christian controversialists no longer to emphasize the Jewish "materialistic" interpretation as foreign to its spirit.

At the same time, realizing that offense was the best method of defense, many Spanish Jewish apologists made an intensive study of Christian sources, thus reciprocating the Christian interest in rabbinics. Rather than repeating the crude aspersions cast at the persons of Jesus and Mary in the old folkloristic *Toledot Yeshu* (Life of Jesus), they critically pointed out the numerous inconsistencies in the New Testament and argued that some Christian dogmas could not be reconciled with human reason. Most remarkably, the writers took for granted the familiarity of their Hebrew readers with such teachings, perhaps even with specific New Testament passages to which they briefly alluded. Sometimes they did it so subtly as to mislead the censors, who first considered, for instance, Profiat Duran's early tract, "Be Not Like Thy Fathers," a defense of Christian teaching. Only in time was its satirical intent detected and the whole tract consigned to the flames. More overtly, in his second apologetic tract, "The Shame of Gentiles," Duran as a true rationalist attacked the doctrine of the Trinity by associating it with the much-disparaged Kabbalah. "In my youth," he asserted, "while attending the academy of my masters, I have heard from a German talmudist and also from students of the Kabbalah that Jesus the Nazarene and his disciples were kabbalists, though their Kabbalah was erroneous. Utilizing the practical methods of that discipline, Jesus performed those various strange acts extraneous to the natural course of events." In "practical Kabbalah" Jews came to see something akin to magic arts. By implication Duran repeated here the older equation of Jesus' miracles with magic, an equation which, under the guise of the invocation of the divine name surreptitiously secured by Jesus, had played such a focal role in the legendary *Toledot Yeshu*.[14]

The association of Christian teachings with the Kabbalah in this manner was far from displeasing to Christian mystics. In fact, Raymond Lull (or rather one of his disciples, possibly Pietro Mainardi), Arnaldo de Vilanova, and Abner of Burgos were among the first authors to perceive clearly the extent to which kabbalistic doctrines could be used for the defense of Christianity. Vilanova, who may have had personal contacts with the kabbalist Abraham Abulafia, betrays some kabbalistic influences also in his anti-Jewish polemics, particularly in his *Allocutio,* written in 1292, which may have come to Abner's attention when he was still wrestling with his inner doubts. Before long Christian Hebraists began to immerse themselves systematically in the mystical lore of

Judaism, finding therein a confirmation and elaboration of their own cherished beliefs. Ultimately, Giovanni Pico della Mirandola, an assiduous reader of kabbalistic works (a number of which have been identified in his library), exclaimed, "No science can be more efficacious in demonstrating the divinity of Christ than magic and Kabbalah." [15]

Obviously the Jewish apologists had little hope, and hardly evinced any real desire, to convert their Gentile readers to Judaism; most of them merely argued for the legitimacy and peaceful coexistence of the various faiths. At a time when he was still groping for religious truths, Joshua ha-Lorqi raised the old question, frequently debated especially in Muslim philosophic circles, whether man was entitled to cast doubts on his ancestral religion. Joshua asked whether such freedom of inquiry would not subject each faith to individual whims, the result being "that no man in the world would remain faithful to his creed." Moreover, he insisted, divine justice could not possibly condemn a Christian living in England, where there were neither Jews nor Muslims, or a Muslim residing in distant regions of the Orient uninhabited by Jews or Christians, for his failure to reexamine the validity of his faith in comparison with rivaling religions. Few Jewish leaders, to be sure, were ready to subscribe to the equivalence of all creeds, but they certainly would have echoed the inherent demand for mutual toleration.

## DOCTRINAL CONTROVERSIES

In contrast to the novelty of methods and variety of interests on both sides, the substantive issues under debate at first changed relatively little. The same problems which had been discussed by representatives of the two faiths in ancient times and during the High Middle Ages still preoccupied the minds of most controversialists in England, France and the Iberian Peninsula during the later medieval period. Only the original mind of Abner of Burgos, stimulated by his ever-deepening hatred of his ancestral faith, added a new dimension to his attacks on the ethics of Judaism. Among the fifteenth- and sixteenth-century writers, especially in northern Italy and Germany where Jewish status had interveningly undergone great changes, the economic factor began to over-shadow all others in importance.

Nor must we lose sight of the fact that many Jewish apologists were forced to fight, so to say, a two-front war. They had to defend all of Judaism against the onslaughts of Christian controversialists and at the same time explain their particular brand of Judaism to the masses of their coreligionists. They knew that they faced a vast array of internal opponents ranging from extreme fundamentalists to radical rationalists and even to believers in astrological deter-minism. Typical of these divergent lines of defense is Isaac Pollegar's *Support of Faith,* in which he divided his Jewish oppo-nents into five major groups. Correspondingly, he composed his tract in five sections, described by him as follows:

In the first section I have shown to all nations the glory of our faith and the perfection of its exponents among those of all other religions; in the second section I have demonstrated the identity of its teachings with those of the true sciences, its agreement and intermingling with them . . . ; the third section is devoted to controverting the views of the astrologers and to showing the nature of the alternative courses [open to man] from all their angles; in the fourth section I shall answer the fools who indulge in imaginary realities, exaggerations and matters whose existence cannot be sustained [an allusion to literal believers in aggadic statements and more recent folklore]; the fifth section will explain to the best of my ability the preservation of the thinking soul after its separation from the body.

Clearly, Pollegar anticipated that only a segment of Spanish Jewry would subscribe to his entire presentation, even if many others might appreciate his taking up the cudgel in behalf of their an-cestral faith.[16]

The focal point in the Judeo-Christian controversy still was the personality of Jesus and his messianic as well as divine qualities. The related subjects of the Virgin Birth, Original Sin, the redemption of mankind by the incarnate Son of God, and the doc-trine of Transubstantiation, also continued to engage the close at-tention of the spokesmen of both sides. Connected with these doc-trines were the problems of the immutability or abrogation of the Old Testament laws, and the relative claims of the two faiths to chosenness.

Perhaps the briefest summary of these issues is offered in Profiat

Duran's satirical Epistle, describing the differences between what Duran's converted friend, Paul of Burgos, was expected to believe as a Christian and what his Jewish forebears had believed. "Be not like thy fathers," read the first ironical injunction, "who believed in a God of simple oneness and totally denied any multiplicity in Him. . . . You are different; you will believe in Him as being one and three and the three being one . . . a matter which the mouth cannot express and which the ear can hardly perceive." Secondly, the forefathers had believed in a God who is not subject to change, and rejected any kind of corporeality in Him. Philosophically, they viewed Him as a pure intellect and interpreted the anthropomorphic phrases of the Torah as a mere oversimplification for the masses. The new convert, however, must believe that in one of His manifestations God had become flesh, shed His blood to redeem His people, for His wisdom had found no other way to secure its salvation, and that He had been born from the womb of the 'Alma which the Christians equate with virgin, but which, Profiat intimated, in the Bible really stands for a nonvirgin. Similarly, the forefathers had investigated and tried to explain the deeper meaning of the ramified story of creation in Genesis. But a convert must believe that the first man had loaded upon himself and his successors a permanent sin from which they could be redeemed only by a supernatural savior. Furthermore, the forefathers refused to eat the bread of idols, whereas as a convert one must consume the host containing the flesh and blood of the redeemer. More remarkably he, Profiat, had read the Acts of the Apostles and found nowhere an abrogation of the six hundred and thirteen commandments of the Torah for the children of Abraham. "Those [early Christians] who had been of Jewish descent fulfilled the precepts of the Torah after the death of Christ and after their baptism in his name. You will find it thus written in the Book [Gospel] of Matthew." Nevertheless, the new convert may now indulge in any kind of forbidden food, violate the Sabbath, fail to circumcise his sons, and generally break the law.[17]

So convinced were Profiat and his fellow intellectuals of the validity of their philosophic preconceptions that they disregarded the substantial segment of Jewish public opinion which refused to reinterpret allegorically all biblical passages implying God's corporeality. In this approach Duran followed in the footsteps of his teacher, Ḥisdai Crescas, who in a more directly scholastic vein had argued against the Trinitarian dogma and its acceptability to Jews. "This principle," he wrote, "is contrary to the religion of Israel which teaches that God is one in perfect simplicity and the only omnipotent one possessing all perfection. In Him are combined power, wisdom, and will and other eternal attributes without any partnership. . . . If it were as the Christians contend that the Son born from the Father was identical with his Father, then the Father was likewise born; if the Father is born then He is caused and exists through something else and hence does not possess necessary existence. . . . Nor can one believe that the Father has all perfection for why did He need to beget a Son who would be a God like Himself and why did He have to emanate the Holy Ghost likewise to be a God like Himself?" Nor was this a late medieval Spanish innovation. In the mid-thirteenth century Moses b. Solomon of Salerno devoted the larger part of his philisophic tract to precisely such scholastic arguments against the combined doctrines of Trinity and Incarnation. Addressing his Christian interlocutor the Jewish spokesman made, for instance, the following point:

You believe that the Godhead had assumed a corporeal form. I shall accept that for the moment, but please let me know whether the Godhead assumed that corporeal form in toto or only in part. For there are only two alternatives: if you contend that the entire Godhead became a body you place measurement, quantity and limits on an entity which has none of it, namely, it is not subject to any measurement, quantity or limit. If, on the other hand, you contend that only a part of the Godhead assumed a physical shape you introduce a division and split in an entity which cannot be split or subject to division.

At this juncture a young monk named Philip is said to have offered a lengthy explanation related to the then current scholastic efforts to reconcile the doctrines of Trinity and Incarnation. This preeminently philosophic orientation and the facile identification, by some latter-day Jewish scholastics, of the "refined" findings of human reason with incontrovertible principles of their faith opened the gate widely to antirationalist counterattacks. The rising tide of mysticism, both Christian and Jewish, often brushed aside the rationalistic speculations as irrelevant, if not altogether

heretical. To Isaac Pollegar's rationalistic assault on his mystically
colored arguments, Abner of Burgos replied that, if the Bible had
intended to impose upon Israel these philosophic doctrines, it
would have stated them as clearly and explicitly as all other commandments. In fact, however, Scripture constantly uses anthropomorphic expressions running diametrically counter to these
philosophic concepts.[18]

Apologists of either faith were never short of answers. Addressing the Jews directly, Joachim of Floris contended, "When
we Christians speak of God having a Son, you must not depict it in
your heart as anything human or corporeal, for just as we view
God the Father as an ineffable idea [virtus], so do we think of His
Son only in terms of the divine idea. . . . Nor shall you believe
that the sacred Gospels have given us a new faith alien to the
prophets and contrary to the faith of your fathers, but rather that,
while the latter but enigmatically had alluded [to certain teach-
ings], they [the Gospels] have spelled them out for us more explicitly." Along somewhat different historiosophic lines Abner
pointed to the numerous pantheistic passages in rabbinic letters,
such as that "there is no place in the universe without the She-
khinah [divine presence]." In these statements, and in similar expressions of Gentile philosophers, Abner saw oblique references to
the divine presence incarnate in all beings. He thus explained
even the mistaken notions of ancient idolaters who worshiped
objects only because of that presence incarnate in them. The same
idea accounted, in his opinion, for both Roman imperial worship
and the ancient Jewish sages' endeavor to measure the divine
stature. The importance of the latter, he claimed with reference to
a medieval Hebrew apocryph, had been stressed by such eminent
authorities as R. Ishmael and R. 'Aqiba. The only reason Scripture was less outspoken with respect to both the Trinity and the
Incarnation, was that belief in one God was so novel a doctrine in
the days of ancient Israel that it had to be implanted in the hearts
of men to the exclusion of all those subsidiary teachings which
might have created confusion.[19]

Christian apologists explained the Trinitarian dogma in various
ways. Some reverted scholastically to the time-honored doctrine of
attributes; others referred merely to the revelation embodied in

the New Testament to which one must unquestioningly submit; still others contended that these were matters of belief rather than reason. Even the difficult concepts of three-in-oneness and the Virgin Birth could be explained as miracles outside the realm of natural law through God's omnipotence and omniscience. The first man, one teacher contended, was created by God without the assistance of either male or female, the first woman was formed out of a male body alone, the subsequent generations were born from the union of father and mother. Thus, to complete the circle, Christ was invested with humanity through a female body alone. Even Raymond Lull, otherwise often more understanding than his confreres, sharply contrasted the modified acceptance of Jesus by the Muslims with his total rejection by the Jews. "They love not Our Lady," he exclaimed, "but blaspheme and despise and scorn her, saying and affirming and believing that her glorious Son was not conceived by the Holy Spirit, but was the son of a man; and is not united with the Deity, but was false, and a liar and a deceiver, and a greater sinner and wrongdoer than any other man soever." Nevertheless, Lull and other missionaries believed that they could break down the Jews' stubborn resistance if only the latter could be persuaded that their own Scriptures, or the Talmud which they considered equally revealed, confirmed the pluralistic essence in the one and only God, as well as the miraculous nature and actual arrival of the redeemer. Above all, they felt that they were, through the Gospels, in the possession of an indubitable divine revelation. Out of that feeling of "certainty," Paul of Burgos rejected Joshua ha-Lorqi's aforementioned assertion that allowing every individual to reexamine the fundamentals of his faith by comparison with other religions would lead to spiritual anarchy. He felt that one need not bother to examine, for example, the validity of the Muslim doctrines, whereas any believer in Moses' Torah, which foretells the coming of the messiah, was indeed in duty bound to investigate whether the Christian redeemer was the predicted messiah. "This investigation was the gate of hope through which I have entered into the new covenant, I and my associates, and this is the gate of the Lord through which the righteous shall enter. It becomes evident, therefore, that the Muslim religion is not subject to such investigation, since it [the

Torah of Moses] does not fall within the purview of the principles of Islam." [20]

Under the impact of these incessant controversies, Jewish apologists began minimizing the very messianic idea, which previous generations had cherished as the life buoy of their people on the ship of exile. They denied not only the messiahship of Jesus but also his Davidic descent, occasionally stressing the contradictions in the genealogies in the Gospels of Matthew and Luke and pointing out that that of Joseph had no bearing on Jesus' birth by Mary, because the Virgin Birth would have removed any blood relationship between her husband and her son. More fundamentally, following Naḥmanides, they insisted that the messianic idea played a far less important role in Judaism than in Christianity. What appeared in 1263 in Barcelona as a temporary expedient to dispose of an embarrassing argument before a biased jury was later developed into a theologoumenon by such outstanding thinkers of that age of controversy as Crescas and Albo. Agreeing with Maimonides that denial of the ultimate coming of the redeemer stamped a Jew a heretic, Crescas nevertheless refused to include belief in a messiah among the fundamental principles of Judaism. By eliminating it and several other doctrines from this classification, he reduced the thirteen Maimonidean "principles" to six. His pupil, Albo, reduced them further to a mere three. This demotion of the messianic idea hardly represented the majority opinion, however, even among the learned Jews of Spain. It left the masses there completely untouched and had no effect on basic Jewish attitudes in other lands. On the contrary, messianic speculations, even actual messianic movements, were soon to reach a new peak as a result of the great upheavals accompanying the transition from the Middle Ages to modern times. Yet the new philosophic teachings helped point up one of the basic differences between the two faiths, and demonstrated anew how impossible it was for the parties, starting as they did from different premises, to reach a genuine meeting of minds. Admittedly, this was a goal which neither group really sought.[21]

Apart from gainsaying Jesus' messiahship and Davidic descent, some Jewish apologists sought to demonstrate other serious inconsistencies in the Christian tradition. In the twelfth century Jacob b. Reuben (together with Joseph Qimḥi, a pioneer in the field) hesitantly employed this method. He claimed to have yielded only to entreaties by his friends to divulge publicly his critique of the New Testament as expressed in his oral disputations, and added, "I have mentioned only a few mistakes and errors of their Scripture, though I have not revealed a tenth of a tenth because I was afraid." This abbreviated treatment, circumspectly phrased, occupies the entire Chapter XI of his apologetic tract and is an integral part of his defense of Judaism. Somewhat more courageously and in a more popular vein, Profiat Duran, more than two centuries later, argued in his *Kelimat ha-goyim* that the New Testament often contradicted itself and almost invariably misquoted the Old Testament.

There is no question [he asserted] that Jesus, his disciples and apostles were uneducated people. This is evident from those disciples' occupations: one was a fisherman, another a shepherd, a third a publican. This is also manifest from the proofs they adduced from the Bible in confirming Jesus' conduct and their citations from the narratives of the Torah and the Prophets, in all of which they erred. For this reason the Jews called the believers in Jesus by the name of *Marranos,* a term derived from alteration, for they were altering and twisting the meaning of biblical verses and uncovering untrue interpretations of the Torah. For this reason until today every Jew believing in Jesus is called by the Gentiles a *Marrano.*

To buttress this assertion, the apologist cited numerous passages from the Gospels and the Pauline epistles. Profiat's namesake, Simon b. Ṣemaḥ Duran, whose tract was devoted to a critique of Islam as well as of Christianity, made effective use of the mutual recriminations of the spokesmen of those two faiths. The Christians rightly criticized the Qur'an, he wrote, because of its numerous unethical and historically inaccurate statements. With equal justification the Muslims repudiated the New Testament because of its corporeal conception of the Godhead, its doctrine of salvation which makes it appear that until the coming of Jesus even Moses and Abraham had lingered in Hell unredeemed, and its manifold inconsistencies. "You will thus find that each of these sects is justified in refuting the other. Hence they both stay refuted, while the true Torah perseveres." [22]

Profiat insisted that many original sayings of Jesus had connotations different from those attributed to them in later Christian tradition and that a number of Christian dogmas also were but innovations of later ages. He attacked the Papacy's position within the Church as equally far removed from the original intent of the Gospels. Crescas declared that the Christian world had mistakenly interpreted the well-known verses in Matthew (16:13–19) as meaning "that Jesus had given Peter the permission to renew the Torah, to add to it, or to remove from it as he pleased. But all this contradicts what he had said before . . . [Matthew 5:17–18]. If the master cannot alter the Torah, how much less can his disciple do so! And how could Pope Sylvester, who arose in the year 338 of their era, remove the Sabbath day to Sunday? Who gave him the permission to nullify the Sabbath day which had been observed by Jesus and all his disciples and apostles?" Crescas further argued that, from the outset, Peter had possessed little authority in his own circle and was not even followed by his fellow apostles. Not surprisingly, therefore, after several centuries many Christian sects separated themselves from the Catholic Church and wholly repudiated the authority of the pope. Some of them, Crescas emphasized, believed that Jesus' resurrection had taken place on Saturday rather than Sunday, and were still observing their weekly Sabbath on the former day.[23]

Jewish apologists thus tried to repay in kind the concentrated attacks of Christian controversialists on Jewish law and its institutions. Some Jewish converts hated the "yoke" of Jewish law even more than Judaism's spiritual tenets. John Duns Scotus, otherwise a vigorous Jew-baiter, was relatively moderate when he exclaimed, "How insipid are their [the Jews'] ceremonies without [the belief in] Christ!" The armory of medieval Jewish antinomians, dating back to ancient polemics, was refurbished in the course of the numerous internal sectarian controversies. Salmon b. Yeruḥim's compilation of the *Ḥuqqim lo ṭobim* (Laws which are not Good) and Yehudah Hadassi's long list of allegedly wrong or wicked statements in the Talmud could now be used to good advantage by Christian polemists. The fourteenth-century Latin translator(?), Alphonso Bonhomo, attributed to the alleged convert Samuel Maroccanus a remarkable demonstration, from the Old Testament itself, of the definitive abrogation of Jewish law. He cited a purported Arabic text of Zech. 7:4 which, in addition to the masoretic text: "When ye fasted and mourned . . . even these seventy years, did ye at all fast unto Me?" contained the crucial reading: "Ego tale jejunium nolui a vobis" (I did not want such a fast from you). This was grist in the mill of "Samuel's" recurrent theme that the Babylonian Exile, lasting seventy years, had been but a temporary punishment for the grave sins of the ancient Israelites, whereas the Second Exile, which by his day had lasted more than a thousand years, was a permanent chastisement for the much greater sin of the later Jews in repudiating Christ. He interpreted the Zechariah passage to mean that during the Babylonian Exile God had repudiated the fasts of the Jews, as well as their Sabbaths, circumcision, and other commandments. Now during the permanent Second Exile, called by Daniel, "the perpetual desolation," Jews lived under far greater divine wrath, and "hence our [the Jews'] works are even less pleasing to Him." [24]

On somewhat less shaky foundations rested the antihalakhic arguments of the better informed convert, Abner of Burgos, doubtless stimulated by certain antinomian tendencies among Spanish Jews themselves. There is at least a possibility that the *Kol Sakhal* (Voice of a Fool), reputedly written in Alcalá de Henares by one R. Amitai b. Yedaiah aben Ras in the year 1500, which underlay Leon of Modena's much debated reply under the same title, was not a wholly imaginary target invented by this seventeenth-century Venetian rabbi to serve as a sounding board for his own unorthodox views. It may, indeed, have reflected certain genuine reformatory trends among the Spanish Marranos after the expulsion of 1492. Some such trends may well have been anticipated by Abner of Burgos. His repudiation of basic Jewish laws could nevertheless go hand in hand with his acceptance of fundamental Christian canonical regulations. Abner's critique may even have been nurtured from still older underground springs of Jewish heterodoxy, the very title of his major book, *Moreh ṣedeq* (Teacher of Righteousness; in Spanish *Mostrador de Justicia*) bearing perhaps a more than accidental resemblance to the title of the leader of the ancient Qumran sectarians.[25]

## SOCIOPOLITICAL WRANGLINGS

While these theological and dogmatic considerations still played an eminent role, contemporary conditions assumed an ever increasing significance in the Judeo-Christian dialogue. In the very debate about the messiahship of Jesus the Jewish apologists pointed out that, according to prophetic enunciations, the advent of the redeemer was to be followed not only by spectacular miraculous events but also by a reign of permanent peace. "But we see," wrote Joshua ha-Lorqi, "the very opposite. From the time of his [Jesus'] appearance until today wars and quarrels have increased infinitely in the world until they [the Christians] have assailed the followers of Islam who are double their number. All their reliance in upholding their faith rests with the sword and the spear." Yom Ṭob Lipmann-Mühlhausen, on the other hand, emphasized that the predicted universal reign "had neither been fulfilled in Jesus nor in his adherents. They do not have dominion even over his sepulchre." Indeed, Christian apologists had great difficulty in explaining the warlike conditions of their day, as Christianity itself had undergone a great transformation from the pacifist religion it was in its early centuries to one constantly preaching Crusades in both East and West. They usually replied that the era of eternal peace was to come only after the second coming of Christ.[26]

Some polemists conceded that a Jewish messiah was yet to arrive, but they identified him with Antichrist (a counterpart to the Jewish Armilus) who was to usher in the final age ending in the total conversion of the Jewish people to Christianity and the second advent of Christ. Quoting St. Isidore of Seville and the Venerable Bede, Alphonso de Spina predicted that the Jewish Antichrist would be born in Babylon from the tribe of Dan (many Muslims placed their equivalent, the *dajjal,* further east in the Jewish quarter of Isfahan) and even enumerated nine portents of his coming. Others drew the more fundamental distinction between the Jews' "materialistic" expectation of a redeemer who would merely release them from bondage through military action and reestablish their kingdom in the Holy Land, and the Christian spiritual conception of a savior who died to redeem mankind from original sin. Still others, like Paul of Burgos, ridiculed the various unsuccessful Jewish chronological computations of the end. Perhaps with tongue in cheek, he pointed out that the Maimonidean family tradition that the messiah was due to arrive in 1210 C.E. coincided with the rise of the Dominican and Franciscan orders.

"Who can estimate the number of souls redeemed by [them] . . . from the devil's captivity?" We shall see that the Jewish response to these challenges was no less equivocal. If, under the stress of controversy, Naḥmanides overemphasized the earthly and nationalistic ingredients of the Jewish messianic idea, others pursued the old lines of apocalyptic visions and depicted in glowing colors the cosmic impact of the coming of the messiah.[27]

On their part, Christian controversialists played up the old theme of Jewish political inferiority. Like "Samuel Maroccanus," many stressed the endless duration of the postcrucifixion Jewish dispersion, which had far exceeded the 400 years of Egyptian bondage and the 70 years of Babylonian Exile. Paul of Burgos devoted a lengthy chapter in the second part of his *Scrutinium* to a discussion of the position of the Jews "in the middle period between the first and the second coming of Christ" and claimed that, because of their repudiation of Christ, their punishment was greater than that of Sodom or that of Dathan and Abiram. The latter had been sudden and local, whereas the Jewish exile was both long and universal, for all Jews shared in that sin and the penalty had to be commensurate with the enormity of the crime. This argument did not prevent him and other writers, with the typical inconsistency of propagandists, from clamoring against alleged Jewish domination over the Christian masses. Reasonings of this kind must have made a particular impression upon sensitive Jews during that era of grave Spanish persecutions. The closer were their social and intellectual contacts with the Gentile world and the higher their economic and intellectual achievements, the more bitterly did they resent their low legal and political status and their growing feeling of insecurity, a feeling well illustrated by Abner's narrative about how he came to write his controversial tract:

I reflected about the oppression of the Jews, the people to which I belong, who live in that long captivity, pursued, broken and frightened by the taxes, the people which descended from their dignity and fame and now find no help and support. So it happened one day, when I thought a great deal about this question that I entered the synagogue with much weeping and bitterness of heart and prayed to God as follows. . . . Because of the great sorrow in my heart and exhaustion I fell asleep, and saw in a dream a great man telling me: "Why do you slumber? Listen to the words which I tell you and be prepared. For I am telling you that the Jews live for so long a time in that captivity because of their own negligence and unworthiness and because they do not have a teacher of righteousness from whom they might learn the truth."

It is this lack of a teacher that Abner tried to remedy by writing his treatise. Not surprisingly, however, when it suited his purpose, he blandly accused his former coreligionists of taking their exile too lightly. According to him, some Spanish Jews actually did not wish to be redeemed. They allegedly rationalized with respect to taxation—that constant refrain in medieval Jewish complaints about the hardships of exile—that after their return to the Holy Land they would be worse off, for they would be paying taxes to their own kings while having no opportunity to amass riches through usury. "Moreover, we are now free from the burden of offering sacrifices and observing other commandments obligatory for us in the Promised Land." [28]

In reply, Jewish authors needed but repeat their old contention that political success was no proof of the veracity of one's religious convictions. Now Albo simply stressed the fact that, according to accepted chronology, for two thousand years before the Sinaitic Revelation none of the successful and prosperous nations had professed the true religion. Even after the Torah had been given to Israel no other nation believed in the true God, and yet many of them were far more powerful. "Surely the fact that Sennacherib, Nebukadrezzar or Alexander succeeded in ruling over Israel, is no proof that their faiths were superior to that of Israel." Nor is the Muslim domination over a large part of the world evidence of the divine origin of Islam. The only real proof of authenticity consists in the continuity of miracles, such as had fallen to the lot of Israel while it lived in its own land but had never happened to Christians or Muslims. Nathan b. Meshullam of the family of the "zealous" Frenchmen, who could still afford at times to be more "smart-alecky" than serious, contended that the Babylonian Exile had come to the Jews because of their frequent relapse into idol worship. Since the idols had been built from materials and with instruments of a transitory nature, the penalty of exile was correspondingly of but short duration. In contrast thereto, the Jews of the Second Commonwealth had allowed the rise of the permanent worship of Christ as God. Hence their punishment was exile to the end of days, that is to the advent of the Jewish messiah.[29]

From time to time Christian apologists echoed the old accusations of the Jews' deep-rooted enmity toward Christians, and rehearsed certain despicable acts attributed to them. On the whole, the more enlightened controversialists abstained from repeating the folkloristic tales concerning Jewish ritual murders, the desecration of hosts, and the poisoning of wells. Especially those born and trained as Jews knew how groundless the accusations were and how little their repetition would impress the Jewish public. Yet Alphonso de Spina, though holding the responsible post of general of the Franciscan order, gave vent to those popular superstitions. Evidently ignorant of Hebrew and familiar with rabbinic writings only secondhand, he devoted an entire chapter of his *Fortress of the Faith* to a discussion of "the Jews' parentage according to the doctrine of the Talmud," which, in his opinion, demonstrated that they all were children of demons. In another chapter he gloated over the various expulsions of Jews from the Holy Land, Visigothic Spain, England, and France, and described with gusto a number of miracles which had failed to persuade the Jews of the truth of Christianity. In this context he mentioned the sudden miraculous appearance of the crosses in 1295 which had allegedly so deeply impressed Abner. He also described how—only a few years before his writing in 1455—a Jewish boy had acquired from a venal sacristan in Segovia a host which had wrought such miracles that it had to be restored to the church.[30]

As spokesman for these deep-seated popular prejudices, De Spina did not mind deviating from official Church doctrine concerning the toleration of Jews. He belonged to the minority of churchmen who welcomed the conversion of Jewish children even against the will of their parents, and advocated the forcible conversion of adults as well, citing in support John Duns Scotus' wrathful exclamation, "that it is better for them [the Jews] to be compelled to do good than to do evil with impunity as they do now." With equal acerbity he attacked the numerous Spanish *conversos* of his day, trying to prove their utter unreliability as Christian believers. He insisted that many observed circumcision and other Jewish rituals and, at the first opportunity, emigrated to the Muslim East where they openly reverted to their former faith; some even dared to criticize the New Testament. Here, too, this Franciscan leader tried to prove historically that unreliability characterized Jewish converts at all times. He even told a story, allegedly found in an old English chronicle, about the expulsion of Jews from England and the ensuing mass conversion of those who remained behind. Only through a ruse was the king able to uncover the deceit of those new converts. De Spina was rather an exception among leading churchmen, however. For the most part such miracle tales and venomous denunciations were left to popular preachers and writers, and form part of the anti-Jewish folkloristic heritage which was so deeply to envenom the relations between medieval Jews and their neighbors.[31]

Even the more sophisticated controversialists, however, were deeply convinced of the Jewish hatred of Christians, and attributed to it much of the Jews' stubborn refusal to join the Church. In this area former Jews from Donin to Geronimo de Santa Fé, filled with the self-hatred frequently characteristic of minority groups, helped stoke the fires of mutual hostility by culling from the rabbinic literature various anti-Gentile utterances. This accusation sounded doubly persuasive to Christian listeners and readers, as their own growing anti-Jewish feelings made them expect that the Jew would pay back his tormentors in kind.

Most extreme among those accusers was Abner of Burgos. In his general denunciation of Jewish Oral Law which, he claimed, distorted rather than supplemented the Written Law of the Torah, he contrasted especially what he chose to call the rabbinic Ten Commandments with those recorded in the Bible. According to him, Jews were enjoined by their rabbinic leaders "to steal, rob, bear false witness, miscarry justice, cheat, swear false oaths, murder, fornicate, lend on usury, and worship idols." In evidence, he adduced for each of these "commandments" certain talmudic regulations and utterances in his own forced interpretation. In his opinion, this unethical code was upheld only by the excessive power of rabbis and communal elders, who lorded over the masses of the population and propagated false doctrines in order to maintain their own control. "With the downfall of these overlords, judges and watchmen, salvation will come to the multitude." [32]

Needless to say, these violent diatribes bore little resemblance to either the rabbinic teachings or the medieval Jewish realities. Not surprisingly, Abner's vituperations and ruthlessness in mistinterpreting talmudic regulations made him suspect to his Jewish contemporaries. At least, the distinguished philosopher Moses b. Joshua Narboni (also known as Vidal Blasom) seriously impugned his motives. Upon receiving his astrological treatise, called *Iggeret ha-gezerah* (Epistle on Determinism) in the 1340s while Abner was still alive, Narboni clearly intimated that the latter's conversion had been the result of both the repudiation of his astrological and deterministic teachings by the Jewish leaders and his unwillingness to exist on the low standard of life characteristic of Jewish scholars of his time. [33]

Jewish preachers, to be sure, like homilists of other faiths, also fulminated against their coreligionists and censured particular moral shortcomings. Even the apologist Solomon ibn Verga conceded much misconduct on the part of Spanish Jews, and on it—in line with the ancient prophetic denunciations—he blamed the great cataclysm of 1492. He aired many such controversial issues in a lengthy imaginary dialogue between the king and "Thomas," a Christian dignitary who shuddered at the thought of being considered of Jewish descent but who nevertheless was moderate and well-meaning enough to defend the Jews from time to time. In one characteristic passage, Thomas tried to explain the length of the period of exile by the Jews' moral deficiencies. Insisting that transgressions against fellow men were even more serious than those against God, Thomas claimed that "the Christians carefully abstain from robbery, cheating, usury and the like, though they are less exacting with respect to duties toward God, and many a Gentile does not pray even once a year. In contrast, the Jew will not miss a single prayer, but he will be less careful with respect to theft, cheating and robbery." But such moralistic censures of individual behavior were a far cry from the blanket accusation that abuses of that nature were the guiding principles of rabbinic law! [34]

Abner's distortions can, of course, readily be disproved from the whole array of rabbinic sources, both ancient and medieval. For

one example, in his demonstration of the alleged rabbinic commandment to fornicate, he adduced only the rabbinic regulations
permitting a husband to cohabit with his wife in any posture and
at any time even during her menstruation—the latter Abner's pure
invention. Rabbinic moralists, including Ibn Verga, on the other
hand, scolded their coreligionists (we shall see, not without reason) for maintaining Christian concubines. A Jew of Foligno was
actually hailed before an ecclesiastical court because he had
allegedly taught that "it is not sinful for Christian women to
cohabit with Jews." He was acquitted because of lack of sufficient
evidence, a sentence confirmed by Boniface IX on July 18, 1399.
Most Jewish apologists, however, less intent on teaching their
coreligionists a lesson in morals than on defending them against
their accusers, generally boasted of the superiority of Jewish ethics
and particularly of Jewish sex morality over those of Gentiles. In
the northern countries especially that contrast seems to have been
quite marked. Presenting these issues in the customary form of a
dialogue between a "believer" and a "heretic," a Jewish polemist
observed:

I shall now begin to demonstrate the Jews' good deeds, which are
perfectly evident. Whether old or young, Jews study the Torah and
teach their children from infancy to read books, attend houses of
prayer, abstain from profanities, but to speak in a clean language, and
be careful about taking oaths. They also watch their daughters lest they
become licentious and run around with rather than stay away from
men; thus there is no apparent promiscuity among them. Nor do they
break through walls to steal, or hold up travelers on the roads. But *you*
profane your speech and swear by the name of God, His head, mouth,
hands, feet, eyes, and entire body, even His genitals, and your daughters
are licentious, some living in houses of prostitution; many of you are
thieves and robbers. In deeds the Jews are pious, take pity on their
brethren lest they beg from door to door; they bring the poor to their
houses and give them food and drink. They also give away a portion of
their wealth so that they [the poor] may marry off their daughters or
ransom captives. They also properly observe their Sabbaths and holidays. In your case the opposite is true.

A German apologist even threw out a wild suggestion as to why
Catholic priests so greatly stressed confession. The question of confession was an old bone of contention between spokesmen of the
two faiths, the Jews often being blamed for lacking that method of

purifying themselves of their sins. Our polemist explained that confession helped licentious priests to satisfy their sexual desires. After listening to paramours describe their adulterous relations with married women, they sought out the unfaithful wives and forced them to submit to their advances. This, too, was evidently but a generalization from some individual cases.[35]

During all the raging Spanish debates the economic issues played but a secondary role. While Peter of Cluny's attacks on the Talmud were greatly elaborated, his major assault on Jewish usury and exploitation found relatively few literary followers on the Iberian Peninsula. True, there were occasional references to Jewish courtiers and public officials who abused their authority, and in fact should never have had that authority; but the Jewish socio-economic stratification in Spain and the intensive participation of Jews in nearly all occupations prevented their enemies from identifying all Jews with usurers and from blaming the Jews for whatever economic crises befell the country. Even Abner of Burgos laid little stress on Jewish usury, although he included the right to charge interest among the reprehensible rabbinic Ten Commandments. In justification he adduced mainly the rabbinic provision allowing scholars to charge interest to one another. Only the popular writers, preachers, and such rabble rousers as Ferrant Martinez more directly responded to the growing disaffection of the middle classes and particularly the debtors. This agitation achieved, as we shall see, signal success in the stormy period of 1391–1415. Jewish apologists, too, could not close their eyes to that festering wound. At least in retrospect, Ibn Verga was prepared to place part of the blame for the expulsion on the haughty behavior of wealthy Jewish moneylenders, their and their wives' conspicuous display of luxuries in contrast to the more moderate attire of the Spanish aristocracy, and the evils of usury. Although arguing that the Torah did not really permit Jews to charge interest to Christians who were included in the category of "brethren," Ibn Verga's "Thomas" suggested to the king, "Proclaim in thy kingdom that all the estates which came to the Jews as a result of their usury, should, in the judges' discretion, be returned to their owners, that no Jews be allowed to wear silken garments, and also that they display a red badge so that they be recognized as Jews." [36]

Usury was a far more important issue in pre-expulsion England and France, where an increasing number of Jews directly or indirectly derived their livelihood from moneylending and related occupations. We recall the pertinent defense of moneylending offered about 1245 by the French-Jewish apologist, Meir b. Simon of Narbonne. While Meir stressed above all the economic indispensability of credit even for monarchs, his successor, Jacob b. Elijah, a native of the Provence, though writing in Valencia, more defensively contrasted the fiscal system under Islam, where the Jews were uniformly taxed according to regulations, with the anarchical exploitation of their resources in the West. "Our kings and lords think only of how they can best attack and fall upon us and take away our gold and silver." Hence came the necessity for Jews to secure greater income through usury, which, moreover, was vastly exceeded by the usurious transactions practiced by the Roman court itself—an obvious allusion to the so-called "papal usurers," the Lombards. "Blessed be our God, the God of our salvation," concludes Jacob, "who has increased our wealth, wherewith we may defend our lives and the lives of our sons and daughters and defeat the evil designs of our enemies." [37]

This issue was even more heatedly debated in Germany and northern Italy, where constant deterioration in the quality of Jewish economic endeavor reduced many communities to a few branches of the economy. In Italy a number of cities specifically invited small groups of Jews to settle and provide credit for the needy population. Before long the evils of moneylending at the then excessive rates of interest began affecting both Christians and Jews adversely. In the ensuing tensions, particularly as a result of the preachment of such counter remedies as the *monti di pietà*, Jewish moneylending became a major target. In fact, while still mouthing the old theological and juridical arguments, many Italian controversialists of the fifteenth and sixteenth centuries, including Giacomo della Marca, Bernardino da Feltre, and Bernardino de' Busti, began focusing their attacks on "nefarious" Jewish business activities. De' Busti, for example, not only wrote special tracts in favor of the *monti* and against Jews generally in his *Contra Hebraeos* and other essays, but he also compiled a *Rosarium sermonum praedicabilium,* a collection of ready-made sermons for the use of preachers. Girolamo Tiraboschi may be right in saying that De' Busti's sermons, "instead of being conducive to piety and meditation, make us laugh, not only on account of their crude style, but also because of their puerile naïveté and the ridiculous stories with which they are filled." Yet perhaps precisely for this reason his *Rosarium* proved a sort of international best seller. In their replies, too, Jews now more and more frequently stressed the economic factors.[38]

Finally, there began to emerge a somewhat better understanding of the historical background of the religious conflicts. An awakened interest in ancient history and a progressive deepening of factual knowledge of the past also made the religious disputants slightly more historically minded. Alphonso de Spina tried to bolster many accusations by historical references, authentic and spurious. Similarly, in their critique of the New Testament, Jewish apologists utilized to their advantage some of the historical literature on the early Church. Josephus began to be quoted with considerable effect, although no one had yet raised any question about the authenticity of the *Testimonium Flavianum*. This testimony seems to have been invoked by Christian polemists with sufficient effect for Ḥayyim ibn Musa to counsel his Hebrew readers in 1456 not to listen to arguments taken from Josephus any more than to those derived from the New Testament. They should only be persuaded by demonstrations from their own authentic sources, namely the Old Testament and rabbinic literature. Nevertheless, more frequent reference was now made to events during the Herodian regime and other factors surrounding the rise of Christianity, just as the prolonged Jewish exile and sufferings were adduced, often with much detail, by Christian assailants as proof positive for divine wrath over the Jews' repudiation of Christ. These incipient historical approaches, however crude and rudimentary, were harbingers of a new era.[39]

Religious controversies thus intermingled with practically all political and socioeconomic debates and permeated the entire fabric of Jewish life under medieval Christendom. Whether stemming from polemical writings by apologists or from practical postulates voiced by churchmen, canon jurists, or schoolmen, or whether they were formulated by secular legislators, business rivals, or generally bigoted individuals, the religious arguments were often linked with all other anti-Jewish contentions in order to cover the latter with a more reputable idealistic veneer. They will have to be considered, therefore, from various angles also in the forthcoming chapters.

## FLEXIBLE AMBIVALENCE

Sharp repudiation of Judaism and most of its teachings, aspersions against its ethics as well as theology, and yet basic toleration of it in the Christian world uniquely among all non-Christian faiths and unorthodox Christian sects—were the principles governing the medieval Church's attitude toward the mother religion. Similarly, the Jewish people, permanently accused of "blindness," stubbornness, and even baser motives, discriminated against economically and rigidly segregated socially, was nevertheless to be allowed to continue its historic career to the very end of days, which would be ushered in by its final conversion. Interveningly, it was to exercise full self-determination in its inner affairs, observe its religious teachings and legal regulations, however obnoxious some of them appeared to the Christian world, under the directives of their own freely chosen leaders, and live a full Jewish life within the walls of its ghettos, physical or spiritual.

This polarity in attitudes bore in itself many germs of irreconcilable conflict and generated a state of permanent tension between the adherents of the two faiths which often resulted in, or at least contributed to, violent outbreaks. But it also offered to the Papacy and its subordinate ecclesiastical organs a high degree of flexibility in dealing with the perennial "Jewish question," and in helping to adjust the status of their Jewish subjects in the Papal States and of Jews living in other parts of the Christian West in accordance with changing social conditions, individual tempers, or even personal whims of rulers, jurists, and theologians. A powerful and farsighted statesman like Innocent III developed the old canonical doctrines to fit into the framework of his ambitious schemes for the supremacy of the Church over the Christian state and for the ultimate world domination of the Holy See. Other popes and Church councils reacted to more temporary exigencies.

It was a far cry from the intolerant policies of Antipope Benedict XIII to the relative "liberalism" of his immediate successor, Martin V. Even a single pope, like Eugenius IV, could swing back and forth from considerable friendliness toward Jews to the kind of repression promulgated in his bull, *Dudum ad nostram,* of 1442. There was even greater leeway for the lower clergy and individual thinkers in the provinces of the Church to treat Jews almost as equals or, at the other extreme, to advocate their total elimination from a particular country or city. But even the more radical Jew-baiters could not completely gainsay the basic doctrine of the Church, based upon a limited and well-circumscribed toleration of Jews.

Beyond the force of tradition and the general power of custom and precedent in all medieval life, this ambiguity was based upon deeper theological and psychological feelings of the indispensability of the Jewish people to the Christian world. Quoting Seneca (or rather Boethius) to the effect that "no pest is more efficacious in doing harm than a familiar foe," Raymond Martini nonetheless insisted that "no enemy of the Christian faith . . . is more indispensable for us, than the Jew." This indispensability had long been motivated by the unwitting testimony which the Jews, through both their Scripture and their unhappy fate, were offering for the truth of Christianity, an argument which continued to be played up in all discussions of Jewish status from the standard papal privilege, *Sicut Judaeis,* to the doctrinal deliberations of leading scholastics. It certainly appeared more acceptable than the practical, and hence "sordid," consideration of the indispensability of the Jewish moneylender, international trader, and taxpayer to the Christian societies and states including those under direct papal sovereignty. More profoundly, the Jewish destiny appeared to leading thinkers intimately tied up with the Christian *corpus mysticum,* which embraced all Christianity despite the enormous diversity within it of nations, races, and linguistic and cultural groups. Among that heterogeneous multitude Jews occupied a certain mystic position, owing to ancient complexities created by the intertwining of the historic destinies of the two faiths. Symbolized by the *corpus Christi* which, according to the same medieval theorists, embraced also the entire non-Christian world of Muslims and pagans, this universal body of humanity included preeminently not only the new Israel of the spirit but also the Israel of the flesh, the generally admitted chosen people of bygone days. The most persistent deniers of Christ were thus paradoxically counted among the foremost and most indispensable members of the body of Christ.[40]

On their part, the Jews not only felt a peculiar kinship to the Christian faith and general outlook on life, which they had helped to mold, but also increasingly sensed the inextricable linkage of their historic destinies with those of the Christian West. In their resistance to Christian polemical onslaughts they were forced to reformulate their own doctrines and reshape their own lives to meet the changing demands of the new expansive civilization. Some individuals yielded ground to pressure or persuasion; some even became ardent self-haters and joined the ranks of the most vociferous anti-Jewish polemists. But despite severe numerical losses, which particularly in Spain after 1391 assumed menacing proportions, the Jewish people weathered the storms and emerged from the medieval trials and tribulations spiritually unscathed and mentally prepared to partake of the marvelous newer forms of human life gradually unfolding in the modern era.

# SERF OF THE CHAMBER

IN CONTRAST to this more or less consistent policy of the central organs of the Church, the medieval states helped to mold the destinies of the Jewish people in Europe in a spasmodic fashion. Particularly in the crucible of the perennial conflicts between state and Church, which reached their climax in the two and a half centuries of the struggle between the Papacy and the Empire from Gregory VII to Boniface VIII, and the equally endless tricornered contest between king, baron, and city, the position of the Jew took ever new turns, mostly for the worse. Defying the basic ecclesiastical postulate of a strictly circumscribed toleration of Jews, state legislations ranged from most favorable treatment, on a level almost egalitarian with the corresponding groups in Christian society, to extreme intolerance and total exclusion.

In all these multifarious changes, one relationship remained fairly constant: the Jews' attachment to the ruling power of the state, be it imperial, royal, episcopal, ducal, or municipal. Whoever enjoyed the sovereign power (in its burgeoning medieval sense) in the state or city, also exercised the most direct control over its Jewish community and expected in return the latter's full-fledged allegiance. This alliance with the dominant authority at times cost the Jews quite dearly. But apart from adhering to their deep-rooted tradition from the days of Jeremiah of "praying for the welfare of the city" (or country, 29:7) in which they lived, Jews had profound realistic reasons to seek shelter under the reigning power of each state. They repaid in money and services, as well as in emotional attachment, for the protection they thus received, a protection which they valued the more highly, as their own feeling of security had been deeply undermined by the recurrent massacres since 1096 and the growing environmental conflicts. Before long this mutual relationship between the Jewish people and its diverse protectors began to be equated with that of "serfs" and masters.

## UNDER CHURCH OR EMPIRE

Medieval political theory never developed a comprehensive and clear-cut formulation of that *servitus Judaeorum*. At first the Church doctrine of Jewish status colored all other interpretations, but with the progressive emancipation of the West-European state from ecclesiastical tutelage and the concomitant rise of the various national movements, new explanations were offered for the peculiar position of Jews in the Christian world. Understandably, the Jews themselves tried to comprehend their status in the light of their own traditions and desires. There thus emerged different doctrines of Jewish "serfdom" which, with some oversimplification, we might classify as the ecclesiastical, imperial, royal, and Jewish concepts. In agreement on some points, those ideologies radically differed in many other aspects.

All these doctrines went back to the original Judeo-Christian controversies under the ancient Roman Empire. After the loss of their national independence, Jewish leaders depicted in ever darker colors the position of their people smarting under foreign domination. Jewish subjection (*shi'abud,* which could also be rendered by "serfdom") became a standard designation of Jewish political inferiority. We need but recall the Babylonian Mar Samuel's famous pronunciamento, "The only difference between our days and those of the messiah is the subjection to [foreign] kingdoms." This theme was readily taken over by the Church Fathers and teachers, from the jurist Tertullian to the theologian Augustine. Particularly after Constantine, they viewed the Jewish exile as but a permanent punishment of the recalcitrant people for its repudiation of Christ. We have seen how deeply this theological concept colored the entire Judeo-Christian debate. True, the first *legal* application of the principle that all Jewish persons were "subject to perpetual serfdom" (*perpetuae subjectae servituti*) was made by the Seventeenth Council of Toledo of 694, which invoked it to justify its threat to sell into slavery all insincere Jewish converts. Clearly this was an exceptional measure intended as a sanction against specific violations of existing laws, rather than as a justification for the establishment of a new regular legal status.

Nonetheless this declaration, frequently cited thereafter in canonistic literature, opened the gate for the full juristic utilization of this theological concept.[1]

Matters remained largely in abeyance until the Crusades and the struggle between the Papacy and the Empire. The Church always claimed supremacy over Jews. For instance, Gregory I felt free, in reply to questions submitted to him, to intervene in their behalf, or, less frequently, in their disfavor, in various parts of Italy and France. On one occasion Pope Leo VII took it upon himself to legitimize their expulsion from Mayence, although he still strenuously objected to their forcible conversion. Some popes responded to appeals by Jews threatened with persecution, as on the occasion of the journey of Jacob b. Yequtiel to Rome early in the eleventh century, and the request for papal help by two Jews who were trying to collect money from a debtor in a neighboring locality. Nonetheless, the Church generally refrained from clarifying the legal aspects of the doctrine of Jewish serfdom, and made little effort to direct the destinies of Jews outside the Papal States. This situation changed when, on the one hand, Jewish security had been undermined by the massacres of the First Crusade and when, on the other hand, their enhanced power from the middle of the eleventh century raised the popes' sights with respect to their own control over all Western Jewry.[2]

It is not surprising, then, that Innocent III and his thirteenth-century successors began playing up the theme of Jewish serfdom in an unprecedented fashion. The very *Constitutio pro Judaeis,* first hesitantly enacted by Calixtus II, became an instrument in the hands of his powerful successors for the reassertion of the Papacy's ultimate control over Jews. That is why Innocent III, anything but a friend of Jews, considered it his duty to renew that bull on September 15, 1199, within a year after his ascendancy to the see of Saint Peter. He formulated his general position more clearly in his much-quoted epistle of July 15, 1205 to his former teacher, Archbishop Peter de Corbeil of Sens, and to Bishop Odo de Sully of Paris:

The Jews, whom their own guilt consigned to perpetual serfdom because they had crucified the Lord whose appearance in the flesh for Israel's redemption had been predicted by their own prophets, have been received by Christian piety and allowed to live together with Christians. This despite the fact that, because of their infidelity, even the Saracens, who persecute the Christian faith and do not believe in Him they [the Jews] had crucified, cannot tolerate them but rather expel them from their borders. . . . These Jews ought not to be ungrateful to us and not to requite the Christians' graciousness with contumely and intimacy with contempt. . . . We have, therefore, requested our dearest son in Christ, Philip the Illustrious, King of France, . . . and also the noble . . . Duke of Burgundy and . . . Countess of Troyes so to restrain the excesses of the Jews that they should not dare to raise their heads submitted to the yoke of perpetual serfdom against the [due] reverence for the Christian faith.

The immediate occasion for this fulmination was Innocent's anger over the Jews' employment of Christian nurses, an offense compounded by the rumor that Jewish masters refused to allow their infants to suckle the milk of such nurses for three days after they had partaken of the host during Easter. The bishops were ordered to prevail upon the king and the barons to see to it "that the infidel Jews should in no way behave insolently but rather, living under servile fear, should always attest the truth of their guilt." This intemperate outburst may have made little impression upon Philip II Augustus of France, who had recalled the Jews to the royal possessions in 1198, but the long-range effects of the phraseology used by Innocent were felt for many generations. The phrasing, *quos propria culpa submisit perpetue servituti* and *sub timore servili* became standard usage in the vocabulary of later popes and canon jurists.[3]

Innocent drew many practical conclusions from this doctrine. In his far-flung correspondence with many European countries he actively intervened in their Jewish affairs without awaiting their inquiries. He often took the initiative in teaching not only his ecclesiastical subordinates but also the Christian princes how to treat their Jewish subjects. The initiative was but a facet of the ever expanding "plenitude of apostolic power," of which he was a most vigorous exponent, claiming that "the spiritual power, having been instituted by God, is both prior in time and higher in dignity" than the royal power. He invoked the example of the Old Testament, which showed that the *sacerdotium* had been conferred upon the people of God by divine order, while the *regnum* had been the effect of human pressures (contrasting Exod. 28:1 with I Sam. 8:7). The priesthood's historic priority was likewise evident, since during the centuries which had elapsed from Moses and Aaron to Samuel and Saul there were priests but no kings. Innocent's views were further expanded by his successors, particularly Gregory IX, Innocent IV, and Boniface VIII, and their experts in canon law. These doctrines, including that of the Jews' subjection to the Church, could also be used for the former's protection, as when Gregory IX urged the king of France to stave off their massacre by Crusaders in 1236, or when Innocent IV universally outlawed the Blood Accusation. Even if such protective bulls were secured by Jewish petitions supported by tangible *douceurs* to the papal Treasury or individual cardinals (there is no documentary evidence for either), the popes clearly felt entitled to issue decrees binding upon the whole Christian world in almost all matters of Judeo-Christian coexistence, which naturally had religious as well as secular features.[4]

Such extraordinary papal claims understandably evoked a reaction first from the German emperors and subsequently from other Christian monarchs. The German Empire always claimed succession not only to the Carolingian monarchy but also to the ancient Roman imperial rule. It inherited from the Carolingians a special protective relationship with the Jews based on the Jewish privileges issued by Charlemagne and Louis the Pious. Possibly some contemporaries began viewing this special nexus as an adjustment of the Teuton "law of aliens." After the expulsions and forced conversions of the seventh century most Western Jewish communities had to make a fresh start, at least outwardly, under the more benevolent rule of the heterogeneous Carolingian Empire. Many new Jewish settlers actually came from Mediterranean lands and could technically be regarded as aliens living under the king's protection, which removed from them the rightlessness attached to aliens by many Teuton laws. Clearly, this mental association, which incidentally found no expression in any contemporary source, bore little resemblance to the historic and legal realities of communities which often antedated the barbarian migrations and which, from the outset, enjoyed the right of owning land, a right usually denied to genuine aliens. We need but remember the vociferous denunciations of Jewish domination and "insolence" by Archbishops Agobard and Amulo of Lyons. Nonetheless there were sufficient socioeconomic and cultural divergences between the Jews and the native majorities to create the illusion of their legally enforced "alienage" and to help in time to forge ever closer ties between the protective monarchy and its Jewish subjects. Ultimately, Jews came to be called royal "serfs." [5]

Nothing definite happened along these lines until the eleventh century, when a combination of the protracted Church and state struggles with Jewish helplessness led to the intensification of the Judeo-royal alliance. Not by mere chance were Henry IV, Frederick I, and Frederick II, the three emperors who made the most clear-cut statements concerning Jewish dependence on the imperial throne, all deeply embroiled in conflicts with the Papacy.

Controverting Gregory VII's attempt at expanding the papal *plenitudo potestatis,* Henry IV wrote in 1076: "Me has our Lord Jesus Christ called to the kingdom—not, however, having called Thee [Gregory] to the priesthood." The emperor found support among many German ecclesiastics, who were antagonized by Gregory's overbearing behavior, which threatened their own independence. Among the leaders was Bishop Rüdiger-Huozmann of Spires who, together with eighteen other bishops, issued a sharp antipapal declaration in 1080. It was he who invited the Jews to settle in his city four years later, in order to "increase the dignity of Our locality a thousandfold." In 1090, shortly before his demise, he was instrumental in persuading Henry IV to renew a privilege of Spires Jewry which was doubtless based upon older Carolingian-Italian models. In the same year Worms Jewry obtained from the emperor a privilege which, though differently and less archaically worded, pursued the same protective aims. Henry IV seems to have enacted a similar privilege in behalf of Ratisbon Jewry in 1097, shortly after the massacres staged by the crusading mobs. In these privileges the emperor not only allowed the Jews to travel and trade freely through the length and breadth of the Empire but he also inserted provisions which controverted certain postulates of the Church. He insisted, for instance, that Jewish converts to Christianity be deprived of all their possessions, that a converted slave of a Jew must still obey his master, and that no

Jewish defendant should be condemned on the testimony of Christian witnesses alone. In 1097 he disregarded canon law even more flagrantly when he indiscriminately allowed the Jewish converts of 1096 to return to Judaism, thus evoking the sharp protest of Antipope Clement III. On these occasions Henry used phrases which were to play a considerable role in the future. In the Spires privilege he declared that he was "accepting and keeping [the Jews] under Our protection [*tuicionem*]." In Worms he prohibited bishops and other officials from intervening in Jewish affairs and insisted that only representatives elected by them and placed at their head by the emperor should have exclusive jurisdiction, "since they belong to Our Chamber [*cum ad cameram nostram attineant*]." [6]

Beginning in 1157, Frederick I Barbarossa felt induced to repeat these privileges for German Jewry. His protective efforts were climaxed in 1179 and 1182, coinciding not by pure chance with Alexander III's convocation of the Third Lateran Council in 1179. Just as under Alexander's guidance the Council adopted several regulations concerning Jews and as the pope considered it his duty to renew the old bull, *Sicut judaeis* (in fact, we possess only Alexander's confirmation, rather than the earlier texts), so did the emperor reassert his protective rights over Jews, particularly by adding his eloquent preamble to the Ratisbon privilege of 1182 which apparently expanded that enacted by Henry IV in 1097. "Deeply concerned," Frederick wrote, "with the welfare of all Jews living in Our Empire who are known to belong to the Imperial Chamber by virtue of a special prerogative of Our dignity, We concede to Our Ratisbon Jews and confirm with Our imperial authority their good customs." [7]

The final step was taken by both pope and emperor in the first half of the thirteenth century, when Innocent III combined the doctrine of Jewish serfdom under the Church with his growing insistence upon his "plenitude" of apostolic powers. So long as Frederick II was a minor and under Innocent's tutelage, the conflict for supremacy had been allowed to simmer quietly. But under Gregory IX's regime (1227–41) the controversy came to a head, and it also focused in a minor way on the imperial versus the papal rights over Jews. By virtue of Frederick's domination over both

Sicily as a hereditary kingdom and Germany through his elective imperial office, the Papal States felt surrounded by Hohenstaufen power, from which Gregory tried to extricate himself by various means. Ultimately, the opposing principles proved unbridgeable and Gregory excommunicated Frederick for the second time in 1239 and absolved all of the emperor's subjects from their oath of allegiance. During the preceding years of growing tension, the pope and his advisers sharpened their insistence upon papal supremacy in temporal matters and propagated the slowly evolving doctrine that both swords, the temporal as well as the spiritual, had been handed by God to the pope, who voluntarily transferred the temporal sword to the emperor, subject to withdrawal at any time. Frederick and his advisers, as well as most experts in Roman law, taught to the contrary that the emperor, as successor of the ancient Roman rulers, independently ruled over the Western world and that his *regnum* or *imperium* antedated the papal *sacerdotium*.[8]

All these controversies naturally affected the position of the Jews, first in Sicily and then in Germany. In Sicily and Naples Frederick at first acknowledged that he held the kingdom by the Church's grace, but subsequently he began to erect "the first modern state in Europe." His semitotalitarian aspirations led him to decree, for instance, that his vassals could not marry without prior royal permission. Strongly governed by centralized royal power, his state utilized to best advantage the services of numerous Greek, Saracen, and Jewish inhabitants in the intellectual and economic spheres. Similar latitude was exercised in the growing royal independence of papal regulations. While Frederick, having meekly followed the Church in his early years, decreed in 1221 that Jews and Muslims must wear distinguishing badges in accordance with the canon adopted by the Fourth Lateran Council six years previously, no such provision was inserted in the basic constitution of Melfi of 1231, proclaimed by the king over papal protests. There Frederick made the broad statement, "We cannot allow the Jews and Saracens, whom the diversity from the Christian faith renders vulnerable [*infestos*] and destitute of any other help, to be deprived of the protection of Our power." He paid no heed to the accusation hurled against him by Jordanus, the second general of the newly formed Dominican order, who reported, "You favor too much the Jews and Saracens." Nor was he discouraged by rumors concerning his infidelity, as when Gregory IX accused him of saying that "the Christian faith is impossible, that of the Jews is a religion of children, that of Islam a religion of hogs." He allegedly also inspired the widely circulating antireligious tract, *De tribus impostoribus* (which in fact originated from earlier agnostic circles under Islam), describing Moses, Jesus, and Mohammed as three great impostors who had misled mankind into believing in three wholly erroneous faiths. This impression was reinforced by news about his utterances during his stay in Palestine. According to the Muslim historian, Sibṭ ibn al-Jauzi of Damascus (died 1257), "his speeches made it perfectly clear that he was an atheist who poked fun at Christianity." Pursuing his moderately pro-Jewish policies, Frederick also issued another remarkable decree in favor of two Jewish petitioners (unfortunately its date cannot be precisely ascertained) which read in part:

Considering the weakness of the Jewish people and that the Jews, all of them collectively and each individually, living anywhere in the lands subjected to Our jurisdiction by virtue of the Christian law and imperial prerogative under which We rule and live are special serfs of Our Chamber [*servi sunt nostrae camerae speciales*], We are accepting under Our and the Empire's special protection the persons, sons, daughters, and all the possessions of Our serfs C. and O. [*sic*] as per their supplication.

This seems to be the first occurrence of the term *servi camerae* in legislation. Frederick used it again in connection with a privilege he issued in November 1237 in favor of Magister Busach, a Jewish physician of Palermo.[9]

From Sicily the term was soon transplanted to Germany. In renewing the privilege of Worms Jewry in July 1236, the emperor emphasized that he had done so on the petition of "all the serfs of Our Chamber in Germany [*universi Alemannie servi camere nostre*]," and that this privilege extended to the Jews of the whole Empire "who directly relate to Our Chamber [*omnibus iudeis ad cameram nostram immediate spectantibus*]." In the following year Frederick combined the old canonical legislation with his insistence on imperial supremacy when, in his charter for the city of Vienna, he accommodated the burghers and prohibited the appointment of Jews to public office, "since from olden times the imperial authority had imposed upon the Jews perpetual serfdom in revenge for the crime committed by them." But he felt free in August 1238 to take the Jews of Vienna, "the serfs of Our Chamber," under direct imperial protection. During the same period Frederick made it clear in international negotiations that he would not budge from his imperial prerogative to protect Jews anywhere in his realm. When in 1236 Gregory IX drew up a list of the emperor's alleged violations of the rights of the Church, it included the indictment that some Sicilian churches had been deprived of their customary controls over Jews. To this accusation the emperor answered curtly: "The Jews in both Our Empire and Our Kingdom are, by virtue of common law, directly subject to Us. We have not taken them away from any church entitled to claim special rights over them which would in any way have precedence in common law over Our authority." To demonstrate his broad interterritorial overlordship over Jews, Frederick utilized the Blood Accusation in Fulda in 1236, which had resulted in the slaying of thirty-two Jews by the Crusaders, to convoke a major assembly of princes, nobles, and abbots of the Empire. At their advice he requested all Western kings to dispatch to him neophytes familiar with Jewish law. Utimately, this commission of Christian experts reached the conclusion that Jews were not allowed to use even the blood of animals and that they abhorred the consumption of human blood in any form. Thereupon the emperor forbade anyone to attack Jews on this score in a sermon or on any other occasion.[10]

It is quite possible that in response to this imperial move, Gregory on his part issued the aforementioned bull against the Crusaders then rioting in France. Eleven years later, in 1247, Innocent IV promulgated his famous decree against the Blood Accusation, with special reference to the events in Fulda. On the other hand, even before his struggle with Frederick reached its climax Gregory had appealed over the emperor's head to the German episcopate to stem the Jews' purported abuses and anticanonical behavior (March 4, 1233). Similarly, the international action initiated by Frederick with respect to the Blood Accusation may have persuaded Gregory that the Papacy ought to re-emphasize its supremacy in all international Jewish matters by initiating the large-scale investigation of the Talmud. This is probably the reason for the delay, which has puzzled all students of the subject, between Nicholas Donin's denunciation of this Jewish classic before the pope in 1236 and Gregory's circular letter addressed in 1239 to the kings of France, England, Aragon, Castile, and Portugal, but not to the emperor or any other German ruler, demanding the seizure and ultimate burning of all "obnoxious" rabbinic works. In 1246, doubtless to underscore the papal *plenitudo potestatis*, Innocent IV confirmed the fiscal authority long exercised by the bishop of Marseilles over the Jews of that district, including Arles, on the basis of privileges granted him by the Hohenstaufen sovereigns, Frederick I and Frederick II. "Whatever is contributed to God's sacred churches," the pope wrote, "and ecclesiastical persons by the munificence of princes inspired by grace divine is worthy, we believe, of being reinforced by the firm backing of Apostolic power." When, under the unstable German conditions after Frederick's death in 1251, the bishop of Würzburg seized control over the Jews of his diocese and issued in their behalf a general decree of protection, the community considered it the better part of wisdom to solicit in 1253 from Innocent IV a confirmation of that decree under the authority of the Apostolic See. At the same time Innocent did not hesitate to authorize the archbishop of Vienne to expel all Jews from his archdiocese, "particularly since they do not observe the statutes enacted with respect to them by the Apostolic See." Opponents of this measure, if Christian (including royal officials), should be overcome with the aid of ecclesiastical censure without appeal.[11]

As in other matters, the protagonists of the rivaling ecclesiastical and imperial theories of Jewish serfdom sought historical justifications. The Church merely had to invoke the evidence of the New Testament concerning the Jews' repudiation of Christ and their ultimate culpability. Combined with the general interpretation of the Old Testament's antimonarchical passages and the twist given to the *donatio Constantini* by Gregory IX and some canonists, the direct subjection of the Jewish people to the Church universal could easily be explained. On their part, the emperors could fall back only on their alleged inheritance of the Roman imperial

Crown. It required some ingenuity to prove that the Jews had been "serfs" of the ancient Roman emperors, who transmitted the control over them to their medieval successors. Here the old Roman-Jewish war under Vespasian and Titus, as reported by Josephus, Hegesippus, and the Church Fathers, was elaborated to indicate that after the destruction of the Temple the Jews had been taken captive by Titus and thus came under the direct over-lordship of the ancient Roman emperors. Not only were the subsequent developments readily forgotten, but medieval jurists and historians rarely hesitated to adorn traditional tales with the fruits of their fertile imagination, particularly if the ensuing amalgams could be utilized to buttress certain ideological positions or practical claims. Even outright forgeries of entire documents were quite common; most famous among them was the very deed allegedly proving Constantine's "donation" to Pope Sylvester.[12]

With reference to the Jewish legal status, this harking back to the events of 70 C.E. occurs first in the influential law book compiled in the 1220s by Eike von Repgow. Without entering into the general merits of papal versus imperial claims, which were in a somewhat quiescent state during the pontificate of Honorius III, Eike's *Sachsenspiegel* tried to explain the competence of imperial courts in prosecuting crimes against Jews. "If a Christian slays a Jew," Eike wrote, "or commits some other wrong against a Jew, he shall be judged under the king's peace which he has broken. Josephus had secured this peace for them from King Vespasian for having cured his son Titus of the gout." The very use of the title "king," rather than "emperor," is characteristic, and shows that the original version did not pursue particularly propagandistic aims. Eike repeated substantially the same story in his *World Chronicle,* but added the legend that after the fall of Jerusalem the Jewish captives had been sold "thirty for a penny, just as they had sold Christ for thirty pennies." This revenge for the act of Judas played a considerable role in medieval historiography and fiction; it had, for instance, induced Tancred, after the Crusaders' conquest of Jerusalem in 1099, thus to rationalize his sale of Jew-ish prisoners at a very low price. However, the elaboration of the *World Chronicle* in the so-called "C" recension, composed in the years between 1237 and 1251, added significantly that, as a result of Titus' conquest, the Jews "were deprived of status and rights, of hereditary possessions and property, so that they also should be bondsmen henceforth. Thus the enemies of God suffered for the offense against God." [13]

Such elaboration, fitting well into the novel image of Jewish status in Frederick II's phraseology, found increasing acceptance in German ecclesiastical and juridical circles. By the time an unknown author composed the so-called Swabian lawbook in 1274–75, this rationale had snowballed into a comprehensive narrative of how Titus had become the protector of his Jewish "serfs."

All the favors and rights in the Jews' possession [the generally Church-minded *Schwabenspiegel* tells us] were secured for them by Josephus from King Titus. . . . Three times eighty thousand Jews were besieged in Jerusalem; one third died of hunger, another third was killed, and the last third was fed by Josephus. These were put up for sale, and were disposed of, thirty for one bad penny. King Titus handed them over to the chamber of the Roman kings, and therefore they shall be servants of the Empire and the Roman king shall protect them.

Here we have a dim recollection also of the ancient *fiscus judaicus* and the *aurum coronarium,* those special taxes imposed upon Jews in the ancient Roman Empire, which could now be construed as the forerunners of special Jewish taxation in the medieval Empire. With this historic rationale, imperial overlordship could be claimed not only over the Jews of Germany, but also over all others, since they all were descendants of Titus' captives and the emperor could invoke his right to temporal world dominion. If we are to believe the fourteenth-century Austrian chronicler, Ottokar von Horneck, Emperor Albert I emphatically asserted that "by right Jews belong to the Empire and to no one else," and thereby brought about the expulsion of Jews from France in 1306, since the French king allegedly refused to tolerate on his territory persons owing allegiance to a foreign monarch.[14]

## HOLY ROMAN EMPIRE

High-sounding declarations of this kind represented, in fact, imperial wishes much more than existing realities. At no time, not even under Frederick Barbarossa, did imperial authority really extend over the entire Holy Roman Empire. As a result of constant internal dissensions, further nurtured by papal interventions, the emperor had to look for allies among his ecclesiastical and lay vassals. The expanding German colonization east of the Elbe was in the hands of conquering princes who paid only nominal allegiance to the emperor. If Frederick II expected by his decree of 1236 extending the privilege of Worms Jewry over the whole Empire, and by his new designation of *servi camerae,* to establish effective imperial control over all German Jews, he failed utterly. Only in Sicily were his centralizing efforts crowned with some success. While earlier in the century he followed his predecessors in awarding the revenue from Jews to local churches and municipalities for definite or indefinite periods, he never gave up his ultimate overlordship. In his later years he actually withdrew many such awards and resumed direct control over the Jewish communities. After the Hohenstaufen regime, southern Italian Jewry was, indeed, almost wholly lorded over by the royal officials of the Angevin and the Aragonese dynasties. In Germany no such centralization could be achieved so long as Frederick was engaged in a life-and-death struggle with the Papacy, which ultimately led to a prolonged civil war.

As a result, Frederick himself had to abandon his centralizing efforts when, in several significant decrees between 1220 and 1235, he recognized the authority of the *dominus terrae* in each locality and region. Moreover, like most other medieval monarchs constantly plagued by a shortage of funds, he followed the example of Philip of Swabia and mortgaged his rights to a number of cities, including the ancient imperial capital of Aix-la-Chapelle, in return for financial and military assistance. He thereby pointed the way for large-scale disposals of imperial property. While outright donations could only take place with the concurrence of the princes (or, after 1281, of the electors), such "temporary" transfers as a rule became permanent alienations. This method was soon extensively employed by the emperors in handing over control over Jews of various localities. At the same time Frederick did not dare to abrogate long-established princely or episcopal powers over such Jewish communities as those of Merseburg or Magdeburg. This gradual erosion of imperial authority over Jewish taxes is well illustrated by the important tax record of 1241, which fails to mention any revenue from such prosperous communities as Mayence or Würzburg. Evidently the income from these communities flowed into the episcopal treasuries rather than the imperial Chamber.[15]

A most portentous change took place in Austria. During the years of his conflict with his namesake, Frederick II of Austria, the last duke of the Babenberg dynasty, the emperor sought to convert both ancient Vienna and, if the pertinent text is authentic, also the newly founded (1192) city of Wiener Neustadt into imperial cities, removing them from the duke's sovereignty. For this purpose he tried to enlist the support first of the burghers by giving them imperial charters, which included the aforementioned piously worded provision against the appointment of Jewish officials, and then of the Jews by granting them the privilege of 1238. Upon the duke's return these imperial provisions went into discard, but in order to retain the loyalty of both the burghers and the Jews of Vienna the Austrian Frederick replaced them by his own charters. In 1239 he enacted one in favor of the municipality, in which he leaned heavily on an earlier privilege granted the city by his predecessor Leopold VI in 1221, but he also incorporated certain provisions from the emperor's decree of 1237. Similarly, when in 1244 he issued a privilege for the Viennese Jews, he closely followed that granted by the emperor six years earlier. By elaborating it in many details, he proved even more liberal toward his Jewish subjects than their imperial overlord. He also extended the validity of this privilege to all Austrian Jews, emphasizing in particular their right of free travel throughout the March.

Wherever a Jew journeys in Our dominion [reads Art. 12] no one shall place an obstacle in his path, nor molest him nor give him cause for complaint. If he transports merchandise or any other thing from which tolls are collectible, he shall pay at all custom stations only such tolls as are paid by any burgher of that city in which the Jew resides at that time.

In contrast to the imperial decree, which had provided that if Jews "should be accused in some major cause, they should be cited before the emperor" (Art. 9), the duke reserved to himself the exclusive right of ultimate judgment and evocation (Art. 29). If much of the ducal charter is devoted to safeguards for Jewish moneylenders, this stress was doubtless owing to the growing importance of Jewish credit transactions in Austria's economy, where in the preceding two decades the Jew Teka, perhaps of Spanish or Khazarian origin, had played an outstanding role. In 1225 Teka served as the guarantor of the peace treaty between Austria and Hungary, while seven years later he was cited with the distinguished title of *comes camerae* (Count of the Chamber), nearly the equivalent of a modern finance minister.[16]

Unwittingly, the Austrian duke thus set up a legislative chain reaction which proved of enormous historical significance for all the Jewries of east-central Europe. His decree was used as a basis, indeed largely copied verbatim, by several neighboring monarchs, especially Bela IV of Hungary in 1251, Přemysl Ottakar II of Bohemia-Moravia in 1254, and a number of Silesian princes in the following years. It was also emulated in 1264 by the Polish duke, Boleslas the Pious of Kalisz, whose charter, as we shall see, was subsequently expanded with additions and modifications by Casimir the Great to embrace all of Poland. Since Grand Duke Vitovt later enacted similar charters for Lithuanian communities in 1388, the combined kingdom of Poland and Lithuania used this law, with minor modifications, under all subsequent regimes. The two Fredericks thus became the unconscious progenitors of the constitutional law which shaped the destinies of Polish-Lithuanian Jewry, the largest Jewish community in the early modern period. Its provisions were renewed by every Polish king, including the last, Stanislaus Augustus Poniatowski, on his election in 1764.[17]

So independent had these eastern princes become that Přemysl Ottakar considered it incumbent upon himself to confirm both the imperial and the papal enactments in favor of Jews. Under existing power conditions of the 1250s, the enforcement of these provisions depended, indeed, much more on the princes than on those more exalted heads of Empire or Church. After Emperor Frederick II's death, especially, there followed a period of chaotic instability in Germany, the so-called *Interregnum,* during which might preceded right in almost all walks of life.

Among the rivaling candidates for the imperial Throne, the foreign princes William of Holland and Richard of Cornwall tried to win the benevolence of some dukes and bishops by transferring to them protection over their Jews. On one occasion William even granted a private Spires burgher, Ebelin vor dem Münster, and his heirs an annual income of 10 marks *titulo perpetuo* from the revenue collected from Spires Jews, "serfs of Our Chamber" (1255). These kings, however, did not give away the imperial rights indiscriminately, as may be seen from William's privilege for the city of Goslar in 1252, in which he pledged himself to "protect them [the Jews] amicably and benevolently as special serfs of Our Chamber." Similarly, in his confirmation of the privileges of the Hagenau burghers in 1262, Richard insisted that the Jews of that city, "serfs of Our Chamber, shall serve only Our Chamber and according to Our patents." How little the princes of that period as yet enjoyed exclusive control over Jews may be seen from the Duke of Brunswick's futile attempt in 1263 to borrow money from Jews; he simply could not enforce such a loan. In the long run, nevertheless, the imperial power could not extend to the Jews effective protection, doubly needed in that era of lawlessness, and they had to seek shelter closer to home. On entering Worms in 1258, Richard confirmed to "the Christian and Jewish burghers of the city all their privileges, and gave them 1000 marks silver." Yet the Worms Jews felt so little reassured that they voluntarily paid the bishop and the city 200 marks, in order that the latter "should maintain them in their rights." Even the various "peace" treaties initiated by Henry IV in 1103, now became the principal responsibility of the various regional authorities. Archbishop Werner of Mayence, several West-German counts, and the cities of Frankfort, Friedberg, Wetzlar, and Gelnhausen, concluded in 1265 a treaty guaranteeing peace "to all men according to [their law], condition and custom, as well as the dignity owing each of them and observed from olden times, even to the Jews." In explaining this clause, they declared that:

Since some lawless persons in the cities, defying God's will, in the memory of whose passion His sacred Church maintains the Jews, nor even deferring to the [wishes of the] Empire to whose Chamber the Jews are known to belong, frequently are prone to riot against them and to insult them, sometimes even inhumanely and miserably to murder them, it is decreed that whosoever will be guilty of such riot and insult against them be punished as the public breaker of the peace.

In this way many imperial prerogatives gradually devolved on the lesser authorities, a process which was not stemmed by the reestablishment of the imperial overlordship over the Jews and the full-fledged reassertion of the latter's Chamber serfdom by Rudolph I and his immediate successors.[18]

For the most part the emperors transferred their Jewish rights for financial or political reasons. In 1251, Conrad IV mortgaged the entire city of Rothenburg with her burghers and Jews in return for a loan, just as he had nine years previously secured a loan by temporarily transferring his revenue from three Jewish individuals. Such temporary transfers often became permanent either through express prolongation, the power of custom, or sheer forgetfulness. Frequently, on the other hand, the kings suddenly reasserted their overlordship even without repaying their original indebtedness; they could invoke the established medieval principle that each grant did not extend beyond the lifetime of its grantor. Unless renewed by the monarch's successor, moreover, all such transactions, and even more basic enactments and privileges, would have automatically expired, were it not for the power of custom. One can easily visualize the legal uncertainties plaguing all groups, and particularly one so defenseless as the Jews, and the opportunity thus given for the free play of force and arbitrary decision. Because of such transfers and the ensuing clashes of authority, the Jews often had to satisfy more than one superior. In an interesting case brought before Meir b. Baruch of Rothenburg, the plaintiff won an indemnity for damages caused him by his guarantee that the defendant would not leave his locality. Although the latter had secured a permit from the local lord to move to another province, the guarantor had been held responsible by a local official who had thereby sustained a loss of revenue. Meir was not exaggerating when, in another responsum, he described the conditions in Germany in the latter part of the thirteenth century by saying that "now, every lord is in his estate like a king and who would dare tell him what to do?" [19]

## FROM RUDOLPH I TO CHARLES IV

Rudolph I of Habsburg (1272–91) tried to restore the imperial overlordship. With respect to Jews, too, he issued regulations affecting the entire empire; and while greatly indebted to the

Church, he underscored the empire's complete independence of it. By officially reconfirming in 1275 the bull outlawing the Blood Accusation, issued by Innocent IV and confirmed by Gregory X, he clearly indicated that papal decrees achieved new validity by an imperial confirmation. At the same time he pledged the resources of the imperial administration (or what was left of it) to protect the Jewish communities against this dangerous libel. *Qua* emperor he also confirmed the Jewish liberties in Ratisbon, though not long thereafter he ordered the Jews of that city to spend the entire Passion Week behind closed doors (1274, 1281). More significantly, when after his defeat of Přemysl Ottakar II he took over the latter's hereditary possessions, he renewed on March 4, 1277 the important Austrian decree of 1244, but he did it in the capacity of Roman emperor rather than as duke of Austria. "Because We wish," the preamble of that renewal read, "that persons of whatever condition living under the Roman Empire should find themselves participants of [Our] grace and benevolence, We institute the following laws in behalf of all the Jews residing in the district of Austria which are inviolably to be observed in their behalf." Accordingly, he also replaced every word *dux* in the original Frederician privilege by the term *rex*. On the other hand, he also tried to pacify the Viennese burghers by repeating, in 1278, the prohibition against the appointment of Jews to public office in that city.[20]

Most radically, Rudolph interpreted the Jewish allegiance to the German Crown as unrestricted fiscal dependence. Going beyond his predecessors, he decreed in 1286 that some Jews of Spires, Worms, Mayence, Oppenheim, and the district of Wetterau, who had left the country for overseas, had done so unlawfully and that hence all their property, both movable and immovable, should be confiscated for the benefit of the imperial Treasury. In justification, he made the following far-reaching statement:

Since the Jews, collectively and individually, in their capacity of serfs of Our Chamber specifically belong to Us with their persons and all their property, just as some belong to princes to whom they have been transferred as a feudal benefice by Us and the Empire, it is right and proper . . . that if any such Jews become fugitives and, without Our special license and consent as their master, render themselves beyond the seas and thus alienate themselves from their true lord, that We

as the lord to whom they belong may freely enter into all their possessions, objects and property, both movable and immovable, wherever
they may be found and not undeservedly take them under Our control.

He was, nevertheless, no more consistent in his fiscal policies than
were his predecessors. Though generally bent upon recapturing
for the Empire the properties lost during the *Interregnum,* he rewarded Bishop Henry of Basel for his services by mortgaging to
him in 1279–80 the Jews of the dioceses of both Basel and Strasbourg for 3,000 marks.[21]

Perhaps unwittingly, the Habsburg emperor thus emphasized
the fiscal aspects of Jewish serfdom above the previous stress on
the mutual responsibility of ruler and Jew. This precedent was
further elaborated by Rudolph's successors. Adolph of Nassau
(1291–98) made use of his fiscal powers not only to transfer the
authority over the Jews of the city and diocese of Mayence to its
archbishop, but soon thereafter also to grant the latter a lifelong
income of 200 marks from the Jewish revenue. In the ensuing controversy between archbishop and burghers concerning the administration of Jewish affairs (1292–95), he decided in favor of the
former in accordance with the award of an arbiter appointed by
him. On the other hand, in 1297 Adolph donated 10 marks
annually to his host, the burgher Ebelin vor dem Münster of
Spires, from the Jewish revenue *titulo iusti feodi* in return for a
promise that Ebelin would always hospitably entertain the king
and his successors at his home. A year later Adolph did not hesitate to mortgage to the burghers of Spires the entire imperial revenue from the local Jews. Such inconsistencies were to become
the rule in subsequent imperial policies. They were but a reflection of the growing royal impotence which, at the end of Adolph's
heavily contested reign, came to the fore also in widespread massacres of Jews, led by a nobleman named Rindfleisch, in parts of
Franconia and Bavaria. To be sure, when Adolph fell in battle
and was succeeded by his original rival, Albert I of Habsburg
(1298–1308), the new German king tried to reassert the imperial
supremacy. He not only severely punished individuals involved in
the Rindfleisch massacres, but he also imposed substantial fines on
the cities of Würzburg, Nuremberg, and others, because they had
tolerated that bloodshed and had subsequently appropriated the

possessions of its Jewish victims. Yet, he himself recognized the right of the archbishop of Mayence to take over the heirless property of all slain Jews. Nor did he interfere when his son Rudolph, to whom he had entrusted the Austrian duchies, passively suffered attacks on Jews, often connected with alleged desecrations of hosts. Nonetheless, he never relinquished the general principle of the imperial obligation to protect Jews, which he had restated at the very inception of his reign at the Nuremberg Diet. According to a romanticizing Austrian chronicler, he even claimed supremacy over the Jews of the entire Christian world.[22]

Upon Albert's assassination in 1308, the campaign for the election of a new king pointed up the monarch's unrestrained freedom in disposing of Jewish revenue. In trying to secure the votes of the archbishops of Mayence and Cologne, the future king Henry VII of Luxembourg (1308–13) promised them the income from Jews of various localities. He also made use of outstanding Jewish loans to reward groups and individuals for their services in his war with the count of Württemberg. The burghers of Esslingen were first granted a two-year moratorium on all debts they owed Jews, and later they were assigned 200 pounds out of the revenue from Frankfort Jewry. A nobleman's debts to Jews were completely canceled so that he might perform better services against Württemberg, while the count of Katzenellenbogen was granted permission to settle twelve Jews each in that city and in Lichtenberg as a reward for his services in Italy (1311–12). In his award of 1309 to Bishop Philip of Eichstädt, Henry even emphasized that thenceforth the Jews of that diocese were to serve the bishop and not the Empire. Perhaps realizing shortly before his demise the deleterious effects of such reckless dissipation of imperial assets, he ordered his official in Nuremberg not only to protect the local Jews but also freely to admit new Jewish settlers to burghers' rights in the city even over the objections of the Jewish community.[23]

More far-reaching was the reign of Louis IV of Bavaria (1314–47). Louis, who during the first sixteen years of his regime had to contend with a rival monarch, Frederick the Handsome, often used this imperial prerogative to punish alleged Jewish adherents of his opponent. On this score he freed the city of Esslingen in 1315 of its financial obligations to the Jews of Überlingen. He also entertained wholly anachronistic Italian ambitions. The ensuing adventurous Italian campaigns were to prove costly both to German and to Italian Jewish communities. Even more regularly short of funds than some of his predecessors, he finally devised a new general poll tax for Jews. In a decree of 1342 he declared that he had reached an agreement with the Jewries of the Empire, according to which each and every Jewish male or widow aged twelve or over and possessing a minimum of twenty guilders was to pay him an annual tax of one guilder. This tax, which came to be designated the *güldener Opferpfennig*, soon turned out to be insignificant in its financial returns, since the number of Jews residing in Germany after 1349 was relatively small and the Empire had at its disposal other means of collecting taxes from them. But it remained a permanent sign of the Jews' attachment to the royal Crown, at least in those areas where the imperial administration was strong enough to enforce its collection.[24]

In return for this tax Louis promised the Jews enhanced protection, a need clearly demonstrated by the widespread massacres of 1337–38 which had been led by two nobles, known as Armleder because they wore leather patches on their sleeves. This was a period of such anarchy that some princes and cities in southwest Germany formed special alliances for the maintenance of public order. One such regional compact was entered into, in 1338, by Bishop Berthold of Strasbourg with a number of Alsatian lords and cities including those of Strasbourg, Colmar, and Hagenau. At its renewal seven years later they were joined by the cities of Basel, Freiburg, and others. They promised to prevent riots whether directed against priests, other Christians, or Jews. Louis himself, whom a contemporary chronicler (probably a Bavarian monk) was soon to extol as "a glorious emperor, father of peace, lover of the clergy and the people, most fortunate triumpher, generous, faithful, prudent and a good Catholic," had to appeal to the archbishop of Mayence and the municipal council of Frankfort to protect his Jewish protégés against the Armleder hordes. Only after the event did he institute an investigation which led to the condemnation of some of the pogromists. Louis' fiscal relations with the Jews, too, were characterized by the customary inconsistencies. In 1330 he transferred "all imperial rights" (*omnia iura imperialia*) over the Jews of Naumburg, Zeitz, and Halle to Margrave Frederick II. In 1333, on the other hand, he reduced the taxes owed by Ratisbon Jewry until it regained its financial health. In the following year he agreed, with the bishop's concurrence, that the Jews of Würzburg pay him only 400 pounds heller. Sometimes he accepted a lump sum in lieu of annual payments. When in 1336 the Rothenburg burghers and Jews paid off a royal loan, the emperor promised that they would be free from taxation and would never be mortgaged again. He similarly accepted a lump sum of 300 marks from the Jews of Goslar in return for a pledge of both freedom from taxation and better protection. At times Louis also regulated various internal affairs, such as permission for the Jews of Nördlingen to punish misbehaving coreligionists and to maintain two or three Jewish butcher stores, provided that they would not sell meat to Christians. All of which did not prevent him from time and again renouncing his imperial revenue in favor of princes or cities and from canceling debts owed to Jews, such as those incurred by the burgrave of Nuremburg up to 1343.[25]

The disturbances of 1337–38 adumbrated one of the greatest tragedies of European Jewry. We shall see that anti-Jewish hostility had became so intense throughout Germany before the Black Death of 1348–49 that in many places Jews were attacked even before any neighbors were stricken by the plague. As a result, they were eliminated from most German territories, some ghost communities never regaining their strength. The reigning emperor of the period, Charles IV of Luxembourg, king of Bohemia (1346–76), proved wholly ineffectual in stemming the bloodshed.

Personally, the new emperor was not anti-Jewish. Soon after his accession to the throne he renewed Přemysl Ottakar II's old Bohemian privilege of 1254. In September 1347 he recommended the Jews of Breslau, "the serfs of his Chamber," to the protection of the city council, allowing the latter in return to raise the Jewish taxes. He also appointed a Prague Jew, Trostlin, as general collec-

tor of the royal revenue from his Bohemian Jews. In the following
year he set his sights higher and endeavored to centralize the collection of the Jewish taxes throughout the Empire in the hands of
a trusted Treves Jew, Samuel. Charles also founded a new city
(Neustadt) on the outskirts of his old capital, Prague. To attract
settlers, he allowed it to organize itself as a municipality apart and
granted its residents special privileges. Jews from outside Prague
were promised tax exemption for twelve years if they settled permanently and erected stone houses in Neustadt. As a matter of
principle, too, he defined the imperial authority over Jews more
sharply than did his predecessors. In 1347 he roundly declared:
"All Jews with their bodies and properties belong to Our Chamber and are in Our hands and power so that We may do with them
in accordance with Our authority as We please." To increase the
Jewish revenue he tried to appropriate for the benefit of the
Treasury also the fines imposed by Jewish courts for insubordina-
tion. In a lengthy decree of September 9, 1348, he ordered Archbishop Baldwin of Treves to collect the fines owed by Jews dis-
obeying orders of royal officials, as well as those who remained
under a Jewish ban for more than thirty days, cited a fellow Jew
before a Christian court, falsely denounced him to royal authorities, or assailed him in the synagogue or elsewhere.[26]

However, when the storm broke loose, Charles had to compromise with the territorial authorities. Only in Breslau, within his
own dominion, did he authorize the captain and city council to
punish the assassins, promising them his active support. But elsewhere he usually absolved the local officials of all responsibility for
the acts of violence committed in their areas. He could no more
poignantly express the breakdown of his own protective devices
than when, on February 17, 1349, he attested that he had given
Archbishop Baldwin "all the property of the Jews who had been
slain in Alsace and elsewhere or yet might be slain, for the Jews
and their possessions belong to the king and the imperial Chamber." Typical of such acts of forgiveness even in Bohemia is the
privilege granted on May 16, 1350 to the burghers of Eger.
Emphasizing that the populace had been "animated by vulgar
prejudice, bad advice and reprobate feelings" when it attacked
Jews and thus caused much damage to the royal Treasury, he

nevertheless accepted the regrets and satisfaction offered him by the city elders:

After a preliminary mature consultation [he added] with Our princes, barons and nobles, we have by Our imperial grace forgiven the afore-mentioned burghers, the municipality, their heirs and successors forever in Our name and in that of the Empire and Our successors, both Roman emperors and Bohemian kings. This forgiveness is for every transgression which was committed by the slaying and destruction of Jews without the positive knowledge, or in ignorance, of the leading citizens or in whatever other fashion. [It is granted] without further reservation for Us and Our successors, the Roman emperors and Bohemian kings, concerning any claim or intervention against those burghers, the municipality or their heirs and successors on account of these excesses and transgressions.

It is small wonder, then, that during those years imperial prestige sank lower and lower and, in his famous Golden Bull of 1356, Charles had to concede to the electors of Germany nearly total independence. Jews residing in the electorates were handed over, together with some other sources of imperial revenue like mints and customs duties, to these powerful princes, both ecclesiastical and secular.[27]

By that time the imperial authority had in any case been re-duced to the areas under the rule of lesser bishops and barons and, particularly, to the imperial cities. This ambivalence is also illus-trated by Charles IV's privilege of December 13, 1360, for Rudolph IV of Austria and his brothers, allowing them to settle Jews in their Austrian lands, as well as in Swabia and Alsace. As king of Bohemia he simultaneously promised, also in behalf of his brother, Margrave John of Moravia, not to admit any Austrian Jews into his dominions without the particular duke's consent. In exchange, Rudolph and his brothers obligated themselves to admit Bohemian or Moravian Jews only with Charles' or John's permis-sion, respectively. Apart from the general oddity of these treaties which, introduced by Philip Augustus and his vassals in France, were then going into oblivion in France and had never been ex-tensively emulated in Germany, their very conclusion bore clear testimony to the far-advanced erosion of imperial power. For the Austrian dukes, notwithstanding Rudolph IV's strenuous efforts, were not even enjoying the status of German electors, upon whom Charles had four years previously conferred the mastery over their Jewries.[28]

## FROM WENCESLAUS TO MAXIMILIAN I

Not that the emperor thereby completely surrendered his control over Jews. Just as the earlier transfers of local Jewries to various lords had not involved renunciation of all imperial rights, so did the over-all "serfdom of the Chamber" now continue unabatedly throughout the Empire, at least in theory. In practice, to be sure, this was a question of the relative strength of emperor versus territorial prince, and depended on the personalities involved as well as on a variety of local circumstances. Charles IV's immediate successor, his son Wenceslaus (1376–1400; he served for another nineteen years as Bohemian king after his deposition from the German throne in 1400), twice issued startling enactments which documented that imperial mastery. Having failed in 1383 to persuade the Rhenish and Swabian cities to pay him one-tenth of their income from Jews, his envoys met with representatives of the Swabian cities (Augsburg, Basel, Nuremberg, and others) at a conference in Ulm which resulted in a remarkable treaty of June 12, 1385. This detailed agreement, which will be more fully analyzed elsewhere, stipulated that all debts owed to Jews for less than one year would carry no interest, and that older debts were to be computed as to capital and interest and the total reduced by 25 percent, with the cities administering the pawns. More significantly, the king provided that Jews fleeing from one city to another should be returned to their former residences, and that the contracting cities should pledge themselves not to accept each other's Jews. In return, the king was to receive a total indemnity of 40,000 florins. Five years later, after threatening at the Diet of Eger that he would demand from the cities the restoration of all Jews to direct imperial authority (1389), Wenceslaus concluded another agreement with the duke of Bavaria, the bishops of Bamberg, Würzburg, and Augsburg, and a number of counts, promising the total cancellation of Jewish debts in favor of the contracting parties and certain cities, in return for their payment to him of specified indemnities. The duke of Bavaria and the bishop of Würzburg were to pay 15,000 florins each, whereas most of the others got off with lesser sums. Understandably, these measures may have temporarily alleviated the pleasure-loving king's financial stringency, but they rapidly undermined all confidence and brought about such chaotic conditions that in 1398 Wenceslaus himself had to promise never again to cancel debts owed to Jews.[29]

Even from the Treasury's standpoint the operation was not an unqualified success. Almost immediately after making the arrangement with the Swabian cities, Wenceslaus started giving away thousands of florins to friendly individuals. In the few days between July 9 and 17, 1385 he disposed of 10,000 florins in addition to 1,000 shock of the large Prague coinage out of the total of 40,000 florins he was to collect. (A few months later 1,500 shock of the same coinage were converted in Rothenburg for 5,000 florins.) Nor were all beneficiaries of the second cancellation ready to pay the promised 15 percent. Within a year of his second agreement (September 16, 1391) he had to threaten the Bavarian estates that anyone failing to deliver the stipulated sum would not only find himself in royal disfavor, but would also automatically become liable for the full payment of his obligations to Jews. At the same time the king insisted upon the undiminished delivery of the annual Jewish poll tax. On the very day of the second cancellation (September 16, 1390) he ordered the city elders of Rothenburg to collect that tax also from newly settled Jews, whom they were freely to admit and to protect, and, on the other hand, to sell all the property of Jews leaving without authorization. The revenue thus yielded was to be equally divided between the imperial Treasury and the city. In 1394, he also summoned the Jewish elders of Ratisbon to explain why the "golden penny" had not been paid.[30]

Wenceslaus' successor, Rupert of the Palatinate (1400–10), not only confirmed in 1401 a number of privileges of local Jewish communities, but also repeated Wenceslaus' pledge not to cancel Jewish debts, although he limited this promise to but three years. He repeated it for another three years in 1404; of course, without thereby creating sufficient security for long-term planning. But the

Jews had long become accustomed to adjusting their lives in Germany, Italy, and elsewhere to legal guarantees extended for a few years only. In some areas their very settlement depended on such temporary permits renewable before expiration. To some extent a privilege issued for a definite term was more reassuring than one which could be revoked at the legislator's whim. Though of generally friendly disposition (he was nicknamed Clem, or Clement) and though the Jewish historian, David Gans, was to call him "a man, wise and understanding, humble, God-fearing, loving justice and merciful to the poor," Rupert seems to have disliked Jews. He was probably coresponsible for their expulsion from the Palatinate in 1390, ten years before his election to the German throne. Yet he had a keen eye for the fiscal possibilities inherent in the Jewish dependence on the Crown and he tried to exploit them to the full.[31]

One of Rupert's greatest innovations, which went far beyond similar stillborn efforts by Charles IV in 1347–48, was to enlist the aid of Jewish tax collectors in increasing the imperial revenue from Jewish communities. Shortly after his election, he ordered the Jewries of the whole Empire to pay their dues to Elias of Weinheim and Isaac of Oppenheim. Rupert hoped that, by allowing the Jewish collectors a share of one-quarter (the two collectors paid their own expenses), he would greatly increase his net income. This expectation was reinforced by his sad experience with the Christian official, Johannes Kirchheim, whom he sent out in 1402 to collect the Jewish poll tax and other royal imposts in Augsburg, Constance, and thirty other communities. On his journey Kirchheim seems to have expended almost the entire revenue of 287 florins he had gathered from the weak and depopulated Jewish settlements. The two Jewish collectors energetically took up their task and organized a regular corporation with local subcollectors who were promised support by many cities. Nevertheless, the whole enterprise proved rewarding for neither the emperor nor his agents. Possibly in order to reinforce future collections, Rupert tried to buttress them by spiritual means. In 1407 he appointed a rabbi Israel as "chief rabbi [Hochmeister] above all Jewish chief rabbis as well as all other Jews and Jewesses in German lands." Israel received the authority to convoke all-

German Jewish assemblies, to issue judgments, and to proclaim bans on all Jews in the Empire. But this appointment, too, so obviously pursued fiscal aims that German Jewry effectively boycotted the new institution.[32]

No less fiscally oriented was Rupert's successor, King Sigismund (1411–37; king of Hungary since 1387, of Bohemia since 1419, emperor since 1433), the half brother of Wenceslaus. Ever impecunious and living at the expense of often unwilling hosts, Sigismund constantly devised new means of exploiting his Jewish subjects. Although Jews had no direct interest in the Ecumenical Council of Constance convoked by Sigismund in 1414, he made them contribute to its expenses through an extraordinary impost. Ultimately, it turned out that they did benefit from the Council, which deposed the three rivaling popes, including the Jews' archenemy Pedro de Luna, and elected in their stead the friendly Martin V. At Sigismund's request (for a Jewish consideration), Martin renewed the Papacy's older Jewish privileges on February 14, 1418, with particular reference to Germany. During most of Sigismund's reign the imperial armies fought against the Hussite troops, often suffering defeats in the field. Jews, though trying to hold aloof from this religious conflict, sustained considerable losses in the war-ravaged areas. Nevertheless, Sigismund exacted from them another special tax to defray the costs of the war. On September 11, 1422 he authorized Margrave Bernhard I of Baden to collect from all Jews in the Empire, "wherever they live, the third penny [one-third] of all their property, movable or immovable, without exception." Finally, he introduced still another enormous Jewish tax on the occasion of his coronation as emperor in 1434, the Jews being threatened with punishment for any delay in payment. To assuage the ruffled feelings of some German princes, Sigismund assured them that this innovation would by no means impinge on their established rights. He gave such assurance, for instance, to his own son-in-law, Duke Albert V of Austria (1411–39, later German king, Albert II, 1437–39). Otherwise, too, he had to exert considerable efforts to make the Jews pay even the ordinary "golden penny" or the fines they owed the Treasury, since their usual taxpayers' resistance was often stiffened in opposition to their immediate lords. To overcome it Sigismund, like Rupert, tried to entrust the collection to leading Jews themselves. At first he used Chief Rabbi Israel for this purpose. Probably disappointed with the latter's achievements, the emperor appointed in 1426 a group of three rabbis, including the generally revered Rabbi Jacob ha-Levi Mölln (Maharil), but this collegium probably never even started to function. Sigismund reverted, therefore, to a single official and in 1435 his treasurer, Conrad von Weinsberg, selected on his behalf a far less eminent leader, Anselm of Cologne, then residing in Worms, and entrusted him with the "spiritual" leadership of the Jewries in the western and central parts of the Empire—obviously, with equally indifferent results.[33]

Notwithstanding this overwhelming concern with Jewish revenue, the general impression left by Sigismund's Jewish legislation is one of relative fairness. One may mention especially his decree of April 4, 1416, in which as Roman king he took the Jews of Nuremberg, Nördlingen, Windsheim, and Weissenburg in Bayern under his protection. It began by stating that no one, including himself, should impose upon Jews against their will any tax other than the customary annual imposts. Nor should anyone encourage the Jews' debtors not to meet their obligations. On later occasions Sigismund likewise promised the Jews protection against arbitrary tax collections, pledged himself not to proclaim any cancellation of or moratoria on debts owed them, and issued a general permit for all princes and city elders who had expelled Jews, to the "Reich's detriment," to readmit them. In individual cases he went even further. In the privilege he issued quite early in his reign (September 7, 1413) in favor of several Jews in Lindau, Ravensburg, and Überlingen, he not only promised them protection under the king's peace and freedom of movement with a royal safe-conduct, but also provided that they be exempted from the specific Jewish taxes, not be summoned before any court except in their places of residence, and not be subject to any Jewish ban. While such favoritism often played havoc with Jewish communal controls and also shifted the burden of Jewish taxation to the nonfavored Jews, it revealed the extent to which some Jews had access to the king. Under the circumstances the accolade given him a century and a half later by David Gans was not altogether undeserved. The Jewish historian called Sigismund, too, "a wise, understanding, humble and God-fearing man." [34]

After Sigismund's death in 1437 the imperial Crown permanently reverted to the Habsburg dynasty, first through Albert II and two years later through Frederick III (1439–93). Albert, under whose princely regime Austrian Jewry had suffered severely, reigned as emperor too short a time to do much damage to the other German Jews. At the beginning of his reign (May 10, 1438) he invited representatives of imperial Jewry to Nuremberg and made them agree to a new general impost for his coronation at Aix-la-Chapelle and for other royal needs. Soon thereafter, however, he frittered away some of that Jewish revenue (for instance, to the cities of Nuremberg and Augsburg) in return for immediate cash payments. He also mortgaged the income from the bishopric of Constance to one of his officials. Probably before Conrad von Weinsberg, who continued serving as treasurer in charge of all imposts, taxes, tithes, and the "golden penny" due from Jews, had much chance to collect, he was ordered to pay out of that revenue 1,000 Rhenish florins annually to the hereditary marshal of the empire. Nor shall we look for any more consistency in Albert's Jewish policies than had been manifested by his predecessors. When the city of Schweinfurt, in need of funds to pay for lands newly acquired from the Teutonic Order, suddenly imposed an excessive tax upon her Jewry, Conrad reacted forcefully and imposed upon the city a fine of 1,800 florins. On the other hand when, as a result of an epidemic of 1436, emotions ran high in Augsburg and the burghers decided three years later to expel the Jews, they had little difficulty in securing royal permission.[35]

Frederick III (V, as Austrian duke) was likewise deeply interested in the imperial revenue from Jews. He improved upon Sigismund's fiscal policies by making the Jews pay the coronation tax twice—when he was crowned German king, and again in 1452 when he became Roman emperor. Nor was he moderate in assessing that tax. Since every new monarch was free to let lapse all existing Jewish privileges, he ordered the Jews to part with one-third of their entire property in return for their release from the rightlessness which might result from such expiration. One of his partisans, Margrave Albert III Achilles of Brandenburg, justified these exactions by pushing the interpretation of Chamber serfdom to unprecedented lengths. "Be it known in the empire [he succinctly declared in 1463] that, as soon as a Roman king is elected, or as soon as he achieves imperial dignity and is crowned emperor, he is entitled by old custom either to burn all Jews, or else to bestow upon them his grace and take from them a third penny of their property, so that they may save their lives." No wonder the Jews often resisted and, in September 1454, Frederick ordered a jurist, Hartung von Cappel, to collect the two-year-old arrears or else to summon the recalcitrant communities before the Imperial Tribunal (*Kammergericht*).[36]

In practice, however, the emperor had to strike a compromise. Several communities (for instance, that of Ulm in 1453) were granted a five-year immunity from any future extraordinary taxes in return for their payment of the coronation taxes. In 1456 Frederick threatened the Jews of Ratisbon and Salzburg with sharp reprisals for their failure to pay those taxes, yet he extended his personal protection to the former in the great crisis which ultimately resulted in their expulsion in 1519. From time to time he also imposed upon the Jews emergency taxes for his wars with the Turks (1471), the Burgundians (1475), and others. Like Sigismund he tried to enlist the cooperation of the Jewish leaders themselves. In 1470 he convoked at Ratisbon an assembly of Jewish elders from the leading German communities. Sensing his fiscal intentions, the Frankfort elders tried to stay away. When they finally sent two delegates they limited their authority by stipulating that no commitment should be made without the approval of the city council—which was, of course, interested in safeguarding Jewish resources for its own benefit. After arriving in Ratisbon, the Frankfort representatives, together with the elders of Worms and Spires, negotiated at length with the imperial officials. The discussion was supposed to be concerned with broader legal and political issues, but the officials evinced real interest only in new ways to increase the Jewish revenue, a procedure which understandably did not appeal to the Jews. The assembly adjourned without achieving any tangible results.[37]

It would be a mistake, however, to view Frederick III's regime entirely from the aspect of his fiscal administration. Generous and well-educated, though weak and moody, he was genuinely interested in the welfare of his Jewish "serfs" while meeting the basic requirements of canon law. To weather the gathering storms of anti-Jewish hostility, which led the Austrian Estates reiteratedly to demand the expulsion of Jews, Frederick secured from his friend, Pope Nicholas V, the bull *Romanus Pontifex* of September 20, 1451. After a long and wordy preamble, the pope made it perfectly clear that Christian rulers were entitled to maintain Jews in their dominions and to treat them humanely without running counter to any apostolic constitutions. This bull, although introducing no innovation into canon law, was considered so useful by the Austrian Jews that they secured a number of copies, including one certified in Wiener Neustadt in 1452 by Ennea Silvio Piccolomini, the later Pope Pius II. On learning in 1470 that Margrave Carl of Baden had lent a willing ear to a Blood Accusation in Endingen, tortured and executed many Jews, and confiscated their property, the emperor ordered all princes and other officials to assist him in forcing the margrave to release the Jews still imprisoned and to return their property, under a fine of 100 gold marks. To this effect he invoked both the papal bulls against the Blood Accusation and his own rights, according to which "all of Jewry in the Holy Empire is subject directly to Us as Roman emperor in behalf of the Holy Empire." [38]

On the other hand, Frederick was greatly instrumental, as we recollect, in establishing the later famous Frankfort ghetto, although he did it out of Christian piety rather than anti-Jewish animus. He also often lent a willing ear to denunciations of Jewish usury. However, when trying to stem "abuses," he insisted that these had no bearing upon the general toleration of Jews. In his attempt to achieve a proper balance, on July 20, 1465 he authorized his brother-in-law, Count Ulrich of Württemberg, to administer the affairs of the Jewries in the provinces of Mayence, Treves, Salzburg, and Besançon (all bishoprics, it may be noted), and wrote:

We give you thereby the full authority of the Roman imperial power, until its revocation by Us or Our successors or until you are assigned to other tasks, to receive and accept all and every Jew and Jewess residing in the aforementioned provinces under Our and your protection and truce in Our and the Holy Empire's behalf. You are to maintain and safeguard them to the best of your ability in their rights and privileges.

Ulrich was, on the other hand, to listen to complaints about Jewish misdeeds, hold the necessary hearings, and institute remedial actions. Frederick was reputed to have often stressed the biblical saying, "And yet for all that, when they are in the land of their enemies, I will not reject them, neither will I abhor them, to destroy them utterly and to break My covenant with them; for I am the Lord, their God" (Lev. 26:44). With the smattering of Hebrew he had learned, he punned on the first word of that verse, *Ve-af,* and said that Jews have an *Affe* (monkey) in their Bible, which word they should inscribe with golden letters. Nor did he hesitate to employ a Jewish physician, Jacob Loans, who often attended him at his castle in Linz and whom he raised to noble rank —the first nonofficial Jew to attain that distinction. Not surprisingly, Frederick also evinced great interest in the inner administration of the Jewish communities, particularly in Austria, without too deeply interfering in their operation. It is small wonder, then, that some contemporaries condemned him as a friend of Jews, a Bavarian writer stating that the emperor had "defended no people more vigorously than the Hebrews. In so far as it depended on him, he did not permit the killing of Jews for whatever reason." The Austrian chronicler, Matthias Döring, asserted that Frederick "was generally styled a king of the Jews, rather than of the Romans." [39]

A similarly moderate position was taken by Frederick's son and, for a while, coregent, Maximilian I (1485–1519). According to a rumor widely circulated among Jews, Frederick on his deathbed enjoined his son to "do good to Jews." This knightly monarch, crowned Roman emperor in 1508, laid the foundations for the great extension of Habsburg rule to the Netherlands, Spain, and the New World. But his costly ventures often forced him, too, fully to exploit his Jewish resource. After certifying on August 4, 1491 that the Jews of Rothenburg had paid their 200 florins of the special impost voted at the Nuremberg diet, he sent, in 1497, a circular letter to the rabbis and elders of Ratisbon, Worms,

Nuremberg, Frankfort, Ulm, Rothenburg, and other cities, to see to it that the regular "golden penny" be paid. At the same time, like his father he tried to treat his Jewish subjects fairly. Until the end he succeeded in forestalling their expulsion from Ratisbon. On the other hand, he had to approve a similar expulsion from Nuremberg in 1498. He may have been swayed by a brief, submitted to him by Nuremberg lawyers at the request of the Council, which recited the Jewish misdeeds and argued, on legal grounds, for the legitimacy of their banishment. In several subsequent enactments he merely tried to regulate a more orderly disposal of the property left behind by the exiles, but he finally consented to its appropriation by the city council for the payment of 8,000 florins to the Crown. More significantly, in his own Austrian hereditary possessions he cooperated in 1496 in the expulsion of the Jews from Styria after its Estates consented to indemnify the Treasury by the payment of 38,000 florins. However, in contrast to his predecessors, Maximilian convoked a Jewish assembly in 1510, not in order to extort more money from its constituents but rather in compliance with the suggestions of Frankfort Jewry, which was then seeking concerted action against the accusations of the renegade, Johann Pfefferkorn. Before long there appeared at Maximilian's court that superlative defender of Jewish rights in the sixteenth century, Josel of Rosheim, a relative of Frederick III's court physician, Jacob Loans. All these events were an augury of the great transformations which were to take place in Germany and the rest of Europe in the following several generations and which were to affect profoundly also the destinies of German Jewry.[40]

In the thirteenth to the fifteenth centuries, control over Jews thus gradually shifted from the imperial Crown to the respective German princes and cities. Of course, where the emperor himself was the reigning hereditary prince he exercised his sovereign powers over Jews with little restraint. This applied particularly to the Habsburg rulers of Austria and the Luxembourg kings of Bohemia, since from the outset imperial supremacy in that region had often been quite nominal. As tensions increased and the security of the Jewish population declined, the inadequacy of imperial protection against recurrent local attacks became manifest, reinforcing the trend toward the atomization of, and the ensuing conflicts over, the mastery over Jews.

## ARCHBISHOPS-ELECTORS

Jewish settlements had deep roots in the three archbishoprics of Mayence, Cologne, and Treves. Cologne could look back on a history reaching at least to the days of Constantine the Great. The Jewry of Treves, too, may well have dated back to the second century C.E. If no such early evidence is available for Mayence, its community easily made up by the quality of its leadership for its lack of chronological priority. From the days of Gershom b. Yehudah, the Light of the Exile, to the First Crusade it enjoyed intellectual preeminence in all German, and to some extent also in all Ashkenazic, Jewry.

In other respects, too, Mayence held a unique position through its archbishop-elector. As chancellor of the Holy Roman Empire he served as a sort of viceroy, acting in the emperor's behalf especially during the latter's frequent absences from Germany. In this capacity he also served as coprotector of imperial Jewry, being rewarded by one-tenth of the imperial revenue from Jews. In addition he was collecting taxes from the Jews of his own archbishopric. A document of 1248–49, before the death of Frederick II, records such revenue from Mayence ("five pounds from the Jews and five which the wife of the Master of the Jews gave"), and other places in the electorate including Frankfort and Erfurt. This position of the archbishop was recognized by the author of the *Schwabenspiegel*, who wrote: "He [the king] shall also recommend his Jews living in German lands to his chancellor [the bishop of Mayence]. If he fails to do so, the bishop nevertheless takes care of them." Of course, such protection availed the Jews little during the chaotic period of the *Interregnum*. Propelled by the growing feeling of insecurity, which was aggravated by a blood libel in 1282–83 and the subsequent confiscation of much Jewish property, many Jews left Mayence and its environs. Thereupon their property, including some fifty-four houses in the best quarter of town, was confiscated by the city. Ever since, these houses carried the designation of *Judenerben*. Not surprisingly, the archbishop protested and in the ensuing litigation he secured a favorable judgment in 1286 from Rudolph I. Because the emperor tried at the same time to appropriate all goods left behind by the Jewish refugees, the city refused to return the houses and defied the emperor's threat of placing it under a ban. Finally, in return for the city's pledge to pay him an annual tax of 112 marks, Archbishop Gerhard II von Eppenstein conceded, in 1295, the city's right not only to retain the houses but also "to tax the Jews according to its judgment and to use the revenue for the benefit of the municipality." Thenceforth the archbishop shared control over Mayence Jews with the city, but retained his undiminished authority in the rest of the electorate. In 1287 Rudolph had actually assigned to him the protection of Jews in Thuringia and other outlying districts. Albert I also authorized the archbishop, on January 6, 1299, to take over all heirless estates of slain Jews. Eighteen years later Louis the Bavarian confirmed his tithe of the imperial revenue and assigned to him the entire imperial income from the Jews of Spires.[41]

Here, too, the Black Death and the accompanying massacres of Jews put a temporary end to their community. However, the energetic Archbishop Gerlach von Nassau (1346–71) soon thereafter invited a Jew from Bischofsheim to settle in Mayence and empowered him to bring in additional Jews. The old legal status was restored, the Jews being given the express right to depart at will, provided only that they paid up their taxes for the current year. The first of the twenty-eight extant letters of admission is dated October 6, 1355, showing that Charles IV's Golden Bull issued in the following year merely confirmed the archbishop's existing right freely to admit Jews. Two years later a number of Jews led by a gifted organizer, their Magister Froudel, made an agreement with Erfurt's city council concerning their annual contributions, the archbishop having in the meantime relinquished all controls over the local Jewry in favor of the city, as he did soon thereafter with respect to that of Frankfort. Before long this new Jewish settlement, the third in Erfurt's history, exceeded in populousness and economic influence that of the electoral capital. Gerlach's successors followed his favorable policies toward Jews, even suppressing the theretofore widely enforced "dice toll" (*Würfelzoll*) which produced more annoyance for the Jews than revenue for the Treasury. This toll was restored by King Rupert in 1401, largely to spite the archbishop, but it was abolished again in 1422.[42]

In general, the fifteenth-century archbishops sought to safeguard their Jewish fiscal preserve against royal encroachments. John II von Nassau (1397–1419) may, in 1405, have reduced all indebtedness to Jews by 20 percent and allowed the debtors to pay the balance in four instalments, but he supported the Mayence community in 1414 in whittling down Emperor Sigismund's demand of one-third of their property to the moderate sum of 2,000 florins. When the emperor tried to collect another large tax from Mayence Jewry in 1429, Archbishop Conrad III (1419–34) resisted even more adamantly. But he finally had to compromise on a total payment of 4,000 florins, just as five years later he yielded on the coronation tax, helping out the Jewish taxpayers only by advancing them 500 florins from his own Treasury. A similar mixture of enlightened self-interest with humanity also animated Archbishop Diethrich von Erbach (1434–59). To be sure, the provincial synod of Mayence, meeting under his chairmanship in 1451, adopted a number of anti-Jewish provisions, particularly relating to the badge. But apart from his inability to controvert long-accepted provisions of canon law, Diethrich acted under the combined pressures of the general membership of the synod and of the papal legate, Nicolaus Cusanus, under whose prompting other German church councils adopted similar resolutions. The archbishop's own inclination revealed itself when he failed to implement these resolutions for five years, and then only for a short time. Diethrich was also involved in a protracted controversy with the city over its attempted expulsion of Jews in 1438. The briefs submitted by the jurists on both sides shed considerable light also on the previous legal history of the Mayence community. The archbishop insisted that the city should indemnify him for the ensuing loss of 140,000 marks. Next to the emperor, his lawyers argued, he was the true overlord of the Jews, while the rights of the city were limited to their use (*usufructus*) for which it was traditionally paying 112 marks a year. Just as a tenant may use a house but must not destroy it, so was the city to maintain the archbishop's Jewish property intact. On its part, the city claimed unrestricted control. The controversy found a tragic finale under Diethrich's successor, Diether von Isenburg (1459–62), when the city was occupied by Adolph II of Nassau, who expelled many burghers along with the Jews. If he soon thereafter started read-mitting some wealthy Jews, Adolph could not prevent their second expulsion from Mayence in 1471. After his death in 1475, Archbishop Diether, during his second occupancy, reopened the Mayence gates to a few hardy souls, but the community never recovered from these successive blows.[43]

Equally dramatic were the vicissitudes of the Jewish communities under the regime of the archbishop-elector of Cologne. Here, too, the archbishop's difficulties lay more with the aspirations of the city than with the imperial claims. From the twelfth century on the municipality fought for nearly total independence in its inner affairs, including mastery over Jews. Under Archbishop Conrad von Hochstaden (1238–61) it came to open warfare, in which the Jewish community helped the burghers to defend the city against the archbishop's troops. Nevertheless when peace was established in 1252, Conrad issued a pro-Jewish decree. Addressing himself to all officials of the archbishopric, he wrote on April 27, 1252:

We believe that it will contribute much to Our welfare and Our honor if the Jews, who confide in Us and submit themselves to Our dominion in the hope of Our protection and Our grace, should receive from Us the expected good treatment [*beneficenciam*]. We wish you all to know that, guided by this consideration, We have taken the Jews who reside in Cologne, as well as those who intend to settle in the city as soon as they move within its walls, under Our protection with respect to their persons and property. They should be fostered by Us and Our officials in all their transactions throughout Our territory. . . . In order that the Jews who already reside in the city the more willingly remain with Us and that foreign Jews be induced to settle here by the example of the good treatment of those residents, We order Our faithful officials, the judges, mayors, sheriffs, and aldermen of Cologne who, at Our request had pledged themselves to contribute to the observance of the above provisions . . . that you grant the Jews protection, aid, and help to the extent of your ability and not tolerate that they be injured or offended by anyone, this privilege to the contrary.

More specifically, the privilege provided that the Jews be obliged to pay only two semiannual taxes and be free from other imposts for the next two years, after which new arrangements would be made if the Jews decided to stay. Jews were also to enjoy full judicial autonomy, except in cases of theft, forgery, assault and battery, failure to obey a ban, or adultery with a Jewish or Christian woman, all of which were to be submitted to the general courts. In such criminal prosecutions the guilty person alone, not the community as a whole, was to be held responsible. Whenever the communal majority should wish to exclude an unworthy member, the archbishop was to expel him. Jews should elect annually a new head (*Judenbischoff*), on which occasion they were to pay the Treasury a fee of 5 marks. The municipality, at that time relatively pro-Jewish, agreed with these provisions and subsequently accused the archbishop of illegally incarcerating a few Jews. This controversy was finally settled by arbitration with the participation of Albertus Magnus. The arbiters agreed that, in principle, the archbishop had been enfiefed by the emperor, but that the city also had certain traditional rights. In 1266 Archbishop Engelbert II (1262–67) added the provision that no one dare to collect tolls on Jewish corpses brought to burial in the Cologne cemetery. He also significantly prescribed that "no Cahorsins [*Cavwercini*] nor [other] Christians who manifestly lend on usury should be allowed to reside in the city of Cologne, since their [the Jews'] interests would thereby be prejudiced." To reinforce this decree the archbishop ordered that it be inscribed on two stone tablets. The tablets (3 by 2½ feet in size) were subsequently immured in the walls of the famous Cologne cathedral, and have thus been preserved to the present day.[44]

These provisions remained intact and, in fact were expanded further for the benefit of the Jews in a decree issued by Archbishop Wicbold von Holte (1297–1304). To be sure, the new decree of 1302 was at the outset limited to nine years, but it was subsequently renewed for ten-year periods in 1311, 1321, and 1331. The two latter renewals came from the municipal authorities, which had full control over the Jews ever since 1321, although the archbishop's authority had been reinforced by the promises made by Henry of Luxembourg as a candidate for the royal throne in 1308. Similar promises had also been made by

Frederick the Handsome to the archbishop during his campaign against Louis the Bavarian in 1314. Yet in 1338 Archbishop Walram (1332–49) had to request the city council to protect the Jews' rights in accordance with the privileges recently enacted, and four years later he felt it incumbent upon himself reciprocally to confirm the city's renewal of Jewish privileges, this time prolonged for thirteen years. In the meantime the number of Jews and their holdings of the city's houses increased rapidly. According to local real estate records, the Jews owned or rented a total of about 50 houses in 1235. In contrast, they were able to acquire in the year 1300 alone some 60, and in 1325 some 70, structures. These acquisitions so deeply aroused the Christian burghers that in 1341 the municipality forbade any further Jewish expansion.[45]

All of these legal safeguards did not save the Jews of the electorate from reiterated assaults by hostile mobs. At times the burghers of a provincial community turned against the Jews, as when they expelled them from Andernach in 1287 despite the archbishop's belated intervention. However, the elector prevailed upon the municipality to readmit them and to promise them protection. Persons guilty of the disturbances were to be punished, while those who had killed an assailant of Jews were not to be prosecuted but rather praised as an example for the future. Despite these favorable developments, the authorities could not rescue the Jews from nearly total annihilation during the Black Death. It took Cologne longer than Mayence to reassure the Jews and to reestablish a community in 1372. This date is significant in so far as it coincided with the victory of the patrician party over the artisan groups, which had been trying for several years to share fully in the municipal regime. In essence, the new privileges were but a renewal of those granted by the archbishops before the tragedy of 1349, except that now the Jews were limited to renting rather than owning their houses. Like the former decrees, that enacted in 1372 was limited to ten years, but was decennially renewed from 1384 to 1414. Apart from the general protection for Jewish lives and property and safeguards for the Jewish courts, the decree of 1372 went into some detail in regulating Jewish moneylending and the holding of pledges. While freed from military service, the Jews were supposed, as before 1349, to guard the Jewish gate in case of attack. The revenue from Jews was to be equally divided between the archbishop and the city.[46]

Nevertheless the community was now but a shadow of its former self. Almost immediately upon their resettlement the Jews became involved in a controversy between the archbishop and the city because of two Jews accused by episcopal officials whose jurisdiction the city impugned. The municipal elders disregarded a summons from Charles IV in 1375, as well as the subsequent imperial fine of 10,000 gold marks. But the emperor's ensuing ban on the city entailed such hardships that the elders yielded in 1377 and agreed to share the authority with the bishop. In the meantime the two Jewish defendants were executed, the wife of one being saved from burial alive only by her timely conversion to Christianity. On that occasion a contemporary poet, Menaḥem Ṣiyyon b. Meir, composed a dirge, Ṣiyyon me'on ḥishqi (Zion, Dwelling of My Delight). Since during that period the number of Jews at no time exceeded 200 souls or 31 taxpaying households and the revenue from them was correspondingly slight, a new quarrel broke out between the city and the archbishop in 1415. After Emperor Sigismund had reaffirmed, on November 8, 1414 the archbishop's extensive rights, including his authority over Jews, the city complained that the latter took undue advantage of his right to summon them before his court. During the trial before the royal commissioners much of the complex legal status of Cologne Jewry and the often contradictory rights of city, bishop, and king were as thoroughly aired here as the parallel problems of Mayence were some three decades later, except that the municipality of Cologne was more powerful and independent. The litigation was settled by arbitration in 1419, the Jews bearing the brunt by being forced to pay 25,000 florins to the archepiscopal Treasury. The difficulties with the archbishop were compounded by the fiscal demands of the emperor, the city's involvement in the Hussite wars, and rumors that the Jews sided with the heretics. Finally, in 1423, the city council unanimously passed a resolution not to renew the Jewish privileges expiring in the following year. Although both emperor and Pope Martin V intervened, that decision was firmly upheld. Notwithstanding Sigismund's reiterated warnings, the city proceeded in 1424 with the expulsion, the final judgment of the arbiter reaching it on July 24, 1425, several months after the Jews had been forced to depart.[47]

It must be borne in mind, however, that although the expulsion from Cologne was followed by those from Siegburg in the 1440s, Neuss in 1462, and the neighboring duchy of Jülich-Berg in 1461, the Jews did not completely disappear from the Cologne electorate. They continued to live in a number of smaller localities, inducing a church synod of 1452 to renew the old regulations concerning the badge. But no comprehensive legislation is recorded in the electorate until a completely new regime enacted it in 1599.[48]

Jews in Treves, too, speedily recovered from the shock of the First Crusade after Emperor Henry IV permitted those who had been forcibly baptized to return to the Jewish fold. Their history during the following century seems to have been less dramatic and, hence, less fully recorded, than that of their coreligionists in the other two episcopal electorates. An interesting early decree of 1215–19 contains some noteworthy provisions, such as that when a Jew was accused of breaking the peace outside the Jewish quarter he was to be hailed before the city sheriff. But if he succeeded in returning to the Jewish street he was responsible only to the episcopal treasurer serving as master of the Jewish community (*magister Judeorum*). The decree also goes into great detail concerning Jewish fiscal obligations. For example, the "Jew bishop" was expected to lend the archbishop annually 10 marks without interest. In return the archbishop was supposed to give the Jewish leader a cow, a pitcher of wine, two bushels of wheat, and an old coat which he himself "no longer wishes to wear." Yet enough animosities accumulated locally for the archbishop to expel the Jews in 1262 and to replace them with Lombard moneylenders. This was the more remarkable as the archepiscopal Treasury was then, as later, employing Jewish fiscal administrators. This first expulsion was evidently short-lived, for the Lombards charged even more exorbitant rates of interest. Two years later the same archbishop, jointly with Coblenz, admitted Jews to that city. By 1299 the Coblenz community had grown sufficiently wealthy to pay 300 marks annually to the Treasury. In 1309 Emperor Henry VII transferred to his brother, Archbishop Baldwin (1307–1354), to whom he largely owed his royal crown, the income from the Jews of various parts of the electorate. So important had this revenue become that, according to the historian Karl Lamprecht, it served as the basis for the whole accounting system of the Treasury, particularly under the administration of the Jewish court banker, Jacob Daniels (1336–41), and his son Michael (1341–45 or 1349). Nevertheless, like many of their coreligionists, the Treves Jews suffered from the Armleder massacre in 1339 and from those accompanying the Black Death in 1349.[49]

No sooner did the Jews begin to recover after Archbishop Cuno had made an agreement concerning them with the burghers of Treves, when in 1418 Archbishop Otto von Ziegenhain expelled them again. Before departing, the Jews were forced to deliver to the latter's officials all writs of indebtedness on Treves subjects. Yet communities seem to have persisted, at least in the rest of the electorate, for Emperor Frederick III included them with those of Mayence and Cologne in the order given in 1445 to his brother Albert to collect the coronation tax of one-third of their property. Similarly, twenty years later Frederick entrusted the protection of Treves Jewry, together with those of Mayence, Salzburg, and Besançon, to Count Ulrich of Württemberg. We also possess several certificates of admission of individual Jewish families in the years 1499–1540. On July 21, 1518, Archbishop Reichart even cited imperial privileges, confirmed by Maximilian I, which entitled him

freely to settle Jews coming from whatever lands, together with their property, in Our cities of Treves and Coblenz, and Our other fortresses and castles, as well as to maintain these Jews as Our and Our Chapter's property. [They also forbade the cities] to demand or solicit from the Jews any tax, impost, rent, gift or contribution, or to collect such by force, if they wished to avoid His Majesty's severe displeasure and some major financial penalties.

Nevertheless, the number of Jews thus admitted remained very small. A list issued by the then newly elected archbishop in 1547 mentioned only 34 Jewish heads of families residing in 19 different electoral localities. To such an extent had the atomization of the Jewish communities progressed! While this process must have seriously interfered with the development of Jewish communal and cultural life, it was at least a safeguard against total expulsions, which continued locally in the sixteenth century. These intolerant edicts are as a rule recorded, however, only in connection with exceptions granted to individual Jews and their families. In the city of Treves, too, a residual community seems to have carried on until it received a new privilege in 1555, renewed in 1679.[50]

## OTHER BISHOPS

Perhaps nowhere did the inconsistencies of imperial policy play greater havoc with the legal status of Jews than in the two other ancient communities of Worms and Spires. Emerging severely weakened from the first three crusades, they carried on valiantly, and Worms in particular remained an important center of Jewish learning. Among its distinguished rabbis were Baruch b. Meir and his son, Meir (better known from his residence in Rothenburg), as well as Jacob b. Moses Mölln (often cited under the abbreviation Maharil). One of Meir's responsa offers a noteworthy testimony to the anarchy prevailing during the long *Interregnum* and for some time thereafter. The Jewish court of Spires had permitted a member of the community forcibly to break into the house of a recalcitrant debtor and to seize some possessions in satisfaction of the debt. Pointing out that the Talmud had permitted such self-help only for the vindication of particular objects unlawfully appropriated, R. Meir censured his Spires colleagues for their unduly broad interpretation of the talmudic provision. Later, too, the Worms community was not seriously impeded by Bishop Emmerich's unusual decree of 1312 reserving for himself the appointment of its official head. Although with the aid of the burghers it successfully resisted the bishop's efforts also to appoint the entire communal board, it chose as the lesser evil the latter's self-perpetuation, which sharply contrasted with the more democratic methods of election in other German communities. It had to promise, moreover, to pay the bishop 20 pounds annually for the confirmation of these elders; in 1439 this contribution was converted into a regular tax.[51]

Far more disturbing, however, were the contradictory claims to overlordship over both communities by kings, bishops, and cities.

Louis the Bavarian (as well as Charles IV) was particularly responsible for that confusion. After mortgaging the Spires Jews with the bishop on January 13, 1315 until the repayment of his substantial debt, Louis turned around fourteen months later and assured the Spires burghers that he had no intention of infringing on their rights. Perhaps to underscore his good will, he increased the city's Jewish revenue from 300 to 400 pounds. On the same day he also extended a similar privilege to the burghers of Worms. All of this did not prevent him, however, in 1335, from mortgaging the same Spires and Worms Jews (together with those of Ladenburg) with his cousin, Rupert I of the Palatinate, as security for a reward of 5,200 pounds heller. True, the emperor specified that the mortgage applied only to Jewish revenues not otherwise committed, but such clauses were rarely respected by powerful creditors. Four years later Louis again mortgaged the Jews of Spires to Rupert for a loan of 2,000 pounds, this time with the approval of Bishop Gerhard. In 1346 Louis gave Rupert still another mortgage on the Jews of Spires and Worms, first for six years and then until its revocation. To double that confusion, in 1338 Louis himself confirmed the right of the Spires bishop to collect 700 pounds annually from Jews. He and other emperors also mortgaged some Jewish revenue from the same communities with individual burghers, particularly with the family Ebelin of Spires. Nor did they respect the territorial boundaries, as when in 1330 Louis assigned to a Worms burgher, Hanemann, 58 pounds annually from the revenue of the Jews of Spires. Independently, the Jews secured from Bishop Gerhard and the city pledges of protection for ten years in return for an annual contribution of 500 and 300 pounds, respectively (December 10–11, 1339). Some four weeks later the bishop himself confirmed an agreement between the municipality and the Jewish community, in which the latter acknowledged the receipt of 1,100 pounds from the city and promised to pay back 100 pounds annually. Another most remarkable compact was made in 1324 by the Spires bishop, Emich, its city council, and the local burgher, Henry of Cologne, concerning the portions of royal revenue from the local Jews respectively assigned to them. The beneficiaries allotted various amounts to Henry and two women named in the document, after which the city council was to receive up to 300 pounds, and the bishop 525 pounds. From a possible surplus the bishop was to collect an additional 225 pounds, while the balance was to be divided equally among the three parties.[52]

These complicated financial transactions are described here at some length because they graphically illustrate the great difficulties confronting the Jewish communities in their relations with their diverse overlords. The effects of such rash attempts to alleviate momentary stringencies were felt for many generations. As late as 1561 they led to a protracted conflict between the bishop and the burghers of Worms, in which the emperor himself ultimately had to take a hand. Unlike the earlier litigations in Cologne and Mayence, this trial before the royal commission lasted for several decades, with each party citing detailed documents to prove its authority over the Jews. It was not seriously interrupted even by the illegal riot and expulsion of Jews from Worms in 1615, being resumed after the Jews returned there within a few months. Less enduring was the Jewish settlement of Spires, which had not only suffered from local riots in 1282 and 1343, but whose inhabitants had nearly all fallen prey to frenzied mobs during the Black Death of 1349. Although the city first had to compromise with the new holders of the Jewish property—and after a protracted controversy with Palatine Rupert had in 1353 to recognize his superior control over its Jewry—the municipal council decided in 1352 to readmit Jews and take them under the city's "peace and protection." Notwithstanding a decree of their banishment promulgated in 1405 and the subsequent threat of rebellious peasants in 1432 to attack the city if their Jewish debts were not canceled, the Jews survived there until their final expulsion in 1435.[53]

Würzburg Jewry, too, suffered greatly during the Second Crusade (the massacre of 1147 happens to be the first reliably recorded fact of its communal life), but it recovered rather speedily and enjoyed imperial protection under Frederick Barbarossa. As late as 1234, King Henry VII, substituting for Frederick II, confirmed its privileges by taking the Jews, together with the burghers and the clergy, under his protection. Voluntarily Jews

contributed some funds also to the episcopal Treasury. The situation changed under the energetic bishop, Hermann I von
Lobdeburg (1225–54), to whom the royal pretender Henry
Raspe, in recognition of the bishop's services during the electoral
campaign, mortgaged the Würzburg Jews for 2,300 marks in 1247.
On the other hand, the burghers of Würzburg tried to appropriate
certain Jewish revenues and, in reaction to the Blood Accusation
of Fulda, staged riots against the Jews for years after the event,
despite the intervening condemnation of the ritual murder libel
by Frederick II and Innocent IV. These riots called forth a direct
papal intervention in Würzburg in 1253. But it was not until 1261
that the new bishop, Iring von Rheinstein (1254–66), reached an
agreement with the burghers, who promised not to molest the
Jews. That promise was quickly broken, when the populace rioted
against the bishop himself in 1265. But soon thereafter the bishop's partisans, Jewish and Christian, were permitted to return
from their exile, the burghers promising to allow them "to enjoy
their honors and liberties." An important step forward was made
in 1281, when the Jewish community paid the bishop 1,200
pounds heller in return for a reduction of its annual taxes to 1,000
pounds for ten years. The bishop also promised to protect the Jews
against undue demands from either the emperor or the city council and, whenever needed, to provide them with passes to other
places of residence. This agreement was partly nullified, however,
by the reassertion of imperial supremacy under Rudolph I. Although severely suffering from the Rindfleisch massacres in 1298
—for the 800 Würzburg names (in addition to those of 100 visitors) enumerated in the "Nuremberg Memorbook" constitute the
largest number of victims of any community included in that list
—the Jews recuperated quickly and Würzburg became an even
more important center of Jewish life than it had been before. In
1336 Pope Benedict XII canceled all debts owed to Jews by Bishop
Otto, even demanding that they hand over the latter's deeds of indebtedness. Otherwise, the pope threatened, he would forbid all
intercourse between Christians and Jews. Nevertheless, the bishop
continued to do business with Jews. Among the latter's debtors
was Queen Elizabeth, Albert I's wife, who borrowed 60 pounds
from them in 1308. Here, too, Louis and Charles IV proved quite

generous toward both bishop and city, particularly after the destruction of the community in 1349, when Charles donated all the remaining Jewish property to the bishop.[54]

Jews soon began returning to Würzburg and, in recognition of the bishop's assistance at the election of his son Wenceslaus, Charles IV specifically authorized the new bishop, Gerhard von Schwarzburg, to admit Jews to his diocese. In the early fifteenth century the Würzburg community again played a major role in the destinies of German Jewry. An interesting controversy in 1406 between the energetic Bishop Johann I von Egloffstein (1400–1411) and a Rabbi Süsslein, whom he had brought to the city, had wide repercussions. Süsslein fled to Frankfort, whose council was requested by the bishop "with all the urgency and seriousness" not to let him stay there, for "he had grossly offended Us and had spoken and written against Our honor." The bishop secured a similar order to the council from King Rupert, who also demanded from all imperial Jewry that it banish Süsslein and have no dealings with him until he gave full satisfaction to the bishop. On the other hand, the archbishop of Mayence asked Frankfort to leave Süsslein unharmed. The conflict ended by a compromise and Süsslein's return to Würzburg. About the same time Rupert extended his special protection to Levy (Lewe) Colner, head of the Würzburg community. In 1415 Sigismund even tried, without success, to employ Levy as the chief tax collector for all German Jewry; similar attempts by the emperor to employ other Würzburg Jews after 1420 proved equally ineffective. In 1422 Bishop John II von Brunn (1411–32), whose regime, ever short of funds, marked a critical period in the destinies of the bishopric, made a compact with the bishop of Bamberg and two margraves of Brandenburg for the imprisonment of all Jews and the confiscation of their property. Although this danger was averted in Würzburg by the payment of a huge ransom of 60,000 florins, many Jews left the city. Another danger loomed under the administration of Gottfried IV von Limburg (1443–55), a genuinely pious man, who tried gradually to rebuild the weakened Jewish community, but he soon found himself exposed to severe anti-Jewish pressures from the papal legates, Nicolaus Cusanus and John Capistrano. Reluctantly, Gottfried at first decided to expel the

Jews in 1453, characteristically without expecting any direct bene-fit to himself. But he noted that, at the request of Frederick III, Pope Nicholas V had overruled his legates and annulled some of the most threatening conciliar decisions aimed at Austria and Nuremberg. Apparently, with Frederick's aid, Gottfried secured from the pope a similar bull for Würzburg Jewry; it was formally promulgated by Nicholas' successor, Calixtus III, on April 20, 1455, nineteen days after Gottfried's demise. More decisive was the anti-Jewish compact entered into by Bishop Rudolph II von Scherenberg (1466–95) with the margraves of Brandenburg and the city of Nuremberg in 1488. Yet some Jews remained after the ensuing decree of banishment, and it was not until 1567 that, with Emperor Ferdinand II's permission, Jews were definitively ex-pelled from Würzburg.[55]

Closely akin to the developments in Würzburg were those in the bishopric of Bamberg. Here, too, the origins of the Jewish com-munity are shrouded in legends such as the story of the miraculous healing of a Jewish boy by the relics of St. Kunigund, which allegedly took place in 1033 but was probably fabricated in 1200 on the occasion of Kunigund's canonization. However, the com-munity of Bamberg was sufficiently well established before the First Crusade for Antipope Clement III to address to its bishop his oblique attack on Henry IV's permission for the forced Jewish converts of 1096 to "relapse" to their former faith. Some seventy years later Benjamin of Tudela found there "many wealthy and learned Jews." Thenceforth, notwithstanding occasional excesses, Jews lived rather peaceably as scholars, merchants, and money-lenders under the bishop's protection. In his code of laws of 1348, Bishop Frederick von Hohenlohe actually contended "that not even the emperor-king . . . has any rights, authority or domin-ion in this locality or city of Bamberg . . . over burghers or Jews . . . but only the aforementioned bishop or his successors." Understandably, the emperors ignored such usurpation of power and in a decree of July 24, 1347 Charles IV promised the Bamberg Jews his royal protection against any future annulment of debts owed them (Jews evidently feared a repetition of Henry VII's cancellation confirmed by Louis the Bavarian in 1332). Two years later, after the tragedy of the Black Death, Charles assigned the

Jewish possessions to the bishop, who divided the spoils with the burghers. In 1400 some newly settled Jews secured a comprehensive privilege from the bishop, which did not prevent their lord from joining hands with the bishop of Würzburg and the margraves of Brandenburg in signing the aforementioned compact of 1422 to expel and never to readmit them to the entire Franconian region. The Jews successfully weathered this storm and also the harsh anti-Jewish provisions enacted by the church synod which met at Bamberg under the presidency of Nicolaus Cusanus in 1451. They fared less well in 1478. Bishop Georg von Schaumberg, who had refused five years earlier to enter a similar alliance with Nuremberg and Margrave Albert III Achilles of Brandenburg, changed his mind under the impact of the Blood Accusation of Trent and banished the Jews from all his lands. If they did not entirely vanish from that region, this was owing to the numerous enclaves belonging to barons who failed to follow the bishop's lead. From these areas Jews soon returned to the city and remained there permanently, although they were threatened by several later decrees of expulsion, apparently enacted in order to secure some tactical advantages for the bishops rather than for definitive implementation.[56]

In the neighboring archbishopric of Salzburg, which extended into various Austrian and Bavarian districts (the bishops of Bamberg likewise had some enclaves in Styria and Carinthia), Jews were incidentally mentioned in connection with liturgical forms associated with the prayer *Pro perfidis Judaeis,* prescribed in the Salzburg *capitulare* of *ca.* 800, and with the alleged request of Archbishop Arno (798–821) that a friend send him a Jewish and a Slavonic physician. But reliable information flows only from the thirteenth century on, when we find Jews settled not only in the city of Salzburg but also in several provincial localities (including two villages bearing the somewhat equivocal name of *Judendorf*). By 1284 they were sufficiently numerous and wealthy to contribute the substantial amount of 20 gold marks to the archepiscopal Treasury. Their growth was but slightly hindered by the antagonistic canons adopted by several Salzburg provincial synods. The municipal ordinance of 1368 merely restated the old sanction of capital punishment for relapsed converts, doubtless reiterated

now because of the frequency of such relapses among forced converts of the Black Death era. In the fifteenth century, however,
governmental chicaneries and popular attacks multiplied rapidly.
Even the intervention of Emperor Frederick III, who had entrusted Count Ulrich of Württemberg with the protection of the
Salzburg Jews, proved of no avail. Finally, in 1498, the ruthless
and tricky Archbishop Leonhard von Keutschach (1495–1519)
not only banished the Jews from all his territories but also made
them individually sign the following pledge:

We swear and promise, by the true oath and conscience of our Judaism,
that neither we nor any of our heirs, friends, or anyone else from among
us will at any future time endeavor or, in any fashion, attempt to look
for a domicile in any of the lands, dominions, bailiwicks, shires, cities,
markets, villages, hamlets or [other] possessions belonging to our grac-
ious Lord of Salzburg . . . or any of his princely successors.

They further promised that they would seek no redress for their
losses by suing any archepiscopal officials for wrongdoings during
that expulsion and expropriation. Evidently, Maximilian I, who
had approved the expulsion of the Jews from neighboring Styria
two years earlier, could not stop the archbishop from carrying out
his design, which spelled the end of Jewish settlement in this entire area for some three centuries.[57]

Situated at the other end of the Empire, the important
bishopric of Strasbourg extended its dominion over large parts of
Alsace and territories later incorporated into Baden and other
adjacent states. The destinies of these Jewish communities, in part
reaching back to the Carolingian age, differed from those of many
other bishoprics inasmuch as the city of Strasbourg had, after a
prolonged struggle, achieved almost total independence in the
middle of the thirteenth century. Beginning in 1263, the fate of
the Jewish community there rested with the city fathers and city
mobs, rather than with the will of bishop or emperor, neither of
whom, however, completely gave up his Jewish rights. In the rest
of the bishopric, however, decisions by the bishop or diocesan
chapter still were decisive, although they too were often determined by varying local and national pressures.

Records for the early Jewish settlements in the bishopric of
Strasbourg are rather sparse. Its major community was seriously

threatened in 1146 by the anti-Jewish preachment of the Cistercian monk, Radulph, until he was restrained by St. Bernard of Clairvaux. Some two decades later Benjamin of Tudela counted it among the main German communities. From about the same time dates a remarkable Hebrew inscription recording the gift of five gold florins by a pious lady for the construction of a synagogue. Jews were at first treated more or less on a par with the burghers. The second Strasbourg municipal statute (*ca.* 1200) mentions that whenever the citizenry marched Jews were to furnish the flag, which seems to reflect some political and military cooperation on their part. During the following turbulent period, the bishop and city of Strasbourg joined, in 1254, a confederacy of West-German bishops, cities, and barons, who among other matters proclaimed a ten-year truce for Jews and the Christian clergy. Shortly thereafter, however, the raging conflict between bishop and city resulted in the transfer of all effective controls over Jews to the municipality, which in its preliminary peace treaty of 1262 merely pledged itself not to tax the Jews for a period of five years. At first the city treated them quite well, but in 1322 it forbade them to acquire real estate in the town or its immediate environs. Nor did it save them from sudden imprisonment in 1328 by the then newly elected Bishop Berthold von Bucheck (1328–54), or spare them the ransom of 6,000 marks exacted from them by the bishop to meet the heavy financial obligations incurred during his electoral campaign. Two years later both city and bishop were overruled by Louis the Bavarian, who took the Jews of Strasbourg under his direct protection in return for the then long-traditional annual payment of 60 marks. This pledge (confirmed by Charles IV in 1347) was reinforced by another regional compact in which the city participated, and by another privilege issued by the municipality in 1338. On the other hand, a blood libel in Mutzig in 1328 led to the expulsion of the local Jewry and its readmission by Bishop Berthold only after the payment of 2,000 marks. Ten years later the Jews of Ruffach and other communities suffered severely from the spread of the Armleder movement.[58]

All these misfortunes were overshadowed by rumors about the approaching Black Death. Although the municipal officials tried hard to protect the Jews, the entire Jewish community, allegedly numbering 2,000 souls, except for some voluntary converts and children forcibly baptized, suffered death "for the sanctification of the name" of the Lord. Having found in the synagogue a *shofar* (horn) used by the worshipers during services on New Year and the Day of Atonement, the hostile crowd readily believed that Jews intended to use it for signals to approaching enemies of Strasbourg. The Cathedral authorities ordered two horns to be cast in bronze and blown every evening to remind the population of this alleged act of treason, a practice which continued down to the French Revolution. Nevertheless, the Jews were readmitted to the city in 1369 on the basis of temporary agreements with the municipal council. The last such compact was dated in 1384 and was to last for six years. (The Jews were made to pay in three years the full amount stipulated for the entire period.) Curiously, by 1377 the bishop's authority in Strasbourg had sunk so low that when he wished to punish two Jews for their alleged assault on a cleric he had to fall back on his purely canonical prerogative of placing the culprits under a Church anathema. He used the traditional canonical phraseology that the Jews were "enemies of the Christian Cross who, through their own guilt, have been subjected to perpetual serfdom and whose life [among the Christians] has been accepted and maintained [only] by Christian mercy. These ungrateful men have repaid the Christians with contumely for grace, with contempt for friendliness." However, this ban was probably no more effective than a similar proclamation made in 1319 by a provost of Freiburg on the order of Pope John XXII. One of the newly settled Jews, Magister Gutleben, was hired by Strasbourg to serve as its physician until 1390. Nonetheless, the community was banished again in 1388. Many refugees settled in neighboring hamlets, and in the course of the following generations some of their descendants were allowed to trade in the city but not to live in it. Jews persisted also in the rest of the bishopric until 1440, when the bishop left it to the discretion of the cities of Molsheim and Zabern to decide whether they wished to keep their Jewries. In 1472 Jews were expelled from Ruffach, and in 1479 from the rest of the bishopric. While some Jews began drifting back in the following decades, several other decrees, culminating in two imperial enactments of 1514 and 1515, put an end to the legalized

Jewish sojourn in Strasbourg almost to the eve of the French Revolution.[59]

Further north was the archbishopric of Magdeburg, where Jews had settled in the Ottonian period (965, 969, 973). It was an important center of Germany's trade with Slavonic Europe, and it was to exercise considerable influence also on the legal relations of the East-European Jews in the following centuries. We first hear about its Jewish settlements again in 1184, when Archbishop Wichmann donated to a newly founded monastery the two marks he had been receiving annually from the community of Halle. In 1207 the Halle populace attacked the Jewish quarter and expelled the Jews, an unlawful act for which the city had to pay Archbishop Albert II an indemnity of 10,000 marks. During the war between Emperor Otto IV and the archbishop six years later, the "Judendorf" of Magdeburg was destroyed. But Jews remained, and apparently were prospering in both Halle and Magdeburg when Archbishop Robert (1260–66) followed the example of other monarchs and tried to pay off some heavy debts by large-scale confiscation of Jewish property and the seizure of wealthy Jews for ransom. This operation of 1261 succeeded in the city of Magdeburg, whereas the Halle burghers resisted fiercely. After a siege of the city, the affair ended with a substantial loss of Jewish property which, for both cities, is exaggeratingly estimated at a total of 100,000 silver marks. Despite this financial bloodletting, however, Jews continued to prosper; in 1287 the abbot of Bergen allegedly sold them his large church bell and other ecclesiastical property.[60]

More significantly, the Jews of the archdiocese, aided by the archbishop and the city council of Magdeburg, weathered the storm of 1349 with fewer losses than elsewhere. Magdeburg actually attracted some Jewish survivors from other parts of Germany and soon thereafter (1361–67) a Jew named Schmoll (Samuel) served as the archbishop's court banker. On the other hand, the Jews of Halle (who apparently had temporarily left the city after the great fire of 1312) suffered severely in 1349, the archbishop handing their quarter over to the city two years later. But he reserved his rights over future Jewish settlers, who before long began rebuilding their community. In Magdeburg, too, a serious anti-Jewish disturbance in 1384 led to a temporary decree of expulsion, but after the payment of 1,000 silver marks to the archbishop and 500 to the city council the Jews were almost immediately reinstated. The legal status of Magdeburg Jewry was placed on a firmer foundation by a privilege extended to them by Archbishop Günther in 1410 for a period of six years. Noteworthy are its provisions that misdeeds of a single Jew should not be avenged on the whole community; that apart from a semiannual tax of 40 silver marks, Jews would not have to pay imposts other than some extraordinary taxes levied also from Christian subjects; and that foreign Jews "who would migrate to the synagogue or the cemetery of the local community" would be given protection. To be sure, within a year Günther tried to expropriate his Jews, but the burghers resisted and the affair ended with a compromise payment of 600 florins by the Jews. These relatively peaceful conditions (except for another Halle riot of 1434, which again led to a temporary exodus of the Jews) did not, however, prevent the tragic dénouement later in the century. Like most other German cities the Magdeburg and Halle communities suffered from the anti-Jewish propaganda of John Capistrano and some less eminent preachers like Gerhard Dobler, whose incitation of the Halle populace led to still another temporary departure of the Halle Jews in 1458. These cumulative hostilities were brought to a final conclusion under the long reign of Archbishop Ernest of Saxony (1476–1513), by a decree of banishment in 1492–93. Although arising from a few trivial incidents, this decree ended all legal Jewish residence in the archbishopric for several generations.[61]

## PARTICULARISM VS. UNIVERSALISM

Such tales of woe can be repeated many times over in connection with the numerous other episcopal cities in late medieval Germany. Although members of the ecclesiastical establishment, the ruling bishops acted toward Jews, as toward other subjects, mainly as territorial lords trying to satisfy their states' or their personal needs. There was, in fact, little difference in principle between their behavior and that of the even more numerous secular princes who, whether electors of Germany or not, were likewise gaining an increasing measure of independence from the imperial Crown.

Bishops, to be sure, had to give consideration not only to the postulates of canon law and the wishes of ecclesiastical superiors up to the pope, but also to the regnant opinions among the clergy of their dioceses. If they happened to preside over a provincial synod, they could hardly prevent the majority from adopting resolutions, based upon canonical considerations or prevailing popular moods even if these ran counter to their avowed public policies. We have seen the awkward behavior of Archbishop Diethrich of Mayence during, and shortly after, the synod which met in his city in 1451. A similar embarrassment was undoubtedly caused to Diethrich's predecessor by the analogous resolutions adopted by an earlier Mayence council which met at Fritzlar in 1259. One or another archdiocesan chapter, moreover, claimed the right to be consulted before the archbishop made final arrangements with his Jewish subjects. Such a controversy arose, for instance, in Cologne in 1336, when Archbishop Walram had to expostulate with his colleagues that his confirmation of the Jewish privilege had been made in the best interest of the Church, since the funds secured from the Jews had alone helped him to redeem Church property pledged to outsiders which might otherwise have been lost to the diocese. True, within five years, Walram broke his promise of future consultations and, on his own, again renewed the Jewish privilege. Nonetheless, neither he nor any of his confreres could wholly disregard the wishes of their most intimate associates. More remarkably, when Archbishop Gerhard of Mayence compromised with the burghers in 1295 and issued a protective decree for the Jews, the Mayence chapter independently issued a similar decree in their behalf. However, truly decisive in the long run were the general considerations, fiscal, military, and political, also governing the decisions of the secular rulers.[62]

In this fashion the two great universalist establishments, Empire and Church, lost much of their universalism in their contact with harsh political and socioeconomic realities. Even the Papacy when ruling over the States of the Church in Italy or in France often had to pursue a *Realpolitik* conflicting with certain general approaches pursued by the Church universal. However, its focus essentially remained ecumenical and its interests far transcended the boundaries of its territorial possessions. In the case of the Empire, political considerations were always paramount; they became doubly so when imperial power was constantly whittled down by the operation of external and internal forces and when its bearers had to rely principally on their hereditary possessions as the mainstay of their authority. While the emperors never gave up their nominal claims to universal supremacy and its corresponding obligations, in practice these exalted claims were less and less respected outside Germany and also mattered less within the very imperial structure. The bishops, too, though owing their personal elevation and even the sovereignty of their states to their spiritual calling, in the ultimate sense had to act more or less like their secular counterparts. Styled "princes of the Church," they behaved much more as princes than as churchmen.

For Jews the growing particularism of the two universalist institutions could only lead to a deterioration of their status. We shall see how many difficulties the rising tide of European nationalism was to create for medieval and early modern Jewry. On a lesser scale, their difficulties manifested themselves also on a local and regional level. Their trials and tribulations were aggravated by the frequent lack of legal clarity and the definite separation of competences among conflicting authorities, particularly those of emperor, prince, and city. While alert individuals were thereby given the opportunity to play one force against the other and to maneuver themselves into positions of affluence, even eminence, the masses of Jewry necessarily suffered. Understandably, they were even worse off under secular princes or city councils whose particularist interests were even less limited by considerations for the universal weal.

In short, if one were to attempt any generalization, one might assert that, next to the emperors, the German hierarchy served as the chief and relatively most consistent protector of Jewry. Certainly the bishops rarely initiated, even though they did not always strongly enough resist, the popular pressures aimed at the total elimination of Jews from their bishoprics.

# XLI

# VICTIM OF FEUDAL ANARCHY

IN CONTRAST to the attitude of emperors and bishops, that of the secular princes and cities shows enormous variations. Side by side with some basic similarities and even an occasional community of action particularly in emergencies, it revealed significant dissimilarities ranging from fully equitable treatment with due attention to traditional Jewish modes of living to completely arbitrary legislative and administrative acts often leading up to total intolerance. True, the princes, barons, and cities usually paid lip service to the teachings of Christianity with respect to Jews. But in practice the polarity inherent in these very teachings gave them enough leeway to choose those which suited their needs or whims of the moment.

Jewish life under secular regimes thus became extremely unstable and unpredictable. The less effectively the emperors were able to intervene in their behalf, the more exposed the Jews became to alternating fits of tolerance and intolerance. Such extremes were characteristic of many of the lesser lordships which included the vast hereditary possessions of the imperial dynasties of Habsburgs and Luxembourgs down to tiny baronies forming but enclaves within larger areas dominated by mighty ecclesiastical or secular princes. The cities were as a rule very small when compared with modern towns. Yet their several thousand inhabitants often lost their sense of proportion and behaved as if they constituted major powers in their own right. Obviously, in decisive moments their weaknesses became quite apparent and they often had to band together in urban leagues in order to defend themselves against more powerful neighbors or even in order to exercise more effective dominion within their own walls. Jews often became pawns in that unending game of petty power politics, further aggravated by the internal class struggle, especially between the patrician and artisan classes.

Any attempt to try to sketch the historic evolution of even the more important centers of Jewish life in late medieval Germany would far transcend the bounds of this presentation. A mere enumeration of localities where Jews are known to have resided between 1200 and 1500 C.E. would require a disproportionate amount of space.[1]

We must restrict our analysis, therefore, to several larger and historically more influential principalities, as well as to certain major communities under the control of burghers. These will show enough variations from one another, as well as within themselves, to illustrate both the growing anarchy in German public life of the period and its macabre effects on Jewish life under their sway.

## HABSBURGS AND LUXEMBOURGS

Among the secular princes, there stood out the kings of Bohemia and the electors of the Palatinate, Saxony, and later Brandenburg, as well as the (arch)dukes of Austria who, without a seat in the electoral college, often enjoyed a special status. From Rudolph I on, the house of Habsburg took over Austria and the adjoining provinces as its hereditary possessions. Naturally, whenever a Habsburg was emperor the laws issued by him for his own territories were often invested with semi-imperial authority. When the imperial Crown was held by the house of Luxembourg, its private dominions in Bohemia and Moravia revealed a similar ambiguity. Only a few emperors clearly separated the postulated treatment of Jews in the Empire from their actual behavior toward the Jewish subjects in their own lands. Rupert of the Palatinate alone evinced little concern for that dichotomy, since shortly before his election as German king the Jews had been expelled from most of his possessions. On the other hand, Jewish destinies in nonelectoral Bavaria, ruled by another branch of the Wittelsbach family, were intertwined with those of the important Jewish communities within the Bavarian area such as Würzburg, Augsburg, Ratisbon, Nuremberg, and Ulm, whose effective authority rested with the bishops or city councils. Among the electorates, Saxony played the least important role in late medieval Jewish history, being overshadowed by the nonelectoral principalities to the north including Brandenburg, Mecklenburg, and Pomerania. Silesia long oscillated between Poland and Germany, and its internal divisions made for little consistency in the policies of its numerous duchies.

In Austria, we recall, the conflict between the imperial and ducal regulations of Jewish status had become manifest under the two Frederick IIs in 1238–44. If the imperial controls weakened during the *Interregnum*, this ambiguity was sharpened by Rudolph I's confirmation of the 1244 Austrian privilege as an imperial law. At the same time the emperor tried to enlist the good will of the cities by confirming some of their privileges, even where they ran counter to this general Jewish statute. Not only did he repeat in 1278 the Viennese prohibition of employing Jews in public office "lest they oppress the Christians," but he had in 1276 slashed the maximum interest rate allowed the Jews in Tulln by one-half (to 21⅔ percent), and in 1277 he renewed "the old custom" that the Jews residing in Laa an der Thaya "should not serve together with the other Jews," but rather that their services be included with those rendered by the burghers. Rudolph's successor, Albert I, pursued a relatively friendly policy, notwithstanding the growing popular hostility toward Jews because of the Blood Accusation of Krems in 1293 and several alleged desecrations of hosts. Albert reacted strongly. Just as in his capacity as emperor he imposed severe fines in 1298 on the cities of Würzburg, Nuremberg, and others which had tried to enrich themselves at the expense of Jewish victims of the Rindfleisch massacres, so he vigorously suppressed these spreading libels. Under his direction the bishop of Passau, Wernhard von Prambach (1285–1313), instituted a careful investigation which revealed that one of the accusations of host desecration was a pure fabrication by a cleric. Albert proceeded even more sharply against the city of St. Pölten in the Passau bishopric. Here Albert's son, Duke Rudolph, who soon thereafter ascended the royal throne of Bohemia, surrounded the city, threatening to level it to the ground and to build another in its vicinity. In 1306 he finally accepted an indemnity of 3,500 "talents." Many contemporaries must have realized, however, that both Albert and Rudolph were far more lenient with Austrian Korneuburg and other cities. Similarly equivocal was the position of Austrian Jewry under King Frederick I the Handsome, who on March 7, 1318 by virtue of his royal authority issued the first recorded letter of cancellation (*Tötbrief*) of a debt owed to a Jew. On the other hand, three months later (June 5) he ordered several officials to help Jews collect their claims from the nobles and other debtors. In general, he followed his predecessors in protecting Jewish rights and in upholding the principle that in their litigations with Christians Jews should repair only to a superior *iudex Judaeorum*, appointed by him, who presumably would be more impartial.[2]

After Frederick's death his successors in the Austrian possessions, Albert II (1330–58) and Otto the Joyous (1330–39), signed a peace treaty with his rival, Louis the Bavarian. In that treaty of 1330 and another decree of the following year, Louis included the promise that the Jews "will be left in the enjoyment of the rights and good usages which they have hitherto enjoyed from olden times until Our election." Under Albert II's regime the Armleder persecution extended to some provincial cities in Austria, where it was sustained by recurrent accusations of host desecration. However, the major communities of Vienna and Wiener Neustadt were protected by the concerted action of duke and city patricians. In recognition, the Jewish community of Vienna voluntarily pledged itself in 1338 to charge no higher interest than 3 pfennigs per pound a week, or approximately 65 percent, which was a substantial reduction from the generally permissible rates ranging from 86.66 to 173.33 percent. The Jewish elders declared in a remarkable Hebrew document:

Having noted the kindness of our City's respected citizens here in Vienna which they showed us at the time of our distress, and which they are willing to continue to show us, as we trust, by the favor of God and their own favor, we, freely and without compulsion, nay with our whole heart and willing spirit and full knowledge, have consented to make them this gift.

Albert, who confirmed that agreement, tried to put an end to the host libels once and for all by appealing to Pope Benedict XII, who in his bull *Ex zelo fidei* of August 29, 1338 promised a thorough investigation through the bishop of Passau. The outcome of this investigation is not recorded, but it stands to reason that had the Jews been condemned the chroniclers would not have failed to mention it. It is not surprising, therefore, that under Albert II's energetic reign even the pogromists of 1349 made little headway in Austria. Vienna in particular, though suffering severely from the pestilence, preserved her Jewish community fairly intact. The numerical losses sustained by the Jews owing to the contagion (the Jewish cemetery had to be enlarged on this score) were more than made up by refugees from other communities as well as by Hungarian exiles in the years 1352–61. Vienna thus became one of the largest Jewish communities in the Empire.[3]

The subsequent ducal regimes of Rudolph IV (1358–65), Albert III (1365–95), and Albert IV (1395–1404) basically maintained the policies established by their predecessors. The treaties of 1360 with Charles IV as king of Bohemia, in which the contracting parties promised not to raid one another's Jewries, confirmed the full overlordship of the Austrian dukes. With an excess of confidence Albert III sought in 1370 to alleviate his financial difficulties by suddenly ordering the imprisonment of all Austrian Jews and the confiscation of their property. This wholesale robbery seems to have proved less rewarding than expected. Within a few years, the duke reversed himself and tried to encourage Jewish trade and moneylending, promising not to issue any further letters of cancellation (1377). In 1397 Jews fleeing from persecution in Styria and Carinthia settled in Vienna and paid the Treasury the substantial amount of 16,000 pounds. While Albert IV added trade restrictions in certain Austrian cities and forbade Jews to practice medicine among Christians, the Jewish communities of Vienna and Wiener Neustadt continued to enjoy a modicum of prosperity. The former speedily overcame the disastrous effects of a fire of 1406 which, starting in the synagogue, practically demolished the entire Jewish quarter and opened the gates to a mob, including some university students, bent on pillage and destruction. A Jewish banker, David Steuss, whose business records have been preserved, belonged to the leading financial magnates of the Empire. Similarly, the Vienna and Wiener Neustadt rabbis included such illustrious names as Meir b. Baruch ha-Levi, Abraham Klausner, and Israel Isserlein, who exerted great spiritual influence on all Ashkenazic communities of their time. But the days of Austrian Jewry were counted. Under the reign of Albert V of Austria (1411–39; as Albert II king of Germany, 1438–39), the wave of intolerance sweeping the German cities during the fifteenth century reached Vienna, which in 1420–21 became the scene of wholesale execution of some 400 Jews and of the total banishment of the rest of the community except for a minority who had accepted baptism. This persecution stood out even within the sanguinary annals of contemporary German-Jewish history, and achieved a special renown under the name of the *Wiener Geserah.*[4]

Expulsion from Vienna and the rest of Albert V's dominions, though reconfirmed by his son Ladislaus Posthumus (1440–57) in two decrees of 1453 and 1455, by no means terminated Jewish settlement in Austrian provinces. In 1438 Albert himself granted a safe-conduct to a Jew. Other individual exceptions were made by Emperor Frederick III, while many lesser lords kept Jews in their localities. Even after their banishment from Wiener Neustadt in 1496 some smaller settlements remained in Lower Austria. Frederick in particular not only resisted reiterated demands by the Austrian Estates that no Jews be readmitted, but he also secured another papal bull, this time from the enlightened Pope Paul II (*Sedis apostolicae copiosa benignitas* of May 31, 1469) specifically addressed to the Austrian clergy, calling for their just treatment. Maximilian I, too, issued a number of permits for individual Jewish bankers and traders. Even regular Jewish communities continued after 1421, particularly in the provinces of Styria, Carinthia, and Carniola, quite apart from the bishoprics of Salzburg and Bamberg and their extensive enclaves in the other provinces. Jews had settled in many towns, including Graz, Marburg, Klagenfurt, and Carniola's Laibach (Ljubljana), their legal status being regulated by Austria's thirteenth-century legislation. While Frederick II's decree of 1244 had been limited to the province of Austria proper, Přemysl Ottakar II's similar privilege of 1254 extended over those provinces as well. If a question might have arisen concerning certain Styrian districts then occupied by the Hungarians, it was settled by Bela IV's reiteration in 1256 of his decree of 1251, which had followed the same Frederician pattern. Moreover, when Přemysl Ottakar reoccupied those districts in 1261, they became subject to his confirmation of his original broad privilege in 1268. This statute remained essentially unchanged after its reconfirmation under Rudolph I's imperial authority.[5]

Jewish moneylending and other commercial activities created resentment in various quarters and contributed to the people's gullibility concerning Jewish desecration of hosts and ritual murder. Those accusations gave rise in Styria and Carinthia, too, to anti-Jewish riots in 1310, 1338, and particularly in 1349. On the other hand, the legend that the Judenburg Jews were planning in 1312 to slay all Christians and that when this conspiracy was revealed by a Jewess to her Christian paramour all local Jews were killed, is more revealing of the popular state of mind than of any historical facts. Nevertheless, despite the additional instability created for Jewish moneylenders by unpredictable ducal letters of cancellation, the Jews of Styria and vicinity, when compared with those in most of the Empire, lived a rather sheltered life until the fifteenth century. At that time, however, they became the targets of increasing attacks both locally by aroused mobs and by the provincial Estates representing the upper classes. The cities resented, in particular, the exemption of Jews from local taxes because of their heavy direct tax liabilities to the Crown, their commercial competition, and the presence of special justices of Jews. Their concerted attacks finally induced Frederick III to issue, in the 1440s, a series of decrees which freed the burghers from any jurisdiction of Jewish courts, abolished compound interest, and reduced interest rates. The latter had, in any case, been dropping in the course of the century from the initially prevailing 86.66 percent to half or even a quarter of that figure. The Styrian population also used, to its advantage, a private but widely accepted legal compilation (before 1425), the so-called *Steiermärkisches Landrecht*, which included ten articles relating to Jews, seven of them lumped together in a separate section at the end of the volume. In 1478 Judenburg secured from the emperor the concession that all writs of indebtedness to Jews must be officially registered with the authorities; otherwise they would lose their validity—a regulation reminiscent of the English "chests" of the thirteenth century. Yet so long as Frederick lived, the Styrian burghers' repeated demands to eliminate the Jews entirely remained unfulfilled. Even the alleged local expulsion from Graz in 1439, at the transition of the reign from Albert to Frederick, is not supported by unequivocal documentary evidence. Only Maximilian I, for reasons which will be explained elsewhere, proved more pliable. His decrees of expulsion of 1496 and 1515 put an end to Jewish community life in Styria, Carinthia, and Carniola, with the exception of the Salzburg and Bamberg enclaves which shared the legal status of those two bishoprics. Thenceforth only a few hardy Jewish pioneers, returning with or without formal permits, maintained a measure of continuity of Jewish life there for several generations.[6]

Bohemia and Moravia had some of the oldest Jewish settlements in Slavic lands; Ibrahim ibn Ya'qub had met them in his travels there in the tenth century. Some Jews were even able to put up a stout resistance to their assailants during the First Crusade. Yet apparently no comprehensive legislation concerning them was enacted until 1254, when Přemysl Ottakar II paraphrased and somewhat enlarged the Austrian decree of 1244. At the same time he also confirmed Innocent IV's protective bull of 1253. In 1268 he renewed the privilege of 1254, emphasizing in the preamble that Jews "belong to Our Chamber" (*ad nostram cameram pertineant*)—the standard phrases of the older imperial charters. Although disavowed by Rudolph I, this decree influenced Rudolph's own legislation and remained the foundation stone of the legal structure of Bohemian Jewry in the subsequent centuries. It was formally confirmed by Wenceslaus II *ca.* 1300, Charles IV in 1348, Wenceslaus IV soon after his accession to the throne in 1378, Ladislaus in 1454, and remained in force under the Habsburgs, being reconfirmed by Ferdinand I in 1527.

Nevertheless, considerable room was left for arbitrary legislation and interpretation. John of Bohemia, who had been formally hailed by the Jews of Brünn (Brno) in 1311, not only collected (from Jews as well as Christians) 10,000 marks in Glatz and 12,000 in Breslau (1331), but he also ordered the Jews of Brünn to contribute one-quarter of the expense for the repair of walls and ditches (1333). Nor did he hesitate to interfere with Jewish religious institutions. In 1336 he ordered diggings in the old synagogue in Prague, and he declared the recovered treasure of 2,000 marks as a legitimate royal prize. According to the chronicle, John followed up this confiscation by the imprisonment of Jews "throughout his dominion" and the collection of a substantial ransom. He also allowed the municipal elders of Breslau to immure stones of the Jewish cemetery in the city walls (1345). At the same time, partially relinquishing Přemysl Ottakar's and his successors' insistence on the royal supremacy over Jews, John acknowledged, for example, the right of his Treasurer, Peter von Rosenberg, to settle four Jews on his estate "with all the liberties, utility and jurisdiction which might in some fashion belong to Us, Our successors and heirs" (1334). Understandably, such concessions led to numerous jurisdictional conflicts. When the sheriffs of the Silesian city of Neisse imprisoned a Jew, they evoked the protest of the Breslau bishop who claimed that all Neisse Jews belonged to the episcopal Chamber (1327). In effect, Jews often depended more on the good will of local authorities than on that of the Crown. In a characteristic decree of 1329, in which he confirmed the privileges of the newly acquired city of Görlitz, Silesia, John recommended the local Jews to the protection of the burghers. Some Bohemian Jewish communities (Časlav, Neuhaus [Jindrichuv Hradec], and Přichowitz) also suffered from the disturbances of 1337–38, while Kauřim Jewry was accused of the desecration of a host.[7]

Prague, however, largely escaped the brunt of the massacres of 1349 as well, although some individuals were murdered in both Prague and Eger, Charles IV dividing the spoils with the nobles. Speedily recovering, the Prague community assumed increasing significance, particularly through its cemetery, which served as a resting place for many provincial Jews. In 1357 Charles IV gave the community the right to display a flag of its own. Prague Jewry cherished this symbol of authority for several centuries and displayed it on many solemn occasions, such as the welcome extended to Ferdinand I in 1527. Next to the capital community, that of Kolin played a considerable role in the economic and intellectual history of Bohemian Jewry, and we are fortunate in possessing documents of the fourteenth century showing numerous real-estate transactions by the Kolin Jews in and outside their quarter. Neighboring Kuttenberg (Kutna Hora), however, an important mining town, admitted Jews only on market and court session days. As late as 1527 its city council ordered the imprisonment and seizure of all property of any Jews caught there at other times.[8]

Under Wenceslaus and his successors, including his half brother Sigismund, and the latter's son-in-law Albert and grandson Ladislaus Posthumus (1440–57), fiscal considerations dominated all relations with Jews. Wenceslaus, who, as we recall, twice canceled debts owed to German Jews, also ordered in 1384 and 1389 the imprisonment of many Jews in Prague and the confiscation of their property. In the latter year a massacre allegedly cost 3,000 Bohemian Jewish lives. Ten years later the denunciation of a Jewish convert, Pesaḥ-Peter, embroiled the Prague community in a serious religious controversy. Scores of Jews, including the distinguished Jewish apologist, Yom Ṭob Lipmann-Mühlhausen, were imprisoned and submitted to a searching investigation concerning the alleged blasphemies against Jesus contained particularly in the prayer, 'Alenu. Lipmann-Mühlhausen, it seems, successfully defended his own position (we possess his report on this subject in his major apologetic treatise) and was released. But he apparently could not save the other defendants, seventy-seven of whom were executed immediately and three more three weeks later. But there is no evidence for the direct involvement of either the king or the city council in this ecclesiastical prosecution.[9]

Wenceslaus, and still more Sigismund, realized the value of Jewish taxpayers. Yet the regime's extraordinary vagaries manifested themselves on numerous occasions, particularly under the weak and impulsive Wenceslaus, sometimes doubtless acting under the influence of liquor for which he displayed an inordinate fondness. Sigismund, too, permitted the temporary expulsion of Jews from Eger in 1430. Two decades later, under the impact of John Capistrano's mission, many Bohemian cities became the scenes of anti-Jewish disturbances; for instance, Skalitz (Skalica), in 1453. True, despite the vagaries of the individual monarchs, the basic law of Přemysl Ottakar II still remained in force. It was never repealed by his successors, although from the standpoint of medieval law one could argue that all laws unless renewed expired at the legislator's death. That such general provisions did not entirely safeguard Jewish rights, however, was clearly demonstrated by Ladislaus when, in 1454, but a few weeks after their confirmation, he permitted the city of Olmütz to banish the Jews and to take over all their possessions in return for a promise to pay the "king and his heirs and successors, the margraves of Moravia," 40 shock groschen annually. In the same and the following years, Ladislaus, or rather his advisers (he was only fourteen years old in 1454), also sanctioned the expulsion of the Jews from Brünn, Breslau (after a prolonged trial for an alleged desecration of a host), and other Silesian communities. In his decree of January 30, 1455 Ladislaus specifically ordered the council and burghers of Breslau "not to admit Jews to residence . . . for ever." [10]

Nor did the Jews, or for that matter the entire country, enjoy a more peaceful and stable existence under the succeeding Slavonic rulers, George Poděbrad (1458–71), a native Bohemian noble, Vladislav (1471–1516) of the Polish-Lithuanian Jagiellon dynasty, and his son Louis (1516–26). George, although ever after fondly remembered as a distinguished ruler by his Bohemian compatriots, could not overcome the combination of external hostility and sharp inner divisions. Vladislav, especially after his election to the Hungarian throne in 1490, altogether despaired of bringing order into the chaotic conditions of his Bohemian territories. In the struggle between the Hussites, themselves plagued with endless internal dissensions, and the pro-Roman party; the drive for mastery of the growingly powerful nobles who likewise often fought hard against one another; the quest of the burghers to maintain and, if possible, enlarge their municipal autonomy; and the hopeless efforts of the masses of peasantry to maintain their traditional liberties against ever expanding villeinage, Jews became the objects of violence and extortion from all sides. When Louis, upon his arrival in Prague in 1522, deposed the overbearing supreme burgrave, Zdeněk Leo of Rožmital (Rosenthal), the latter's theretofore strong controls over, and revenue from, Jews were immediately taken over by the municipality. But no sooner was he reinstated by the king in 1525 than he, too, began reasserting his authority over the Jews. More orderly conditions were established only when, after the death of Louis in the great battle of Mohács in 1526, Ferdinand (later Emperor Ferdinand I) reincorporated the country into the Habsburg dominions, whose destinies it shared during the following four centuries.

Royal weakness came clearly to the fore in such incidents as when George Poděbrad admitted several Jewish individuals to settlement in Eger in 1462, promising them, in return for an annual payment of 150 Rhenish florins, the enjoyment of all rights of the other Jewish serfs of his Chamber. Yet seven years later a local lord, Henry von Gera, had to appeal to the Eger city council not to confiscate the Jewish communal property in which his subjects had a share. In 1480 the elders of Eger unabashedly rejected King Vladislav's request that they continue to tolerate Jews. Moreover, the diets, now dominated by the lords of the kingdom, began issuing decrees seriously interfering with the established Jewish rights. Apart from imposing a new tax on the Jews, the Diet of 1487 threatened with severe punishment Christians advancing money to Jewish moneylenders for a share in the latter's usurious gains. This threat was clearly aimed at some leading statesmen, considered silent partners of Jewish lenders, whom they also helped in other ways; they were powerful enough to disregard the Diet's wishes in this matter. In 1494 another session insisted that Jews lend only on pawns, but not on more confusing writs of indebtedness. That hostile Diet also abrogated the old protective laws for Jewish *bona fide* purchasers of, or pawnbrokers on, stolen objects by demanding their return to the owners without compensation, unless the thieves were named. These regulations affected numerous individuals, for although the Bohemian Jews pursued many other occupations, their moneylending played an increasingly significant role in the fifteenth century. Lists recording the names of the Jewish lenders in Prague in 1497–1500 are still extant.[11]

Such emotional reaction by the diets, of course, could not satisfy society's basic needs of Jewish credit. What the influential Bohemian statesman Wilhelm von Bernstein was to write to his son a few decades later was equally true at the end of the fifteenth century. Referring to a projected ordinance that all Jewish loans must first be registered at court, he contended that it would ruin the peasant population. He disclaimed any particular interest in the Jewish lenders and stated:

I am writing in favor of my subjects whom I have at my vineyards and who would have to leave those vineyards if these regulations were to be

carried into effect. In Blučin they owe the Jew Faitl alone 400 schocks
[coins varying in value from 2 to 7 shillings]. When their crop had
failed he had pity with them and took no money from them. When our
Lord will give us better times they will be able to help themselves. In
contrast thereto some priests and burghers have lent on my estate this
year 5 schocks on a 10-bucket [*Eimer*] barrel of wine. . . . On other
estates they occasionally lent only 4 schocks. This appears to me to be
three times the rate of usury charged by Jews.

It was in response to similar complaints from Jews and non-Jews
that King Vladislav decreed, in 1497, that a Jew should be allowed
to charge twice as high a rate of interest as a Christian, because of
the numerous taxes he was paying and also because this was his
main source of livelihood. In 1499 the king ordered his officials to
protect the Jews, placed Prague Jewry under the jurisdiction of
the court judge, and entrusted all provincial Jews to the supervision of the deputy treasurer. These protective devices, though in
part supported by the Diet of 1501, did not prevent local expulsions of Jews such as those from Pilsen in 1504, and from Budweis
in 1503–1505. (Jews had originally been admitted to that city by
King John in 1341 in order to alleviate the discomfort of its inhabitants who theretofore had to secure loans from residents of
other communities.) In 1509–1510 the administration took under
advisement the possibility of expelling the Jews from the whole
country. This measure was not adopted, but even the subsequent
Habsburg regime could not prevent further local expulsions in the
following decades. It is truly amazing how, under these harrow-
ing conditions, Prague was able to develop into a major center of
Jewish learning which soon also influenced the unparalleled expansion of rabbinic schools in neighboring Poland. Its great eminence, to be sure, was not to be reached until the sixteenth
century. But as early as the 1400s the community could boast of a
number of prominent rabbis and scholars.[12]

## OTHER LEADING PRINCES

Among the multitude of greater and lesser feudal lordships the
three secular electorates of the Palatinate, Saxony, and Brandenburg stood out. The latter joined the ranks of the superior princes
relatively late, but by ultimately developing into the kingdom of

Prussia it gradually became, next to the Habsburgs, the leading power in the Holy Roman Empire. Together with the three arch-bishops of Mayence, Cologne, and Treves, and the kings of Bohemia, these electors formed the electoral college which not only elected each successive emperor but had an important share in the administration of the Empire, especially since the Golden Bull of 1356. In their own territories the electors were to all in-tents and purposes independent princes. In Jewish affairs, in par-ticular, their full autonomy was explicitly safeguarded by the Golden Bull. Their example was emulated by many lesser lords, who behaved in their possessions as if they were absolutely sovereign.

Within the space of this chapter, the evolution of Jewish com-munities under the lesser powers had to be limited largely to the areas of the free cities, which often served as major foci of Jewish economic and cultural activity. Only the developments in north-eastern Germany, as represented especially by Mecklenburg as well as Brandenburg, had to be given special attention because of the gradual shift of the Jewish center of gravity from the Rhine-lands to those areas and to the Habsburg hereditary possessions. Mention also had to be made of the large territory under the control of the Wittelsbach dynasty, those perennial rivals of the Habsburgs, whose highly divided controls extended over Upper and Lower Bavaria as well as the Palatinate.

In Bavaria Jews were first recorded in the Raffelstetten toll ordinance of 906. Subsequently they spread through most of the cities and hamlets of its several duchies with their ever changeable frontiers and inner divisions. In the important city of Landshut, for example, capital of a special subdivision later called Lower Bavaria, the Jews were found from its very foundation in 1204. According to one chronicler, they actually helped to build the city; their quarter, recorded later, was immediately adjacent to the castle. A curious ordinance of 1256 provided that meat of diseased animals should be sold, together with Jewish meats, at a distance of at least seven feet from the regular butcher shops. In Munich Jews reputedly settled in 1210 and acquired a cemetery of their own in 1225. In 1244 Duke Otto II the Illustrious (1231–53) con-cluded with several bishops, counts, and nobles a three-year truce providing, among other matters, that no Christian be entitled to charge interest except to Jews. A similar truce was concluded by his son, Duke Henry I of Lower Bavaria, in 1255, except that here Jews also were limited to an interest rate of 2 pfennigs per pound a week or 43.33 percent. In general, the power of the Wittelsbach dukes increased considerably during the following century, but they were unable to protect their Jews against either the Rind-fleisch or the Armleder pogromists. In 1338 Duke Henry II (1310–39) was actually forced not only to grant a total amnesty to the burghers of Straubing, but he also canceled all their debts to Jews and allowed them to keep the seized Jewish property. A similar local cancellation of debts was granted to the city of Weissenburg by Charles IV in 1350, after the massacres of the Black Death era following the more quiescent period under the seven-year reign of Emperor Louis the Bavarian, who had suc-ceeded in temporarily reunifying Bavaria. No less severely affected by the Black Death were the budding communities of the Palati-nate, many martyrs being recorded in the various *memor* books. Here, however, coregent Rupert I (1329–53, sole palatine 1353–90), with whom Charles IV in 1346 had mortgaged his reve-nue from the Jews of Spires and Worms for six years, saved some refugees from these two communities by admitting them to Heidelberg.[13]

After the catastrophe, Rupert, whose long reign secured for his dominion an unwonted measure of stability, attracted many other Jewish settlers through favorable privileges. In one letter of pro-tection, still extant, he promised the recipient free sojourn in Heidelberg for the annual fee of 5 florins, with the stipulation that, after paying "that annual impost, he may depart wherever he wishes and Our official will provide him with safe-conduct" (*ca.* 1355). In 1362 Rupert took the Jewish physician, Gottlieb, into his services and freed him from all Jewish taxation. The same privilege was extended to a rabbi, Isaac of Bingen, who had resided in Mayence. With Rupert's general encouragement of Jewish autonomy, the small communities of the Palatinate formed a federation in 1381 which was promised not to be assessed more than 600 florins in the following three years. The ruler's ex-ample was followed by local authorities, the University of Heidelberg, for instance, forbidding students in 1387 under severe penalties to molest "the property or person of any burgher or, for that matter, of any Jew." Rupert even invited into his realm in 1367 a number of Jewish lepers, that most despised and feared yet quite numerous class in the Middle Ages. Although charged with very high fees for admission (the first leper was to pay 200 florins annually, his confreres 25 florins each) and told to live apart from their healthy compatriots, with whom they were to maintain no contacts whatsoever, the unfortunates found here a modicum of peace and security. These promising developments were cut short, however, by the demise of Rupert I in 1390. His nephew and successor, Rupert II (1390–98), speedily reversed his policies and in 1391 banished all Jews and confiscated their possessions. He sold many Jewish houses and donated the Heidelberg synagogue to the University. Within a few months this Jewish house of worship was converted into a Christian chapel by the bishop of Worms in a solemn ceremony attended by the palatine and his son, the future king of Germany, as well as by many professors.[14]

If Jews did not completely disappear from the Palatinate, this was owing not to any major change of governmental policy but rather to the country's expansion and its incorporation of several established Jewish communities, such as that of Oppenheim. These Jewish settlements were allowed to carry on. Simultaneously, the other Bavarian dukes largely followed the example of Rupert I, though somewhat more hesitantly, and tried to attract Jews to their areas. In 1375 and 1380, Duke Frederick of the Landshut line granted them extensive privileges, providing especially that foreign Jews not pay higher customs duties for their merchandise than did Christians. In 1377, he permitted the city of Biberach to admit Jews freely. Six years later, together with two other dukes he insisted that the city of Donauwörth treat its present and future Jewish settlers like other burghers and that, if later dukes should withdraw their toleration, the Jews be given a one-year notice. Yet Frederick himself readily became the beneficiary of Wenceslaus' cancellation of Jewish debts in 1390—although in the following year the king had to threaten the Bavarian Estates that failure to deliver the required 15 percent to the imperial Treasury would make them liable for the full amount of the original debt. In 1401, moreover, Dukes Ludwig and Hans promised their father King Rupert (of the Palatinate) that they would neither allow Jews to reside in their castles nor suffer any underlings to admit new Jews. Not surprisingly, therefore, most Bavarian dukes actively participated in the general banishment of Jews from one section or city in Bavaria after another. Duke Henry of Landshut (1393–1450), to be sure, continued to admit Jews and even confirmed their privileges. But his widely known rapacity (he had special sleeves on his garments so that all petitioners and visitors could conveniently drop their gifts there) deprived his benevolence of its possible moral effects. His son Louis IX, the Rich (1450–79), at the beginning of his reign expelled the Jews from Lower Bavaria. Even earlier Albert the Pious of Munich (1440–60), likewise reversing the policies of his predecessors, had banished them from all of Upper Bavaria (1442). Subsequently, these and other dukes allowed the cities of Eichstädt and Passau to remove their Jews in 1477–78, just as they did not oppose the more famous decrees of banishment secured, despite many obstacles, by the cities of Nuremberg in 1498 and Ratisbon in 1519. Finally in 1551 Jews were expelled from the whole country, Albert V (1550–79), son-in-law of the Habsburg King Ferdinand I, even exacting a pledge from Josel of Rosheim that, in return for the liberation of four imprisoned Jews, their coreligionists would promise never to set foot again in Upper or Lower Bavaria. This decree was confirmed by the Land Ordinance of 1553, in which the Jews were designated as "pernicious elements." [15]

Compared with these larger countries of Jewish settlement, the electorate of Saxony had few Jews outside its major bishoprics and free cities, including Magdeburg, Halle, Halberstadt, and Erfurt. These and other territories in Thuringia, Meissen, and vicinity were now embraced under the general designation of Saxony, whose area was gradually shifting from west to east. Reference has already been made to the developments in Magdeburg, Halle, and Erfurt; the latter will be mentioned again in this chapter. After the resettlement following the Black Death massacres, Erfurt belonged to the most populous German-Jewish communities. Halberstadt generally followed the patterns of the other German bishoprics. In all these localities the electors' influence was still rather slight. Next to the local powers, Jews had to deal, therefore, primarily with the imperial administration. The situation was different in the duchies north of Saxony. In Mecklenburg, in particular, which formally became a duchy in 1348 by decree of Charles IV, the impact of the powerful princes, Henry I the Pilgrim, Henry II the Lion, and Albert II the Great was strongly felt in the thirteenth and fourteenth centuries. But there were considerable local variations between the cities of Rostock, Wismar, Güstrow, and others. While Jews got along fairly well with their neighbors in most communities, they were temporarily banished from Wismar in 1290 by burghers venting their spleen against Henry I, then absent as prisoner of war in Muslim hands. In 1330 Jews were persecuted in Güstrow. After suffering severely during the Black Death, they were more permanently victimized by the anarchical conditions in the country during the entire century of 1379–1480. Ultimately, even the limited toleration extended to them during that period was terminated and in 1492 they were banished from the whole duchy.[16]

In the German northeast, Jewish communities began to grow, especially in the territories of the margraviate (later electorate) of Brandenburg and the duchy of Pomerania. Brandenburg's territories, often divided into the so-called Old Mark west of the Elbe, the Middle Mark between the Elbe and the Oder, and the New Mark (Neumark) east of the Oder, suffered from frequent further internal divisions. The New Mark was for a time taken over by the Teutonic Order. Only under Hohenzollern rule, beginning with the investiture of Frederick I by King Sigismund in 1417, and particularly after the *Dispositio Achillea* of 1473 had established the succession through primogeniture, did the country embark upon its remarkable historic career.

Inauspiciously, the first reliable mention of Jews in Brandenburg is connected with a reputed miracle of a host in the town of Beelitz in 1247. However, the ensuing persecution had but a local character and the Jews were allowed to live peacefully in other communities. In Berlin they are mentioned in a document of 1295 or soon after its foundation. A year earlier the community of Frankfort on the Oder had reached an agreement with the Christian butcher guild that it would maintain no more than ten ritual slaughterers, each handling no more than five animals a week. The sale of meat of that quantity obviously presupposed a substantial Jewish clientele in Frankfort and its vicinity. The first known formal decree was also quite favorable. In 1297, Margraves Otto and Conrad granted the city of Stendal the right to settle Jews owning a minimum of 10 marks each; they were to be treated as "burghers" enjoying the same rights as the other inhabitants. Such basic equality is also assumed in later ordinances. True, the rise of the cities and their growing independence created many ominous portents for the future. In his privilege of 1323 for the city of Alstadt-Brandenburg in recognition of its help during his war with Frederick the Handsome, Emperor Louis the Bavarian proclaimed the burghers'

right to hold two or three Jews in their city for its utility and benefit. These Jews should live and dwell there under their constant and permanent protection. Neither We nor any of Our heirs and successors nor Our princes and officials shall at any time in the future force them [the Jews] to pay any impost, contribution or tax of whatever kind.

Twelve years later the sister city, Neustadt-Brandenburg, received a similar privilege to admit five Jews. Before long Jews lived also in a score of other cities. In a more sweeping decree of 1344, Margrave Louis IV, son of Emperor Louis, considerably enlarged the commercial rights of one Maier, "the beloved serf of Our Chamber," and his heirs settled in Havelberg.[17]

Within five years these high-sounding phrases were to stand the acid test of the mass hysteria of the Black Death. Louis' half-hearted attempts to protect the Jews, through his decree of November 30, 1349 which upheld all their rights in the districts beyond the Oder, broke down under the frenzy of the populace, whose good will the embattled margrave could not afford to lose. In 1351 he tolerated the burning of Jews in Königsberg (actually initiated by a royal official who publicly boasted of it), and promised Stendal immunity for its crimes. The massacres practically obliterated all twenty-six communities in the electorate. In the Teutonic Order's ever expanding neighboring possessions in the Baltic area, where Grandmaster Siegfried von Feuchtwangen had in 1309 outlawed any Jewish settlement (along with that of magicians and pagan priests), the mob, unable to vent its wrath upon professing Jews, attacked the few resident Jewish converts. But before long sanity returned, and both Brandenburg and some Pomeranian districts extended relatively favorable privileges to Jews. In the early 1350s the city of Perleberg readmitted Jews under moderate conditions. As early as 1356, a Jew Fritzel of Spandau received from Louis II the Roman, in recognition for his "manifold faithful services," the office of guardian of the local tower as an hereditary feudal benefice. Thirty years later this tower still bore the designation of *turris Judaeorum*. To be sure, the old charters of 1341, 1344, 1349, and 1350 had been nullified by the popular outbreaks. Yet these laws remained on the statute books and reasserted themselves upon the gradual restoration of Jewish life. In 1420 Frederick I of Hohenzollern (1417 [1411]–40) not only renewed the old privilege of 1344 for the New Mark but extended it to the entire electorate for the benefit of his "dear serfs of the Chamber." His son, Frederick II (1440–71), whose ruthlessness was to earn him the nickname "the Iron," confirmed this privilege soon after his accession to the throne. But constantly feuding with the cities and trying to enlarge his territories by negotiation, he was often short of funds. In 1446 (perhaps in some connection with a host miracle in a church of Wilsnack in the diocese of Havelberg) he ordered the sudden imprisonment of all Jews and the confiscation of their property along the then well-trodden paths. While individual Jews persisted in certain localities, in others, Stendal for instance, they were steadfastly refused readmittance. Under Albert III Achilles (1471–86), who often played an important role in imperial affairs, the cities clamored for the expulsion of Jews. They were joined by the clergy and the nobles at the Diet of 1480. But the elector rejected all such demands, pointing out that on previous occasions Christian usurers had exploited their debtors more severely than had the Jews. Perhaps he felt restrained by his own extreme doctrine of the emperor's overlordship over all German Jewry.[18]

The cities finally secured compliance under Joachim I (1499–1535). A Berlin trial involving both host and blood libels was staged in 1510 with great fanfare. It ended with the condemnation and burning of many Jews, headed by their rabbi, Sloman, and the banishment of the rest. Curiously, the exiles were made to take an awesome oath that they would avoid the country in the future, warn their coreligionists against settling in it, and refrain from planning any act of vengeance. After this catastrophe, only few Jews began to trickle back into Brandenburg, notwithstanding their total exoneration by the great reformer Philipp Melanchthon at an assembly of German princes in Frankfort on the Main in 1539. More or less parallel were the developments in Pomerania, whose destinies were generally intimately interwoven with those of Brandenburg. Here, too, the deep internal divisions caused many local disparities, and it was only after Bogislav X had reunified the whole duchy and endeavored to reestablish public order with the aid of Roman law, that he issued in 1481 a relatively tolerant edict in favor of the various Jewries under his reign.[19]

## BURGHERS

Equally far-reaching was the gradual transfer of power to municipal organs. This shift, particularly significant and extensive in the older settlements along the Rhine and in southern Germany, reflected the general expansion of cities and the growing self-assertion of their burgher class. It has been estimated that only some fifty localities deserved to be called cities in 1200. In the course of the following hundred years, this number increased tenfold, while the older towns grew larger and larger. One of the oldest, Cologne, had occupied an area of only 120 hectares (some 300 acres) in 1106; in the thirteenth century it grew to 400 hectares (1,000 acres). Although tiny by modern standards and exceeded in dimension by many medium-sized American farms, Cologne and such other important cities as Erfurt, Frankfort, Augsburg, Nuremberg, or Vienna, none of which extended over more than 500 acres during the Middle Ages, played a significant role in both German and Jewish history. Many cities were originally built for defensive purposes, for instance those of the Hohenstaufen emperors in Swabia. They and the other founders sought to attract new settlers, including Jews, and endowed them all with autonomous rights. Under the ever unstable conditions of the Empire, those privileges facilitated the constantly increasing self-determination of the burghers. Dependent on local conditions and changing constellations of power, some cities remained or came under the control of bishops (of the fifty twelfth-century cities, more than thirty had been episcopal sees); others fell into the hands, or were originally founded, by regional dukes or barons. But still others early attained the status of imperial cities directly dependent only on the emperors. They later sometimes advanced to the status of imperial "free cities," where even the imperial overlordship was more nominal than real. Everywhere, however, the burghers expanded their self-governing activities, particularly in domestic relations, which included some jurisdiction over, and responsibility toward, the local Jews. At times a city secured from its sovereign a blanket privilege *de non tolerandis Judaeis*, or at least the safeguard that no Jew would be admitted to settlement without its consent (for instance, Greifswald in 1289). Elsewhere admission by the Jewish communal elders sufficed to open the gates for new Jewish settlers, a practice specifically emphasized by Charles IV in his privilege for Nuremberg Jewry of 1347.[20]

City councils now became directly or indirectly responsible for the preservation of public order. At all critical junctures, it was really up to the local burghers, rather than the more remote state or imperial organs, to take the necessary protective measures for the Jews, too. Even in 1096, we recall, many Jews were saved from the Crusaders by their patrician friends who considered it a matter of both honor and prudence to extend a helping hand to endangered compatriots. They realized that any disturbance of public order would not only cast reflection on the city's dignity and its ability to restrain unruly mobs and thus weaken its claims to self-governing status, but also that once murder and pillage were given free rein in the Jewish quarter they might spill over to the patrician houses. Reporting about a "large tumult" in some outlying townships whose citizenry demanded the reduction of Jewish interest on loans but was refused by Mayence Jewry with municipal support, an anonymous chronicler stressed the patricians' fear that "if these extraneous townships were allowed to break in by force, they would despoil not only the Jews but also all the wealthy men" of Mayence. Not surprisingly, the burghers expected some recompense from the Jews. As emphasized by Ḥayyim

b. Isaac Or Zaru'a, "If they [the Jews] say to the burghers, 'We shall not pay,' they [the burghers] must not take from them either money or houses. But since, on account of our numerous sins, the Jews have become dependent on the burghers, they fear that the latter will hate them and cause them manifold evils. Hence they must comply with their [the burghers'] demands and pay what they ask for." [21]

In time, the cities' protection of Jews became formalized in specific privileges from their imperial, episcopal, or ducal masters. Thus there gradually evolved a new sort of alliance between the urban patricians and their Jewish protégés, a miniature duplicate of the traditional alliance between kings and Jews. Here, too, such an alliance proved satisfactory only in long quiescent periods, whereas in times of sharp inner conflict the Jews were often victimized by the newly upsurging classes. In the perennial clashes, particularly, between the rising artisan class and the dominant patrician merchants (in various forms this so-called "guild revolution" deeply affected most German cities from the fourteenth to the seventeenth centuries) Jews were the sufferers not only through the ensuing curtailment of trade and increased monopolies of the craft guilds, but also in their sociolegal standing. Ultimately, especially in the critical years of the Black Death, even the upper classes were unable, or unwilling, to extend a helping hand to their Jewish neighbors, and most cities lost their Jewish populations as a result of massacres and the flight of survivors. Only gradually did small Jewish groups resettle in those cities during the latter part of the fourteenth century, but many Jewish communities, particularly along the Rhine, never recovered their former glory.[22]

Burghers, whether patrician or artisan, never considered Jews "serfs" even in the limited sense employed by kings. To them the Jews were a separate and distinct, but for the most part equal, segment of the population. Even when oppressed, the Jews never lacked freedom. Nor were they given or mortgaged away to other authorities, since there were no public-law agencies below the city councils. If the burghers did not wish to have Jews, they would expel them—if need be, with the cooperation of royal, princely, or episcopal powers. Habitation within city limits thus unquestioningly gave the Jews all the personal freedoms they needed, which indeed they largely enjoyed also as royal "serfs."

In this sense, the old Teuton maxim *Stadtluft macht frei* fully applied to Jews. Of course, Jews had to pay manifold, often quite burdensome, municipal imposts, but so had everybody else though in different forms and in differing amounts. In fact, the Jewish communities, through their collective agreements with rulers, actually pioneered in the vital transition from individual to collective taxation, which accrued to the benefit of the burghers as well. On the whole, the city treasuries were somewhat less rapacious and extortionist and employed less drastic means of collecting revenue from Jews than did their royal and ducal overlords. Very frequently they negotiated general agreements with the local Jewish communities about the total amounts due, leaving the task of allocation and collection to the Jewish organs. The latter were also often entrusted with choosing new Jewish settlers through the so-called *herem ha-yishub*.[23]

Nor do we hear of many intercity pacts against mutual raiding of Jewish settlers, such as were concluded between Charles IV and the Austrian dukes in 1360. If the treaty between King Wenceslaus and the Swabian cities of 1385 (primarily a financial transaction to secure 40,000 florins for the king) contained such reciprocal safeguards, those cities, shortly thereafter defeated by the princes, could hardly implement it. Such a pledge by a league of cities is the less surprising as the formation of leagues often pursued administrative objectives as much as foreign policy goals. Still less were the German cities, or for that matter, the majority of princes, prone to follow the French example and conclude mutual extradition treaties affecting fugitive Jews. Occasionally a prominent Jew enjoyed residential rights in more than one city, so long as he met his fiscal obligations to both municipalities. A Mayence Jew, Jocelin of Würzburg, and his wife were accepted in 1366 by the city of Frankfort for an indefinite stay provided they would pay an annual tax of 10 gulden. Such transfers of residence were particularly frequent among rabbis. Meir b. Baruch officiated in Kostnitz, Augsburg, Würzburg, Worms, Nuremberg, Mayence, and, probably for the longest time, in Rothenburg on the Tauber, with which city his name became permanently associated. There is no evidence that he, or any of his less famous confreres, ever encountered legal difficulties in accepting a call to another community. More, in the earlier period of peaceful symbiosis Jews were often treated on the basis of equality. We shall see that in Worms, particularly, where they were under special imperial protection since Henry IV, they long enjoyed the status of burghers. For one example, while paying homage to its new bishop Simon in 1283, the city made its lord promise that he would "observe, increase and not reduce all the privileges, liberties, and good customs enjoyed by his dear citizens of Worms, both Christian and Jewish." But here and elsewhere, even such a favorable designation lent itself to diverse interpretation. In general, medieval Jewish life depended far more on sociopolitical realities than on such juristic formulas.[24]

On this twilight position of their coreligionists in the cities depended also the status of Jews residing in outlying districts, be they suburbs or neighboring villages. In some rural areas Jews may have been excluded by law. Elsewhere they themselves preferred to live in closer urban settlements, where they could regularly attend synagogue services and enjoy the existing cultural amenities. In the later Middle Ages, moreover, even concentrated Jewish quarters were rarely safe from attacks by malevolent individuals or groups. Isolated Jews in villages must have felt totally helpless. Yet there is some evidence of medieval Jewish peddling which doubtless involved lengthy absences from home and temporary changes of residence from manor to manor, and from one village of free peasants to another. Legally the itinerant Jews probably belonged to one or another established Jewish community, to and through which they paid their taxes and whose legal protection and religious safeguards and facilities they shared. This is indeed implied by the general tenor of the few rabbinic references to rural Jews. A fourteenth-century author mentioned an unnamed duke of Lorraine "who had demanded from his Jews that they should concern themselves with their coreligionists living in his villages under petty masters so that they return to his control; otherwise he would expel them all." The rabbi decided that the Jews ought to obey that order.[25]

## LOCAL VARIATIONS

Considerable differences between one locality and another resulted from the variety of general charters they had received from kings or intermediary overlords, special ad hoc arrangements, or gradually evolving customs. Before the end of the Middle Ages a few major cities came under the emperor's immediate overlordship, more or less on a par with bishops and princes. It was nonetheless natural for the royal authority to be more fully exercised in these imperial cities than in the larger electorates and principalities—if not as a matter of law, at least as a reflection of the existing power relationships. With respect to Jews the following illustrations taken from the diverse evolutions of the major communities of Frankfort on the Main, Erfurt, Nuremberg, and Ratisbon may be considered fairly representative.

Frankfort, which was later destined to play a great role in the historic career of the Jewish people, became a center of Jewish life comparatively late. Despite its favorable geographic location it was still designated a hamlet (*oppidum*) in a document of 1142. Only thirty years later was it called a "municipality" and in 1184 a "city." Disregarding various legends, we obtain the first reliable glimpse of a Jewish community there at the time of its demolition. In 1241, the tensions produced by the Empire's losing struggle against the Papacy and internal factionalism were intensified by the panic which seized the masses at the approach of the Mongolian invaders. Widespread suspicion of Jewish collaboration with these irresistible hosts had no other factual background than the observation that some Jews saw in this world terror an adumbration of the wars of Gog and Magog preliminary to the advent of the Messiah, long expected to arrive at the end of the fifth millennium A.M., or about 1240 C.E. A minor incident connected with the intended conversion of an individual Jew or Jewess sparked a mob uprising in Frankfort. Some 160 to 180 victims are recorded in the sources; many others must have perished, and still others escaped annihilation only through flight or conversion. The case of a converted girl, whose fiancé had married someone else but was sued for breach of promise after she reverted to Judaism, raised legal problems discussed by several contemporary and later jurists. Perhaps taught by such experiences, the city of Frankfort readily joined in 1265 with the archbishop of Mayence and several other princes and cities in a compact guaranteeing "peace" to various classes of inhabitants, including Jews, for a period of three years. To counteract the spreading Blood Accusations, the Jews of Frankfort and other communities secured copies of the papal decrees condemning that libel. A transcript of the bull issued by Gregory X in 1274, bearing the signature of Albertus Magnus, is still extant in the Frankfort Municipal Archives, to which it had undoubtedly come from the collections preserved by the local Jewish community.[26]

Basically, the Frankfort Jews during that period were treated on a par with the burghers and entered into the usual burghers' ledgers. Like Christians, Jewish arrivals were admitted after paying a fee of three pounds heller and proving that they had leased a house or a plot of ground for a rental of at least one mark annually. Among the Jewish burghers were women, such as one Hanna Judea, who was made "co-burgher [concivis]" in 1348. Being the objects of conflicting claims by the emperor, the archbishop of Mayence, and the city, the Jews had to accept a steep increase of their originally moderate annual imposts which, including 840 pounds for the archbishop, apparently had not exceeded 2 percent of their property. True, Adolph of Nassau's attempt to make them advance him 20,000 silver marks for his expenses during his lengthy stay in Frankfort was averted by the energetic remonstration of a leading municipal official. Yet between 1241 and 1309 the Jewish taxes grew more than sixfold, only in part owing to the increase in the Jewish population. They became particularly burdensome under the regime of Louis the Bavarian, who in return tried to protect his "dear serfs of the Chamber." In a remarkable decree of July 1331, he informed the Frankfort Council, "We have promised them [the Jews] that . . . no one shall oppress them nor make claims against them whereby they would feel aggrieved and suffer harm. . . . We also order you to comfort them." He repeated a similar injunction six years later (April 15, 1337). Even a serious misunderstanding between him and some Frankfort Jews, which caused the flight in 1346 of some fifty persons—a rather substantial segment of the entire community—was eventually cleared up. But all along Jews had to pay heavily for these imperial favors. In 1316 the community was forced to borrow 333⅓ marks. It secured that loan from a Christian burgher at the moderate rate of 8⅓ percent, compared with the far higher rates charged by Jews on their petty loans. In 1338, these were reduced by law to 32½ percent on loans to Frankfort burghers, and to 43⅓ percent in the case of borrowers from other cities. On the whole, under these fairly peaceful conditions, Frankfort Jewry was able to cultivate its traditional lore and to include among its members such distinguished rabbis as Simon Qara, compiler of the outstanding aggadic collection, the *Yalquṭ Shime'oni,* and, possibly, Eliezer b. Joel ha-Levi who is said to have died in Frankfort in 1224.[27]

In 1349, however, Frankfort Jewry suffered total eclipse. Almost immediately there started a struggle between the city and other claimants, including Charles IV, the archbishop of Mayence, and some neighboring nobles, over the inheritance of the murdered Jews' communal and individual possessions. The city's "mortgage" of 15,200 pounds heller on the imperial dues from Jews arranged with Charles IV on June 25, 1349, but a month before the tragedy (it included a promise of immunity for the city in case of the foreseeable mass murder of Jews), was followed by the archbishop's renunciation, in 1358, of his claims on the Jews for the payment of 7,500 florins. It paved the way for a new compact with the emperor in 1360 which allowed the council freely "to attract Jews, men and women, to the city and to agree with them concerning their annual payments." The Jews' settlement rights thus granted were revocable at any time subject to but a two-months' notice. Not surprisingly, only eight Jewish families availed themselves of the new opportunity, three of them departing within two years. Only after the agreement had been amended and the Jews were guaranteed a stay of at least six years with an additional year's notice did the community embark upon a third period of real growth. It became ever more dependent on the council, which gradually bought out the imperial and archepiscopal rights. The emperors never gave up their overlordship, however, and in the fifteenth century demanded with increasing frequency not only the regular payment of the "golden penny" but the various coronation taxes and other new imposts invented by their ingenious fiscal advisers as well. The Frankfort Jews were also directly affected by King Wenceslaus' cancellation of debts in 1390 (not by the more moderate one of 1385), the city reaching voluntary settlements with both the king and the representatives of princes and gentry about their respective shares. The full liquidation of these debts took more than a decade, and it proved less ruinous to the Jewish community than had been feared. Moreover Wenceslaus himself, and following him, King Rupert, pledged themselves not to cancel Jewish debts in the future. True, Sigismund occasionally "forgave" individual debts, but on the whole he refrained from wholesale annulment of Jewish claims, and in 1414 granted the Jews an extensive privilege which served as a basis for much subsequent imperial legislation.[28]

We need not proceed here with the dreary recital of the fifteenth-century emperors' fiscal exactions and their advisors' endless negotiations with the city and Jewish community of Frankfort. The city council staunchly defended the Jewish rights, not only because of its contractual pledges but also because it wished to preserve the Jewish resources for its own ultimate benefit. These considerations also governed the city's selection of Jews admitted to residence, and its replacement of the theretofore customary simple registration of all Jewish, as well as Christian, newcomers in the general list of burghers by individual Stättigkeiten. The oldest extant permit of this sort, dated in 1336, was quite favorable to its recipient, Jocelin of Würzburg, who, we recall, was able to retain his Mayence burgher's rights as well. Later permits became more and more detailed and exacting. It is small wonder, then, that few Jews were allowed, or willing, to live in the city for a long time. By reviewing the municipal ledgers for the period of 1360–1400, Isidor Kracauer has shown the extraordinary mobility of the Jewish population. Names of many taxpayers constantly disappeared from the rolls and were replaced by new ones. According to his admittedly incomplete table, some 72 percent of all Jewish taxpayers resided in the city but four years or less, 30 percent enjoying less than a year's residence. Only from 1424 did a general Stättigkeit cover the entire community. Limited to one year, so as to enable the city to increase the fees for each renewal, it was annually read in the synagogue in order to remind the Jewish public of its numerous restrictions. The latter included the prohibition, now inserted for the first time, for Jews to retain permanent ownership of any real estate acquired through foreclosure from Christian debtors; they were ordered to dispose of it to Christian owners without delay. Occasionally, the council placed additional restrictions on certain individuals as when, in 1428, a rabbi was allowed to instruct up to twenty pupils only after he promised not to engage in moneylending.[29]

These variations are the more remarkable as the Frankfort Jewish community still was exceedingly small. According to extant tax lists, it reached a maximum of 29 taxpaying households in 1412, and declined sharply to but three such families four years later. Not until 1478 did it recover to embrace 17 households. Of course, there were some nontaxpaying members of the community, but its total size hardly ever reached 200 persons in the fifteenth century. Nor were the usual petty chicaneries absent from the Frankfort scene. The city council evinced a particular fear that the sacred precincts of its city hall might be contaminated by the presence of one or another Jewish passer-by. The records of 1405–1408 include the following momentous council resolution:

Except during fairs no Jew is entitled under penalty of the law to enter the Römer Mountain [on which the city hall was located] without a substantial reason. Only when a Jew brings spices as a New Year's present to the Honorable Council may he come up in a straight line through the Römer Mountain to the city hall and return in the same fashion.

Nevertheless Frederick III's aforementioned initiative to establish a ghetto in Frankfort required some two decades before its realization in 1462. On this occasion the city invested so much money in the newly erected buildings that its elders viewed with alarm the possibility of Jewish emigration. Despite reiterated demands by the local artisan guilds or outside nobles and even serious threats from the dreaded Fehmic courts, the city refused to follow the example of other German municipalities and to expel her Jews. In this way the community was salvaged up to and beyond the period of Maximilian I, when it played an important part in the

Reuchlin-Pfefferkorn controversy. In time it assumed an even more leading role in the affairs of all German Jewry.[30]

Like Frankfort, Erfurt emerged from under the control of the archbishop of Mayence. Its Jewish community had a shorter but equally brilliant career. As usual in the case of medieval cities, its early beginnings are shrouded in darkness. We are grateful for the preservation of tombstones with Hebrew epitaphs showing the presence of Jews and probably of a Jewish cemetery there in the twelfth century. Three of these inscriptions, dated in 1137, commemorate the demise of three brothers on successive new moon days of Iyyar, Sivan, and Tammuz of that year. On the other hand, a holiday prayerbook (*Maḥzor gadol*), allegedly written in 1142, was apparently composed late in the following century. Among other vestiges of early Jewish life in Erfurt is the aforementioned formula of Jewish oath which belongs to the earliest of its kind. In 1212 Emperor Otto IV transferred the authority over Erfurt's Jewry to the archbishop of Mayence, who, despite his proximity, was unable nine years later to prevent an assault on the Jewish community by some Frisians, possibly visiting merchants resentful of Jewish competition. This obscure assault, which almost exterminated the first Jewish community in Erfurt, was long thereafter commemorated by a local fast day. But the community soon recovered sufficiently to call forth, through its expansion into a quarter adjacent to the St. Benedict Church, reiterated complaints by the latter's priest that it was thereby reducing the church's revenues from the tithes of its parishioners (1240 and 1273).[31]

Gradually the control over Jews shifted here, too, from the archbishop to the municipal council, itself first mentioned in a record of 1212 and soon thereafter styled the "noble Senate." If in 1266 Archbishop Werner placed Erfurt under interdict until it gave satisfaction to Jews who had suffered from another riot, his successors made peace with the city, and in 1291 even mortgaged with it their Jewish income for a period of eleven years, subsequently extended. The city took its new responsibilities seriously, especially during the crisis of 1303 when a sudden outburst of popular frenzy again threatened the survival of the Jewish community. A Blood Accusation in neighboring Weissensee had led to the wholesale slaughter of Jews in that and several adjacent cities. "The same would have happened in Erfurt," reports a local chronicler, "were it not for their [the Erfurt Jews'] ample funds which secured them protection from the city council and the other patricians [*meliores*] of the city." The city fathers doubtless saw in the Jews a source of economic and military strength. Within six years, in fact, the Jews were called upon to help defend the city, then besieged by the powerful Margrave Frederick of Meissen. To cite the same chronicler's German version, "the Jews, jointly with the Christians, ascended the walls and towers and fought back." After a fortnight the margrave withdrew. Otherwise the first decades of the fourteenth century passed rather peaceably, despite a pestilence of 1315 which took nearly 8,000 human lives, and various temporary expulsions of Jews from neighboring Thuringian areas. But in 1349, in the face of the approaching Black Death, the community suffered complete destruction at the hand of a panic-stricken mob.[32]

In 1354 two Jews reappeared in Erfurt as visitors; three years later, together with other newcomers, they began rebuilding the community. Its growth was extremely rapid. By 1365 it counted 86 taxpaying households. Nine years later the recorded number dropped to 53, but it rose again to 76 in 1389, during which year an additional 26 families were mentioned as poor and hence without burghers' rights. This was a far greater number than those recorded in Frankfort and in most other communities, Erfurt doubtless belonging to the largest Jewish settlements in the Empire at the end of the fourteenth century. We happen to possess a remarkable documentation of this growth in the so-called "Erfurt Jewry Book," which listed the city's revenue from the Jewish community by individual houses year after year from 1357 to 1407. Next to full-fledged Jewish burghers, whose admission seems to have paralleled that of Christians, we also find Jews living on visitors' permits (*hospitium*) and others enjoying temporary burghers' rights. Jewish taxes, but moderately heavier than those of their Christian compeers, were collected by six Jewish elders, appointed by the city council for three years. According to two extant tax lists of 1433 and 1438, the Erfurt community was assessed at 3,000 and 6,000 florins, respectively, an impost greater than that of any community except Nuremberg—a clear testimony to its size and wealth. In return for earlier payments, Sigismund issued a very favorable decree for Erfurt's Jewry in 1417. To make it ironclad, he provided that "all letters issued, or to be issued, by the King which run counter to this decree shall be considered null and void, and all inhabitants of the Empire shall observe it if they wish to avoid his and the Empire's anger." Sigismund further reinforced this decree in 1429 by ordering the Erfurt council to protect Jews against assaults from any quarter, including the neighboring princes. If his successor, Frederick III, tried in 1453 secretly to conspire with the elders of Erfurt for the collection of the coronation tax after an assessment of all Jewish property there and in other Thuringian localities, three years later he intervened in favor of Jews against the city. He ordered the council to cease and desist from certain actions within six weeks and three days, or else to appear before the imperial court within thirty days to defend them. Ultimately, however, he relented, and on the intervention of the Mayence archbishop he dismissed the case in 1459 without any apparent indemnification for the Jewish plaintiffs.[33]

All during those years the Erfurt community maintained its intellectual eminence. Among the founders of the reconstructed community in 1357 was Froudel of Breslau, styled *magister* in the documents. This did not necessarily mean that he occupied a rabbinic post, for at that time the rabbinate as a salaried institution was still in its formative stages. He is recorded also as a moneylender, which occupation, however, he could well have combined with certain rabbinic functions. He was so effective as a leader that in 1367 he was invited by Margrave Frederick III of Meissen to develop also the Jewish settlements in the margraviate. Among Froudel's successors was Magister Heller of Hiller, recognized in 1406 by the city council as head of the Jewish community, and ten years later appointed by Margrave William II as *magister* of all the Jews in Thuringia. He was cited by R. Moses Menz under the high-sounding title of "prince of the dispersion." Another distinguished leader was Nathaniel Weil, who maintained a school of higher learning in Erfurt. At the same time, domestic and external tensions were constantly increasing. They reached high intensity under the impact of sermons delivered in Erfurt by John Capistrano in 1454. Within four years the Jews were banished from the city, with the approval of Archbishop Diethrich von Erbach of Mayence. Imperial consent was likewise secured by the city's payment of a large sum, despite its intervening condemnation by an imperial tribunal. This delicacy of its legal position doubtless induced the council to indemnify the other claimants on Jewish revenue more lavishly than was usually the case. A family Schlick received 1287 Schock groschen, while the archbishop became the beneficiary of a wholly disproportionate indemnity of 7,000 florins for the mere 100 marks he had been annually collecting from the community. More significantly, the council seems to have raised no objection when some Erfurt Jews withdrew into two neighboring villages and carried on from there their accustomed trade with the city's inhabitants. These were but temporary makeshifts. Deprived of their organized community, these small Jewish settlements apparently vanished after a short time.[34]

Nuremberg's Jewish quarter was even more populous than that of Erfurt. Although interest in the history of that community dates back to Andreas Würfel's volume published more than two centuries ago, its beginnings cannot be ascertained. Certainly the story told by the fifteenth-century chronicler, Sigmund Meisterlin, that in 1105 the Jews had surrendered the city to King Henry V and were allowed to take over the best places in town, is pure legend. Some sixty years later Nuremberg was still but a *burgum* (borough). In 1146 some Jewish refugees from the incendiary sermons of the monk Radulph seem to have fled to this central Bavarian hamlet, where minor riots are recorded in 1180 and 1200. The reliable history of Nuremberg Jewry begins only in 1288, when the city communicated with Weissenburg about the regulation of Jewish pawnbroking. Yet the community had by that time become one of the largest in Germany, since no less than 628 Jews were slain by the Rindfleisch gangs in 1298. Among the victims was the distinguished jurist, Mordecai b. Hillel, together with his wife and five children.[35]

Under the protection of the city, which in that very year had received from the emperor the right to keep Jews, the Jewish settlement started growing again until in 1338 it allegedly reached 2,006 souls. (A more nearly correct figure appears to be 1,060.)

The legal status of Nuremberg Jewry, however, was quite confused, since in 1313 King Henry VII entrusted the sheriff (*Schult-
heiss*) of Nuremberg with the admission of Jews and their protection against all enemies. The city also had to consider the wishes of
the royal burgrave to whom Louis the Bavarian had mortgaged his
Jews, as well as those of the bishop of Bamberg to whose diocese
Nuremberg belonged. These conflicting claims remained, despite
Louis' express privilege of 1322 terminating the mortgage with
the burgrave and granting the Jews of Nuremberg a one-year tax
forgiveness. Louis also extended to his imperial "serfs" a favorable
privilege in 1331 for a period of three years. He wrote:

We declare that We have noted the faithful and useful services rendered
to Us by Our dear Jews of Nuremberg. For this reason We declare them
free and give them the liberty to reside there free and immune from
all taxes and imposts and also from any pressure or imprisonment on
Our part.

For this privilege Jews were to pay 400 florins annually, the city
council being allowed to collect more if in its judgment the Jewish
economic conditions had sufficiently improved. Two years later
Louis went a step further, and in order to enable Nuremberg to
attract more Jews declared that the city should protect its Jewish
residents, present and future, even "against Us and all our officials
and servants." The omission of the burgrave in these decrees was
remedied in 1336, when that officer was specifically entrusted with
the protection of the Jews in Nuremberg, Rothenburg, and the in-
termediate localities. These conditions, essentially undisturbed
even by the emperor's promise of 1344 not to aid Jews in acquiring houses from Christians, were suddenly altered here, too, after
the temporary seizure of power by the artisan guilds in 1348–49.
The new rulers appropriated many Jewish and patrician holdings,
calling forth Charles IV's sharp order to the burgrave in May 1349
to force the artisans to disgorge their loot. Yet any contemplated
action was rudely interrupted by the Black Death and the ensuing
massacres. According to the Nuremberg Memorbook, 562 Jews
were killed and the rest banished from the city.[36]

Nuremberg Jewry staged a speedier recovery than most other
communities. As early as 1351 Charles IV ordered the burgrave to
readmit Jews and to help them reestablish themselves. A year later

he authorized the city to admit and protect such new arrivals, promising not to give away or mortgage his revenue from them. Soon thereafter two Jewish representatives, signing as Nuremberg burghers, reached an agreement with the city whereby the Jews renounced all claims antedating the massacre and promised to move into a new quarter. Their former concentration under the castle in the heart of town was now replaced by a street in the so-called Taschental, which had shortly before been destroyed by fire. In return the Jews were to be free of local taxation, in order the better to serve the Empire. These amicable relations were facilitated by the emperor's intervening conquest of Nuremberg, which had sided with the Bavarian party against him, his abolition of the local guild structure, and the restoration of patrician rule. Charles' decree of 1352 did not prevent him, however, eight years later, from taking the Nuremberg Jews directly under his own protection and from ordering the council to safeguard their rights during the relatively long period of fifteen years. Two-thirds of the Jewish revenues were to go to the imperial Treasury and one-third to the council. For some reason, by 1371 emperor and Jews felt that an advance renewal, this time for twenty years, was in order. Yet in 1382 Wenceslaus, perhaps because of the theoretical expiration of all privileges upon the death of each legislator, again renewed the decree of 1360 for another nineteen years. Whether or not with reference to this decree, Rupert of the Palatinate, soon after his accession to the royal throne, issued still another privilege in 1401 authorizing the city to admit and protect Jews. While the imperial share dropped here to one-half the revenue, it was extended to include also half the property left behind by any future Jewish émigrés. In addition, every adult Jew, man or woman, was to pay to the Treasury one florin annually. But even this decree did not settle all outstanding litigations connected with Wenceslaus' cancellation of debts in 1390, of which several neighborhood nobles had become direct beneficiaries.[37]

Records of the following decades are filled with the usual tale of royal exactions, against which Nuremberg's city council at times halfheartedly tried to shield its Jews. In 1416 Sigismund issued a very favorable decree for the Nuremberg community under the condition that any Jew earning his own livelihood should pay him a huge ten percent property tax annually. In 1433 and 1438 the community was assessed by the imperial officials for the substantial amounts of 4,000 and 10,000 florins, respectively. But in 1442 when Frederick III demanded the enormous sum of 20,000 florins, a Jewish delegation, supported by the city deputies, secured a substantial reduction. These friendly relations with the council did not endure, however. Although the canonical restrictions demanded by the Synod of Bamberg in 1451 were minimized through the cooperation of city and emperor, the council itself imprisoned many Jews in 1463 (probably in connection with Frederick III's second coronation tax), and four years later burned eighteen Jews at the stake because they had allegedly slain four Christian children. Its hostile attitude was also reflected in the new municipal code published in 1479–84, the discriminatory provisions of which the Jews sharply denounced. More, from 1473 on the city council reiteratedly petitioned the emperor for permission to expel the Jews altogether. While Frederick III still staunchly resisted, his successor Maximilian approved their total banishment in 1498, allegedly because their usury had become too ruinous for the Nuremberg population. To prevent likely Jewish evasions, the municipal officials assembled the prospective exiles in the synagogue and made them take an oath that they would leave the city within three months (November, 1498). At first all Jewish property was taken over by imperial officials, but soon thereafter Maximilian transferred his claims to the municipality for a lump sum of 8,000 florins. Jews were given only a few months' grace to visit the city in order to settle outstanding business affairs. Thereafter no Jew was to be allowed ever to come to Nuremberg —a prohibition which was rather strictly observed until 1839.[38]

## RATISBON DRAMA

Somewhat different was the evolution in Ratisbon, one of the oldest and most revered central German communities. More than other communities, Ratisbon Jewry was convinced of its antiquity and claimed an ancestry reaching back to the pre-Christian era. In a detailed topographical study, Adolf Schmetzer has indeed shown that the location of the Jewish quarter indicated its provenance

from the early Bayuvar period (sixth or seventh century), if not
from Roman times. We possess reliable documentary records of
such a quarter only from 1006–28, although as early as 981 the
monastery of St. Emmeram purchased an estate, Schierstadt, from a
Ratisbon Jew, Samuel. Because of the city's importance in international trade, particularly with Slavonic countries, Ratisbon Jewry
maintained close relations with that of Prague as well as with the
West. During the First Crusade, we recall, many members were
forced to adopt Christianity, but they were later allowed to revert
to Judaism. Counted among the more important German Jewish
communities by Benjamin of Tudela, Ratisbon received from
Frederick I in 1182 his aforementioned significant privilege,
which, confirmed "in perpetuity" by Frederick II in 1216, was expected by the emperor to be "observed by everybody." It was
again summarized by Frederick's son, King Henry (VII) in 1230.
Invoking the older laws, Henry stated that the Jews "may buy and
sell gold and silver in the city of Ratisbon. They must not be summoned before a judge other than the one they elect and accept on
their part. Nor may any cleric or layman claim and demand anything from them unless a Jew is part of the testimony and is one of
the witnesses. They shall possess and own without demurrer all
property owned and quietly held by them for ten years." As conditions became less stable, the city of Ratisbon, with its bishop and
several other cities and princes, joined in 1244 in the proclamation
of a truce which included Jews. However, here, too, Jewish life
was greatly complicated by the conflicting jurisdictions of emperor, bishop, Bavarian duke, and municipality. When in 1297
King Adolph, to recompense Duke Otto, assigned to him 2,000
pounds on the Ratisbon Jews, the burghers impulsively expelled
the duke's envoys from the city. The ensuing conflict ended with a
fine of 1,000 pounds paid by the city in addition to the Jewish contribution. All along the city secured privileges from the kings (for
instance, in 1207 and 1251), providing that all inhabitants of
Ratisbon, including its clergy and Jews, must contribute to the
city's imposts and participate in its defense. At times Jews were
indeed called upon to repel attackers on the portion of the wall
adjoining their quarter.[39]

Most significantly, the burghers long effectively protected the
Jews against their assailants. Typical of the city council's attitude

was its order of 1342 to all burghers in the case of riots to help the Jews and "to act in accordance with the advice of mayor and council for the honor and necessity of all of us and of our city." Thus the Jewish community not only escaped the ravages of the Rindfleisch and Armleder massacres but it also suffered little from the hands of pogromists during the Black Death. The events of 1349 are doubly remarkable as the dukes of Bavaria had, in anticipation of the bloodshed, granted the municipality an advance absolution for whatever assassinations of Jews might occur. As observed by the chronicler, Archdeacon Eberhard:

The burghers of Ratisbon, wishing to honor their city, prohibited the slaying or destruction of Jews without judicial judgment. They said that if God himself should desire the death of the Jews, they would not resist; but they wished first to achieve greater conviction that it was God who imposed that penalty upon the Jews. Thus the Jews of Ratisbon, though not without much difficulty, have hitherto escaped death by burning.

This friendly attitude of the patricians stemmed from their high sense of honor, their fear that popular frenzy, once unleashed, would not stop before their own gates, and the direct economic benefits brought to the city's then flourishing economy by the Jews' share in its international trade, their fiscal contributions, and the political connections engendered by their money trade. The credit often extended by the Ratisbon Jewish bankers to outside personages led to their social contacts which, at crucial moments, could also help the city and its patrician leaders. For one example, Jewish bankers mediated, in 1297, between the Bavarian duke and the archbishop of Salzburg, being able to advance the latter 600 silver marks. The document recording this transaction is signed by the bankers and provided with a remarkable seal bearing a Hebrew legend. In times of need both the city and its elders also could borrow money from the Jews.[40]

Even when the city's economic flowering had begun to decline in the fourteenth and fifteenth centuries, the Jewish community maintained its leading position in German Jewry. It was aided therein by a succession of distinguished scholars and the presence of a beautiful synagogue, founded by Yehudah b. Samuel the Pious, the image of which has been preserved for posterity by two woodcuts of Albrecht Altdorfer (died in 1538). Equally significant was the Ratisbon cemetery, which served all Bavarian Jewry ever since 1210. In 1325 its management was granted a special exemption from tolls usually charged for Jewish corpses transported from distant localities. In time, many pilgrimages were made to the graves of "saints" and scholars buried in that renowned "house of eternity." Ratisbon, as we recall, had been the seat of Yehudah the Pious, many of his disciples among the German *Hasidim*, and the traveler Petaḥiah, who had thence embarked on his famous world "circuit." Even in the fifteenth century its community was headed by the distinguished jurist, Israel Bruna (of Brünn). Although imprisoned by hostile city elders in 1474, probably because he was one of the suspects in the alleged admission of some Bohemian Jews without the council's approval, he was released by direct imperial intervention after signing the so-called *Urfehde,* a pledge that he would not retaliate in any form for this unlawful arrest. This combination of relative security, economic well-being, and broad intellectual interests doubtless stimulated somewhat closer social relations between Christians and Jews and also accounted, in part, for certain greater freedoms enjoyed by Ratisbon's Jewish women. In a case brought before Meir of Rothenburg, a "rebellious" wife threatened that if the husband would carry out his design to despoil her of her marriage settlement and make her wait for several years for her divorce, she would leave him and live among Gentiles. In this connection the inquirer contended that "the Ratisbon women had always been haughty toward their husbands and now were even more arrogant than ever." While such generalizations must always be taken with a large grain of salt, we shall see that in this case they contained an element of truth. All through that period, however, Jewish economic strength was sapped by Wenceslaus' debt cancellations and the fiscal exactions. On demanding from Ratisbon Jewry a contribution toward the Hussite Wars in 1421, Sigismund's envoys did not hesitate to imprison its leaders and to exact from them no less than 8,000 Hungarian florins. They overcame the council's resistance by allotting to the city half that amount in accordance with an agreement dating back to 1410. To assuage its guilt feelings, the council reduced the ordinary Jewish taxes to but 60 marks annually for a period of four years. These harsh proceedings did not discourage the royal bureaucrats from demanding another

Hussite tax from the Ratisbon Jews a year later. But this importunity appeared exaggerated to the king himself, and the tax was apparently never collected.[41]

In the mid-fifteenth century the city lost all interest in protecting her Jews against Frederick III's continued exactions. Apart from changing economic factors, and the anti-Jewish clamor of the craft guilds anxious to seize the reins of municipal administration, it was the growth of religious fanaticism, stimulated by the appearance of Nicolaus Cusanus and John Capistrano in Germany, which accounted for the new antagonisms. Rabble-rousing sermons by such preachers as Peter Schwarz (Nigri), likewise turned public opinion in Ratisbon against the Jews. Ratisbon felt the additional pressure from the Bavarian duke, Louis, who after expelling the Jews from his own domains demanded a similar enactment in 1452 from the Ratisbon council. Temporarily the Jews escaped this fate and merely had to submit, apparently for the first time, to effective enforcement of the Jewish badge. But the city council, theretofore their staunchest defender, now turned against them and joined the ever more vociferous chorus demanding their expulsion. Ready excuses were found in successive Blood Accusations. One initiated in 1474 was quashed with relative ease by Frederick III; it ended with the confession and execution of the false informer, a converted Jew. But another, perhaps given greater credence because of the wide publicity attached to the affair of Simeon of Trent in 1475, led to the imprisonment and protracted trial of many leading Jews in 1476–80. The Jewish elders appealed not only to the emperor and imperial courts but also to the papal legate. Characteristically, they now tried to deny the city council's authority altogether. In their petition to the legate they wrote:

Like his predecessors, Emperor Frederick has reserved for himself and his authority all Jews living under his reign and particularly also those of Ratisbon. He did it in consequence of his particular right and his special dominion, lest the Christians eliminate them [the Jews] altogether while they ought to be maintained in memory of the Lord's passion in accordance with the law.

The verbiage of this passage betrays Christian influence; the petition may actually have been written with the aid of a Christian lawyer or cleric. Yet it clearly revealed the preference of the embattled Jews for the imperial, over the then no longer dependable municipal, protection. In the ensuing trial, indeed, Frederick succeeded in preventing the execution of the arrested defendants. At one time he even employed the drastic means of entirely suspending the city's right to criminal jurisdiction (*Blutbann*).[42]

In this tricornered struggle, in which the various Bavarian dukes pursued changeable opportunistic policies, Frederick succeeded in staving off the expulsion of Jews from Ratisbon to the end of his life. This staunch resistance seemed to bear out in the eyes of many contemporaries uncomplimentary characterizations by hostile observers, such as Matthias Döring's "avaricious and negligent," or that the emperor "was generally styled the king of the Jews, rather than of the Romans." More remarkably, Frederick's policy was also undeviatingly pursued by Maximilian, although this "last medieval knight" proved far more accommodating to Nuremberg, Styria, and other anti-Jewish regimes. To the end of his reign Maximilian successfully repudiated all attempts of the Ratisbon council to expel the Jews. Only after the emperor's death in 1519 and the ensuing *interregnum,* during which imperial authority was at a low ebb, did the city finally carry out its design and banish the Jews. It effectively resisted orders of Habsburg officials to readmit them, and in 1521 it persuaded Charles V to grant it pardon and to acknowledge the accomplished fact. Only a small Jewish minority established itself in an adjacent suburb, Stadtamhof (formerly Schierstadt), which was under Bavarian jurisdiction. From there the remnant could carry on for a time some trade with its old and ever nostalgically remembered home town.[43]

## SERFS OF MANY CHAMBERS

Viewed in its totality the fate of late medieval German Jewry was most deeply affected by the gradual crumbling of imperial authority. For notwithstanding the frequent arbitrariness and unmitigated selfishness of many emperors, they were subject to somewhat greater restraints. Jewish representatives could more readily cope with their officials than with the temperamental outbursts with which both the princes and the municipalities often approached the Jewish question. But the emperors were frequently powerless to impose their will upon these lesser authorities. Their very protective rights toward their "serfs of the Chamber" were often nullified by such declarations as those of the Brandenburg margrave, Louis IV. In his significant privilege of 1344, subsequently often renewed (1350 and 1367) and even extended to all of Brandenburg (1420 and 1440), Louis bluntly declared that the Jews were the serfs of *his* chamber. The ensuing diversity of claims to overlordship over Jews was already noticed by the thirteenth-century jurist who composed the so-called *Rechtsbuch nach Distinctionen* (or *Meissener Rechtsbuch*), along the lines of Eike of Repgow's Saxon law book. "I shall not write," he declared, "about the Jews' established courts, for in the various lands it operates by custom, differently than in others." What was said here about the judiciary applied with equal validity to all other phases of the Jews' juridical status, and particularly their varying fiscal obligations and the changing provisions for their security. Ultimately, the imperial police ordinances of 1548 and 1577 acknowledged the long undisputed fact that the protection of Jewish life and property devolved on the whole hierarchical structure of imperial institutions down to the imperial gentry.[44]

By that time, however, the dispersal of authority brought the Holy Roman Empire to such a state of confusion that a general reaction set in. Although, as we shall see, the attempt to reestablish genuine imperial overlordship, undertaken by Charles V with the backing of his vast non-German resources, was quickly frustrated, individual princes were gradually able more effectively to unify their states.

Nor was the earlier atomization of the feudal regimes devoid of a silver lining. Had the dreams of a Frederick Barbarossa come true and had Germany become, under the centralized imperial regime, a national German state, paralleling the achievements of the kings of England and France, the chances are that at some particular historic moment that central power would have enacted a general decree of expulsion of Jews similar to those of its western neighbors. Quite apart, therefore, from whatever effects the instability created by feudal anarchy may have had on the psychological alertness and the pioneering spirit as well as the communal cohesiveness and solidarity of German Jewry—all of them indispensable for its sheer survival—it enabled at least some of the individuals banished from their old homes to find shelter in a neighboring locality under the rule of a lesser bishop or baron. The Jewish settlement in Stadtamhof is a case in point. From these tiny settlements Jews were able not only to maintain a modicum of trade with their older habitats, but also gradually to fan out into some other semirural locations.

In the meantime, the great political and ideological transformations taking place throughout Germany during the early modern period stimulated the rise of several modern states with more or less efficient bureaucracies and standing armies which required the assistance of ingenious bankers and suppliers. The surviving remnant of medieval Jewry was now able to furnish to the princely governments a number of enterprising Jewish counselors, whose presence indirectly led to the establishment of many new Jewish communities. The era of the *Court Jew* had arrived.

# NOTES

# ABBREVIATIONS

| | |
|---|---|
| *AFH* | Archivum franciscanum historicum |
| *AFP* | Archivum fratrum praedicatorum |
| *AKKR* | Archiv für katolisches Kirchenrecht |
| *AS* | Archivio storico |
| | |
| *b.* | ben or bar (son) |
| *Baron Jub. Vol.* | Essays on Jewish Life and Thought in Honor of Salo Wittmayer Baron. New York, 1959. |
| *BH* | Bulletin hispanique |
| | |
| *CH* | Church History |
| | |
| *DAGM* | Deutsches Archiv für Geschichte des Mittelalters |
| | |
| *Freidus Mem. Vol.* | Studies in Jewish Bibliography . . . in Memory of Abraham Solomon Freidus |
| | |
| *GS* | Gesammelte Schriften |
| | |
| *HJ* | Historia Judaica |
| *HJB* | Historisches Jahrbuch |
| *HUCA* | Hebrew Union College Annual |
| *HZ* | Historische Zeitschrift |
| | |
| *JGJCR* | Jahrbuch der Gesellschaft für Geschichte der Juden in der Čechoslowakischen Republik |
| *JJLG* | Jahrbuch der Jüdisch-Literarischen Gesellschaft, Frankfurt a. M. |
| *JJS* | Journal of Jewish Studies |
| *JQR* | Jewish Quarterly Review (new series, unless otherwise stated) |
| *JSS* | Jewish Social Studies |
| | |
| *KA* | Korrespondenzblatt . . . Akademie für Wissenschaft des Judentums |
| *KS* | Kirjath Sepher, Quarterly Bibliographical Review |
| | |
| *MGH* | Monumenta Germaniae Historica |
| *MGWJ* | Monatsschrift für Geschichte und Wissenschaft des Judentums |
| *MIOG* | Mitteilungen des Instituts für österreichische Geschichtsforschung |
| *M.T.* | Moses b. Maimon's Mishneh Torah (Code) |
| *MWJ* | Magazin für die Wissenschaft des Judentums |

| | |
|---|---|
| *Neuman Jub. Vol.* | Studies and Essays in Honor of Abraham A. Neuman. Leiden, 1962. |
| *PAAJR* | Proceedings of the American Academy for Jewish Research |
| *Philippson Festschrift* | Beiträge zur Geschichte der deutschen Juden. Festschrift . . . Martin Philippson. Leipzig, 1916. |
| *PL* | Patrologiae cursus completus, series Latina |
| *RBPH* | Revue Belge de philologie et d'histoire |
| *REJ* | Revue des études juives |
| *RH* | Revue historique |
| *RHE* | Revue d'histoire ecclésiastique |
| *RHPR* | Revue d'histoire et de philosophie religieuses |
| *RHR* | Revue d'histoire des religions |
| *RMI* | Rassegna mensile di Israel |
| *RQH* | Revue des questions historiques |
| *VSW* | Vierteljahrsschrift für Sozial- und Wirtschaftsgeschichte |
| *Weiss Jub. Vol.* | Abraham Weiss Jubilee Volume. New York, 1964. |
| *ZGJD* | Zeitschrift für die Geschichte der Juden in Deutschland (new series, unless otherwise stated) |
| *ZGJT* | Zeitschrift für die Geschichte der Juden in der Tschechoslowakei |
| *ZKG* | Zeitschrift für Kirchengeschichte |
| *ZRG* | Zeitschrift der Savigny-Stiftung für Rechtsgeschichte |

# NOTES

## CHAPTER XXXVII: INFIDEL

1. The numerous variations, chronological as well as geographical, of the Church policies toward Jews under the Christian Roman Empire and during the High Middle Ages, have been discussed in earlier volumes, particularly Vols. II, Chaps. XII–XIII; IV, Chap. XX; and V, Chap. XXIV. Much of the literature listed in the notes to those chapters will prove useful also for the understanding of the developments after 1200 c.e. However, there have been many significant additions in both the primary sources and secondary letters, some of which will be recorded in the forthcoming notes. On the general background, suffice it to refer to the numerous Church histories such as the multivolume *Histoire de l'Église,* ed. by A. Fliche *et al.* The effects on Jewish status of the rising tide of medieval nationalism will be more fully discussed *infra,* Chap. L.

2. A comprehensive scholarly analysis, with full documentation, of the relations between the Roman Church and the Jews is still a major desideratum. In *Le Saint-Siège et les Juifs,* E. Rodocanachi merely scratches the surface. More detailed, though often quite biased, is the long series of articles, still incomplete, by L. Erler in *AKKR,* XLI–XLIV, XLVIII, L, LIII, especially those relating to "Die Päpste and die Juden" in XLVIII, 369–416; L, 3–31. Many data are included in H. Vogelstein and P. Rieger, *Geschichte der Juden in Rom* (more briefly, in the former's English summary, *Rome*) and A. Berliner's work under the same title. Of great value is the documentary collection of papal letters and conciliar canons, in both their Latin originals and an English translation, with a good introduction and notes, in S. Grayzel, *The Church and the Jews in the XIIIth Century,* which, however, covers only the years 1198–1254. The continuation of J. Parkes, *The Jew in the Medieval Community,* which was to deal specifically with the socioreligious aspects of Judeo-Christian relations during the later Middle Ages, has not yet appeared.

Quite useful, however, are numerous monographic studies such as the collection of excerpts by B. Blumenkranz from *Les Auteurs chrétiens latins du moyen âge sur les Juifs et le judaïsme;* P. Browe, *Die Judenmission im Mittelalter und die Päpste;* idem, "Die Religiöse Duldung der Juden im Mittelalter," *AKKR,* CXVIII, 3–76; idem, "Die Kirchenrechtliche Stellung der getauften Juden und ihrer Nachkommen," *ibid.,* CXXI, 3–22, 165–91; idem, "Die Judenbekämpfung im Mittelalter," *Zeitschrift für katholische Theologie,* LXII, 196–231, 349–84; M. Elias, "Die Römische Kurie, besonders Innozenz III, und die Juden," *JJLG,* XII, 37–82; L. Lucas, "Judentaufen und Judaismus zur Zeit des Papstes Innozenz III," *Philippson Festschrift,* pp. 25–38; L. Bardinet, "La Condition civile des Juifs du Comtat Venaissin pendant le séjour des papes à Avignon, 1309–1376," *RH,* XII, 1–47; S. Grayzel, "The Avignon Popes and the Jews," *HJ,* II, 1–12; K. Eubel, "Zu dem Verhalten der Päpste gegen die Juden [1379–1450]," *Römische Quartalschrift,* XIII, 29–42;

idem, "Weitere Urkunden" on the same subject, *ibid.*, XVII, 183–87; F. Vernet, "Le Pape Martin V et les Juifs," *RQH*, LI, 373–423; M. Simonsohn, *Die Kirchliche Judengesetzgebung im Zeitalter der Reformkonzilien von Konstanz und Basel.*

Data of a different kind have been assembled by P. Démann and R. Bloch in their "Catechèse chrétienne et le peuple de la Bible," *Cahiers sioniennes*, VI, and "Formation liturgique et attitude chrétienne envers les Juifs," *ibid.*, VII, 115–78. See also the numerous publications by B. Blumenkranz and others, pertaining particularly to the Judeo-Christian controversy, and cited *supra*, Vol. V, pp. 340 ff. and in forthcoming notes. Of some interest, though more as a reflection of Nazi biases, also are the brief surveys by G. Franz, "Der Jude im katholischen Kirchenrecht," *Deutsche Rechtswissenschaft*, II, 157–66; and J. Roth, "Die Katholische Kirche und die Judenfrage," *Forschungen zur Judenfrage*, IV, 163–76.

3. Alexander of Hales, *Summa theologica*, II, ii.8, 1, 730 f., 740, ed. by the Fathers of the College of St. Bonaventura in Quaracchi, III, 729 f., with reference to the Decretals of Gregory IX, v. 6, 9–15 in *Corpus juris canonici*, ed. by E. Friedberg, II, 771 ff.; and Peter Lombard's *Commentary* on Ps. 40:11, 58:12–13, in *PL*, CXCI, 413, 546 f. See also the editors' introduction to that volume of the *Summa*, pp. liii ff. These views of the distinguished Paris theologian have been briefly analyzed by Jakob Guttmann in *Die Scholastik des dreizehnten Jahrhunderts in ihren Beziehungen zum Judenthum und zur jüdischen Literatur*, pp. 32 ff. See also W. Lampen, "Alexander von Hales und der Antisemitismus," *Franziskanische Studien*, XVI, 1–14. On the basis of Alexander's statements relating to the Talmud, Lampen has plausibly argued that this entire second title in the *Summa* devoted to Jews and pagans was composed in the years 1238–42.

4. Alexander III's and Clement III's bulls of 1179 and 1188, respectively, in the sources cited *supra*, Vol. IV, pp. 8, 235 n. 3; Thomas Aquinas, *Summa theologica*, II, 2, q. 10, art. 11, in his *Opera omnia*, ed. under the sponsorship of Leo XIII [and Benedict XV], VIII, 93; here quoted from the English trans. by the Fathers of the English Dominican Province [IX], 143. Like most other areas of Thomistic theology, the teachings of the great scholastic on the proper attitude of pious Christians to Jews and Judaism have been subjected to careful scrutiny for many years. See especially the monographs by Jakob Guttmann, *Das Verhältniss des Thomas von Aquino zum Judenthum and zur jüdischen Literatur (Avicebron und Maimonides)*; H. Gayraud, *L'Antisémitisme de St. Thomas d'Aquin;* S. Deploige, *St. Thomas et la question juive*, 2d ed.; and the debate of 1935 between B. Mailloux and S. S. Cohon in Mailloux's "Saint Thomas et les Juifs," reprinted from the *Revue Dominicaine* in his *Essais et bilans*, pp. 217–35; and S. S. Cohon's *St. Thomas et les Juifs*. See also H. Liebeschütz's more recent analysis of "Judaism and Jewry in the Social Doctrine of Thomas Aquinas," *JJS*, XIII, 57–81; *infra*, n. 52; and Chap. XXXVIII, n. 26.

These arguments of the leading scholastics and canon jurists were often repeated in the subsequent literature, even where the writers' aims were far more antagonistic to Jews and Judaism; for instance, in fifteenth-century Italy, where the rapid growth of Jewish moneylending to meet the requirements of the speedily expanding economy created much anti-Jewish feeling. Understandably, the lower clergy and the Christian apologists felt the impact of such popular hostility far more than did the central organs of the Church. They readily participated, therefore, in various so-called *Consilia contra Judaeos foenerantes*. Nevertheless, a *consilium* meeting in

Piacenza about 1490, with the participation of the anti-Jewish polemist Bernardino de' Busti and six associates, essentially repeated the traditional arguments for and against Jewish toleration. Its resolution, confirmed by the prior of the local College of Judges, differed only in some relatively minor nuances, particularly in its anti-usurious emphases, from the traditional position of the Church. See the summary by H. Élie in his "Contribution à l'étude du status des Juifs en Italie aux XVe et XVIe siècles. L'opinion de Bernardin de Busti," *RHR*, CXLII, 70 ff.; and *infra*, n. 61.

5. "The number of forgeries in the domain of medieval documents," Horst Fuhrmann observed in a recent paper, "was so overwhelmingly large that, in 1918, Wilhelm Peitz of the Society of Jesus established a special series of publications devoted to *Untersuchungen zu Urkundenfälschungen des Mittelalters*, and the *Monumenta Germaniae Historica* planned in 1940 the preparation of a special *Tafelwerk der Urkundenfälschungen*." See Fuhrmann, "Die Fälschungen im Mittelalter: Ueberlegungen zum mittelalterlichen Wahrheitsbegriff," *HZ*, CXCVII, 532.

6. Marquardus de Susannis, *Tractatus de Judaeis et aliis infidelibus*, I, vii.1, Venice, 1558 ed., fol. 24b, citing numerous earlier juridical authorities. There is no evidence, however, that any secular ruler ever considered the precepts of Christian charity a serious deterrent for withdrawing toleration from Jews. Some popes themselves, such as John XXII in 1321–22 and Pius V in 1569, did not refrain from at least partial expulsions of Jews. The other factors affecting toleration and nontoleration of Jews will be discussed in later chapters, particularly Chap. L. See *infra*, n. 8, and Chap. LIX.

7. Honorius IV's bull of 1285, Art. 9 in *Bullarium romanum*, ed. Taurinensis by A. Tomassetti, IV, 73 (summarized in A. Potthast, *Regesta pontificum romanorum*, II, 1801 No. 22291); *infra*, Chap. XLVI, n. 5. As in the earlier enactments of the *Constitutio pro Judaeis*, we do not have the texts of most of these renewals and often have to rely on the record of their confirmations by later popes. See *supra*, Vol. IV, pp. 7 f., 235 f. n. 3. But, directly or indirectly, we learn that after Innocent III's restatement of 1199, the succeeding thirteenth-century popes reconfirmed it: Honorius III in 1217, Gregory IX in 1235, Innocent IV in 1246 (and again in 1247), Alexander IV in 1255, Urban IV about 1261, Gregory X in 1272 (and again in 1274), Nicholas III in 1278, Honorius IV soon after his succession in 1285, and Nicholas IV soon after 1288. See the excerpts reproduced by A. Potthast in his *Regesta*, I, 79 No. 834, 494 No. 5616, 841 No. 9893; II, 1042 No. 12315; and more fully (for the period of 1198 to 1254) with the English trans. by Grayzel in *The Church*, pp. 92 ff. No. 5, 144 ff. No. 35, 218 f. No. 81, 260 ff. No. 111, 244 f. No. 118. The decrees of Urban IV, Honorius IV, and Nicholas IV are mentioned only by their successors, Urban V and Martin V, in their renewals of that decree in 1365 and 1419, respectively, as reproduced in the *Bullarium Romanum*, IV, 522 f. No. iv, and by O. Raynaldus in his *Annales ecclesiastici*, VIII, 503 No. ii, while that of Nicholas III is quoted by G. B. Depping in *Les Juifs dans le moyen âge*, p. 465.

The latter text was characteristically found in the Paris archives, evidently having been in the possession of the Paris Jewish community before its expulsion from France. Gregory X's renewal, with additions, in 1272, is now found in the Innsbruck archives in a copy provided with notes by a bishop of Trent. Similarly, the bull issued by Innocent IV in 1247 against the Blood Accusation is still extant in the

Cologne archives in a copy of its confirmation by Gregory X of 1274 and Rudolph of Habsburg of 1275. It even bears a Hebrew inscription, "Lying talk must not be believed," an allusion to Exod. 5:9. Another copy, showing the signature of Albertus Magnus, found its way into the Frankfort archives. See A. Kober, *Cologne*, in S. Grayzel's English trans., pp. 34 ff., 351 n. 4; and *infra*, Chaps. XLI, n. 26; and XLIX.

Innocent IV's and Gregory X's repetition of the bull within two years probably stemmed from the need of foreign Jews for additional protection. Not surprisingly, these texts were cited by Přemysl Ottakar II of Bohemia in 1254 and by Emperor Rudolph I in 1275. See G. Bondy and F. Dworský, *Zur Geschichte der Juden in Böhmen, Mähren und Schlesien von 906 bis 1620*, I, 23 ff. Nos. 25 and 27; and M. Wiener, *Regesten zur Geschichte der Juden in Deutschland während des Mittelalters*, I, 9 No. 54. Innocent IV, who also distinguished himself by being the first pope to outlaw the Blood Accusation, may have reissued that protective bull in 1253 as well. This is at least the date given by M. Stern in his *Päpstliche Bullen über die Blutbeschuldigung*, p. 14. See Grayzel, p. 274. See also the data given by L. Erler in *AKKR*, L, 3 ff.; and by P. Browe, *ibid.*, CXVIII, 10 f. The late medieval Blood Accusation, whose earlier manifestations were discussed *supra*, Vols. I, pp. 191 f., 382; IV, pp. 135 ff., 306 ff., will be analyzed *infra*, Chap. XLIX.

The fact that some popes are not recorded as having confirmed the *Constitutio* may be owing to their short tenure of office or other accidental causes, or merely to the failure of subsequent popes to include their names in the list, always selective, of confirming predecessors. The papal archives, though probably better preserved than other West-European repositories, suffered from the frequent riots in Rome, the transfer of the papal residence to Avignon in 1309 and then back to Rome in 1376, and the sheer bulk of the correspondence rapidly accumulating in the papal chancery. A mere glance at the extensive "Registers" of the various thirteenth-century popes, conveniently listed in A. Fliche's *Histoire*, X, 5, and frequently mentioned in these notes, will convey the impression of both their richness and their inevitable incompleteness.

8. Potthast, *Regesta*, I, 870 No. 10243; Grayzel, *The Church*, pp. 226 ff. No. 87; Raynaldus, *Annales*, II, 150 f. No. xlviii; V, 136 ff. Nos. xxi ff. The concluding phrase, *appellatione remota*, in Gregory IX's letter of 1236 was of particular significance. Innocent III had already realized that transgressors often sought to "inject the obstacle of an appeal, so that they may evade the canonical correction." See his various letters of 1202, in his *Epistolae* (or *Regestae*), v.41 ff., in *PL*, CCXIV, 453 ff. Of course, satisfaction for property losses could not bring back to life the victims massacred by the would-be Crusaders. On the bloody persecution by the latter including the Pastoureaux, see *supra*, Vol. IV, pp. 89 ff., and *infra*, Chap. XLIII. At times the popes themselves were swayed by such waves of popular hostility. The same John XXII who had so strongly defended the Jews against the Pastoureaux in 1320 two years later decreed their expulsion from Carpentras, an unprecedented step indeed in the annals of the Papacy. That decree was of short duration, however, and Jews were allowed to return in 1343 and to rebuild a synagogue of exactly the same size. Seven years later, they left Carpentras again, but they returned in 1367—this time for good. See L. Bardinet's data, partly culled from the local archives of Avignon, in *RH*, XII, 39 ff.

9. G. D. Mansi, ed., *Collectio*, XXII, 1172; XXIII, 714; (C. D. Hefele, *Histoire*, V, Part 2, pp. 1429 ff., fails to mention the anti-Jewish provisions); Grayzel, *The*

*Church*, pp. 282 f. No. 123, 314 f. No. xvi, 330 f. No. xxxvi; J. Peckham, *Registrum epistolarum*, ed. by C. T. Martin, I, 212 f. No. clxxix; Potthast, *Regesta*, II, 1937, No. 24175; C. Devic and J. Vaissète, *Histoire générale de Languedoc*, IX, 62 No. xlvii; *supra*, n. 6; Vol. II, pp. 181, 189, 192 f., 398 n. 13; and *infra*, Chap. XLVII.

In his note on Devic and Vaissète, A. Molinier (ed.) connects the resolution of the Paris Parlement with an inquiry instituted by the seneschal of Carcassonne, published by G. Saige in *Les Juifs du Languedoc antérieurment au XIV^e siècle*, pp. 213 ff., though Saige postulates here the date of 1284. See also G. Caumes' dissertation, *Les Jurisdictions royales et seigneurales de la ville de Béziers de 1229 à 1789*.

On learning from a petition of Cistercian monks about the construction of a new synagogue in the city of Pressburg (Pozsonyi or Bratislava), Benedict XII on November 13, 1335 ordered the archbishop of Gran (Esztergom) without much ado to see to it that it was "destroyed without delay." See his *Lettres communes*, ed. by J. M. Vidal, I, 207 No. 2391. The problem of new synagogues often agitated the minds of pious Catholics even in a new country like Poland where Jewish settlers began arriving in increasing numbers during the later Middle Ages. A provincial synod meeting in Piotrków in 1542 asked the king for "an order to destroy the new synagogues including those built in Cracow. While the Church tolerates the Jews in commemoration of the Saviour's passion their number ought not to increase." In 1589, the Synod of Gniezno complained that "contrary to ancient statutes, Jews have built in the royal cities new brick synagogues, larger and more beautiful than the churches; also houses above the permitted number. May the king forbid this severely through an edict." See M. Balaban, *Zabytki historyczne Żydów w Polsce (Historical Remains of the Jews in Poland)*, pp. 54 ff.; and other data assembled by Browe in *AKKR*, CXVIII, 11 ff.

The prohibitions cited by Browe, however, that Jews could not even maintain additional private chapels in their homes (London, 1282, and Strasbourg, 1322), merely illustrate the occasional excesses of zeal. More frequently the Jews had to be given permission to maintain more than one synagogue in localities where they lived in substantial numbers or belonged to congregations praying in accordance with diverse rituals. They are recorded to have possessed twelve houses of worship in fourteenth-century Toledo, while the very capital of Catholic Christianity, Rome, accommodated no less than eleven Jewish congregations in 1519. A compromise solution was found there, however, in the so-called *cinque scuole*, where five different congregations occupied separate chambers in the same building. See D. Kaufmann, "Les Synagogues de Tolède," *REJ*, XXXVIII, 251–56; idem, "Léon X et les Juifs de Rome," *ibid.*, XXI, 288; A. Berliner, *Geschichte der Juden in Rom von der ältesten Zeit bis zur Gegenwart*, I, Part 2, pp. 95 f., 104; and my *The Jewish Community*, III, 148 f. n. 19. The papal vicar general in Ferrara, too, merely adhered to the accepted tenets of canon law when in 1532 he forced the new German-Jewish settlers in the city to hold their independent services in the existing communal synagogue, rather than allowing them to build a synagogue of their own. See Perugini, "L'Inquisition romaine et les Israélites," *REJ*, III, 95. See also *infra*, Chap. XLVII.

10. E. Levy, "Un Document sur les Juifs du Barrois en 1321–23," *REJ*, XIX, 246–58; E. Florez, *España sagrada*, XLIV, 297 f.; J. Régné, "Catalogue des Actes de Jaime I^er, Pedro III et Alfonso III, rois d'Aragon, concernant les Juifs (1213–1291)," *REJ*, LXIII, 252 No. 696; *supra*, Vol. IV, pp. 8 f., 236 n. 4. Later the famous preacher

Menaḥem Azariah da Fano permitted communities to sell tombstones "when they are persecuted by men bent upon stealing the stones and using them in the construction of their theaters [churches] or for sepulchers upon their own dead, and there is no escape." See J. E. Scherer, *Die Rechtsverhältnisse der Juden in den deutsch-österreichischen Ländern*, pp. 182 (Art. xiv), 225 f.; Menaḥem Azariah da Fano, *Resp.*, fol. 26b No. 44, 32ab No. 56. See also Browe in *AKKR*, CXVIII, 21 ff.; and my *The Jewish Community*, II, 150 f.; III, 153 n. 25, 154 n. 28.

11. Augustine, *In Ioan.* xxvi.2, in *PL*, XXXV, 1607 ("credere non potest nisi volens"); Thomas Aquinas, *Summa theologica*, II, ii, q.10, art. 8, with the *Commentary* thereon by Cajetan (Gaetanus, originally Tommaso de Vio), in *Opera omnia*, ed. under Leo XIII's sponsorship, VIII, 89 f.; in the English trans. [IX], 134; Vicente Ferrer, *Sermones*, cited from a Valencia MS by V. Genovés, *San Vicente Ferrer en la política de su tiempo*, p. 23; his correspondence with King Ferdinand I of Aragon of 1414, published in Raynaldus, *Annales*, VIII, 386 f. No. 19 (*ad* 1414); and P. Reid, "St. Thomas' Christmas Gift: Conversion of Two Prominent Jews," *Dominicana*, XXXVI, 279–84. See also *supra*, Vol. III, pp. 26 ff., 241 n. 31, 242 n. 34; this Chap. n. 4; and *infra*, Chap. XXXVIII, n. 26.

Facing the peculiar situation of early thirteenth-century Spain, with its large Muslim populations even in the Christian states, the decretist Laurentius wished to extend the doctrine of nonforcible conversion to all unbelievers. He claimed that the first real Roman emperor was Constantine, who had the right to use force only with regard to those subject peoples who had previously recognized him. Otherwise "they ought not to be injured, any more than the Jews, so long as they conduct themselves quietly and do not attempt to create any disturbance." See his gloss (written about 1210), cited by F. Kempf in his *Papsttum und Kaisertum bei Innocenz III*, pp. 242 ff. But on the whole, canonical jurisprudence drew a line between Judaism, which had a special claim on the Christian world, and the other faiths which did not have to be tolerated at all.

Needless to say, not all churchmen lived up to this principle. We recall how many monks and lower clergy had been involved, directly or indirectly, in the massacres of Jews during the first Crusades, and that only the intervention of St. Bernard of Clairvaux stopped the bloodshed instigated by the Cistercian monk Radulph in 1146. See *supra*, Vol. IV, pp. 120, 126, 300 n. 40. Similar violations recurred in the later Middle Ages and in modern times. In periods of great tension, particularly, new rationalizations for the outright use of force were sought by such English scholastics as John Duns Scotus or Francisco de Vitoria, the Spanish commentator of the Thomistic *Summa*. See *infra*, n. 13; and Chaps. XLIX and L. Nevertheless it was of vital importance for European Jewry to be able, at critical moments, to invoke protective regulations that were reinforced by ancient tradition.

See additional data assembled by Browe in *Die Judenmission*, pp. 231 ff. On the varying attitudes of secular authorities, see *infra*, Chaps. XXXVIII and XLVII. The complexities of the canonical regulations governing the conversion of Jews in modern times are analyzed by D. Grasso in his "Contrasti e problemi nella conversione degli Ebrei," *Civiltà cattolica*, CVI, 393–407.

12. Alexander of Hales, *Summa theologica*, II, ii.8, 1, 743, Quaracchi ed., III, 731. Innocent III's epistle of September or October 1201 was subsequently incorporated in the Gregorian Decretals and thus became part and parcel of the main code of

canon law. See Potthast, *Regesta*, I, 131 No. 1479; *Decretales Greg*. iii.42, 3, in *Corpus*, ed. by Friedberg, II, 644 ff. (in substance repeated by Boniface VIII and restated in the *Liber Sextus*, v.2, 13, *ibid.*, col. 1075); Grayzel, *The Church*, pp. 100 ff. No. 12; Marquardus de Susannis, *Tractatus de Judaeis et aliis infidelibus*, III, ii.7, Venice, 1558 ed., pp. 133 f. Like other letters from the fourth year of Innocent III's pontificate, that addressed to the archbishop of Arles was not available to Etienne Baluze, the first compiler (in 1682) of the pope's epistles from the pontifical archives. They are, therefore, missing also from the reprint in *PL*, CCXIV, 945 ff., and had to be reconstructed from the quotation in the Gregorian Decretals, hence the absence of a more precise date. See F. Kempf, *Die Register Innocenz' III: Eine paläographisch-diplomatische Untersuchung*; L. Santifaller *et al.*, "Studien und Vorarbeiten zur Edition der Register Papst Innocenz' III, Parts 1–3," *MIOG*, LXV, 237–368; "Parts 4–9," *Römische historische Mitteilungen*, I, 77–105; II, 9–50; III, 129–85; IV, 26–36, 37–62; and *infra*, Chap. XL, n. 4. On Leo VII's letter of 937–38, see *supra*, Vol. IV, pp. 6 f., 235 n. 2.

We may also note that the baptismal act need not have been performed by a priest, nor even by a Christian. In line with Augustine and other predecessors, Thomas Aquinas taught that baptism is an internal process in which Christ uses any human being as an instrument. See N. M. Haring, "A Brief Historical Comment on St. Thomas, *Summa Theol*. III. qu. 67, a. 5: *Utrum non baptizatus possit sacramentum baptismi conferre*," *Mediaeval Studies*, XIV, 153–59. On the other hand, baptism performed by a Jew on himself, even on his deathbed, was declared null and void by Innocent III in his reply of August 28, 1206, to the Bishop of Metz. See his *Epistolae*, ix.159, in *PL*, CCXIV, 985 ff.; and therefrom in the *Decretales Greg*. iii.42, 4 in *Corpus*, ed. by Friedberg, II, 646 f.

13. Mansi, *Collectio*, XXII, 1058; Hefele, *Histoire*, V, Part 2, p. 1388; Grayzel, *The Church*, pp. 310 f. No. xii; Durandus of San Porciano, *Commentary* on the *Sententiae theologicae* by Peter Lombard, iv, dist. 4, qu. 6, Lyons, 1563 ed., fols. 259b f.; *Decret. Greg.* and Innocent III's letter of 1201, *loc. cit.* (*supra*, n. 12); Clement IV's, Gregory X's, and Nicholas IV's bulls *Turbato corde* in *Bullarium*, III, 785 f. No. xxiv; IV, 24 f. No. vii, 88 No. ii; Potthast, *Regesta*, II, 1619, No. 20095, 1675 No. 20798, 1840 No. 22795; and *supra*, Vol. IV, pp. 106 f., 293 n. 21. In his frequently quoted bull *Nimis in partibus* of 1286, Pope Honorius IV urged the English bishops to take all necessary steps to secure Jewish compliance with the requirements of canon law and particularly to prevent Jews from seducing the faithful into their sect. According to the pope, Jews were particularly anxious to persuade former coreligionists to return to Judaism by offering them gifts. While some relapsed converts moved away to other localities where they were unknown, many others remained in the same parishes where they had received their baptism, openly lived together with Jews, and observed all Jewish laws and rituals. See Raynaldus, *Annales*, IV, 10 No. xxv; and more briefly Potthast, *Regesta*, II, 1819 No. 22541. Such complaints were frequently voiced by later popes also. They swelled into a chorus after the mass conversion of Spanish Jews following the massacres of 1391. On the early modern developments, see *infra*, Chap. LV.

14. Thomas' *Summa theologica*, II, ii, q.10, art. 12, in *Opera omnia* (Leo XIII's ed.), VIII, 94, with Cajetan's commentary thereon; in the English trans. by the Fathers of the English Dominican Province [IX], 145 f.; Innocent III's aforemen-

tioned letter to the archbishop of Arles of September or October 1201, and Innocent IV's letter to the king of Navarre of October 7, 1246, both in Potthast, *Regesta*, I, 131 No. 1479; II, 1040 No. 1229; and Grayzel, *The Church*, pp. 14, 100 ff. No. 12, 260 f. No. 110; Martin V's bull, *Licet Judaeorum*, issued about 1420 in reply to complaints of some German and Italian Jews, and cited by F. Vernet in *RQH*, LI, 400 n. 6, and Appendix, p. 422 No. 81. See also *ibid.*, pp. 411 ff. Nos. 8, 9, 17, 38. The age of twelve, at which time, according to Jewish law, girls reached maturity (boys a year later), may actually have been suggested to the pope, or at least tacitly accepted, by the "vigilance committee" appointed by a convention of Jewish communities of the Papal States, Tuscany, Ferrara, and Padua, which had met in Bologna in 1416. This committee, which reconvened in Forlì in 1418 and in Perugia in 1423, was doubtless instrumental in securing various concessions from the papal chancery. See my *The Jewish Community*, I, 320 f.; III, 79 n. 35; and the sources cited there. See also, more generally, P. Partner, *The Papal State under Martin V* (quoting, among other matters, a proclamation of June 3, 1427, in Ancona that no one "presume to cause any injury, villainy or displeasure, or say any word of blame or opprobrium against any of the said Jews"; p. 118 n. 1).

15. Vincent of Beauvais, *Speculum doctrinale*, ix.42; John Duns Scotus, *Questiones in librum quartum Sententiarum*, dist. 4 q. 9 in *Opera omnia*, XVI, 487 ff. (tortuously elaborated in the commentary thereon by Antonius Highaeus, *ad loc.*); Rodocanachi, *Le Saint-Siège et les Juifs*, p. 149 n. 1 (from a Vatican MS). Among Duns Scotus' English predecessors, Robert Grosseteste represented the far more moderate attitude of the leading clergy in the early decades of the thirteenth century. Evidently he not only contributed to the considerable restraint exercised by Simon of Monfort, Earl of Leicester, but in his letter to Countess Margaret of Winchester of 1231 he insisted that "it is the duty of the lords who hold them [the Jews] captive to protect them from being killed, and at the same time to use the severest measures to prevent them from oppressing Christians by usury; and to see that they may gain their livelihood by the lawful work of their hands." See his *Epistolae*, ed. by H. R. Luard, p. 34 No. 5; and the English trans. by L. M. Friedman in his *Robert Grosseteste and the Jews*, pp. 12 ff. On the developments leading up to the expulsion of 1290 and the reputed mass conversion of Jewish children at that time, see *infra*, Chap. L.

16. Ulrich (Uldericus) Zasius, *Opera*, Frankfort, 1590 ed., V, 103–116, esp. p. 111; Antonine of Florence, *Summa theologica*, III, xiv.13, 9, cited by J. Schröteler in his comprehensive analysis of *Das Elternrecht in der katholischen theologischen Auseinandersetzung*, p. 234. On the impact of the Freiburg incident on the debates of the early 1500s, see *infra*, Chap. LVII.

17. *Decretum Gratiani*, iii. De consecratione 4, 93 and 98, in *Corpus*, ed. by Friedberg, I, 1392 f.; Alexander of Hales, *Summa*, II, ii.8, 1, 744, in Quaracchi ed., III, 744. The story of the English *Domus Conversorum* is told in full detail by M. Adler in his *Jews of Medieval England*, pp. 277–379. The most amazing part of that story is the continued functioning of that institution for generations after the expulsion of the Jews from England, when all converts must have come from the Continent. (See the list of inmates of the *Domus* from 1330 to 1606 totaling 41 men and 10 women, pp. 376 ff.) Wherever the Jewish population was sufficiently large and the number of likely catechumens quite substantial, the cost of maintaining such houses

probably discouraged emulation. That is probably why even in Rome no such concentrated care was provided for the prospective neophytes until the days of the Renaissance popes. See A. Milano, "L'Impari lotta della comunità di Roma contro la Casa dei catecumeni," *RMI*, XVI, 355–68; and *infra*, Chap. LIX.

18. A. Warschauer, "Mitteilungen aus einem mittelalterlichen Formelbuche," *ZGJD*, [o.s.] IV, 278 (this formula seems to have been of Iberian origin); Third Lateran Council, canon 26, and the Council of Valladolid, canon 21, in Mansi, *Collectio*, XXII, 231; XXV, 719 f.; Hefele, *Histoire*, V, Part 2, pp. 1105 f.; VI, Part 2, pp. 797 f.; Innocent III's letter to Peter of Corbeil, archbishop of Sens, of June 10, 1213, in his *Epistolae*, xvi.84, *PL*, CCXVI, 885 f.; and in Grayzel, *The Church*, pp. 136 ff. No. 29; P. Sambin's ed. of *Lettere inedite di Innocenzo IV*, Nos. 70, 103, 106; and his earlier comments thereon in his *Problemi politici attraverso lettere inedite di Innocenzo IV*, pp. 9 f. See also Grayzel, *The Church*, pp. 16 ff.; Browe, *Die Judenmission*, pp. 187 n. 33, 197 ff. The tone of Innocent's letter is doubly remarkable, as he had been Peter's appreciative pupil in Paris. In fact, that teacher's elevation to the metropolitan see of Sens was entirely owing to Innocent who had overruled the objections of both the king of France and the canons of Sens. See A. Luchaire, *Innocent III—Rome et Italie*, pp. 3 f. On the age-old antecedents of the converts' financial plight, see *supra*, Vols. II, pp. 180 f., 398 f. nn. 12–13; III, pp. 40 ff.; IV, pp. 15 ff.

19. *Leges Visigothorum*, xii.2, 18, ed. by K. Zeumer in *MGH, Leges*, I, Part 1, p. 427 (on the exceptional character of that legislation, however, see *supra*, Vol. III, pp. 43 ff., 249 f.); Emperor Henry IV's and his successor's privileges, Alexander III's epistle and the canon of the Third Lateran Council, all analyzed *supra*, Vol. IV, pp. 16, 67 ff., 240 n. 15, 272 n. 86: Edward I's letter of 1280 to the custodian of the *Domus Conversorum* in T. Rymer and R. Sanderson, *Foedera, conventiones, litterae et cuiuscunque generis acta publica inter reges Angliae et alios quosvis*, rev. ed. by A. Clarke and F. Holbrooke, I, Part 2, p. 582. See also the additional data on "Die Kirchenrechtliche Stellung der getauften Juden und ihrer Nachkommen," assembled by P. Browe in *AKKR*, CXXI, 3 ff., 165 ff.

20. James I's decree of 1242, cited with warm approval by Innocent IV in his epistle to the archbishop of Tarragona of August 20, 1245, in Potthast, *Regesta*, II, 1004 No. 11822, and Grayzel, *The Church*, pp. 254 ff. No. 105; Alphonso X's restatement of the Castilian law in *Las Siete Partidas*, vii.24, 6, ed. by G. Lopez, new ed. Paris, 1847, IV, 646 f.; Grayzel, *The Church*, pp. 18 f., 222 ff. No. 85; John XXII's bull, *Cum sit absurdum*, of June 19, 1320, in *Bullarium*, IV, 294 No. xxvii, repeated in the *Extravagantes communes*, v.2, 2, in *Corpus*, ed. by Friedberg, II, 1290; the debates and resolutions of the Council of Basel in *Monumenta conciliorum generalium seculi XV*: Concilium Basiliense, II, Part 1, pp. 750 f., 758. The date of John XXII's bull is given as July 23, 1320, in L. Bardinet's quotation from an Avignon MS in *RH*, XII, 14 n. 1. In his comprehensive edition of John XXII's *Lettres communes*, however, G. Mollat gives the summaries of three pertinent bulls; one, more general, dated July 22, 1320, concerned all Jewish converts, while another issued nine days later ruled in favor of an individual, Arnaldus de Sorriano of Arles (III, 134 Nos. 11842–43, 166 No. 12205). See also Grayzel, "References to the Jews in the Correspondence of John XXII," *HUCA*, XXIII, Part 2, pp. 46 f. No. ix, 52 ff.

Nos. xiv–xv, with his comments thereon; M. Simonsohn's analysis in *Die Kirchliche Judengesetzgebung*, pp. 37 ff.; and, more generally, Browe, *Die Judenmission*, pp. 183 ff. The procedure adopted in Amalfi, where in 1292 Jewish neophytes were indiscriminately freed from all state and municipal taxes, was quite exceptional, however. See R. Straus, *Die Juden im Königreich Sizilien*, p. 61 (citing M. Camera's *Memorie storico-diplomatiche dell'antica città e ducato di Amalfi*, I, 348).

On the problem of restitution of usurious gains and the ensuing complications in the case of the lender's conversion, see *infra*, n. 58. An additional reason for the protection of the pecuniary resources of neophytes, frequently advanced in the canon legislation and papal correspondence, was the likelihood that they might otherwise relapse into their former faith. This danger was understandably heightened wherever the new converts maintained their old social ties with former coreligionists. Jewish families, on their part, fiercely resisted the conversion of their members, giving rise to atrocity stories such as that recorded in a twelfth-century MS now at the Salisbury Cathedral concerning a Jewish glassworker who became so incensed by the apostasy of his son that he threw him into a burning furnace. The son miraculously escaped injury. See M. Adler, *Jews of Medieval England*, p. 257. Similar miracle tales elsewhere became part of medieval Christian folklore, on which see *infra*, Chap. XLIX.

21. Innocent III's letters to William of Tyre of December 30, 1198, to Bishop Ugo of Ferrara of May 1, 1199, and to Bishop Albert de Buxhoevden of Livonia of April 19, 1201, in his *Epistolae* i.514, ii.50, in *PL*, CCXIV, 475, 588 f.; CCXVI, 1268 f. (Appendix, tit. xi), and in Grayzel, *The Church*, pp. 19 f., 88 ff. No. 3, 101 No. 11; James I's decree and Innocent IV's praise thereof cited *supra*, n. 20. Innocent III's two epistles of 1199 and 1201 achieved even greater recognition by their inclusion in the *Decretales Greg*. iv.19, 7 and 9, in *Corpus*, ed. by Friedberg, II, 722 ff. See also Thomas Aquinas' *Summa theologica*, III, Suppl., q. 59, art. 3 *ad* 2; and G. Fransen, "Les 'Questiones' des canonistes. Essai de dépouillement et de classement," *Traditio*, XIII, 482, placing the problem of a baptized couple married in the second grade of consanguinity near the top of the list of complex questions (Question 2). See also, more generally, C. E. Smith, *Papal Enforcement of Some Medieval Marriage Laws*, showing the numerous perplexities and inconsistencies of the papal legislation concerning marriage impediments among Christians.

On their part, rabbis, too, often faced difficult problems, especially in periods of numerous conversions such as occurred during the age of the Crusades and after the Spanish outbreaks in 1391. See *supra*, Vol. IV, pp. 146, 310 n. 68; and Isaac b. Sheshet Perfet, *Resp.*, Constantinople, 1544 ed., No. 6 (denying the Jewish validity of a church wedding of two *conversos*). See also L. Lucas' observations in *Philippson Festschrift*, pp. 25 ff.; A. M. Herschman, *Rabbi Isaac ben Sheshet Perfet and His Times*, pp. 71, 218, and *infra*, Chap. LVI.

22. Stephen of Tournai, *Epistolae*, ii.42 in *PL*, CCXI, 333 No. xxxii; G. Carano-Donvito, "Gli Ebrei nella storia economica di Puglia," *Rivista di Politica economica*, XXIII, 838; Yehudah b. Samuel the Pious, *Sefer Ḥasidim* (Book of the Pious), ed. by J. Wistinetzki, pp. 72 No. 183, 73 Nos. 189–90, 74 No. 193, 75 Nos. 200–203, 76 Nos. 208–10, etc. See on the latter M. A. Beck's "On the Relations between Jews and Christians in the Thirteenth Century According to the Book of the Pious" (Dutch), *Nederlandsch Archief voor Kerkegeschiedenis*, XXXIX, 91–99. On the effects of the

disputation of Tortosa and, more generally, on the *conversos* in Spain and Portugal, see *infra*, Chap. XXXVIII, nn. 44 ff. In *Die Judenmission*, pp. 203 ff., P. Browe collected many illustrations of recorded conversions, both voluntary and enforced. Although his list is incomplete, it nevertheless does convey a general impression of the comparative paucity of recorded baptisms.

Nor is his argument altogether farfetched that the failure of sources to mention prominent churchmen, scholars, or statesmen as descendants of Jews is another reflection of that paucity. Otherwise, with their generally high economic and intellectual preconversion status many new Christians would undoubtedly have been admitted into the upper classes of Christian society, and would have also given their children and grandchildren greater opportunities to achieve prominence in their chosen careers. Many doubtless would have secured ecclesiastical offices, in accordance with the aforementioned Valladolid canon of 1322. Only after the Iberian mass conversions of the fifteenth century did this issue loom large. By 1512, an anonymous memorialist, enumerating the pertinent subjects for the deliberations of the forthcoming Lateran Council convoked by Julius II, urged consideration of the overweening influence of the New Christians in Rome; he thus joined the growing chorus of objectors to entrusting the newcomers with important offices in the papal capital "against the common law." See J. J. I. von Döllinger, *Beiträge*, III, 204; *supra*, n. 18; and more generally, *infra*, Chap. LVI. The few records, therefore, of what the Nazis would call "non-Aryan" clergy before that period are, indeed, an indication that not too many European Jews had given up their faith in the earlier period.

23. Honorius IV's bulls of November 18 and 30, 1286, in Raynaldus, *Annales*, IV, 10 f. Nos. xxv–xxvii; Potthast, *Regesta*, II, 1819 f. No. 22541; Yehudah b. Samuel, *Sefer Ḥasidim*, ed. by Wistinetzki, pp. 73 No. 189, 77 Nos. 214–16; Abraham Abulafia's *Sefer 'Edut*. On the date of Abulafia's dramatic effort, see Vogelstein and Rieger, *Geschichte der Juden in Rom*, I, 248 f., and, more generally, *infra*, Chap. XLVI.

24. See *supra*, n. 11; Raynaldus, *Annales*, IV, 92 No. xlix; *Bullarium franciscanum Romanorum pontificum*, ed. by J. H. Sbaralea, IV, 136 No. ccxx; Potthast, *Regesta*, II, 1866 No. 23185. See also the various provisions by Boniface VIII restated in the *Liber Sextus* of the *Decretales*, v.2, 12 ff., in *Corpus*, ed. by Friedberg, II, 1075 f. There must also have existed quite a few would-be proselytes who, like the aforementioned German described in the "Book of the Pious" (p. 77 No. 214), were prepared to observe all Jewish commandments, but whose formal conversion was delayed by the community's fear lest the act of circumcision bring down upon it the wrath of the authorities. See B. Z. Wacholder, "Cases of Proselytizing in the Tosafist Responsa," *JQR*, LI, 288–315; and, more generally, the few data assembled by N. Sampter in his *Judenthum und Proselytismus;* and by L. I. Newman in his *Jewish Influence on Christian Reform Movements*, pp. 393 ff. Much yet remains to be done before the story of medieval Jewish proselytism will be more fully clarified.

25. Innocent III's letters to Alphonso VIII of Castile of May 5, 1205, and to the clergy of Barcelona of August 26, 1206, in his *Epistolae*, viii.50, ix.150, in *PL*, CCXV, 616 f., 977 f.; Grayzel, *The Church*, pp. 112 ff. Nos. 17 and 19; Martin V's bull, *Sedes Apostolica*, of June 3, 1425, excerpted by Vernet in *RQH*, LI, 383 f., 416 No. 39. Since the Saracens allegedly were prepared to pay for the East-European slaves ten times the Jews' purchase price, Martin suggested the confiscation of all property of such

Jewish traders. He also ordered their expulsion from Christian territories and demanded that all foreign Jews be made to wear distinguishing marks. See also Simonsohn, *Die Kirchliche Judengesetzgebung*, p. 23 n. 1. On Innocent's correspondence and the vicissitudes of Jewish slave traders in the early Middle Ages, see *supra*, Vol. IV, pp. 42, 187 ff., 255 n. 53, 333 ff.; and, more generally, C. Verlinden, *L'Esclavage dans l'Europe médiévale*, I, esp. pp. 291 ff., 303 ff., 318; and his "Esclaves alains en Italie et dans les colonies italiennes au XIVᵉ siècle," *RBPH*, XXXVI, 451–57, showing that East-European slaves were recorded as far apart as Rapallo, Tana, Modon, and Candia. The fact, therefore, that as late as 1462 a Jew could be arrested in Caltagirone, Sicily for purchasing a Christian slave girl is not so incredible as it first appears. See Lagumina and Lagumina, *Codice diplomatico*, ii, 21 f. Nos. 485–86.

26. Innocent III's letters to a French priest, Peter, of January 20, 1204, and to the archbishop of Sens and the bishop of Paris of July 15, 1205, in his *Epistolae*, vii.194, viii.121, in *PL*, CCXV, 507, 694 f.; *Decretales* Greg., v.6, 13, in *Corpus*, ed. by Friedberg, II, 775 f.; Council of Oxford of 1222, canon 39; of Valladolid of 1322, canon 22 (following the lengthy canon "de Judeis et Saracenis"); of Prague of 1346, canon 55; of Palencia of 1388, canon 7—all in Mansi, *Collectio*, XXII, 1172; XXV, 713 f.; XXVI, 97 (with minor variations, col. 403), 744 f.; Hefele, *Histoire*, V, Part 2, pp. 1429 ff. (which fails to mention the anti-Jewish provisions); VI, Part 2, pp. 797 f., 906 f., 1428; Grayzel, *The Church*, pp. 110 f. No. 15, 114 ff. No. 18, 314 f. No. xvi. See also Gregory IX's sharp letter of March 4, 1233, censuring the whole German episcopate for allowing Jews to employ Christian servants whom they allegedly circumcised and nurses "with whom they committed enormous" sins, as well as to hold important offices, and for not requiring them to be distinguished by their clothing from the Christians. See *Epistolae saeculi XIII e regestis pontificum Romanorum selectae*, ed. by C. Rodenberg, I, 414 f. No. 515; Potthast, *Regesta*, I, 781 No. 9112; Grayzel, pp. 198 ff. No. 69. As pointed out by Grayzel (p. 314 n. 4), the implementation of the Oxford resolutions, which incidentally included a sharp castigation of the clergy but not of Jews for keeping concubines, caused considerable complications between the leading ecclesiastics and the king of England, and even within the clergy itself. (The general problems of mixed Judeo-Christian matrimonial unions and sex relations will be discussed in later chapters.)

The Prague Council's acceptance of otherwise unverified rumors concerning the Jewish rejection of the milk of nurses undergoing communion can be understood only against the background of the widespread folkloristic accusation of Jews' desecrating the host, a practice which, in the popular imagination, was almost invariably followed by miracles. See P. Browe, "Die Hostienschändungen der Juden im Mittelalter," *Römische Quartalschrift*, XXXIV, 167–97; and *infra*, Chap. XLIX. The Council of Prague evidently forgot that many canonical regulations had gone much further and demanded that no Christians, whether employed by Jews or not, and particularly no females, ever live in Jewish houses. See *infra*, nn. 34 ff. This example, as well as the very fact of the constant reiteration of the same prohibition, is a clear indication of its widespread violation.

27. *Monumenta conciliorum generalium saeculi XV.: Concilium Basiliense*, II, Part 1, pp. 757 ff. (also Mansi, *Collectio*, XXIX, 98 ff.); St. Bernardino da Siena, *Opera omnia*, ed. by the College of St. Bonaventura, III, 362; Lagumina and Lagumina, *Codice diplomatico*; *supra*, Vols. II, pp. 210, 406 n. 42; IV, pp. 50, 252 n. 63. The

Council of Basel specifically emphasized that this regulation was but a "renewal of canonical provisions." Among its predecessors we need but mention the important Councils of Valladolid of 1322 and of several Languedoc provinces which met at Lavaur near Toulouse in 1368 under the presidency of the archbishops of Toulouse and Narbonne, both of whom had resolved that no Christians be allowed to partici- pate at Jewish weddings or funerals. See Mansi, *Collectio*, XXVI, 527; and Hefele, *Histoire*, VI, Part 2, pp. 962 f. This provision, too, was but a variation on the old theme of prohibiting conviviality among members of the two faiths, set in motion by the Council of Elvira about 300 c.e. Remarkably, the Council of Basel also refused to reenact several other innovations of Antipope Benedict XIII's bull, *Et si doctoris*, of May 11, 1415; in J. Amador de los Rios, *Historia social, política y religiosa de los Judios de España y Portugal*, II, 630 f. Of particular importance, as we shall see, was the Council's restraint in impeding commercial relations between Jews and Chris- tians and its passing over in silence Benedict XIII's stringent antiusurious provisions. See the Council's resolution in *Monumenta, loc. cit.*; and Simonsohn's remarks thereon in *Die Kirchliche Judengesetzgebung*, pp. 7, 41. See also P. Thureau-Dangin biography, *Saint Bernardine of Siena*, English trans. by Baroness G. von Hugel.

28. A. Fliche *et al., Historie de l'Église*, X, 195 n. 1; A. Luchaire, *Innocent III—Le Concile de Latran et la Réforme de l'Église*, pp. 9 ff.; Fourth Lateran Council, canon 68, in Mansi, *Collectio*, XXII, 1055; Hefele, *Histoire*, V, Part 2, pp. 1386 f.; Grayzel, *The Church*, pp. 308 f. No. x. These provisions of the universal Council were expanded by many lesser gatherings. For example, the important provincial council of Albi of 1254, which repeated some older canons of Toulouse of 1229, provided that each Jew should carry on his breast a circular patch of cloth a digit wide and half a palm in height (canon 65). The Ravenna synod of 1311 prescribed a red wheel (canon 23); that of Avignon of 1326 imposed the wearing of such a wheel, 3 to 4 fingers wide, upon all males over fourteen, and a coiffure with horns upon all females over twelve years of age (canon 57); that of Prague of 1346 stressed the hat for men. See Mansi, *Collectio*, XXIII, 851; XXV, 462, 773; XXVI, 97; Hefele, *Histoire*, VI, Part 1, pp. 82, 638; Part 2, p. 806 (vague); Grayzel, pp. 334 ff. No. xli; Bardinet in *RH*, XII, 27. A comparative study of the various badges of shame was offered, some seventy years ago, by U. Robert in *Les Signes d'infamie au moyen âge: Juifs, Sarrasins, hérétiques, lépreux, cagots et filles publiques*. See also the additional literature listed *infra*, n. 33; and the more general legislative, admin- istrative and social aspects of the "Jewish badge," discussed *infra*, Chap. XLVIII.

29. Innocent III's letter to the French episcopate of 1215–16 in his *Epistolae* in *PL*, CCXVI, 994 end (a summary from *Rubricella*); the two Councils of Arles of 1234 and 1236, canons 16, in Mansi, *Collectio*, XXIII, 340, 342 end; Hefele, *Histoire*, V, Part 2, pp. 1560 f.; Grayzel, *The Church*, pp. 140 f. No. 31, 326 f. Nos. xxix–xxx. See *ibid.*, p. 69 n. 123; and the comprehensive, though still incomplete, list of medieval councils which dealt with the Jewish badge in Scherer, *Die Rechtsverhält- nisse der Juden*, pp. 41 f. If, as E. Rodocanachi suggests, the Council of Arles acted at the prompting of Pope Gregory IX, its passing reference to the suspension of the badge during journeys indicates that the intervening practice doubtless went back to Innocent himself. See *Le Saint-Siège et les Juifs*, p. 223.

30. Solomon ibn Verga, *Shebeṭ Yehudah* (Judah's Rod: a Chronicle), ed. by M. Wiener, pp. 114 (Hebrew), 233 (German); ed. by A. Shohet, p. 148; J. P. Papon,

*Histoire générale de Provence*, III, 61, Appendix, Preuve xv (although an abbot, this eighteenth-century historian praises Charles); A. de Boüard, *Actes et lettres de Charles I, roi de Sicile concernant la France* (1257–84), pp. 57 No. 217, 83 No. 316, 173 f. No. 643; and Willy Cohn, "Die Judenpolitik König Karls I von Sizilien in Anjou und in der Provence," *MGWJ*, LXXIV, 429 ff. Ibn Verga (or his anonymous source used by Shem Ṭob Sonzolo) probably exaggerated when he claimed that the inquisitorial ordinance concerning the badge included the sanction of the extreme penalty. See the resolution of the difficulties in Ibn Verga's and Papon's accounts in H. Gross, *Gallia judaica*, pp. 3 f., 249. See also *supra*, Vol. IV, p. 238 n. 9. Curiously, the Council of Vienna, held in 1267, passed over in silence the motivation of the Fourth Lateran Council and insisted that distinguishing clothes were needed because of the Jews' overbearing behavior which, "as they say," was affecting the purity of the faith among many Christians (canon 15). Despite this constant reiteration, the Council of Aschaffenburg took cognizance in 1292 of the fact that the old canons concerning the Jewish badge had not been uniformly observed. It resolved, there-fore, to order all towns, castles, and other localities in the province of Mayence within two months after the promulgation of that statute to make all Jewish men and women wear such clothing or signs whereby they would be easily recognizable from Christians (canon 18). See Mansi, *Collectio*, XXIII, 1174 f.; XXIV, 1091 f.; Hefele, *Histoire*, VI, Part 1, pp. 137, 343 f. In view of the great diversity of local sociopolitical factors and popular prejudices which shaped the development of the Jewish badge, numerous additional data will be supplied *infra*, Chaps. XLVII and XLVIII.

31. L. Erler in *AKKR*, XLVIII, 37; Lagumina and Lagumina, *Codice diplomatico*, I, 383 f. No. 307, 387 f. No. 315; the decree republished by De Boüard, *Actes*, 173 f. No. 643; with Willy Cohn's comments thereon in *MGWJ*, LXXIV, 431; the text of the 1465 arbitration agreement in *Memorias de Don Enrique IV de Castilla*, published by the R. Academia de la Historia, II, 335 f. No. 109, Art. 100; and its brief summary in F. Baer, *Die Juden im christlischen Spanien*, I, Part 2, p. 330 No. 318.

32. C. Roth, *Venice*, p. 114; I. Kracauer, *Geschichte der Juden in Frankfurt a. M. (1150–1824)*, I, 194 ff.; and S. Salfeld, "Zur Geschichte des Judenschutzes in Kurmainz," *Philippson Festschrift*, pp. 161 f. On Nicolaus Cusanus' role in the struggle for universalizing the Jewish badge, especially as papal legate and presiding officer at the Councils of Bamberg of 1451 and Mayence of 1452, see the summaries in Mansi, *Collectio*, XXXII, 131; XXXV, 89 f. (which dates the Mayence Council in 1451); Hefele, *Histoire*, VII, Part 2, pp. 1208 f. n. 2 (citing from Pastor a Wolfenbüt-tel MS entitled *Nicolai Cusani decreta quaedam, quae fecit in synodo Bembergensi*, which included 2 folios [22–24b]: "De Judaeis"); K. A. Schaab, *Diplomatische Geschichte der Juden zu Mainz*, pp. 120 f.; M. Stern, *Urkundliche Beiträge über die Stellung der Päpste zu den Juden*, I, 52 ff. No. 47, 58 ff. No. 53, 62 f. Nos. 55, 57; J. S. Menczel, *Beiträge zur Geschichte der Juden von Mainz im XV. Jahrhundert*, pp. 26 f.; and, more generally, K. Grube, "Die Legationsreise des Cardinals Nicolaus von Cusa durch Norddeutschland im Jahre 1451," *HJB*, I, 393–412. Typical of John Capistrano's anti-Jewish harangues is his sermon, in R. Cessi, "Notizie e documenti intorno alla vita di S. Giovanni da Capistrano, ricercati negli archivi e nelle biblioteche di Padova," *Bolletino della Società di storia patria*, XX, 2nd ser. XIX,

60 ff. (placing the badge high on the list of the twenty-one provisions needed for the realization of the postulates of the "holy fathers"). See also, more generally, J. Hofer, *Johannes von Capestrano*, pp. 498 f.

In all these matters the central authorities of the Church evidently left much to the discretion of the local bishops and princes. Even when a papal legate like Cusanus appeared as the moving spirit of a conciliar resolution, he need not have acted on direct instructions from the pope, or necessarily represented the Papacy's deliberate policy. In Cusanus' case the text of his original instructions before his departure for Germany, dated December 22 and 29, 1450, contained many detailed orders regarding the general ecclesiastical reforms advocated by the Papacy, but included no provisions concerning Jews. And yet on his arrival in Germany, the cardinal-legate evidently had a well prepared draft of injunctions concerning the Jewish badge for submission to the various synods. See his correspondence in the *Cusanus-Texte*, IV, ed. by J. Koch, pp. 12 f. Nos. 67–70, 111 ff.; and Koch's observations in his *Nikolaus von Cues and seine Umwelt*, IV, Part 2, pp. 111 f.

33. Council of Salzburg of 1418, canon xxxiii, in Mansi, *Collectio*, XXVIII, 1004 f. (erroneously dating it in 1420); Hefele, *Histoire*, VII, Part I, p. 599 (with reference to *ibid.*, VI, Part 1, p. 137); Wiener, *Regesten*, p. 193 No. 582; the Cologne ordinance of 1404, published by C. Brisch in his *Geschichte der Juden in Cöln und Umgebung*, II, 26 ff.; Ferdinand I's decree of August 1, 1551, reproduced from the Vienna Archives by A. F. Pribram in his *Urkunden und Akten zur Geschichte der Juden in Wein*, I, 10 ff. Notwithstanding the great interest evinced by modern scholars in the history of the Jewish badge, much work is yet to be done before that institution will be fully known. The monographs by: U. Robert, *Les Signes d'infamie*; G. Rezasco, "Del segno degli Ebrei," *Giornale ligustico di archeologia*, XV, 241–66, 321–51; XVI, 31–61, 259–84; F. Singermann, *Die Kennzeichnung der Juden im Mittelalter*; T. Jakobovits, "Die Judenabzeichen in Böhmen," *JGJC*, III, 145–84; G. Kisch, "The Yellow Badge in History," *HJ*, IV, 95–144; and others, furnish good material for France and the Holy Roman Empire, but are totally inadequate for the rest of Europe. The influence, in particular, of Islamic prototypes (on which see *supra*, Vol. III, pp. 139 ff., 298 n. 22) requires further elucidation. Once the practice had been imported into Europe, pretexts for it were easily found. Just as Innocent III pretended that the badge would prevent errors in love, King John I of Aragon in 1393 demanded an outward symbol to distinguish *conversos* from professing Jews. See F. Baer, *Die Juden im christlichen Spanien*, I, Part 1, p. 717 No. 456; and *infra*, Chaps. XLVIII and LVI. The manifold variations of the badge and its effects on the Jewish costume and on general Judeo-Christian relations will be discussed more fully in the context of medieval Jewish social life.

34. Mansi, *Collectio*, XXIII, 1167 f. can. xii. The fuller text of the Breslau resolution is reproduced from R. Hube's collection by J. Aronius in his *Regesten zur Geschichte der Juden im fränkischen und deutschen Reiche*, pp. 301 ff. No. 724. On the defensive aspects of the Jewish quarters, see also *infra*, Chap. XLVIII. The phrase relating to Judeo-Christian common living in canon xxvi of the Third Lateran Council is equivocal. The canon begins with the prohibition against the holding of Christian slaves in the homes of Jews or Saracens. Then it adds: "Those who should dare to live with them shall be excommunicated." Since such a threat could hardly be addressed to slaves who were not free to dispose of their places of residence, the

churchmen assembled in Rome must have wished to expand the prohibition to any Christian living together with infidels. See Mansi, XXII, 231; Hefele, *Histoire*, V, Part 2, pp. 1105 f.; Grayzel, *The Church*, pp. 296 f. No. i.

35. F. Baer, *Die Juden*, I, Part 2, pp. 253 ff. No. 267; my *The Jewish Community*, II, 139; III, 147 n. 16. As early as 1478, Ferrant Martinez justified his anti-Jewish agitation in Seville by invoking the canonical demands for separate Jewish habitations and the prohibitions against new synagogues. The Jews of the city, he claimed, had erected twenty-three houses of worship "against God and against the law." Baer, *ibid.*, p. 217 No. 221. On the early history of separate Jewish quarters, see *supra*, Vols. I, pp. 188, 380 f. n. 29; II, pp. 148 f.; III, pp. 144 f., 195, 301 n. 29; IV, pp. 74, 275 n. 96; V, pp. 219 f., 393 n. 12. The origin of the term "ghetto," and the gradual growth of that institution as a result of Jewish wishes as much as external pressure, will be discussed more fully *infra*, Chap. XLVIII.

36. Benedict XII's letter of 1340 to Pedro IV of Aragon, and Eugenius IV's bull of 1442, *Dudum ad nostram*, in Raynaldus, *Annales*, VI, 222 f. Nos. lvi–lvii, and IX, 398 ff. No. xv; Mansi, *Collectio*, XXIV, 176 (Bourges, 1276); XXV, 462 (Ravenna, 1311), 1055 f. (Salamanca, 1335); Hefele, *Histoire*, VI, Part 1, pp. 133, 233, 638; Part 2, p. 835. Perhaps it was the influence of the papal legate Pedro de Luna, who later as Antipope Benedict XIII was to enact many anti-Jewish measures, that the Council of Palencia adopted, in 1388, a general canon (5) demanding that Jews and Saracens live in quarters of their own. See Mansi, XXVI, 743 f.; Hefele, VI, Part 2, p. 1428.

37. Lagumina and Lagumina, *Codice diplomatico*, I, 35 f., No. xxxv; *Memorias de Don Enrique IV*, pp. 335 ff. No. 109, Arts. 98–99; Baer, *Die Juden im christlichen Spanien*, I, Part 2, p. 330 No. 318.

38. Lagumina and Lagumina, *Codice diplomatico*, II, 102 f. No. 533; M. Stern, *Urkundliche Beiträge*, I, 64 f. No. 59; I. Kracauer, "Geschichte der Judengasse in Frankfurt a. M.," *Festschrift zur Jahrhundertfeier der Realschule . . . der israelitischen Gemeinde (Philanthropin) zu Frankfurt am Main 1804–1904*, Part 2, p. 307; idem, *Geschichte der Juden in Frankfurt a. M.*, I, 197 ff.; and *supra*, Vol. III, pp. 29 f., 243 n. 36. The architectural layout of the Frankfort ghetto and other medieval and early modern Jewish quarters, as well as the pertinent legislation and the impact of both on Jews and Gentiles, will be analyzed in later chapters. Some of the more important studies from the vast literature available on this subject—general, regional, and local—will also be listed. However, the specific role of ecclesiastical authorities, both central and provincial, in the promotion of the topographical segregation of Jews is yet to be fully explored.

39. Innocent III's *Epistolae*, vii.186, in *PL*, CCXV, 501 ff.; Grayzel, *The Church*, pp. 104 ff. No. 14. The two statues in front of the Strasbourg Cathedral have often been reproduced. See especially the fine photographs by J. Roubier, with an intro. by J. Walter, in *La Cathédrale de Strasbourg*, Plates ii–v; and the general study by H. Haug *et al.*, *La Cathédrale de Strasbourg*, with a foreword by E. Fels. In view of the artists' general anonymity during that period it is difficult to ascertain to what, if any, extent the sculptors were influenced by their living contacts with contem-

porary Jews. See M. Ginsburger, "La Première communauté israélite de Strasbourg," *Publications* of the University of Strasbourg, Fac. des Lettres, CIV (*Mélanges*, 1945, 1), which deals with the period of 1150–1349. These statues were probably erected around 1230. On the meaning of Jewish "bondage" in its ecclesiastical interpretation, see *infra*, Chap. XLVII. See also, *supra*, Vol. IV, pp. 15, 240 n. 14.

40. *Decretales Greg.* v.6, 8, in *Corpus*, ed. by Friedberg, II, 773 f.; Alexander of Hales, *Summa*, II.ii.81, 734, Quaracchi ed., III, 734; the oaths of the Provençal authorities included in the acts of the Council of Montelimar of 1209 in Mansi, *Collectio*, XXII, 767 ff., 782; Hefele, *Histoire*, V, Part 2, pp. 1280 f.; Gregory IX's letter to the archbishop of Gran of March 3, 1231, in Raynaldus, *Annales*, II (*ad* 1231), fol. 45 f. Nos. 39–41; Potthast, *Regesta*, I, 744 No. 8671; Grayzel, *The Church*, pp. 184 ff. No. 61, 302 f. No. v; and *supra*, Vol. II, pp. 180 f., 398 f. nn. 12–13. The situation in Hungary was, indeed, complicated by the perennial squabbles between the monarchy and the nobility, whose national fervor often aroused antipapal sentiments. The relative youth of Christianity, the propinquity of such pagan tribes as the Cumani, and influences emanating from the not-too-distant Muslim countries, all contributed to moderation in the treatment of religious minorities. See *infra*, Chap. XLII, nn. 23 ff. Understandably, the Church evinced special anxiety whenever a ruler entrusted Jewish tax farmers with the collection of ecclesiastical dues. On this score Nicholas III addressed a sharp letter to Alphonso X of Castile on March 23, 1279. See Raynaldus, III, 492 f. Nos. xxiv–xxvi; Potthast, II, 1741 No. 21556 (which omits the crucial reference to "Judaeos Christianis praeponit multipliciter").

41. Council of Valladolid of 1322, in Mansi, *Collectio*, XXV, 720; Hefele, *Histoire*, VI, Part 2, p. 798 (more fully given by Tejada y Ramiro, in his *Colección de canones y todos los concilios de la Iglesia española*, III, 477 ff., and J. Saenz de Aguirre, *Collectio maxima conciliorum*, V, 250 f.; see Baer, *Die Juden im christlichen Spanien*, I, Part 2, p. 141); Vogelstein and Rieger, *Geschichte der Juden im Rom*, I, 252 ff.; Arnaldo de Vilanova, cited by M. Menéndez y Pelayo, *Ensayo histórico su Arnaldo de Vilanova*, p. 96. See *infra*, Chap. XXXIX, n. 4 item 6. A motivation similar to that of Valladolid was offered by the Council of Salamanca in 1335 (canon 12) while the earlier Council of Albi, 1254 (canon 69) and others limited themselves merely to the general prohibition of employing Jewish physicians. The qualification permitting such use in emergencies occurs, for instance, in the resolution of the Council of Avignon of 1337 (canon 69). See Mansi, *Collectio*, XXIII, 852 (Albi, 1254); XXV, 1055 (Salamanca, 1335), 1105 f. (Avignon, 1337); Hefele, *Histoire*, VI, Part 1, p. 82; Part 2, pp. 835, 840; Grayzel, *The Church*, pp. 334 ff. No. xli; Bardinet in *RH*, XII, 27.
Neither the date nor the identity of the pope who employed Gaio is known, since our information is limited to a brief mention in a Paris manuscript. See Vogelstein and Rieger, *loc. cit.* Of course, secular rulers could be even more liberal. The general progress of Jewish medical studies, especially during the Renaissance, will be discussed in later chapters.

42. Mansi, *Collectio*, XXIII, 851; Hefele, *Histoire*, VI, Part 1, p. 82; G. Bessin, ed., *Concilia Rotomagensis provinciae*, p. 175; Innocent III's letter to the Count of Nevers of January 17, 1208, in his *Epistolae*, x.190, in *PL*, CCXV, 1291 ff.; Grayzel, *The Church*, pp. 72 f., 126 ff. No. 24, 334 ff. No. xli. On the importance of the wine

trade in Latin countries during the Middle Ages see *supra*, Vol. IV, pp. 162 f., 317 n. 14. In his letter Innocent III also censured the purchase of milk allegedly spurned by Jewish mothers.

Since these prohibitions played into the hands of Christian butchers and food merchants, we shall not be surprised to find that they engendered an enormous variety of detailed regulations, both ecclesiastical and secular. While the Council of Narbonne of 1227 (canon 2) had limited itself to the prohibition against Jews' publicly consuming (*publice vescantur*) meat or selling it in Christian butcher shops or on days when Christians abstained from eating it (Mansi, XXIII, 21; Hefele, V, Part 2, pp. 1452 f.; Grayzel, pp. 316 f.), that of Albi temperamentally added that "since Jews disdainfully refuse to consume some of our food and drink, we strictly forbid any Christian to make use of theirs" (*loc. cit.*). More extremely, the Council of Breslau of 1267 accused Jews of attempting to poison meats sold to Christians. See the sources mentioned *supra*, n. 34; and Grayzel, p. 72 n. 139, where many other regulations are cited.

43. Alexander of Hales, *Summa*, II.ii.81, 2, 746, Quaracchi ed., III, 732 f.; *supra*, Vol. IV, pp. 48 f.; and *infra*, Chap. XLVIII. The Council of Vienne apparently debated, but did not formally adopt, the resolution, *Cum Judaei*. See E. Müller, *Das Konzil von Vienne*, pp. 640 f. In this struggle with state officials the Church was at a great disadvantage, since its organs could not impose their will upon recalcitrant Jews through purely spiritual sanctions nor otherwise penalize them without the cooperation of those very secular authorities. Even the recurrent threats of a Christian boycott of obstreperous individuals or communities, under the sanction of severe ecclesiastical penalties, were gradually losing their deterring force among Christians themselves. In the churchmen's "determination to maintain law and order," rightly observes Rosalind Hill, "they used the sentence of excommunication so freely that at last it degenerated from a tremendous spiritual sanction into a minor inconvenience." See her "The Theory and Practice of Excommunication in Medieval England," in *History*, XLII, 11. Jews could even more readily disregard this ecclesiastical sanction. For one example, when, in 1319, two Strasbourg Jews failed to appear before a Freiburg prior appointed by Pope John XXII to adjudicate their litigation with the marquess of Baden, the irate prior placed them under a ban. Yet the city council of Strasbourg continued unperturbedly to do business with them. See A. Glaser, *Geschichte der Juden in Strassburg*, p. 9. See also *infra*, n. 50.

44. Gregory X's bull, *Sicut Judaeis*, of October 7, 1272 (slightly over a year after his ascension to the see of St. Peter) in M. Stern, *Urkundliche Beiträge*, I, 1 ff. No. 1; N. Ferorelli, *Gli Ebrei nell'Italia meridionale dall'età romana al secolo XVIII*, p. 182. The alleged offering of the heart of a child victim seems to appear here for the first time. It will be discussed in connection with the other facets of the Blood Accusation, *infra*, Chap. XLIX. Remarkably, the problem of Jewish testimony against non-Jews rarely engaged the attention of canon jurists, and still less of popes and councils. Nonetheless, the Dominican inquisitor, Bartolomeo Fumi, voiced a fairly widespread notion among his fellow prosecutors when he declared that generally Jews should not be allowed to incriminate Christians, but that in matters pertaining to the faith anybody revealing secret deviations ought to be heard. See his *Summa aurea armilla*, summarized by Élie in *RHR*, CXLII, 93 f.

45. T. J. Lacomblet, *Urkundenbuch für die Geschichte des Niederrheins*, III, 18 No. 24; Brisch, *Geschichte der Juden in Cöln*, pp. 104 ff.; *Decretum Gratiani*, II. xxii.1, 16, in *Corpus*, ed. by Friedberg, I, 865 f. A provision similar to that of Cologne was also enacted by the Bishop of Würzburg in 1414. See Wiener, *Regesten*, pp. 172 f. No. 475; and, more generally, O. Stobbe, *Die Juden in Deutschland während des Mittelalters*, pp. 153 ff.; H. K. Claussen, "Der Judeneid," *Deutsche Rechtswissenchaft*, II, 166–89; and other literature listed *infra*, n. 46, and in Chap. XLVIII.

The terms *perfidia* and *infidelis* underwent various mutations of meaning in the course of centuries. See the extensive analysis by E. Peterson, "Perfidia judaica," *Ephemerides liturgicae*, L, 296–311; H. Schmeck, "Infidelis. Ein Beitrag zur Wortgeschichte," *Vigiliae christianae*, V, 129–47, esp. pp. 138 f.; B. Blumenkranz, "Perfidia," *Bulletin du Cange*, XXII, 157–70. But in the minds of ordinary clerics and laymen, the connotation of malevolence and hatred of true believers must have loomed prominently at all times. Similarly, the purely religious accusation of Jewish stubbornness in denying the truth of Christianity was readily transferred into the realm of private relationships. When a relatively mild preacher like Martin de León complained of the "foolishness" of the Jews' "pestiferous unbelief" and called them "enemies of truth" (*Sermones*, iv.16, 25 in *PL*, CCVIII, 247, 350 ff.), he undoubtedly evoked in the minds of many listeners the picture of the Jew as a hater of truth, one who would commit perjury on the slightest provocation. See also A. Viñayo Gonzalez, ed., *San Martín de León y su apologética antijudía*, with a Foreword by R. G. Villoslada, pp. 97 f.; and other data cited by Browe in *Die Judenmission*, pp. 290 ff.

46. Abraham ben David's stricture on Maimonides, *M.T.* Shebu'ot xi.13, based on numerous geonic sources (apparently known to him only from hearsay), as analyzed by H. Tykocinski in *Die Gaonäischen Verordnungen*. See *supra*, Vol. III, pp. 184, 194 f., 318 n. 14, 322 n. 28. This situation continued to affect civil procedure in Jewish and in general courts, including the Jewish oath. Hence this problem became the center of heated controversy in the 1840s and 1850s, and brought to light much excellent material. See especially Z. Frankel, *Die Eidesleistung der Juden in theologischer und historischer Beziehung;* and L. Zunz, "Die Vorschriften uber die Eidesleistung der Juden" (1859), reprinted in his *GS*, II, 241–64 (listing the large earlier literature). A definite departure from the traditional explanation of the oath, as exclusively a product of the antisemitic animus of Christian legislators, was marked by F. Baer's excursus in *Die Juden im christlichen Spanien*, I, 1024 ff.; as well as in H. Voltelini, "Der Wiener und Kremser Judeneid," *Mitteilungen des Vereines für Geschichte der Stadt Wien*, XII, 64–70. See also R. Straus, "Ein Landshuter Judeneid aus dem 14 Jahrhundert," *ZGJD*, V, 42–49 (with facsimile): J. Weill's note "Source de la formule du serment juif codifiée dans les 'Partidas' d'Alphonse X [III.xi.19–21]," *REJ*, LXXXVI, 58–60, referring to a royal letter of 1260 concerning the various types of oaths provided for members of the three denominations in *Las Siete Partidas*, iii.11, 19–21 (Paris, 1847 ed., II, 545 ff.); Amador de los Rios, *Historia social......de los Judios*, I, 558–66, giving formulas current in various parts of Spain; Lagumina and Lagumina, *Codice diplomatico*, I, 106 No. 74, giving a fourteenth-century Sicilian *sacramentum Judaeorum;* and U. Inchiostri, "Accenni agli Ebrei nei documenti e statuti dalmati del medio evo," *AS per la Dalmazia*, VIII, 479 f., citing two relatively mild formulas from Arbe and Fermo.

The great variety and arbitrariness of existing formulas of Jewish oaths is well illustrated by those employed more or less simultaneously in such neighboring North-Italian cities as Milan, Brescia, and Padua. See the texts cited by L. Fumi in "L'Inquisizione romana e lo stato di Milano," *AS Lombardo*, XXXVII, 289 f.; F. Glissenti in *Gli Ebrei nel Bresciano al tempo della dominazione veneta*, pp. 16 f.; and A. Ciscato in *Gli Ebrei in Padova (1300–1800)*, p. 284 No. xxv. A good survey of medieval German practices, together with some new documentation, is offered by G. Kisch in his interrelated essays, "Studien zur Geschichte des Judeneides im Mittelalter," "Ein süddeutscher Judeneid aus dem 14. Jahrhundert," and "Nürnberger Judeneide," reprinted in his *Forschungen zur Rechts- und Sozialgeschichte der Juden in Deutschland während des Mittelalters*, pp. 137 ff., 166 ff., 172 ff. (The latter two essays are also available in English, in *Speculum*, XV, 331–37; and in *HJ*, II, 23–38, respectively.) On the Jewish law of oaths, see I. Bernfeld's brief sketch of *Eid und Gelübde nach Talmud und Schulchan Aruch;* and B. Cohen, "The Testimonial Oath," *HJ*, VII, 51–74. See also M. Calamari, "Ricerche sul giuramento nel diritto canonico," *Rivista di storia del diritto italiano*, XI, 127–83, 420–30.

The most crucial problem in the origin of the oath *more judaico* is that of its Byzantine or Islamic antecedents. In the West the first mention of a special formula is found in the Carolingian *Capitulare de Judaeis*, Section 4 (J. Aronius, *Regesten zur Geschichte der Juden*, pp. 28 f. No. 77), supposedly issued before the year 814. This law is, however, of dubious authenticity. See *supra*, Vol. IV, pp. 260 f. n. 62. Neither are the Byzantine sources older than the tenth or eleventh century. The formula mentioned, for instance, in the Croatian regulation of 892 c.e., and published in F. Rački's *Documenta historiae Chroaticae periodum antiquam illustrantia*, No. 12, probably represents general Byzantine practice without reference to Jews, although it contains most of the characteristic biblical curses for transgressors, such as that "Naaman the Syrian's leprosy may never recede from them; that the earth may swallow them as it swallowed Dathan and Abiram." The oath of abjuration of Judaism, moreover, which apparently paved the way for the oath in courts, is much older both in Byzantium and in Visigothic Spain. See J. Juster, *Les Juifs dans l'empire romain*, I, 114 ff.; and particularly the data cited *supra*, Vol. III, pp. 184, 194 f., 318 n. 14, 322 n. 28. On the parallel Islamic developments see the long formula composed in the thirteenth century by the Egyptian qadi, Shihab ad-din ibn al-'Umari, and soon administered to Jews throughout the Mameluk kingdom, in I. Goldziher, "Mélanges judéo-arabes, XIII: Les serments des Juifs," *REJ*, XLV, 1–8. Somewhat later E. Fagnan detected in a Paris MS of *Diwan al-Insha*, written about 1436, a Jewish oath (the formula of which he gives in an incomplete French translation), supposedly drafted by Āl-Fadhl ibn ar-Rabi', Harun ar-Rashid's chancellor, which allegedly served as a model for the Muslim courts ever after. See his "Arabo-Judaica," *REJ*, LIX, 228 f.

Should this Muslim tradition be even partially correct and the aforementioned *Capitulare* in this point reflect some more or less authentic Carolingian survivals, the Jewish oath would have been simultaneously developed by Harun and Charlemagne. This would not necessarily be a strange coincidence, inasmuch as Jewish immigrants from Muslim lands, who were mainly instrumental in reviving the Jewish communities in the Carolingian Empire, may well have brought with them certain peculiar forms of Jewish oaths which were later elaborated and modified in the growingly hostile Christian environment. See *supra*, Vol. IV, pp. 43 ff.

47. See *supra*, Vol. IV, pp. 219 f., 351 n. 90. The Council of Palencia held in 1388 under the leadership of the papal legate Pedro de Luna, later Antipope Benedict XIII, was most specific in prohibiting Jews from engaging in commerce and handicrafts on Christian holidays. See Mansi, *Collectio*, XXVI, 744; Hefele, *Histoire*, VI, Part 2, p. 1428. Eugenius IV, after reversing his earlier pro-Jewish policies, also took up the cudgel in behalf of Sunday rest observance. He who in 1435 had forbidden Christian preachers to arouse the populace against Jews or prevent their listeners from kindling lights or baking bread for Jews on the Jewish Sabbath, not only revoked that order in 1442 but also included in his aforementioned sharply anti-Jewish bull, *Dudum ad nostram*, addressed to Pedro IV of Aragon, an express censure against Jews (and Saracens) working on Sundays and Christian holidays. See Stern, *Urkundliche Beiträge*, I, 45 f. Nos. 38, 40; and *supra*, n. 36.

48. Mansi, *Collectio*, XXIII, 1000; XXIV, 1092 f.; Hefele, *Histoire*, VI, Part 1, pp. 92 f., 344; *Memorias de don Enrique IV de Castilla*, II, 355 f. No. 109, summarized by F. Baer in *Die Juden*, I, Part 2, p. 330 No. 318 (Art. 105); and *supra*, Vol. IV, pp. 55 f., 266 n. 72. There were many variations on this fundamental theme, especially in the Holy Roman Empire. Without prescribing the size of the fine, the synod of the newly founded archbishopric of Prague demanded in 1349 that Jews not be allowed to leave their dwellings on Good Friday and even be made to shut all their gates and windows (canon 50). See Mansi, *Collectio*, XXVI, 97 (in the version of 1355, *ibid.*, col. 404); Hefele, *Histoire*, VI, Part 2, p. 906.

49. Boniface IX's bull of April 6, 1399 in G. L. Marini, *Degli archiatri pontifici*, II, 68; C. Rè, ed., *Statuti di Roma*, ii.199, iii.89 (88), pp. 191, 246 f.; Vogelstein and Rieger, *Geschichte*, I, 314 f., 344 ff.; Bardinet in *RH*, XII, 39 ff.; M. Stern, *Urkundliche Beiträge*, I, 18 ff. No. 7. In granting this far-reaching privilege to Elia di Sabbato, the Roman Senate felt obliged to mouth in its preamble the usual phrases about Jewish perfidy and stubbornness, but emphasized the great services rendered by this physician to Christian patients. It passed over in silence the canonical prohibition against employing Jewish doctors. More remarkably, twenty-eight years later Pope Eugenius IV renewed both Elia's Roman citizenship and his pension. Similar tax immunities had been granted in 1376 to the Jewish physicians Manuel and his son Angelo; see Stern, *ibid.*, pp. 14 ff. No. 3, 45 No. 37. On the meaning of citizens' rights in Rome and elsewhere, see *infra*, Chap. XLVII.

50. F. Vernet's data in "Le Pape Martin V," in *RQH*, LI, 384 f., 419 No. 62; *Registres d'Alexandre IV*, ed. by C. Bourel de la Roncière *et al.*, I, 26 No. 101, 55 f. Nos. 201–202; and, more generally, Vogelstein and Rieger, *Geschichte, passim*; Bardinet in *RH*, XII, 1 ff.; and *supra*, Vol. IV, pp. 13 f., 239 f. n. 12. The support extended by Innocent IV to the bishops of Sicily and Germany in securing fiscal supremacy over Jews is illustrated by the data assembled by M. Elias in *JJLG*, XII, 43 ff. But this was only a facet of the general struggle between Papacy and Empire, particularly of their conflicting interpretations of Jewish "serfdom," on which see *infra*, Chaps. XL and XLVII. On their part, Jewish communities sought relief from such oppressive legislation by concerted action and more or less effective "lobbying" at the papal court. Martin V's punitive action in connection with the events in Jerusalem was the subject of discussion at a conference of many Italian communities

held in Florence in 1428. See my *Jewish Community*, I, 320; III, 79 n. 35; and *supra*, n. 12.

The fiscal picture of alternating benevolence and repression toward Jewries of the Papal States is delineated here with considerable diffidence. Even Rome's general financial history is far from fully clarified. See, for instance, V. Pfaff's recent analysis of the "Aufgaben und Probleme der päpstlichen Finanzverwaltung am Ende des 12. Jahrhunderts," *MIOG*, LXIV, 1–24; the various texts published in the series of *Vatikanische Quellen zur Geschichte der päpstlichen Hof- und Finanzverwaltung, 1316–1378*, Vols. I–VII; P. Partner's largely administrative data on *The Papal State under Martin V*, pp. 111 ff., 140 ff.; and M. Monaco, "Le Finanze pontificie al tempo di Clemente VII (1523–1534)," *Studi romani*, VI, 278–96. The story of fiscal exactions from Jews in the Papacy's Italian and French possessions is yet to be made the subject of detailed monographic study. See also *infra*, Chaps. XLVI and L.

51. Raymond Martini, *Pugio fidei adversus Mauros et Judaeos*, Preface, ed. by J. B. Carpzov, p. 20. The fiscal vicissitudes and changing moods of Roman Jewry are well illustrated by its behavior during the tragic episode of Cola di Rienzo's rapid rise and decline. See *infra*, Chap. XLVI. However, in all such affairs Jews seem to have acted more as Romans than as members of the Jewish community. Involvement in the general affairs of the city is also illustrated by Honorius III's attempt to collect from Jews, as well as other inhabitants, of the distant city of Worms amounts owing by the Church of Worms to certain Roman citizens. See his letters of July 8, 1225 and June 4, 1226 to the archbishop of Mayence in *Epistolae saeculi XIII*, ed. by C. Rodenberg (*MGH*), I, 195 f. No. 273, 226 No. 298; Potthast, *Regesta*, I, 640 No. 7437, 653 No. 7582.

52. Thomas Aquinas, *De regimine Judaeorum*, Art. 1, in his *Opera omnia*, Parma, 1865 ed., XVI, 292 f.; J. F. Willems, *Les Gestes des ducs de Brabant*, I, 665. The circumstances which led to this correspondence in the spring of 1261 and the precipitancy of the thinker's reply, which explains some of his inconsiderate statements in this anti-Jewish pamphlet, are well brought out by H. Pirenne in "La Duchesse Aleyde de Brabant et le 'De regimine Judaeorum' de Saint Thomas d'Aquin," *Bulletin de l'Académie royale de Belgique*, Classe de lettres, 5th series, XIV, 43–55. The duchess' concern doubtless arose from the will left behind by her husband, Duke Henry III, who demanded that "Jews and Cahorsins be expelled from the land of Brabant and totally excluded so that not one remain there, except for those who would be willing to do business like the other merchants and give up their habitual moneylending and usury." See C. Demeure in "Les Juifs en Belgique," *Revue de droit international*, XX, 246; and G. Boland's analysis of "Le Testament d'Henri III, duc de Brabant," *RHE*, XXXVIII, 59–96, esp. pp. 81 f., 94. See also Pope Urban IV's letter of February 8, 1263, in *Les Registres d'Urbain IV*, ed. by J. Guiraud, I, 57 No. 204 (allaying similar compunctions); as well as some of the older writings listed by Aronius in his *Regesten*, pp. 279 No. 669, 324 ff. No. 770; and J. Stengers, *Les Juifs dans les Pays Bas au Moyen Age*, pp. 13 f., 48 ff., 98 f., 173 f. Stengers has cast doubt on the identity of Thomas' correspondent and the date of his tract. Many years before him, P. Glorieu and others suggested that instead of Aleyde, the mother of John I, it was the latter's wife, Margaret, Louis IX's daughter, who—perhaps during her husband's absence on a Crusade together with her father —had been troubled by the incongruity of using revenue from forbidden Jewish

usury. This feeling may indeed have been reinforced by Louis' prohibiting French Jews from engaging in usurious transactions. In that case, the exchange probably took place in 1270, rather than nine years earlier. Martin Grabmann, who in an earlier edition of his work had accepted Pirenne's date, later reversed himself and adopted Glorieu's theory. See his third (1949) ed. of *Die Werke des hl. Thomas von Aquin*, pp. 336 ff. In this case, Thomas' relative moderation would be doubly meaningful as he had lived many years in Paris under Louis' regime. On the great impact of custom on all phases of canon law and ecclesiastical thinking and on its ancient antecedents, see the pertinent remarks of F. Guilfoyle in his "Custom in the Justinian Law and Its Influence on Canon Law," *Bulletino* of the Istituto di diritto romano, III, 427 ff.

53. Grayzel, *The Church*, pp. 48 f., 232 ff. Nos. 90–92, 272 f. No. 117; J. Amador de los Rios, *Historia social*, II, 22 f.; *Les Registres de Boniface VIII*, ed. by G. Digard *et al.*, I, 814 No. 2120. Restitution of usury, or its replacement by some such pious cause as the financing of a Crusade, was demanded as a matter of principle by several later medieval popes such as Urban VI (1367), Eugenius IV (in his oft-quoted bull of 1442), and Calixtus III (1456). See Wiener, *Regesten*, p. 135 No. 246; Raynaldus, *Annales*, IX, 398 ff. No. xv; X, 95 ff. No. lxviii; and Erler in *AKKR*, L, 14, 23 f., 27.

54. *Raccolta di costituzioni pontificie, sentenze, decisioni, voti e pareri concernenti il gius di gazagà degli Israeliti sulle case del già ghetto di Roma (1877);* E. Natali, *Il Ghetto del Roma,* I; and *infra,* Chap. LIX. Of course, such opposition to Jewish ownership of houses did not prevent the papal authorities from making use of Jewish housing whenever the occasion arose. In 1316, when the papal residence was transferred to Avignon, two Jewish houses were used to accommodate John XXII's cardinals. See Bardinet in *RH*, XII, 39. See also A. Baccelli's juridical analysis in his "Brevi note intorno al carattere del 'Jus di gazagà' in Roma," *Legge*, XXXII, Part 1, pp. 712–20.

55. Alexander of Hales, *Summa*, II, ii.81, 2, 746, Quaracchi ed., III, 745 ff.; Gregory IX's letter of Aug. 17, 1236, in *Epistolae saeculi XIII*, ed. by Rodenberg, I, 592 f. Nos. 695, 700; Potthast, *Regesta*, Add. Nos. 10227a, 22899, 26265; Raynaldus, *Annales*, IV, 57 No. xxvii; and *supra*, Vol. IV, pp. 12 f., 153 f., 239 n. 11, 313 f. n. 5. In their letters of August 22, 1231, and July 21, 1245, Gregory IX and Innocent IV tried to restrain clergymen from collecting tithes from gardens and houses belonging to friars, "as if they were houses of Jews." The secular clergy's reasoning, that had unbelievers not occupied those premises the clergy would have been able to collect revenue from their former Christian owners, essentially applied also to monks. See J. H. Sbaralea, *Bullarium franciscanum*, I, 75 No. lxv, 369 No. lxxxv; Potthast, *Regesta*, I, 754 No. 8788; Grayzel, *The Church*, pp. 190 f. No. 63.

56. Bonifatius de Vitelinis, *Commentarius in Clementinam*, p. 68, cited by Bardinet in *RH*, XII, 27. The efficacy of a threatened boycott depended mainly on the disciplinary power of the excommunication on those Christians who failed to join it, a power which was constantly diminishing both because of its excessive use and the widespread criticisms of the Church in the later Middle Ages. See *supra*, n. 43.

57. M. Stern, *Urkundliche Beiträge*, I, 54 f. No. 49. The Council of Montpellier of 1258 (canon 5) actually demanded that any Christian debtor should be enabled to secure the cancellation of all or part of his debt by taking an oath that it represented accumulated interest. James I of Aragon tried to forestall such cancellations by enjoining both Jewish creditors and Christian debtors to swear on the Law of Moses and the Gospels, respectively, that their contracts involved neither fraud nor usury. Similarly the notaries were ordered not to execute any usurious contracts (1259). See Mansi, *Collectio*, XXIII, 992; Hefele, *Histoire*, VI, Part 1, p. 91; S. Kahn, "Documents inédits sur les Juifs de Montpellier au moyen âge," *REJ*, XIX, 261 f. On the mistaken interpretation of Luke 6:35, see T. Reinach, "Mutuum date nihil inde sperantes," *Revue des études grecques*, VII, 52–58, pointing out that the original Greek text indicates a more radical demand of lending money without any expectation of repayment. Reinach concludes that this "fatal mistake transformed a precept of ideal charity—too ideal to be dangerous—into a more limited, and hence seemingly more realizable, prohibition. This injunction was destined to assume in the civic code of the Church an importance equally calamitous to Christans condemned to misery and to Jews condemned to usury." In any case, from this original misunderstanding sprang the ramified canonical regulations concerning usury which have been the subject of extended discussions and ample scholarly treatment. See L. dalle Molle, *Il Contratto di cambio nei moralisti dal secolo XIII alla metà del secolo XVII* (with a Foreword by B. R. Ragazzi); and, more generally, A. Dauphin-Meunier's survey of *La Doctrine économique de l'Eglise;* the literature cited *supra*, Vol. IV, pp. 338 ff. nn. 61–78, esp. n. 64. Further data will be cited *infra*, Chaps. XLVI and LIII.

58. Mansi, *Collectio*, XXVIII, 347 (Avvisamenta, v.5); XXIX, 99 (Sessio XIX, Art. 6); Hefele, *Histoire*, VII, Part 2, pp. 878 f.; *Acta concilii Constanciensis*, ed. by H. Fincke *et al.*, II, 666; and other data assembled by Browe in *Die Judenmission*, pp. 195 ff. In passing we may also recall the difficulties created by canon law for Jewish moneylenders through the moratoria extended to Crusaders until their return. See *supra*, Vol. IV. At times popes felt entitled to reduce or cancel debts owed to Jews. This happened not only in the Papal States, where popes acted as sovereign overlords of Jewish property, but also in other lands. In 1335, for example, Benedict XII freed Bishop Otto of Würzburg of all his debts owed to Jews. See M. Wiener, *Regesten*, pp. 50 No. 176, 119 No. 119.

59. M. Lattes, "Documents et notices sur l'histoire politique et littéraire des Juifs en Italie," *REJ*, V, 219 ff., 228 ff. (publishing the text of a typical *condotta* of 1521); see *infra*, Chap. XLVI; Stern, *Urkundliche Beiträge*, I, 60 ff. No. 54, 66 ff. No. 63. A similar dispensation had been granted "for the salvation of the souls" of the city elders of Frankfort by Pope Sixtus IV in 1478. *Ibid.*, pp. 65 f. No. 62. The initiative for this papal act had doubtless come from the Frankfort elders themselves. Evidently the earlier protracted controversy over the alleged Jewish "usury from usury," the recurrent attempts by the ecclesiastical authorities to arrogate to themselves the jurisdiction over Jewish moneylending, and the pro-Jewish intervention of Emperor Frederick III in 1470, had failed to assuage the compunctions of many elders concerning the legality of the Jews' charging interest and the protection extended to such transactions by the municipal authorities. See I. Kracauer, *Geschichte der Juden in Frankfurt*, I, 218 ff.

60. A. Ghinato, "Primi tentativi per la fondazione di un Monte di pietà a Terni (1464–1472)," *AFH*, L, 379–440; and "I Francescani e il Monte di Pietà di Terni da Fra Agostino da Perugia al B. Bernardino da Feltre (1471–1489)," *ibid.*, LI, 95–160, esp. pp. 123 ff., 154 ff., where the text of the *condotta* of 1474 for the new Jewish settlers of Terni is published and analyzed. See also the related archival studies by Ghinato (*Monte di pietà e monti frumentarii di Amelia*), which includes the text of the convention between the city and the Jews of Amelia of 1460; "L'Apostolato religioso e sociale di S. Giacomo della Marca in Terni," *AFH*, XLIX, 106–42, 352–90; and "Un Propagatore dei Monti di pietà del' 400, P. Fortunato Coppoli da Perugia, O.F.M.+ 1477," *Rivista di storia della chiesa in Italia*, X, 193–211; E. Lazzareschi, "Il Beato Bernardino da Feltre, gli ebrei e il Monte di Pietà in Lucca," *Bollettino storico lucchese*, XIII, 12–43; E. Patriarca, *Il Monte di Pietà di S. Daniele dei Friuli;* and *infra*, n. 61.

61. The first *monte di pietà* was established in Perugia in 1462; it was followed by that of Orvieto in 1464 (sanctioned later by Popes Pius II and Paul II) and many others. A collection of ecclesiastical apologias, published in Venice, 1498, bore the title, *Pro monte pietatis: Consilia sacrorum theologorum et collegiorum Patavii*. Among his various anti-Jewish tracts Bernardino de' Busti also included a *Defensorium montis pietatis contra figmenta omnia emule falsitatis* (1497; published in 1503). See also, more generally, H. Holzapfel, *Die Anfänge der Montes Pietatis (1462–1515)*; M. Weber, *Les Origines des monts-de-piété;* and A. Milano, "Considerazioni sulla lotta dei Monti di pietà contro il prestito ebraico," *Scritti in Memoria di Sally Mayer*, pp. 199–223. On the Venetian "ghetto banks," see idem, "I 'banchi dei poveri' a Venezia," *RMI*, XVII, 250–65; and particularly the comprehensive *Compilazione delle leggi . . . . . . in materia d'offici e banchi del ghetto*, ed. by A. A. Viola, which was published in 6 volumes in Venice, 1785–88, while these banks still were in operation. (The decree of 1534 is cited in IV, 381 f.) The fuller story of the origin of that significant institution is only now beginning to emerge from the archival researches by A. Ghinato (see *supra*, n. 60) and others. Its profound impact on the political and economic status of Italian Jewry will be analyzed *infra*, Chaps. XLVI and LIII, where much additional literature will be listed.

# CHAPTER XXXVIII: STUBBORN DISSENTER

1. Gregory VII's letter to King Vratislav of Bohemia of 1079 in his *Epistolae* (*Registrum*), vii.11, *PL*, CXLVIII, 554 f.; that of Innocent III to the diocese of Metz of July 12, 1199 in his *Epistolae*, ii.141, *PL*, CCXIV, 695 ff.; Council of Toulouse of 1229, canon 14, and James I's statute at the Council of Tarragona of 1234, canon 2, in Mansi, *Collectio*, XXIII, 197, 329; Hefele, *Histoire*, V, Part 2, p. 1559; Berthold of Ratisbon (Regensburg), *Vollständige Ausgabe seiner Predigten*, ed. by F. Pfeiffer and J. Strobl, I, pp. xxi Nos. 6–8, xxvii No. 25. See also the additional data assembled by M. Deanesly in her *Lollard Bible and Other Medieval Biblical Versions*, pp. 18 ff. and *passim;* and G. G. Coulton's eloquent description of "Bible Christians" in his *Inquisition and Liberty*, pp. 182 ff.

2. *Chronica Ordinis fratrum predicatorum*, ed. by B. M. Reichert, pp. 82 f. No. 113. This chronicle, variously attributed to Humbert de Romans or to Galuagni de la Flamma, has been shown by H. Denifle to be but Part VI of the *Vitae fratrum ordinis praedicatorum, 1203–1254* by Gerardus de Fracheto. See C. Bémont, *Simon de Montfort, Earl of Leicester, 1208–1265*, new ed. trans. by E. F. Jacob, p. xxxiii. At first the Church viewed with suspicion the Twelfth-Century Renaissance, particularly in so far as it opened the gates to the influx of Aristotelian doctrines. The popes from Innocent III to Gregory IX did not hesitate to forbid the study of Aristotle outright. See esp. M. Grabmann, *I Papi del Duecento e l'Aristotelismo*, I. Only in the latter part of the thirteenth century, when Albertus Magnus and Thomas Aquinas had synthesized Aristotelianism with the Christian tradition, did that hostility gradually diminish; it finally gave way to whole-hearted approval.

3. Bernard Gui (Guidonis), *Practica inquisitionis hereticae pravitatis*, v.5, ed. by C. Douais, p. 288, in G. Mollat's French translation in collaboration with C. Drioux entitled *Manuel de l'inquisiteur*, II, 6 f.; Nicholas Eymeric, *Directorium inquisitorum*, ed. and annotated by F. Pegna, Venice, 1607 ed., fol. 353b. See also data supplied by L. I. Newman in his *Jewish Influence in Christian Reform Movements*, pp. 303 ff.; and, on the widespread practice of concealing heretics, J. Guiraud, *Histoire de l'Inquisition au moyen âge*, II, 83 f. (Guiraud avowedly offered only a few selected cases and mentioned no Jewish *receptatores hereticorum*, probably because he merely wished to document the latter's presence in all classes of Christian society.)

The nexus between Christian sectarian movements and internal Jewish dissension had existed, though less ostensibly, in sect-ridden Byzantium under Justinian and his successors. As late as *ca.* 1240 (see *supra*, Chap. XXXVII, n. 3), Alexander of Hales discussed at some length the ecclesiastical right to interfere with Jewish supporters and instigators of Christian heterodoxy, but he had nothing to say about internal Jewish sectarian trends, despite the burning of Maimonides' *Guide* in Montpellier a few years before. See his *Summa theologica*, II.ii.3, 8, 745, Quaracchi ed., Vol. III, pp. 732 f. (with reference to I Cor. 5:12). It is questionable, however, whether a merely passive attitude toward heresy was as punishable in the case of a Jew as it was in that of a Christian. Certainly, the old formulation of Pope Leo the Great that "he who is able but does not prevent others from erring proves that he himself errs," could hardly apply to a Jewish bystander who was supposed to live in error anyway. See *Decretales Greg.,* v.7, 2 in *Corpus,* ed. by Friedberg, II, 778. In most cases Jewish neutrality in sectarian controversies was taken for granted, if not always viewed with favor by the interested parties.

4. Lucas of Túy (Tudensis), *De altera vita fideique controversis adversus Albigensium errores, libri tres,* iii.3, ed. by J. Mariana and J. Gretser, p. 278; Innocent III's letter of 1198 in his *Epistolae,* i.94, in *PL,* CCXIV, 81 ff.; C. Devic and J. Vaissète, *Histoire générale de Languedoc,* VIII, Preuves, col. 572. Evidently, Jews had to be constantly on their guard lest any remark made by them in the presence of heretics, actual or suspected, be taken as an invitation to heterodoxy. Any passer-by hearing a Jew utter a remotely "blasphemous" statement could denounce the speaker to the inquisitors, and embroil not only that individual but the entire community in endless difficulties. On one occasion, as we shall see, the community of Palermo strained its resources to secure the release of several members condemned to death for allegedly blaspheming against Jesus and Mary.

5. I. von Döllinger, *Beiträge zur Sektengeschichte des Mittelalters,* Vol. II: *Dokumente vornehmlich zur Geschichte der Valdesier und Katharer,* pp. 60 f., 195 f., 220; *La Somme des autorités à l'usage des prédicateurs méridionaux du XIII siècle,* ed. by C. Douais, pp. 126 ff.; Raynier Sacconi in his *Summa de Catharis et Leonistis seu pauperibus de Lugduno,* in E. Martène and U. Durand, *Thesaurus novus anecdotorum,* V, 1769; and other sources cited by J. Guiraud, *Histoire de l'Inquisition,* I, 60 ff. The Catharist arguments for identification of the Old Testament God with Satan are summarized in a thirteenth-century tract quoted from a Carcassonne MS by H. C. Lea in *A History of the Inquisition of the Middle Ages,* I, 92 f. note, 563–67 App. i. These arguments were in part answered by the Dominican, Monetta of Cremona, in his *Adversus Catharos et Valdenses,* ii.5–6, ed. by T. A. Ricchini, fols. 166 ff. See also the chapter on "Le Dieu de l'Ancien Testament est le Dieu Mauvais" in C. Schmidt, *Histoire et doctrine de la secte des Cathares ou Albigeois,* II, 20 ff.; L. I. Newman, *Jewish Influence on Christian Reform Movements,* pp. 156 ff.; G. Saige, *Les Juifs du Languedoc,* pp. 235 f. App. 20; and *infra,* Chap. LV.

Our knowledge of Catharism has only recently entered into a decisive stage, owing to the publication of many Catharist texts and of some penetrating studies by both sympathizers and opponents. See esp. R. Nelli, *Écritures cathares. La Cène secrète. Le Livre des deux principes. Le Rituel latin. Le Rituel occident.* (Textes pré-cathares et cathares); D. Roché, *Le Catharisme,* new ed. enlarged; A. Borst, *Die Katharer;* S. Savini, *Il Catarismo italiano ed i suoi vescovi nei secoli XIII e XIV.* The reaction of the official Church has been analyzed, among others, by M. Dmitrevsky, "Notes sur le catharisme et l'inquisition dans le Midi de France," *Annales de Midi,* XXXV–VI, 294–311; XXXVII–VIII, 190–213; D. Roché, *L'Eglise romaine et les cathares albigeois.*

The indebtedness of many of these heresies to ancient gnosticism and Manichaeism, whose anti-Jewish ingredients have been discussed *supra,* Vols. II, pp. 72 f., 167 f., 394 n. 50, 408 n. 3; III, pp. 57 ff.; VI, 298, has often been analyzed. According to some recent studies, it resulted from a combination of underground survivals of ancient religious trends, the return of Crusaders from the Middle East, and even some active missionary propaganda by the Balkan Bogomils. See S. Runciman, *The Medieval Manichee: a Study of the Christian Dualist Heresy*, 2d ed.; J. Russell, "Interpretations of the Origin of Medieval Heresy," *Mediaeval Studies*, XXV, 26–53, esp. pp. 37 ff. Runciman also points out that many heretics sharply deprecated the veneration of the Virgin, a veneration which was then reaching new heights in southern France as a result of the glorification of the "lady" by the troubadours. This deprecation, which may have added zest to the legends concerning Jewish desecrations of paintings or statues of the Virgin, characteristically found enthusiastic support among high-ranking ladies of the French aristocracy. See *infra*, Chap. XLIX. From another angle, J. P. Faure compared the Inquisition's sharp repression of heretical trends with twentieth-century reactions of societies in dissolution which feel endangered by the rise of new movements. See his "Reflexions sur l'Albigéisme," *Europe*, XXVIII, No. 59, pp. 39–54. A partial answer to this social revolt was the new stress laid within the Church upon poverty, indubitably a major factor contributing to the speedy evolution of the Franciscan movement. See Mlle. C. Thouzellier's pertinent remarks in "La Pauvreté, arme contre l'albigéisme, en 1206," *RHR*, CLI, 79–92 (with special reference to Innocent III's epistle of November 17, 1206, in his *Epistolae*, ix.185, Migne's *PL*, CCXV, 1024 f.). See also other writings listed in P. de Berne-Lagarde's *Bibliographie du catharisme languedocien*, with a Preface by R. Nelli; E. Delaruelle, "Le Catharisme en Languedoc vers 1200: Une enquète," *Annales de Midi*, LXXII, 149–67. We have gone into unusual length in listing sources and researches pertaining to southern French heresies, not only because they shared with Jews the inimical vigilance of the Inquisition, but also because of the persistent underground contacts between Christian and Jewish mysticism in the crucial phase of their European evolution. See *supra*, Vol. VIII, pp. 37 ff.

6. The report of the inquisitor of Passau in Marguerin de la Bigne's ed. of *Maxima bibliotheca veterum patrum*, XXV, 273; Lucas of Túy (Tudensis), *De altera vita, passim;* Charles I's order of July 4, 1276 in A. de Boüard, *Actes et lettres de Charles I*, p. 305 No. 985. See esp. G. Gonnet, "Waldensia," *RHPR*, XXXIII, 202–54; and his bibliographical studies, "Il Movimento valdese in Europa secondo le più recenti ricerche (secoli XII–XVI)," *Bollettino* of the Società di studi valdesi, LVIII, 21–30 (which divides that evolution into three major periods of 1176–84; 1184–1525; 1526 to the present); idem, "Sulle fonti del valdismo medioevale," *Protestantesimo*, I, 17–32.

Relatively less information has been forthcoming in recent years concerning the Passagii. Nor have any recent investigations contributed much to the clarification of the relation between Jews and these sectarian currents as discussed four decades ago by L. I. Newman in his *Jewish Influence*, which still offers the most comprehensive treatment of the subject. See also my review of this volume in *JQR*, XXIII, 405–10; and P. Alphandéry's comments, "Sur les Passagiens," *REJ*, LXXXII, 353–61 (arguing for the classification of the *Passagii* as a mere subdivision of the Waldenses).

7. Gregory IX, *Registres*, ed. by L. Auvray, cols. 351 f. No. 539, 780 f. No. 1391; C. Rodenberg, ed., *Epistolae saeculi XIII*, pp. 432 ff. No. 537; and Lucius III's definition in his bull, *Ad abolendum* of 1184, Art. 4, in *Bullarium romanum*, III, 20 ff., quoted in Gregory IX's *Decretales*, v.7, 9, in *Corpus juris canonici*, ed. by E. Fried-

berg, II, 780 ff. On some ancient antecedents see A. Berger's data on "La Concezione di eretico nelle fonti giustinianee," *Rendiconti* of the Accademia Nazionale dei Lincei, Classe di scienze morali, 8th ser. X, 353–68. See also Innocent III's letter to the French episcopate of April, 1198, in *PL*, CCXIV, 81 ff.; H. C. Lea, *History of the Inquisition of the Middle Ages*, I, 88, 114 f. note; the debate between R. Morghen in his *Medioevo cristiano*, 3d ed., pp. 204–81 and A. Dondaine in "L'Origine de l'hérésie médiévale. A propos d'un livre récent," *Rivista di storia della Chiesa in Italia*, VI, 47–78; R. Manselli, *Studi sulle eresie del secolo XII*; and the bibliographical survey by L. Sommariva, "Studi recenti sulle eresie medievali (1939–1952)," *RSI*, LXIV, 237–68.

8. C. Douais, *L'Inquisition, ses origines, sa procédure*, pp. 36 f., 186; Innocent III's letter to the French archbishops of 1208, in his *Epistolae*, xi.26, *PL*, CCXV, 1357; Devic and Vaissète, *Histoire générale de Languedoc*, IX, 270 n. 1; X, preuves, cols. 232 f. No. 58; G. Saige, *Les Juifs du Languedoc*, pp. 231 ff.; R. Straus, *Die Juden im Königreich Sizilien*, p. 61. See also Philip IV's decree protecting Jews against prosecutions by inquisitors on account of alleged usury, sorcery, and "other matters for which the said inquisitors are not competent by virtue of their inquisitorial office," published by C. V. Langlois in his "Formulaires des lettres du XII^e, du XIII^e et du XIV^e siècle," in *Notices et extraits des Manuscrits de la Bibliothèque Nationale*, XXIV, Part 1, pp. 19 f. No. 14; and R. Anchel, *Les Juifs de France*, pp. 98, 103. That only relatively few papal letters of the thirteenth century deal with problems of heresy and the struggle against it is emphasized, with the aid of some statistics, by A. C. Shannon in *The Popes and Heresy in the Thirteenth Century*, pp. 11 f. Here are also listed many of the more recent studies on the rise and early evolution of the papal Inquisition in France. Additional bibliographical and analytical data will be given *infra*, Chap. LV.

9. Alexander of Hales, *Summa theologica*, II.ii.3, 8, 1, 740, Quaracchi ed., III, 729. On the earlier procedures see the partial analysis, largely based on Ralph Niger's observations, by G. B. Flahiff in "Ecclesiastical Censorship of Books in the Twelfth Century," *Mediaeval Studies*, IV, 1–22. See also, more generally, the recent analyses and apologias, in part relating to the provisions of the canon law code of 1918, by D. H. Wiest, *The Precensorship of Books (Canon 1384–1386, 1392–1394, 2318 § 2): a History and a Commentary*; H. C. Gardiner, *Catholic Viewpoint on Censorship* (apologetically reviewing contemporary conditions especially, and reproducing "The United States Bishops' Statement of 1957 on Censorship," pp. 185 ff.); and *supra*, Vol. V, pp. 133 f. Understandably, Hebrew books almost wholly escaped the attention of Christian censors until the thirteenth century. We do not even have any information concerning the methods of suppression employed by the Byzantine police in executing Justinian's aforementioned outlawry of the Jewish *deuterosis* (Second Torah). See *supra*, Vols. III, pp. 12, 233 n. 11; VII, pp. 94 f., 261 n. 41. A. Berliner, *Censur und Confiscation hebräischer Bücher im Kirchenstaate*, and W. Popper, *The Censorship of Hebrew Books* furnish significant materials only for the period after the spread of Hebrew printing from 1475. See *infra*, Chaps. LV and LIX.

10. The Dominicans of Montpellier acted only in accordance with the papal opposition to Aristotelianism in any form. See *supra*, n. 2. On the various aspects of the anti-Maimonidean controversy see J. Sarachek, *Faith and Reason: the Conflict*

*over the Rationalism of Maimonides;* and our analysis in a later chapter. The nexus between the burning of Maimonides' *Guide* and the subsequent suppression of the Talmud seems rather tenuous. Pro-Maimonists, like the thirteenth-century philosopher Hillel b. Samuel of Verona, connected the two events and thus placed the blame on the southern French obscurantists. According to Hillel, the Paris auto-da-fé of 1,200 rabbinic volumes (or, more likely, 12,000, that is 500 per carload; see *infra,* n. 20) took place within forty days of the burning of the *Guide* in Montpellier "and the ashes of the talmudic books commingled with the ashes of the *Guide* and the book of knowledge [the first section of the Maimonidean Code]." See his *Iggeret* (Epistle) to the papal court physician Isaac Gaio in E. Aschkenazi's ed. of *Ṭa'am zekenim* (Taste of Ancients; a Collection of Manuscript Fragments), fol. 71b. However, as we shall presently see, this second conflagration did not occur until 1242, the interval of almost nine years having been dominated by strong anti-Jewish and antiheretical movements.

11. See *supra,* Vols. IV, pp. 122 f., 301 f. nn. 43-44; V, pp. 108 ff.; VI, p. 462 n. 51; and *infra,* nn. 17 and 22. These scholars must have realized that the biblical exegesis of medieval rabbis was, in part, based on the teachings of ancient sages. Yet secondhand information, when transmitted by generally trustworthy authorities, was too much in vogue to call for direct consultation of the original sources. On the late medieval Christian Hebraists, see more fully *infra,* Chap. LVII.

12. Gregory IX's letter to Nivello and Anselm of May 5, 1236 and his bull, *Lachrymabilem Judaeorum* of Sept. 5, or 9, 1236, in his *Registres,* ed. by L. Auvray, II, 385 No. 3144, 471 f. No. 3308; and in Grayzel, *The Church,* pp. 222 ff. Nos. 85, 87. The condemnation of the Talmud and other rabbinic books has frequently been discussed. Few new details have come to light since H. Graetz's treatment of this subject in his *Geschichte der Juden,* 4th ed., VII, 92 ff., 405 ff. The pertinent papal letters and other documents have often been reprinted; they are readily available, for instance, in Grayzel, pp. 29 ff., Nos. 95-98, 250 ff. No. 104, 339 ff. Only the disputation of Paris, which formed a part of the trial, has been subjected, by F. Y. Baer and others, to a renewed analysis. See *infra,* nn. 13, 30 ff.

The background of Donin's original antitalmudic fervor, which led to his excommunication, has not yet been fully clarified. We recall that Karaism had made some inroads into the Iberian Peninsula during the eleventh century and had to be suppressed by Jewish leaders. See *supra,* Vols. IV, pp. 38, 253 n. 47; V, pp. 271, 412 n. 72. However, little is known about its penetration into French possessions, particularly the vicinity of La Rochelle, Donin's apparent birthplace. We may rather assume that his heretical leanings were nurtured from old antirabbinic trends which had preceded Karaism and were more widespread in the West than the schism as such. See *supra,* Vols. VI, pp. 171 f., 410 f., nn. 23-24; VIII, pp. 32, 38, 288 ff. n. 35, 291 f. n. 42.

13. Potthast, *Regesta,* I, 911 Nos. 10759-60, 10767-68; Grayzel, *The Church,* pp. 238 ff. Nos. 95-98; and other data assembled by A. Lewin in "Die Religionsdisputation des R. Jechiel von Paris 1240," *MGWJ,* XVIII, 97-110, 145-56, 193-210; A. Kisch in "Die Anklageartikel gegen den Talmud und ihre Vertheidigung durch R. Jechiel ben Joseph vor Ludwig dem Heiligen in Paris," *ibid.,* XXIII, 10-18, 62-75, 123-30, 155-63, 204-12; idem, *Papst Gregor des Neunten Anklageartikel gegen den*

*Talmud;* I. Loeb, "La Controverse de 1240 sur le Talmud," *REJ*, I, 247–61; II, 248–70; III, 39–57; and his "Bulles inédites des papes," *ibid.*, I, 114–18, 293–98, esp. pp. 117, 295 f. On the likely nexus between the all-pervading papal-imperial conflict and the papal circular see my "'Plenitude of Apostolic Powers' and Medieval 'Jewish Serfdom'" (Hebrew), *Sefer ha-Yobel le-Yitzhak Baer* (Yitzhak F. Baer Jubilee Volume), pp. 102–24, esp. p. 121.

William of Auvergne, though not unappreciative of Jewish philosophy (he was indebted, as we shall see, to both Ibn Gabirol and Maimonides), was far from friendly to his Jewish compatriots or to Judaism as a religion. While praising the Jews for their agreement with some articles of Christian faith, he declared that "where they disagree, they try to give the prophetic annunciations [*eloquentia*] not only false but ridiculous interpretations in order to adapt them to their error." See his *De fide* in his *Opera*, Nuremberg 1496 ed., fol. 13c; Jakob Guttmann, *Die Scholastik des dreizehnten Jahrhunderts*, pp. 13 ff.; and N. Valois, *Guillaume d'Auvergne, évêque de Paris (1228–1249), sa vie et ses ouvrages*, pp. 118–37, with A. Darmesteter's comments thereon in his review of that thesis in *REJ*, I, 140–45; and *infra*, n. 47. Although before the Council of Vienne of 1311 Hebrew studies among Christians were quite limited, there undoubtedly were some theologians, especially in Paris, then a great center of both Christian and Jewish studies, who evinced interest in rabbinic books.

14. Innocent IV's *Registres*, ed. by Berger, I, 115 No. 682; Potthast, *Regesta*, II, 966 No. 11376; Grayzel, *The Church*, pp. 250 f. No. 104, 274 ff. No. 119. No less than forty distinguished ecclesiastics joined William of Auvergne and Albertus Magnus in the final condemnation of the Talmud. See the list reproduced by A. Kisch in *MGWJ*, XXIII, 208 f. and, with good identifications of the signatories, in the *Chartularium Universitatis Parisiensis*, ed. by H. Denifle and E. Chatelain, I, 209 ff. No. 178. See also *ibid.*, pp. 173 ff. No. 131, 201 ff. Nos. 172–73.

The date of the burning of the Talmud, variously reported in Jewish and Latin sources, has been convincingly established as of June 1242 by Graetz in his *Geschichte*, 4th ed., VII, 405 ff. (Excursus 5). The various reservations and strictures by later scholars have largely been dispelled through the recent Hebrew notes by S. C. Kook, "The Date of the Burning of the Talmud in France," *KS*, XXIX, 281; and by D. Tamar, "More About the Date of the Burning of the Talmud," *ibid.*, pp. 430–31. The delay between the disputation of 1240 and the actual burning in 1242 has long been explained through a story reported by the contemporary monk (and Jewish convert), Thomas of Cantimpré, near Cambrai. According to his *Bonum universale de Apibus*, ed. by G. Colvener, p. 16, an archbishop (Gautier Cornut of Sens?), bribed by Jews, intervened in their behalf, but his sudden death in the presence of the king (Cornut died on April 21, 1241) instilled fear in the youthful Louis IX who, under the prompting of a monk, Henry of Cologne, proceeded with the destruction of the Hebrew books. We must not overlook, however, the significance of Louis' intervening return from the Crusade and his growing contacts with members of the new preaching orders. See L. K. Little, "Saint Louis' Involvement with the Friars," *CH*, XXXIII, 125–48.

15. E. J. de Laurière *et al.*, *Ordonnances des roys de France*, I, 275 No. 32, 596 No. 9; G. Saige, *Les Juifs du Languedoc*, pp. 212 f. No. 2, 235 f. No. 20; C. Douais, *L'Inquisition*, pp. 357 ff. nos. i, iv and 5; Mansi, *Collectio*, XXV, 640; Bernard Gui,

*Practica inquisitionis,* ii.48, 50–53; iii.47; v.4, ed. by Douais, pp. 67 ff., 170, 290 ff.; idem, *Liber sententiarum inquisitionis tholosanae,* ed. by P. Limborch, fol. 13b. In his *Historia inquisitionis,* p. 241, Limborch connects Gui's persecution with John XXII's antitalmudic legislation (see *infra,* n. 18) which, however, was not enacted until September 1320. According to a somewhat obscure report, three large carloads filled with Jewish books had also been burned in Paris in 1309. See the *Anonymum S. Martialis chronicon* in M. Bouquet, *Recueil des historiens des Gaules et de la France,* new ed. by L. Delisle, XXI, 813; and the *Chroniques de Saint Martial de Limoges,* ed. by H. Duplès-Algier, p. 144. In *Les Juifs de France,* p. 110 n. 1, R. Anchel has questioned this date because it places the event during the temporary absence of the Jews from Paris between 1306 and 1315. Doubtless for the same reason A. Lewin had suggested in 1869 (in *MGWJ,* XVIII, 209) that this report related to Gui's bonfire in Toulouse. But his emendation of the date to 1319 is unacceptable, since the anonymous chronicler's notation belongs to the original part of his work composed in 1310. See the editor's introduction in Bouquet, p. 807 and, with more circumspection, that by Duplès-Algier, pp. iv f. Most likely these books had been left by the exiles in 1306 and the courts required three years until they consigned them to the flames. Some were still extant in 1315, and they were returned to the exiles.

16. Great Britain, *Close Rolls,* 1242–47, p. 292 (dated March 11, 1245); V. Balaguer, *Historia de Cataluña,* II, 711 ff.; J. Amador de los Rios, *Historia social,* I, 427 f.; Régné, "Catalogue," *REJ,* LXI, 2 ff. Nos. 216, 249; K. Eubel, in *Römische Quartalschrift,* XIII, 36 No. 10; Baer, *Die Juden,* I, Part 1, p. 847, No. 527; Alphonso X's *Las Siete Partidas,* vii.24, 2, Paris, 1847 ed., IV, 644. In another compilation, to be sure, Alphonso X tried to outlaw the possession by Jews of talmudic and other anti-Christian texts, but little was done to implement this provision. See *El Fuero real,* iv.2, 1 in *Opusculos legales del Rey Don Alphonso el Sabio,* II, 118. In Germany, too, there were sporadic attacks on the Talmud by preachers and poets like Berthold of Ratisbon and Konrad of Würzburg, but they did not result in any extended governmental action. See the data cited by M. Güdemann in his *Geschichte des Erziehungswesens und der Cultur der abendländischen Juden,* I, 142 ff.; and by P. Browe in *AKKR,* CXVIII, 42 ff., 56 ff.

17. Nicholas de Lyra, *Postilla litteralis super Biblia,* best available in various eds. of the Bible, such as the Leyden, 1545 ed., entitled *Biblia sacra cum glossis;* H. Hailperin, *Rashi and the Christian Scholars;* idem, "Nicholas de Lyra and Rashi: The Minor Prophets," in *Rashi Anniversary Volume* published by the American Academy for Jewish Research, pp. 115–47; Bernard Gui, *Practica,* v.5, 4, ed. by C. Douais, p. 291; and in G. Mollat's French trans., *Manuel de l'inquisiteur,* II, 18 f. See also Raymond Martini, *Pugio Fidei* (Poniard of the Faith), *passim; supra,* Vols. V, p. 357 n. 8; VI, pp. 410 f. n. 24.

18. John XXII's *Lettres communes,* III, 169 No. 12238 (also Raynaldus, *Annales,* V, 138 [*ad* 1320] No. xxiii); L. Wadding, *Annales Minorum,* IX, 327 ff.; Antipope Benedict XIII's bull, *Et si doctoris,* of May 10, 1415 in Amador de los Rios, *Historia social,* II, 630 f.; I. von Döllinger, *Beiträge zur Sektengeschichte,* II, 394 f.; Geronimo de Santa Fé, *De Judaicis erroribus ex Talmut* in *Bibliotheca Magna Veterum Patrum,* fol. 545b, and on the latter's role at the disputation of Tortosa, see *infra,*

nn. 39 ff. Eugenius IV's bull, *Dudum ad nostram,* of Aug. 8, 1442, addressed to Castile and Leon, and later extended to Italy as well, did not specifically refer to Jewish books. However, in Art. 7 the pope demanded broadly that "secular Christian judges should punish with pecuniary fines and other more severe penalties, as they see fit, those Jews who blaspheme against God, the most glorious Virgin Mary, his mother, or some saints, or else in some other way commit transgressions of this kind." See *Bullarium,* V, 69. The later Jewish chronicler, Gedaliah ibn Yaḥya, refers to that decree in 42 articles (our text includes only 13 provisions; perhaps 42 is a *lapsus* for 12, the letter *mim* having replaced a *yod*) as having included the regulation that "under the sanction of the loss of all their property Jews were forbidden to study their Torah except for the Law of Moses." Only with much effort and lavish expense did representatives of several Italian communities assembled at Tivoli and Rovigo secure a modification of that prohibition. See Gedaliah's *Shalshelet ha-qabbalah* (Chain of Tradition; a chronicle), Amsterdam, 1697 ed., fol. 94ab.

19. Alexander of Hales, *Summa,* and Lampen's comments thereon, cited *supra,* n. 9; Chap. XXXVII, n. 3; Lagumina and Lagumina, *Codice diplomatico,* II, Part 1, pp. 144 f. No. 558, 150 ff. No. 562; Meir b. Baruch's lamentation, *Sha'ali serufah* (Inquire, O Burned One!), reprinted in A. M. Habermann's anthology, *Sefer Gezerot Ashkenaz ve-Ṣarefat* (Records of Anti-Jewish Persecutions in Germany and France), pp. 183 ff., 263 f.; A. Marx, "Report of the Librarian," in the *Register* of the Jewish Theological Seminary of America for 1938–39, p. 69. More information on this interesting *Maḥzor* will be supplied in a later chapter. Jonah b. Abraham Gerondi's repentence, it should be noted, is reported only by the strongly pro-Maimonidean Hillel of Verona in his *Iggeret,* cited *supra,* n. 10.

20. Vogelstein and Rieger, *Geschichte der Juden in Rom,* II, 145 f. and *passim;* Joseph b. Joshua ha-Kohen, *'Emeq ha-bakha* (Valley of Tears), ed. by M. Letteris, p. 71; in the German translation by M. Wiener, p. 57; and *infra,* Chap. LIX. Of course, the loss of twenty-four carloads of Hebrew books certainly reduced the number of copies available to French Jewry, which was then marching in the vanguard of talmudic scholarship. (The figure of twenty-four carloads is indicated by both the Hebrew liturgist, Zedekiah b. Abraham 'Anav, and the Christian author of the *Annales Erfordenses,* who doubtless had derived their information from different sources; see the citations in Graetz, *loc. cit.*) The loss may indeed have amounted to 12,000 manuscripts (the version cited *supra,* n. 10, speaks of only 1,200 MSS) as reported by Hillel of Verona. Nevertheless this number must have constituted but a fraction of the copies then available in the various French territories, where royal control in some places was rather weak. True, in May 1247, the papal legate Odo asserted that he had complete information about the Hebrew books not delivered by the rabbis and pledged himself to "do what was to be done about them." Yet for the most part Jewish leaders must have found ways of concealing these highly treasured possessions, in some cases with the aid of Christian friends. It was against the latter that the threatened decrees of excommunication were to be proclaimed, since the Jews themselves were obviously immune to such threats. See Grayzel, *The Church,* pp. 279, 343; U. Robert, "Catalogue d'actes relatifs aux Juifs pendant le moyen âge," *REJ,* III, 214 f. No. 30. The latter document evidently reproduces a general formula which was to be used whenever the occasion arose. It is dated by Robert at

about 1250, as are three other formulas prepared for use in connection with the seizure and examination of Hebrew books, cited by him, *ibid.*, Nos. 26–28, and quoted more fully, from the MSS in Fond Doat at the Bibliothèque Nationale in Paris, by Grayzel, pp. 341 ff.

21. James I's decree of 1242, quoted with full approval in Innocent IV's letter of Aug. 20, 1245, to Peter de Albalte, Archbishop of Tarragona. See Potthast, *Regesta,* II, 1004 No. 11822; Grayzel, *The Church,* pp. 16, 254 ff. No. 105; H. Denifle, "Quellen zur Disputation Pablos Christiani mit Mose Nachmani zu Barcelona 1263," *HJB,* VIII, 235 ff.; J. Régné, "Catalogue des actes," *REJ,* LX, 201 No. 208, and LXI, 1 f., Nos. 215 and 217, 30 No. 386. Of course, there were many antecedents for missionary sermons among Jews (see, e.g., *supra,* Vol. IV, pp. 51, 264 n. 71), but they were fully regulated only since Nicholas III's bull, *Vineam Soreth* (or *Sorec*) of 1278, published in *Bullarium,* IV, 45 ff. No. iii. See also Potthast, II, 1729 Nos. 21382–83; and Nicholas III, *Les Registres,* ed. by J. Gay and S. Vitte, pp. 408 Nos. 965–66, 411 No. 1004. Since copies seem to have been addressed to the Franciscans in Austria and the Dominican provincials in Lombardy and France (see F. M. Delorme, "En marge du bullaire franciscain," *Documents de théologie, philosophie, histoire,* XXI, 36; and L. Erler in *AKKR,* L, 3 n. 2), it stands to reason that this was a universal decree appealing to the preaching orders to use their persuasive powers on Jewish audiences, however unwilling. See also Browe, *Die Judenmission,* pp. 14 ff.

22. James II's decree of 1299, in A. Rubio y Lluch's collection of *Documents per l'historia de la cultura catalana mig-eval,* I, 13 f. No. 14; the debates and resolution of the Council of Vienne in E. Müller, *Das Konzil von Vienne, 1311–1312,* pp. 155 ff., 636 ff. See also M. Kayserling, "Notes sur l'histoire des Juifs en Espagne," *REJ,* XXVII, 148 f. (discussing Lull's attitude to the Jews); B. Altaner, "Die Fremdsprachliche Ausbildung der Dominikanermissionäre während des 13. und 14. Jahrhunderts," *Zeitschrift für Missionswissenschaft,* XXIII, 233–41; idem, "Die Durchführung des Vienner Konzilsbeschlusses über die Errichtung von Lehrstühlen für orientalische Sprachen," *ZKG,* LII, 226–36; idem, "Glaubenszwang und Glaubensfreiheit in der Missionstheorie des Raymundus Lullus," *HJB,* XLVIII, 586–610; C. Selmer, "Ramon Lull and the Problem of Persuasion," *Thought,* XXIII, 215–22; and the additional data assembled by Browe in *Die Judenmission,* pp. 21 ff., 48 ff. See also, more generally, B. Bischof, "The Study of Foreign Languages in the Middle Ages," *Speculum,* XXXVI, 209–24.

23. I. Loeb, "Polémistes chrétiens et juifs en France et en Espagne," *REJ,* XVIII, 226 f.; Thomas Aquinas, *Summa theologica,* III, q. 42, art. 2, in his *Opera omnia* (Leo XIII's ed.), XI, 411; in the English trans., [XVI], 218; Vicente Ferrer's Sermon, cited from a Valencia MS by V. Genovés in his *San Vicente Ferrer en la politica de su tiempo,* p. 23; Benedict XIII's bull, *Et si doctoris* (or *doctoribus*) of 1415 in I. von Döllinger's *Beiträge zur Sektengeschichte,* II, 401; and J. Amador de los Rios, *Historia social,* II, 627–53 (with a Spanish trans.); F. Baer, *Die Juden im christlichen Spanien,* I, Part 1, pp. 793 f. No. 488, 805 f. No. 498, 816 ff. Nos. 504–505, 825 No. 509, 828 No. 513; Part 2, pp. 271 f. No. 275, 277 No. 282.

24. Lagumina and Lagumina, *Codice diplomatico,* I, 215 f. No. 162, 272 ff. Nos. 207–208, 403 ff. No. 332; II, 59 f. No. 500; Raynaldus, *Annales,* IX, 509 No. xxii; Q.

Senigaglia, "La Condizione giuridica degli Ebrei in Sicilia," *Rivista italiana per le scienze giuridiche*, XLI, 92 f.; Francisco Suárez, *Commentarii in II 2 divi Thomae; de fide theologica catholica*, disp. 18 sect. 2 No. 4, in his *Opera omnia*, new ed. by C. Berton *et al.* The situation in Counter Reformation Rome will be described *infra*, Chap. LIX. For the time being, see A. Zucchi, "Memorie dominicane in Roma: Il predicatore degli Ebrei in Roma," *Memorie dominicane*, LI, 200–205, 255–64, 313–21 (with varying subtitles); and A. Milano, "Un Sottile tormento nella vita del ghetto di Roma; La predica coattiva," *RMI*, XVIII, 517–32, both dealing mainly with the period after the formalization of that institution through Gregory XIII's bulls of 1577 and 1584.

The frequent use of Jewish converts to persuade other Jews to become Christian is also exemplified by one Manoforte of Trani. Formerly head of a synagogue, he was granted, after his conversion in 1267, an annual stipend of six gold ounces from revenue derived by the city from the Jewish dye works. This was to be his reward for his own conversion, his denunciation of Jewish writings, and his promise to convert others. See R. Straus, *Die Juden im Königreich Sizilien unter Normannen und Staufern*, p. 60. Two centuries later (after 1470) another Sicilian Jewish convert, Guglielmo Raimondo Moncada, was praised by the Aragonese administration of the island for his knowledge of Hebrew, Chaldean, Arabic, and Latin, and for his conversionist efforts among his former brethren. He was rewarded by the viceroy with a benefice of 200 ducats. He subsequently made a career within the Catholic hierarchy, becoming chaplain of Cardinal Cibo, the future Pope Innocent VIII, though he seems ultimately to have run afoul of a denunciation for secret Judaizing. See R. Starrabba, "Guglielmo Raimondo Moncada, ebreo convertito siciliano del secolo XV," *AS Siciliano*, n.s. IV, 15–91, particularly the documents published in Appendices v–vi. On Moncada's family background and scientific contributions, see also the concise data supplied by M. Steinschneider in his "Abraham ibn Esra," reprinted in *GS*, ed. by H. Malter and A. Marx, I, 459 f. n. 148; also the data quoted by H. Vogelstein and P. Rieger in their *Geschichte der Juden in Rom*, *passim*. The ramified problem of missionary and Jew-baiting sermons merits fuller monographic treatment.

25. Martin V's bull of February 20, 1422, *Considerantes quod*, reproduced by Raynaldus in his *Annales*, VIII, 560 No. xxxvi; and by F. Vernet in *RQH*, LI, 380 f., 414 No. 24.

26. Yehudah b. Samuel he-Ḥasid (the Pious), *Sefer Ḥasidim*, ed. by Wistinetzki, 2d ed., p. 204 No. 811; Thomas Aquinas, *Summa theologica*, II, ii.10, 7 with Cajetan's *Commentary* thereon, in Leo XIII ed., VIII, 87 f.; Justinian, *Corpus juris civilis*, Codex, I, i.4, ed. by (T. Mommsen and) P. Krüger, p. 6. The story of Thomas Aquinas' conversion of the two wealthy Jews is not without flaws. As told by his two biographers, the Jews were in the habit of spending the Christmas festival in the cardinal's castle. Such extended friendly visits with an ecclesiastical lord would presuppose even closer social relations between members of the two faiths in the Papal States during the 1260s than one would expect on the basis of other extant sources. But it is not impossible that two Jewish traders, who may have resisted for years the blandishments of a friendly prince of the Church, should have yielded to the superior acumen and debating skill of the distinguished Dominican. See Peter Calo's *Life of Thomas*, xiv; that by William Tocco, xxii; and the fuller recital by

Bartholomeo of Capua in the Canonization Inquiries, lxxxvi, all in *Fontes vitae Sancti Thomae Aquinatis,* ed. by D. M. Prümmer *et al.* See also K. Foster, *The Life of Saint Thomas Aquinas: Biographical Documents,* pp. 36, 69 n. 38; and P. Reid, "St. Thomas' Christmas Gift: Conversion of Two Prominent Jews," *Dominicana,* XXXVI, 279–84. The Jewish attitude toward proselytism has been and will be more fully discussed in other chapters. For the time being, see S. Bialoblocki's lecture *Die Beziehungen des Judentums zu Proselyten und Proselytismus;* B. Z. Wacholder, "Cases of Proselytizing in the Tosafist Responsa," *JQR,* LI, 288–315; and the literature listed *supra,* Vol. II, pp. 387 f. n. 27 which, although dealing with ancient times, has a bearing on medieval conditions as well; and Chap. XXXVII, n. 4.

27. Gregory IX's *Registres,* ed. by M. Auvray, I, 351 f. No. 539; the Councils of Treves, 1227, canon 8; Tarragona, 1233, canon 1; Vienna, 1267, canon 19; Freising, 1440, canon 21; Bamberg, 1491, canon 44, in Mansi, *Collectio,* XXIII, 31 ff., 329, 1176; XXXII, 15; J. Hartzheim, ed., *Concilia Germaniae,* III, 636 (canon 18); V, 277, 623; Hefele, *Histoire,* V, Part 2, pp. 1462, 1559; VI, Part 1, pp. 138 ff. (includes a polemic against H. Bärwald, "Die Beschlüsse des Wiener Concil's über die Juden aus den Jahre 1267," *Jahrbuch für Israeliten,* ed. by J. Wertheim, 5620 [1859], 188); VII, Part 1, pp. 1150 f. See also other data assembled by P. Browe in *Die Judenmission,* pp. 55 ff., 87 ff.; and *supra,* Vol. V, pp. 108 ff., 338 ff. The aversion to public and private debates was, understandably, most pronounced in periods of great tension, precisely because of heightened provocations.

Jews, on their part, rarely invoked governmental protection against enforced disputations, as they often did against enforced attendance at missionary sermons. However, Majorcan Jewry secured from Pedro IV in 1383 a decree prohibiting both kinds of enforced participation—a provision immediately extended to all Jewish communities in Aragon. See Baer, *Die Juden,* I, Part 1, pp. 539 ff. No. 356, and the note thereon.

28. Baruch's deposition before the Inquisition of Pamiers, published from a Vatican MS by J. M. Vidal in "L'Emeute des Pastoureaux en 1320," *Annales de Saint Louis des Français,* III, 121–74; S. Grayzel's English trans. in "The Confession of a Medieval Jewish Convert," *HJ,* XVII, 89–120 (a related twelfth-century *Opusculum de mea conversione* by Abbot Hermann of Scheda was discussed *supra,* Vol. V, pp. 112 f., 340 f. n. 39); Ibn Verga, *Shebeṭ Yehudah, passim;* Gilbert Crispin, *Disputatio Judaei cum christiano de fide christiana,* in *PL,* CLIX, 1003–36, and in B. Blumenkranz's new critical ed. in *Stromata patristica et medievalia,* III; Peter de Blois, *Contra perfidiam Judaeorum,* in *PL,* CCVII, 825–70; R. W. Hunt, "The Disputation of Peter of Cornwall against Symon the Jew," *Studies in Medieval History Presented to Frederick Maurice Powicke,* pp. 143–56; F. Baer, "Abner von Burgos," *KA,* X, 20–37; idem, *"Minḥat qena'ot* by Alphonso of Valladolid and Its Influence on Ḥisdai Crescas" (Hebrew), *Tarbiz,* XI, 188–206; Jacob ben Reuben, *Milḥamot ha-Shem* (Wars of the Lord), ed. by J. Rosenthal; Joseph ben Nathan Official, *Teshubot ha-Minim* (Replies to Heretics) or *Sefer Yosef ha-Meqanneh* (Book of Joseph the Zealous), in the Paris MS reviewed by Z. Kahn in his "Etude sur le livre de Joseph le Zélateur: Recueil de controverses religieuses du moyen âge," *REJ,* I, 222–46; III, 1–38; Israel Lévi, "Manuscrits du Hadar Zekénim, Recueil de commentaires exégétiques de rabbins de la France septentrionale," *ibid.,* XLIX, 33–50; Moses Kohen of Tordesillas' aforementioned *'Ezer ha-Emunah* (Aid to Faith; see I.

A. Benjacob, *Ozar ha-Sepharim: Thesaurus librorum hebraicorum*, p. 434 No. 189); Shem Ṭob b. Isaac Shapruṭ, *Eben bohan* (Touchstone; only partially published; see A. Marx's excursus in "The Polemical Manuscripts in the Library of the Jewish Theological Seminary of America," *Freidus Mem. Vol.*, pp. 265 ff. also mentioning the author's debate with Cardinal Pedro de Luna (Antipope Benedict XIII) in Pamplona; and, more generally, I. Loeb, *La Controverse religieuse entre les Chrétiens et les Juifs au moyen âge en France et en Espagne* (reprinted from *RHR*, XVII–XVIII); and his "Polémistes chrétiens et juifs en France et en Espagne," *REJ*, XVIII, 43–70, 219–42; E. Urbach, "Etudes sur la littérature polémique au moyen âge," *ibid.*, C, 49–77; and A. L. Williams, *Adversus Judaeos*, *passim*.

If we are to believe Joseph ben Nathan, he, his father, and his brothers had many occasions to debate the respective merits of Judaism and Christianity with Christians of various classes. Their interlocutors allegedly included many dignitaries of Church and state, among them the pope (Gregory IX?) and the archbishop of Sens. If this archbishop was Gautier Cornut, Joseph may indeed have been instrumental in securing through him a postponement of the burning of the Talmud. See *supra*, n. 14. In all these conversations the Jewish discussants seem to have spoken their minds quite freely. Perhaps Nathan Official's family background in the city of Narbonne, where Jews had enjoyed unusual freedoms (see *supra*, Vol. IV, pp. 45 ff.), explains some of his and his sons' outspoken, often witty responses, which were subsequently quoted by other Jewish apologists.

Another case of frequent and rather friendly debates on a high academic level may be reconstructed from the *Ṭa'anot* (Arguments) by the philosopher Moses b. Solomon of thirteenth-century Salerno. See the text, ed. with a German translation and notes by S. Simon in his dissertation *Mose ben Salomo von Salerno und seine philosophischen Auseinandersetzungen mit den Lehren des Christentums*. These altercations will be discussed more fully in the next chapter in connection with literary polemics, since the borderline between literary and oral controversies of the time is often quite tenuous. See *supra*, n. 27.

29. L. Ennen, *Geschichte der Stadt Köln*, IV, 121 f.; J. Hofer, *Johannes von Capestrano*, pp. 294 f.; Jean de Joinville, *Histoire de Saint Louis*, x.51–53, original text ed. by N. de Wailly, new ed., pp. 22 f.; in the English trans. by J. Evans, entitled *The History of St. Louis*, pp. 15 f.; Berthold of Ratisbon, *Predigten*, ed. by Pfeiffer and Strobl. Z. Kahn suggests, rather timidly, that Nathan Official's discussion at Cluny may have taken place during the assembly there in 1245 of many dignitaries including Louis IX, Innocent IV, and Emperor Baldwin of the Latin Empire of Constantinople, although "Joseph the Zealous" refers to the abbot of Cluny only in connection with a debate in neighboring Moulins. See Kahn's observations in *REJ*, III, 13.

30. Although the documents on both sides, as well as modern historiography, make the encounter in Paris appear as a formal disputation, it actually consisted of only three separate hearings with two of the four rabbis. The protocols, if any were kept, were immediately amplified by the participants' personal recollections; from the outset the official and the Jewish versions doubtless greatly differed from one another. These differences grew in subsequent oral transmission, and gave rise to divergent, dramatized accounts: one in Hebrew known as the *Viqquaḥ de-R. Yeḥiel mi-Paris* (The Disputation of R. Yeḥiel of Paris), and several in Latin, the most

important of which is preserved in a Paris MS, named after its second part, *Extrac-tiones de Talmut* (Extracts from the Talmud), compiled by the convert Thibaut de Sezanne with the aid of two other converts some time between 1248 and 1255. See B. Altaner, "Zur Kenntnis des Hebräischen im Mittelalter," *Biblische Zeitschrift*, XXI, 296. Another MS of these "talmudic extracts" was located by J. M. Millás Vallicrosa and fully described by him in his "Extractos del Talmud y alusiones polémicas de la Biblioteca Catedral de Gerona," *Sefarad*, XX, 17–49. See *infra*, n. 43.

The Hebrew report was probably compiled by Joseph b. Nathan Official (or *ha-Meqanneh*, the Zealous) within two decades after the event. First incompletely published in 1681 by J. C. Wagenseil in his collection of Jewish polemics entitled *Tela Ignea Satanae* (Satan's Fiery Tail), Part 2, pp. 1–23, it was reissued from a fuller Paris MS by S. Grünbaum. It is now conveniently available in J. D. Eisenstein's *Oẓar Wikuḥim* (Collection of Polemics and Disputations), pp. 81–86. An English translation by M. Braude is included in the latter's collection, *Conscience on Trial: Three Public Religious Disputations between Christians and Jews in the Thirteenth and Fifteenth Centuries*. On R. Yeḥiel (in French, Vivo or Vives) and his academy, see Benjamin of Tudela's earlier report, cited *supra*, Vol. IV, p. 60; and the data assembled by E. E. Urbach in his *Baʻale ha-Tosafot* (The Tosaphists: Their History, Writings and Methods), pp. 371 ff.

The Latin sources, on the other hand, have never been fully and critically edited, although parts were published in the early eighteenth century by J. Echard in his *Sancti Thomae Summa suo auctori vindicata*, pp. 572 ff.; and by J. Quétif and him in their ed. of *Scriptores ordinis praedicatorum*, I, 128 ff. Other fragments were published by A. Kisch in *MGWJ*, XXIII, 210 ff.; and particularly by I. Loeb in *REJ*, I–III. A. Lewin, A. Kisch, and Loeb also offered careful analyses of these documents (see *supra*, n. 13), but all three too readily accepted the greater credibility of the He-brew account. More judicious is Y. F. Baer's Hebrew reexamination of these sources in *Tarbiz*, II, 172–87. Baer dismisses too lightly, however, the personal confrontation of the Jewish witnesses with Donin as asserted by the Hebrew narrator, because it runs counter to the established anonymity of accusers in the accepted inquisitorial proce-dure. That procedure still was in its formative stage, and there probably was no one on the Christian side to replace Donin in pointing out specific passages in talmudic literature and debating their meaning. See also J. M. Rosenthal's more recent study of "The Talmud on Trial: the Disputation at Paris in the Year 1240," *JQR*, XLVII, 58–76, 145–69, stressing in particular the Karaite influences on these attacks on the Talmud. On Queen Blanche, often alluded to in the Hebrew record in a friendly vein, see E. Berger's *Histoire de Blanche de Castille*. See also the literature listed *supra*, nn. 10 ff.

31. The thirty-five accusations reproduced in the version of Donin's memoran-dum, originally submitted to Pope Gregory IX in 1236, are supplemented by a second section which cites at some length objectionable passages from the Talmud in the sequence of the talmudic tractates. The original table of contents of the first part well summarizes the main points of the indictment: "The Authority of the Talmud; Sages and Judges; Blasphemies against the Human Nature of Christ; Blasphemies against God; Blasphemies against Christians; Errors; Sorcery; Dreams; The Future Age and the Hereafter; The Messiah; Stupidities; Turpitudes and Impurities; Fables." See the text reproduced by Loeb in *REJ*, I, 259 f. Remarkably, notwithstanding his generally wide readings, Donin did not know the source of the

irate exclamation by R. Simon b. Yoḥai, "The best of Gentiles, kill him!" Less surprisingly, R. Yeḥiel found it for him in the tractate *Soferim* (xv.7, ed. by M. Higger, pp. 281 f.), rather than in the *Mekilta de-R. Ishmael* (on Beshallaḥ 14:7, ed. by J. Z. Lauterbach, I, 201) or the Palestinian Talmud (Quiddushin iv.9, 66c), for neither of the latter works enjoyed wide circulation in the Ashkenazic countries of that period. See *supra*, Vol. VI, pp. 25, 331 n. 25, 346 f. n. 57. Yet one cannot help feeling that the phrasing and context of the posttalmudic *Soferim* lent itself better to Yeḥiel's interpretation that R. Simon had a wartime enemy in mind, whose killing could be justified by both self-defense and patriotic duty.

32. While planning their replies, the four rabbis may have learned about the thirty-five points raised by Donin before Pope Gregory, which now served as the main framework for the debate. They may have agreed in advance, for example, to utilize the chronological divergence between the Christian and the talmudic Jesus clearly asserted by Ibn Daud in the preceding century. See *supra*, Vol. VI, pp. 207 f., 428 n. 70. In all these matters there is fairly substantial agreement between the Hebrew and the Latin reports, although on the whole the Hebrew text goes into many more details and embellishes the story with telling repartees. It is, however, much less articulate concerning the alleged stupidities and follies of the Talmud. Although the attitude to the talmudic Aggadah had been under discussion ever since geonic times (see *supra*, Vol. VI, pp. 175 ff., 412 f.), the French Jewish representatives could not allow themselves the latitude concerning its nonobligatory character which was to be shown twenty-three years later by the Spaniard Naḥmanides. Still less could they expatiate on this point in their apologetic *Viqquaḥ*, compiled for the benefit of the northern Jewish public.

33. The records furnish no explanation for the abrupt termination of the hearings. The suggestion that exaggerated rumors about the proceedings had sufficiently aroused the Paris populace to create a danger of anti-Jewish riots has no support in the sources. Certainly the public bonfire staged with great fanfare two years later might have generated far greater hostility, and yet the royal administration did not hesitate to order it. On the final outcome of the debate and its repercussions during the following decades, see *supra*, n. 16.

34. Raymond de Peñaforte, *Summa*, I, iv.1 (De Judaeis et Saracenis), Verona, 1744 rev. ed. by H. V. Laget, p. 24ab; Gregory I and Raymond Martini cited *supra*, Vols. III, pp. 28 ff., 242 f.; V, p. 357 n. 8; VI, p. 410 n. 24. The main source for the Barcelona disputation on the Jewish side is Moses ben Naḥman's *Viqquaḥ* (Disputation), first ed. by J. C. Wagenseil with a Latin trans. in his *Tela Ignea Satanae*, Part 2, pp. 23–60 (incomplete and defective). This Hebrew text was reedited from two manuscripts by M. Steinschneider under the title, *Naḥmanides Disputatio publica pro fidei Judaica;* and from there with a biographical introduction and additional notes by R. Margulies. It appears in Naḥmanides' *Kitbe* (Collected Writings), ed. by Ḥ. D. Shevel, I, 297–326. It also is conveniently available in J. D. Eisenstein, *Oẓar Wikuḥim*, pp. 86–94; in an English trans. by M. Braude, *Conscience on Trial;* and in one by O. S. Rankin in his *Jewish Religious Polemic*, pp. 177 ff.

The Christian point of view is represented by a protocol called *Instrumentum disputationis de fide cum quodam Rabbi Moyse dicto magistro Gerundensi habitae per fratrem Paulum Christiani Ord. Praed.*, the text of which is available in two versions. An official copy, provided with a royal seal, is extant in the archives of Aragon; it was first published by C. de Tourtoulon in his *Jacme I<sup>er</sup> le conquérant roi d'Aragon*, II, 594 No. 16, and then republished, together with other pertinent documents, by H. Denifle in his "Quellen zur Disputation Pablos Christiani mit Mose Nachmani zu Barcelona 1263," *HJB*, VIII, 231 ff. Though less official, another fairly contemporary copy is extant in Gerona where it may have been prepared at the request of Bishop Don Pedro de Castellnou who, as we shall see, asked Naḥmanides too for a presentation of his side of the story. This version—likewise long known from J. Villanueva, *Viage literario a las iglesias de España*, XIII, 332–35, and C. E. Girbal, *Los Judíos en Gerona*, pp. 66–68—was reproduced by Baer in his aforementioned essay in *Tarbiz*, II, 185–87. See also J. M. Millás Vallicrosa's documentary analysis presently to be mentioned.

The Jewish and Christian accounts differ not only in many details but also in their general approach, although a closer examination reveals more agreement than is usually the case in medieval reportage. Much has been written about the respective merits of the two accounts, but one can certainly learn a good deal from both. See Denifle's aforementioned analysis unrestrainedly condemning, and I. Loeb, "La Controverse de 1263 à Barcelone entre Paulus Christiani et Moise ben Nahman," *REJ*, XV, 1–18, defending the Gerona rabbi. More judicious are Baer's study in *Tarbiz*, II, 177 ff.; and J. M. Millás Vallicrosa's "Sobre las fuentes documentales de la controversia de Barcelona en el año 1263" in *Anales de la Universidad de Barcelona*, Memorias y communicaciones, 1940, pp. 25–44.

A new summary of the debate in English is presented by C. Roth in "The Disputation of Barcelona (1263)," *Harvard Theological Review*, XLIII, 118–44. See also M. A. Cohen's stimulating "Reflections on the Text and Context of the Disputation of Barcelona," *HUCA*, XXXV, 157–92. Although somewhat overstressing Naḥmanides' self-contradictions and other embarrassing situations—all understandable in the light of the antagonistic frame of reference of the whole disputation—Cohen has shed some new light on this much-discussed debate. His explanation, however, of James I's motives as derived from the king's desire to enlist the support of the Dominicans against the nobles is less plausible. The king certainly would not have antagonized the entrenched episcopate merely in order to gain the rather questionable support of the upcoming and growingly influential but still young order of preaching friars.

Like R. Yeḥiel, Naḥmanides was limited to answering questions and generally acting as a witness at hearings rather than as a disputant. The *Instrumentum* calls his occasional admissions "confessions." On the Christian protagonists, see F. Valls Taberner's biography, *San Ramón de Penyafort;* J. Giménez y Martínez de Carvajal, "San Raimundo de Peñafort y las Partidas de Alfonso X el Sabio," *Anthologica annua*, III, 201–338, esp. pp. 324 f.; and the few biographical data pertaining to Pablo Christiani pieced together by E. Renan and A. Neubauer in *Les Rabbins français du commencement du quatorzième siècle*, pp. 562 ff. Naḥmanides' life and works will be analyzed in later chapters.

35. *De sancta vita et miraculis fratris Raimundi de Pennaforti* (a brief fourteenth-century tract perhaps written by Nicholas Eymeric), ed. from a Barcelona MS by F. Balme and C. Paban in their collection of *Raymundiana*, pp. 19 ff., 31 ff. The new orientation toward the Talmud clearly reflected a greater appreciation of non-Christian religious classics by Spanish churchmen. On the antecedents of the decision

of the universal Council of Vienne in 1311–12 to make oriental languages permanent subjects of instruction at leading Western universities, see *supra,* n. 22. Although it is nowhere recorded, the Dominican Hebraist, Raymond Martini, may likewise have served as a member of the royal entourage during the debate; if so, he doubtless exerted a moderating influence.

36. Nahmanides' view of the lesser role of the messianic idea in Judaism was not born under the stress of the disputation only, but represented his well-considered opinion. It is to be understood in the context of his comments on the Isaianic doctrine of the "Servant of the Lord," which were published by A. Neubauer in *The Fifty-Third Chapter of Isaiah according to the Jewish Interpreters,* I, 75–81 (Hebrew); II, 78–85 (in his and S. R. Driver's English trans.); and of his brief tract *Heshbon qeṣ ha-ge'ulah* (Computation of the Final Date of the Redemption), ed. from a British Museum MS with notes by A. A. Warner, by S. N. Marat; or in the more critical ed. entitled *Sefer ha-ge'ulah* (Book of Redemption) in Nahmanides' *Kitbe,* ed. by H. D. Shevel, I, 253–95. See the pertinent observations by S. Schechter in his "Nachmanides," *Studies in Judaism,* I, 99 ff., 106 f.; and, more generally, *supra,* Vols. I, pp. 365 f. n. 29, and V, pp. 159 ff., 363 ff.; and *infra,* n. 37. The newer developments of the Jewish messianic idea in the late medieval period will be analyzed in a later chapter.

37. Nahmanides' sermon, *Torat Adonai temimah* (The Law of the Lord Is Perfect), first published in Prague, 1595, was reedited with notes by A. Jellinek in 1853 and 1873 and again by H. D. Shevel in Nahmanides' *Kitbe,* I, 141–75. The dates of these meetings are nowhere precisely recorded. The only mention in the Latin source of July 20 (where it is treated as if the disputation required only one day) may refer to the beginning or to the end of the disputation. Assuming that it was the beginning, Loeb reconstructed the dates of the four sessions as July 20, 27, 30, and 31, whereas Roth plausibly postulated five encounters on July 20, 23, 26, 27, and August 4. More important is what caused the suspension of the meetings. According to Nahmanides, he had secured from the king in a private audience the permission to return to Gerona and was given a present of 300 solidi for his expenses. (The king actually borrowed that amount from another Jew, Isaac of Barcelona; see Régné, "Catalogue des actes," *REJ,* LXI, 18 f. No. 319.) Perhaps unaware of this permission, Peñaforte and Christiani expected a continuation of the discussion to cover the remaining two points relating to the sufferings of the messiah and the invalidation of ceremonial laws in the messianic era. They claimed that the rabbi had run away from Barcelona during the king's temporary absence on August 9–12, and that he had thus conceded defeat. But they failed to explain why no sessions had been held in the preceding week. Probably in part to counteract that claim, Nahmanides agreed to publish his pamphlet. In it, however, he did not furnish any additional details about his audience with the king. He must simply have persuaded the monarch that little was to be gained by a further arid debate on the remaining points.

38. The aftermath of the debate, and the royal and papal decrees of the following four years, have long been known from various sources. The most important texts have been reproduced by Denifle in *HJB,* VIII, 234 ff., 240 ff.; Régné in his "Catalogues des actes," *REJ,* LX, 198 ff. Nos. 207 and 212; LXI, 1 f. Nos. 215–17, 7 f. No.

249, 10 No. 262, 18 ff. Nos. 315, 318–19 and 323; F. de Bofarull y Sans, "Jaime I y los Judíos," *Congrés d'história de la Corona d'Aragó dedicat a l'alt rei En Jaume I i la seva época;* and Clement IV's bulls in Potthast, *Regesta*, II, 1605 No. 19911, 1618 Nos. 20081–82. See also Y. Baer's brief summary in his *Toledot ha-Yehudim bi-Sefarad ha-noṣrit* (History of the Jews in Christian Spain), pp. 93 ff.; in the English trans. by L. Schoffman, I, 155 ff.; and *supra*, n. 21.

The connection between Naḥmanides' departure from Spain and his original banishment for two years still is unclear. But evidently no penalty was exacted from his family, at least in neighboring Castile, where his son was allowed to serve in an important office. To this son he addressed his description of the pathetic situation of Palestinian Jewry, written on Sept. 2, 1267, soon after his arrival in Jerusalem. This epistle, often printed, is readily available in the appendix to R. Margulies' ed. of the *Viqquaḥ;* or in A. Yaari's collection of *Iggerot Ereṣ Israel* (Letters from Palestine), pp. 83 ff.; and in Schechter's English translation in his *Studies*, I, 108 f. On Naḥmanides' lifelong yearnings for Palestine and his reiterated stress on the importance of living there, see the passages culled, particularly from his *Commentary* on the Pentateuch, by R. Margulies in the introduction to the *Viqquaḥ*, pp. 18 ff. Of course, some of these passages may have been written or added after their author's settlement in the Holy Land.

39. See the summary of the Vatican MS in N. Valois, *La France et le Grand Schisme de l'Occident*, IV, 91 ff., 97. Benedict's anti-Jewish animus revealed itself quite early in his sharply segregationist rescripts of Oct. 27, 1396 to the episcopal see of Grenoble with respect to the Jews of Geneva, summarized by K. Eubel in "Zu dem Verhalten der Päpste gegen die Juden," *Römische Quartalschrift*, XIII, 33. See also *infra*, Chap. XXXIX, n. 1. But in 1412–14 any anti-Jewish move could also prove politically advantageous. That in the state of mind of the Spanish public Benedict's missionary efforts might have served to buttress his claim to the Papal see is not, therefore, necessarily an exaggeration as suggested by F. Baer in his excellent analysis of "Die Disputation von Tortosa (1413–1414)," *Spanische Forschungen der Görresgesellschaft*, 1st ser. III, 309. Public opinion among both clerics and laymen had become so deeply stirred up over the Jewish issue in that period of recurrent massacres and legislative discrimination, that any public demonstration of religious Jew-baiting easily generated a widespread following. See also, more generally, G. Pillemont's biography of *Pedro de Luna. Le dernier pape d'Avignon;* and *infra*, Chap. XLV, n. 6.

40. The brief Hebrew accounts are altogether fragmentary. One, based upon a report by Bonastruch Desmaestre of Gerona, is included in Solomon ibn Verga's *Shebeṭ Yehudah*, xl, ed. by Wiener, I, 67 ff. (Hebrew), II, 134 ff. (German); ed. by A. Shohet, pp. 94 ff. Another, stemming from an anonymous writer, was edited by S. Z. H. Halberstam in "The Disputation of Tortosa" (Hebrew), Kobak's *Jeschurun*, VI, 45–55. These two accounts are carefully reexamined and compared with the Latin sources by F. Baer in his *Untersuchungen über Quellen und Komposition des Schebet Jehuda*, pp. 38 ff. They refer, however, only to the first five of the sixty-nine sessions of the disputation.

The far more comprehensive Latin protocols are extant in three manuscripts at the Escorial, the Vatican, and Gerona. Important excerpts from the Escorial text appeared in J. M. Rodriguez de Castro's *Biblioteca española*, I: Los escritores rabinos españoles; and F. Perez-Aguado, "Un Congreso cristiano-rabbinico celebrado en Tortosa," *Ciudad de Dios*, XXXIV, 29–37, 181–90, 584–90; XXXV, 18–26, 189–200, 513–22; XXXVII, 35–43, 196–203, 401–408; XXXVIII, 501–11; XXXIX, 94–113. The Vatican MS was extensively quoted by F. Ehrle in his ed. of Martin of Alpartil's *Chronica actitatorum temporibus domini Benedicti XIII*, pp. 580 ff. (on the protocols, see pp. 586 f.); and by A. Posnanski in "Le Colloque de Tortose et de San Mateo (7 Février 1413—13 Novembre 1414)," *REJ*, LXXIV, 17–39, 160–68; LXXV, 74–88, 187–204; LXXVI, 37–46. Only a few extracts from the Gerona MS are appended to Baer's essay in *Spanische Forschungen*, III, 330 ff., which offers the most careful analysis of the entire disputation. This examination is renewed, within the broader framework of Spanish-Jewish history, in Baer's *Toledot*, pp. 325 ff. All these studies have retained their value despite the recent comprehensive textual reconstruction from all three manuscripts by A. Pacios Lopez in *La Disputa de Tortosa*. In contrast to Posnanski, Pacios Lopez does not consider the Escorial MS as the original prepared by the Tortosa scribes but rather a copy inferior to the other two and uses it only for variants. His main reliance is on the Gerona MS in which he fills in lacunae (one extends over 127 printed pages) from the Vatican MS. In the first analytical volume he discusses at considerable length the history and contents of the debate.

One of the highlights of the entire disputation was a lengthy memorandum consisting of eight chapters submitted by Rabbi Astruch ha-Levi, some aspects of which were elaborated in the sessions held between February 15 and March 2, 1414. Although more restrained, it substantially argued along the frank lines of Astruch's early impulsive exclamation, "So long as you [Christians] believe in many farfetched matters pertaining to your messiah, allow us to believe in one regarding ours!" (Because it aroused Benedict's wrath, Astruch's exclamation had been speedily disavowed by his colleagues.) According to Baer, this memorandum offers a most comprehensive and courageous statement of the differences between the Jewish and Christian messianic concepts. It may be regretted that, after the final sessions, these memoranda were no longer extensively recorded. The protocol of the sixty-fifth session (Pacios Lopez, II, 574) has but a passing reference to an apparently extended discussion on the Talmud submitted in writing by Joseph Albo and the papal almoner, Andreas Bertrandi. Perhaps we may reconstruct part of Albo's view from his *magnum opus*, the *Sefer 'Iqqarim* (Book of Principles), published eleven years later. We may see the Christian side from Paul of Burgos' *Scrutinium scripturarum*, which appeared nine years after the *Sefer 'Iqqarim*, largely in response to it. See *infra*, Chap. XXXIX, n. 6.

41. Joshua ha-Lorqi, *Iggeret* (Epistle to Paul of Burgos), ed. from a Meknes MS under the title *Nussaḥ Ketab* (Version of a Writing) by E. Aschkenazi in his *Dibre ḥakhamim* (Words of the Wise: a collection of manuscript extracts), pp. 41–46; and with a German translation and notes by L. Landau under the title, *Das apologetische Schreiben*. It was subsequently reprinted in J. D. Eisenstein's *Oẓar Wikuḥim*, pp. 98–103. Its authenticity, occasionally questioned, was successfully upheld by N. Brüll in his "Paulus Burgensis und Geronimo de Santa Fé," *Jahrbücher für jüdische Geschichte und Literatur*, IV, 50–54. See also *infra*, Chap. XXXIX, n. 7.

42. Joseph Albo, *Sefer ha-'Iqqarim* ('*Ikkarim*, Book of Principles); Ibn Verga, *Shebeṭ Yehudah*, ed. by Wiener, I, 69 (Hebrew), II, 137 (German); ed. by Shohet, p.

96. On the impact of the disputation on Albo's philosophic work, see I. Husik's brief remarks in the introduction to his edition, I, xv ff.

Vicente Ferrer's role at the disputation still awaits clarification. In his *San Vicente Ferrer und sein literarischer Nachlass,* pp. 40 f., 71 ff., S. Brettle greatly minimizes the preacher's part in the proceedings. He points out that Ferrer, obeying a royal summons of April 12, personally appeared at the disputation on June 16, 1413, some four months after its beginning, in order to help put an end to the Great Schism. But he refused to interrupt his stay in Majorca when asked by the king on November 20 to come again. See *infra,* n. 44. According to Brettle, the *Tractatus contra Judaeos,* compiled during the disputation and attributed by its copyist of 1440 to Ferrer and three other monks, is identical with Geronimo's *Summula,* or summary of the proceedings from February to August 1413 prepared by Geronimo at Benedict's request at the forty-sixth session of November 30. This summary was doubtless subsequently revised by Geronimo in cooperation with committees appointed by the antipope, but without any collaboration on Ferrer's part. Brettle overstates his case, however. Not only was the whole disputation permeated with Ferrer's conversionist ideas, but Geronimo, his former pupil and personal convert, on one occasion especially invoked the direct testimony of the "very venerable and famous father," which "God willing you will hear from his mouth." See Martin of Alpartil, *Chronica actitatorum,* ed. by Ehrle, p. 581 n. 3. Vicente, who in one of his Valencia sermons had exclaimed, "We have no worse enemies than the Jews," and who, during the four years preceding the disputation, had revealed an intensive preoccupation with the Jewish question and the methods of either converting or segregating Jews, must now have refrained from playing a more prominent public role only because of his somewhat tenuous relations with the antipope. Although he had been Benedict's father confessor, he doubtless realized that the latter's retirement from the Papacy was being demanded by an ever growing number of protagonists of a fresh start in the affairs of the Church. See S. Mitrani-Samarian, "Un Sermon valencien de Saint Vincent Ferrer," *REJ,* LIV, 241–45; V. Genovés, *San Vicente Ferrer en la politica de su tiempo,* esp. pp. 20 ff., 73 ff.; J. E. Martínez Ferrando, *San Vicente Ferrer y la casa real de Aragón;* and *infra,* nn. 45–46.

43. Ibn Verga, *Shebeṭ Yehudah, loc. cit.;* Antipope Benedict XIII's address of January 8, 1414 and Geronimo de Santa Fé's statement summarized in the Latin protocol, ed. by Pacios Lopez, II, 405, 570; and in French by Posnanski in *REJ,* LXXV, 200; LXXVI, 44; Geronimo's *De Judaicis erroribus ex Talmut,* published with his other polemical tract in Zurich 1552; and *supra,* n. 30. Despite these brief allusions, the economic problems, heatedly debated throughout the Peninsula, were given but scant consideration at the disputation. From the meager records about the sessions at San Mateo it appears that practically the entire dialogue centered on the allegedly obnoxious passages in the Talmud. The Christian spokesmen must have realized the incongruity of first using the Talmud to prove the advent of the messiah and then condemning it as blasphemous and unethical. Geronimo, clever debater that he was, anticipated that objection by asserting that the Talmud had no authority for him or other Christians, but that the Jewish believers in it must accept its confirmation of the Christian tradition. The rabbis, on their part, reverted to Naḥmanides' contention that the Aggadah had no binding character. The talmudic outlook, they asserted, could only be viewed in its totality, particularly from

the standpoint of its truly authoritative halakhic elements. Like the Bible, it contained passages which must be interpreted figuratively in the spirit of the whole work. See *supra*, n. 35.

44. Ehrle's summary of Alpartil's chronicle, pp. 599 ff.; Pacios Lopez, *La Disputa*, I, 70 ff.; II, 555 f.; Posnanski in *REJ*, LXXV, 195, 201; LXXVI, 43, 45. As pointed out by Ehrle (p. 602), some of these reports were inserted by the papal scribes in summary form, perhaps without Geronimo's cooperation.

45. F. Baer, *Die Juden im christlichen Spanien*, I, Part 1, pp. 786 f. No. 481, 793 f. No. 488, 795 No. 491, 802 ff. No. 495, 807 ff. No. 500, 810 ff. No. 502; his *Toledot*, pp. 357 f.; A. Gimenez Soler, "Los Judíos españoles a fines del siglo XIV y principios del XV," *Universidad*, XXVIII, 361–414, esp. p. 401; J. Goñi Gaztambide, "Conversión de la aljama de Fraga," *Hispania sacra*, XIII, 205–206. (Both petitions are preserved in the Vatican Archives.) Not surprisingly, Ferrer's missionary activities among Jews have intrigued many scholars. Within a short time of one another there appeared the following three essays which, though necessarily repetitious in part, well complement one another: F. Vendrell Gallostra, "La Actividad proselitista de San Vicente Ferrer durante el reinado de Fernando I de Aragón," *Sefarad*, XIII, 57–104; V. Beltrán de Heredia, "San Vicente Ferrer, predicador de las sinagogas," *Salmanticensis*, II, 669–76; and B. Llorca, "San Vicente Ferrer y su labor en la conversión de los Judíos. En el centenario de su canonización," *Razón y fé*, CLII, 277–96. Llorca also furnishes an impressive list of earlier Spanish publications. See also the new documentation offered by J. E. Martínez Ferrando in his *San Vicente Ferrer y la casa real de Aragón;* and *infra*, n. 46.

The leading members of the house of Cavalleria, Bonifos and Don Vidal (Benveniste), were invited by King Ferdinand to help him in the fiscal administration of the country during that critical period. Within a few months after their conversion they appeared as influential statesmen. Bonifos, now called Fernando de Cavalleria, received the title of "Councilor and Treasurer of the King of Aragon." The conversion of Don Vidal (he was renamed Gonzalo) made the greater impression, as he had been a Hebrew author and an early Jewish participant at the disputation, though probably not the leading spokesman as he appears in Ibn Verga's report. He had wished to leave Tortosa but was prevented from doing so by Benedict, who consented to his departure, requested by the king, only after his conversion. See Baer, *Die Juden*, I, Part 1, pp. 796 ff. No. 492; and his *Toledot*, pp. 346 ff. On the other hand, the conversion of the septuagenarian poet, Solomon da Piera, suggested by Samuel David Luzzatto and supported by Baer on the basis of an erroneous heading over two of his poems, has been contradicted by S. Bernstein in "The Diwan of Sacred Poems by Solomon b. Meschullam da Piera," *HUCA*, XIX, Hebrew Section, pp. 2 ff.

46. Benedict's bull, *Et si doctoris*, ed. by Amador de los Rios in his *Historia social*, II, 627 ff.; ed. by Von Döllinger in his *Beiträge zur Sektengeschichte*, II, 393 ff.; the antipope's several rescripts of 1414–16, summarized by K. Eubel in *Römische Quartalschrift*, XIII, 36 ff. Nos. 11 ff.; Mitrani-Samarian, "Un Sermon valencien" in *REJ*, LIV, 242; M. M. Gorce, *Saint Vincent Ferrier (1350–1419)*, pp. 229 ff., 241; V. Genovés, *San Vicente Ferrer*, pp. 24 f.; the chronicles by Joseph ibn Ṣaddiq and Abraham b. Solomon of Torrutiel, both ed. by A. Neubauer in his *Mediaeval Jewish*

*Chronicles,* I, 98, 110; in F. Cantera Burgos's Spanish trans., pp. 36, 61; *infra,* Chap. XLV, nn. 2 ff. Other estimates of the number of converts made by Ferrer are mentioned by Llorca in *Razón y fé,* CLII, 296. Curiously Alphonso himself had been accused of having imprisoned a large number of Jews of Saragossa for their failure to appear promptly at a missionary sermon which was to be delivered by Ferrer. Ferdinand ordered him to release the Jews with the preacher's "patience and good will." See Baer, *Die Juden,* I, Part 1, p. 825 No. 509. See also H. Fagés, *Histoire de Saint Vincent Ferrier,* I, 193; II, 106; idem, *Notes et documents de l'histoire de Saint Vincent Ferrier,* p. 209; and V. Galduf Blaseo's more recent *Vida de San Vicente Ferrer* which, though generally overapologetic, has an interesting epilogue concerning the evaluations of the preacher by his contemporaries. It may be noted that a complete critical edition of Ferrer's sermons and tracts is not yet available, the 1909 ed. of his *Oeuvres* by H. Fagés being quite incomplete.

47. William of Auvergne, *De Universo,* toward end, Nuremberg, 1496 ed., fol. 149d. See also *supra,* n. 13.

# CHAPTER XXXIX: SPIRITED APOLOGIST

1. Martin de León, *Sermones*, iv.2, in his *Opera omnia, PL,* CCVIII, 107; A. Viñayo Gonzalez, *San Martín de León y su apologética antijudia,* esp. p. 96; J. Amador de los Rios, *Historia social,* I, 450 n. 1. The generally growing awareness of non-Christian cultures and the incipient source criticism which manifested themselves during the so-called Twelfth-Century Renaissance and which came to fuller fruition during the following three centuries, contributed their share to the quest for understanding the "enemy" from his own tradition. It was still possible, as it is possible today, to put up fictitious straw men in order the more easily to demolish them, but such an undertaking became doubly perilous not only in a direct disputation but also in a literary controversy.

2. P. Galindo Romeo, "La Biblioteca de Benedicto XIII," *Universidad* (Saragossa), V, 724; and, more generally, J. Zunzunegui, *La Legación en España del Card. Pedro de Luna, 1379–1390;* J.-A. Rubio, *La Política de Benedicto XIII desde la ṣubstracción de Aragón a su obediencia hasta su destitución en el Concilio dẹ Constanza (enero de 1416 a julio de 1417).* See also A. Pacios Lopez, *La Disputa de Tortosa,* I, 41 f. n. 20; A. Maier, "Der Katalog der päpstlichen Bibliothek in Avignon vom Jahr 1411," *Archivum historiae pontificiae,* I, 97–107; and, more generally, M. Faucon, *La Librairie des papes d'Avignon. Sa formation, sa composition, ses catalogues (1316–1420).* Ironically, two Jewish scribes were employed by Pedro in 1396 to copy the Hebrew parts of Martini's *Pugio,* of which cherished work he kept no less than three different copies in his library. A Jewish bookbinder bound at least one copy for him. See the excerpts published by F. Ehrle in his *Historia bibliotecae Romanorum Pontificum,* I, 172, No. 55. Evidently, De Luna had little choice in the matter, for at least in Barcelona the Jewish bookbinders had long held practically a monopoly of their trade. See J. M. Madurell Marimón, *Documentos para la historia de la imprenta y librería en Barcelona (1474–1553),* with annotations by J. Rubió y Balaguer, pp. 34 f.

A former Salamanca manuscript list includes a *Tractatus contra Judaeos compositus a papa olim Benedicto de Luna.* But F. Ehrle, who called attention to that entry in 1900, has questioned whether it did not merely refer to the protocols of the disputation of Tortosa. See his "Die Kirchenrechtlichen Schriften Peters von Luna (Benedikts XIII)," *Archiv für Literatur- und Kirchengeschichte des Mittelalters,* VII, 516. Certainly it would appear very surprising if such a tractate of the much-debated antipope should have left no other traces. One wonders to what extent Pedro de Luna's anti-Jewish feelings were reinforced by his friends San Vicente Ferrer and Paul of Burgos, the most active preachers against Jews of his day. See *supra,* Chap. XXXVIII, nn. 45–46.

3. M. Sepet, "Les Prophètes du Christ. Etude sur les origines du théâtre au moyen âge," *Bibliothèque de l'Ecole de Chartes,* XXVIII, 1–27, 211–64; XXIX, 105–39, 261–93; XXXVIII, 397–443 (also reprint); H. Pflaum, "Les Scènes des Juifs dans la littérature dramatique du moyen âge," *REJ,* LXXXIX, 111–34; idem, *Die*

*Religiöse Disputation in der europäischen Dichtung des Mittelalters*, I: Der allegorische Streit zwischen Synagoge und Kirche. See also, more generally, O. Zöckler, *Der Dialog in Dienste der Apologetik*. Many passion plays were written without direct reference to contemporary Jews. However, in graphically depicting the fateful role played at the crucifixion of Christ by the ancient Jews of Jerusalem, the dramatists, consciously or unconsciously, modeled their Jewish figures after Jews of their acquaintance. See *infra*, Chap. XLIX. No unconscious design need be attributed to the writers of polemical tracts who pursued outright defensive or offensive purposes.

4. Many of these writers merely included expositions of their anti-Jewish views in treatises of a broader nature. Thomas Aquinas wrote a small tract on the Jewish question; this was but a minor essay, hastily composed in reply to an urgent inquiry from the Duchess of Brabant. The various references to Jews scattered through the *Summa theologica* are generally of a more tolerant nature. Only in his *Summa de veritate catholicae fidei contra gentiles* (better known as the *Summa contra gentiles*) did the "angelic doctor" undertake to present the Catholic faith in a positive fashion with numerous polemical asides against all unbelievers. This presentation appeared so persuasive to Bishop Joseph Ciantes that in 1657 he republished a large part of it with a readable, though at times a bit awkward, Hebrew translation. He may have calculated that at least some Jews were familiar with Thomas' reputation (particularly through the Hebrew translations of some of his tracts) as the man whom Don Isaac Abravanel had called "the greatest of the great" among Christian thinkers. See A. Jellinek's *Thomas von Aquino in der jüdischen Litteratur;* H. Liebeschütz, "Judaism and Jewry in the Social Doctrine of Thomas Aquinas," *JJS*, XII, 57–81; and, more fully, in our forthcoming treatment of the interrelations between Christian and Jewish scholasticism. Similarly, Robert Grosseteste in his *De cessatione legalium* (written in 1231 but published only in an abridged form in London, 1658), who argued for the supremacy of the New Testament over the Old, and Vincent of Beauvais in his *Speculum historiale* (the third part of his comprehensive *Speculum majus)*, were not primarily concerned with the Jewish problem but wrote occasional, even fairly sharp, anti-Jewish passages. For instance, Vincent included lengthy excerpts from Petrus Alphonsi's *Dialogus* in that *Speculum*, xxv.119–39. See also Jakob Guttmann, "Die Beziehungen des Vincenz von Beauvais zum Judenthum," *MGWJ*, XXXIX, 207–221; and, more generally, idem, *Die Scholastik des dreizehnten Jahrhunderts*, pp. 121 ff. On Grosseteste, see the essays on his seventh centenary, ed. by D. A. Callus under the title, *Robert Grosseteste, Scholar and Bishop*, especially B. Smalley's discussion of Grosseteste as "The Biblical Scholar," pp. 80 ff. (denying that the bishop was seriously concerned with the contemporary Jewish religious observance); and L. M. Friedman, *Robert Grosseteste and the Jews*, pp. 21 ff.

More directly aimed at Jews were the polemical treatises by the following leading controversialists:

(1) Raymond Martini. About 1257, before publishing his *Pugio fidei adversus Mauros et Judaeos* in 1278, Martini had written his *Explanatio symboli apostolorum ad institutionem fidelium*, ed. from a Tortosa MS with an Intro. by J. M. March in his "En Ramón Martí y la sua Explanatio symboli apostolorum," *Anuari* of the Institut d'estudis catalans, 1908, pp. 443–96. In 1267 he wrote his *Capistrum Judaeorum*, since lost, although Jacques Echard saw a MS copy in Bologna in the eighteenth century. See J. Quétif and his *Scriptores ordinis praedicatorum*, II, 818b:

A. Berthier's fine bibliographical review of Martini's works in "Un Maître orientaliste du XIIIᵉ siècle: Raymond Martin, O.P.," *AFP*, VI, 278 ff., 287 ff., 304 ff.; and *infra*, n. 9.

(2) Raymond Lull. Among the approximately 280 tracts written by Lull (240 of them still extant), several deal directly with the problems of Jews and Judaism. See esp. his *Flagellum Judaeorum*, describing a disputation between a Christian and a Jewish doctor in Majorca in 1286; and his *Liber predicationis contra Judeos*, recently ed. with an intro. and notes by J. M. Millás Vallicrosa. See, however, A. Soria's review of that work in *Estudios Lulianos*, II, 335–38, showing that other MSS have better readings than that of Palma preferentially used by Millás. Another treatise by Lull, *Tractatus de modo convertendi infideles*, written in 1291–92, was first published in the *Llibre de Passatge*, ed. by J. Rambaud Buhaud in Lull's *Opera latina*, Majorca, 1954 ed., Vol. III (see below), with comments thereon by R. Sugranyes de Franch in "Els Projectos de Creuada en la doctrina missional de Ramón Llull," *Estudios Lulianos*, IV, 275–90. Of interest also are his (or one of his pupils'; see *infra*, n. 15) *De auditu kabbalistico;* his *The Art of Contemplation* (part of his prose romance *Blanquerna* or *Blaquerna*), trans. into English with an introductory essay by E. A. Peers; and particularly his *Liber de Gentili et tribus sapientibus*, of which Book II is entirely devoted to an analysis and critique of Judaism. See also R. Brummer, "Un Poème latin de controverse religieuse et le 'Libre de Gentil y los tres savis' de Ramon Llull," *Estudios Lulianos*, VI, 275–81, arguing that its author was a subtle missionary rather than a preacher of religious toleration.

Many of these writings are included in the old collected edition of his *Opera ea quae ad adinventam ab ipso artem universalem scientiarum artumque omnium brevi compendio . . . pertinent*, provided with commentaries by Giordano Bruno and H. C. Agrippa von Nettersheim; and more fully in *Beati Raymundi Lulli doctoris illuminati et martyri opera*, ed. by I. Salzinger, Vols. I–VI, IX–X (VII–VIII were never published). The incompleteness and other deficiencies of even this important eighteenth-century Mayence edition have been rightly stressed by A. Gottron and other scholars. See the "Select Bibliography" in E. A. Peers's *Ramon Lull*, pp. 421 ff. A new ed. of Lull's *Opera latina* by F. Stegmüller *et al.* began to appear in 1959, the editors claiming that up to that time no less than one hundred and five works by Lull had remained unpublished. See also Stegmüller's comments on this edition in "La Edición de las obras latinas de Ramón Lull (Principios–Problemas–Experiencias)," *Estudios Lulianos*, V, 217–41. A comprehensive Catalan edition of Lull's *Obras*, begun in 1906 by Hieronymus Rosselló y Ribera *et al.*, for a special Commissio Editora Lulliania, had progressed to Vol. XXI by 1950. The work was resumed in 1961 by R. D. F. Pring-Mill. See the note in "La Edición de las obras catalanas de Ramón Llull", *Estudios Lulianos*, V, 371. More readily accessible is the recent briefer Catalan edition of Lull's *Obras essencials*, sponsored by R. Rierra i Sala *et al.* See also J. M. Batllori's observations thereon in "En torno a una nueva edición de Ramón Llull," *Arbor*, XL, 283–90, stressing in particular Lull's influence on European thought. There is of course an enormous secondary literature on Lull and his works. See, for instance, the sixty-seven entries mainly covering the years 1940–46 in the "Bibliographia Franciscana," VII, compiled by the Istituto Storico dei Fr. Minori Cappucini and appended to the *Collectanea franciscana*, XVIII, 117*–21* Nos. 1771–1837; and B. Mendia's "Bibliografia luliana contemporanea (años 1935–1950)," *AFH*, XLIV, 436–58.

We have gone to unusual lengths in discussing this confusing bibliographical situation because of the manifold Jewish aspects of Lull's teachings and practical activities, which have hitherto but briefly been referred to in Jakob Guttmann's *Die Scholastik des dreizehnten Jahrhunderts*, pp. 150 ff.; A. L. Williams's *Adversus Judaeos*, pp. 256 ff.; and Y. Baer's *Toledot*, 2d ed., pp. 109 f., 496 n. 5; and *A History of the Jews in Christian Spain*, I, 183 f., 417 f. n. 81. A special monograph on this subject now appears both feasible and desirable.

(3) Nicholas de Lyra. He wrote at least two anti-Jewish tracts, the *Tractatus de Christi adventu et divinitate adversus Judaeos*, and *Tractatus contra quemdam judaeum ex verbis evangelii s. Matthaei Christum . . . impugnantem*, both appended to his *Expositio super universa biblia* in *Biblia sacra*, Antwerp, 1634 ed., Vol. VI.

Other Christian polemists have been treated in the following recent editions and studies:

(4) A. Viñayo Gonzalez, ed., *San Martin de León y su apologética antijudía* (includes his *Sermones*, esp. Nos. 4, 30, 34, long familiar from *PL*, CCVIII).

(5) J. M. Millás Vallicrosa, "Un Tratado anónimo contra Judíos," *Sefarad*, XIII, 3–34.

(6) J. Carreras y Artau, "Arnaldo de Vilanova, apologista antijudaico," *Sefarad*, VII, 49–61; idem, "La 'Allocutio super Tetragrammaton' de Arnaldo de Vilanova," *ibid.*, IX, 75–105 (includes the full text from an authoritative Vatican MS); idem, *L'Epistolari d'Arnau de Vilanova* (a review of the extant correspondence, see esp. pp. 21 f.); R. Manselli, "La Religiosità d'Arnaldo da Villanova," *Bulletino* of the Istituto italiano per il medio evo, LXIII, 1–100. See also J. M. Millàs Vallicrosa, "Nota bibliográfica acerca de las relaciones entre Arnaldo de Vilanova y la cultura judaica," *Sefarad*, XVI, 149–53.

(7) Porcheto de Salvatici, a Genoese Carthusian monk, wrote a tract in 1303 under the expressive title, *Victoria Porcheti adversus impios Hebraeos in qua tum ex sacris literis, tum ex dictis Talmud ac Cabalisticarum . . . monstratur veritas catholicae fidei*.

(8) Bernardo Oliver, *Tractatus . . . contra perfidiam* (or *caecitatem*) *Judaeorum*, an excerpt of which is published from an Aragonese MS by F. Vendrell in "La Obra de polémica antijudaica de Fray Bernardo Oliver," *Sefarad*, V, 303–36. In his Postscript thereto F. Cantera mentions another, more complete MS extant in the Cathedral Library of Burgo de Osma. See also his "El Obispo Bernardo Oliver y la tradición manuscrita de su tratado *Contra caecitatem Judaeorum*," *Estudios ecclesiaticos*, XXXIV, 413–18. Vilanova's influence on Oliver is discussed by J. Carreras y Artau in his aforementioned essay. "Arnaldo de Vilanova, apologista antijudaico," *Sefarad*, VII, 49, 58 n.10.

(9) Alphonso de Spina, *Fortalitium fidei contra Judeos, Sarracenos, aliosque christiane fidei inimicos* (Fortress of Faith against Jews, Saracens and Other Enemies of the Faith); see M. Esposito's "Notes sur le Fortalitium fidei d'Alphonse de Spina," *RHE*, 1948.

(10) L. Castán Lacoma, "Un Apologista antijudío aragonés desconocido: Jaime Civeroso," *Revista española de teología*, XXII, 153–77.

(11) Giannozzo Manetti, *Contra Judaeos et Gentes*. Dedicated to the generally liberal King Alphonso V of Naples, this work is extant in an Urbino MS. On this distinguished Florentine Hebraist see *infra*, Chap. LVII.

(12) Nicolaus Cusanus (of Cusa), *Dialogus de pace seu concordantia fidei* in his *Opera*, Basel 1565 ed., pp. 862–79. Cusanus, as we recall, had the opportunity to

employ his anti-Jewish bias in practice, especially while serving as papal legate in Germany in 1451. See *supra*, Chap. XXXVII, n. 32.

(13) Marsilio Ficino, *De religione christiana et fide*, esp. Chaps. XXVI-XXXV, in his *Opera*, I, 29 ff.; with the comments and textual variants thereon by P. O. Kristeller in his *Supplementum Ficinianum. Marsilii Ficini . . . Opuscula inedita et dispersa*, I, pp. lxxvii ff., 7 ff. Ficino's essay was translated into French by the sixteenth-century Hebraist, S. Le Fèvre de la Boderie (1578). See also Kristeller, "The Scholastic Background of Marsilio Ficino," *Traditio*, II, 257–318, esp. pp. 260 f.

(14) Antonius Bonromeus (Borromeus), [professor of Roman law at Padua, 1490–94, died 1509], *Opusculum lepidissimum . . . De christiana religione contra hebraeos*. Probably Venice after 1491 (a rare incunabulum available at the Jewish Theological Seminary of America).

(15) Juan Luis Vives, *De veritate fidei christianae* in his *Opera omnia*, ed. by G. Majansius, Vol. III; with Paul Graf's analysis in his study, *Ludwig Vives als Apologet*, or in its Spanish trans. by J. M. Millás Vallicrosa, entitled *Luis Vives como apologeta*; and Millás's more specific comments in "La Apologética de Luis Vives y el judaismo," *Sefarad*, II, 293–323.

(16) Francisco Suárez, "Contra Judaeos" in his *Commentary* on the *Tertia Pars Summae Theologiae* of Thomas Aquinas, in his *Opera omnia*, new ed. by C. Berton, XVII, 5–25.

The four distinguished thinkers (12, 13, 15, and 16 above), betray some of the new approaches of the Renaissance age. See *infra*, Chap. LVII. Some older apologias, too, such as those by the widely revered St. Isidore of Seville and by the convert Petrus Alphonsi, continued to circulate freely and were found, for instance, in the afore-mentioned library of Pedro de Luna; see *supra*, n. 2. Latin writings were often translated into local languages to make them more accessible to the growing lay intelligentsia. See *infra*, n. 6. Sometimes regular collections of polemical tracts were prepared for propagandistic or defensive purposes. For example, the aforementioned thirteenth-century *Tratado anónimo* (item 5) is included in a MS containing also Petrus' *Dialogus* and Bernardo Oliver's *Tractatus*.

The list of anti-Jewish writers here given could easily be enlarged. As early as 1694, C. J. Imbonati was able to publish a substantial bibliographical volume under the title *Bibliotheca latino-hebraica sive de scriptoribus Latinis, qui ex diversis nationibus contra Judaeos, vel de re Hebraica utcumque scribere*, which forms Vol. V of J. Bartoloccius, *Bibliotheca magna rabbinica*. Of considerable value also are the comprehensive bibliography by M. Steinschneider in his *Polemische und apologetische Literatur in arabischer Sprache, zwischen Muslimen, Christen und Juden*, dealing with the Judeo-Christian controversy in Muslim lands, but occasionally shedding light also on the Western debates; the summaries by C. Werner, *Der heilige Thomas von Aquino*, new ed., I, 621–63; idem, *Geschichte der apologetischen und polemischen Litteratur der christlichen Theologie*, esp. Vol. III, pp. 466 ff.; F. Vernet, "Juifs (Controverses avec les)," *Dictionnaire de théologie catholique*, VIII, Part 1, 1870–1914; Browe, *Die Judenmission*, pp. 95 ff. (includes an extensive chrono-logical list of Christian polemical writings from the seventh century to *ca.* 1560); A. L. Williams, *Adversus Judaeos*; and the literature listed there and in our earlier notes. Interesting bibliographical data on many of these tracts are supplied by M. Marx in "A Catalogue of the Non-Hebrew Books Printed in the Fifteenth Century Now in the Library of the Hebrew Union College," *Studies in Bibliography and*

*Booklore,* V, 62–91. The full story of Christian-Jewish polemics, however, with a thoroughgoing analysis of the issues involved and their social backgrounds is still a desideratum. For the time being the older monographs by I. Loeb, *La Controverse religieuse* (*RHR,* XVII–XVIII) and "Polémistes chrétiens et juifs," *REJ,* XVIII, though merely scratching the surface, still offer the best general introduction.

5. Joachim of Floris, *Adversus Judaeos,* ed. by A. Frugoni, pp. 57 f.; B. Hirsch-Reich, "Ein bisher unedierter Traktat Joachims von Fiore zur Bekehrung der Juden," *Recherches de théologie ancienne et médiévale,* XXVII, 141–48; Sanhedrin 97ab; *supra,* Vol. II, pp. 167 f., 394 n. 50. See also F. Russo, *Bibliografia joachimita;* and the detailed analyses of Joachim's life and works in C. Baraut's review of "Las Antiguas biografías de Joaquín de Fiore y sus fuentes," *Analecta sacra Tarraconensia,* XXVI, 195–232; H. Grundmann's *Neue Forschungen über Joachim von Fiore;* and M. W. Bloomfield's "Joachim of Flora: a Critical Survey of His Canon, Teachings, Sources, Biography, and Influence," *Traditio,* XIII, 249–311. Unfamiliar with Joachim's *Adversus Judaeos,* published about the same time, Bloomfield could only consider the more implicit anti-Jewish arguments included in the mystic's *Concordantiae novi et veteris Testamenti.* Joachim's family background, like the rest of his biography, is very obscure. (See Grundmann, pp. 31 ff.) Although his native Calabria had a substantial Jewish population, there is no real evidence for his Jewish origin. Yet some interesting Jewish parallels to his philosophy of history have been shown by G. G. Scholem in "The Meaning of the Torah in Jewish Mysticism," *Diogenes,* XV, 68, 86, 92 f. These and other interrelations between Jewish and Christian mysticism will be more fully analyzed in a later chapter.

6. Among the outstanding converts who turned polemists against their former faith we need but mention:

(1) Abner of Burgos (Alphonso de Valladolid). His extensive apologetical treatise bearing the Hebrew title, *Moreh ṣedeq* (Teacher of Righteousness), is known only in the Spanish translation entitled *Mostrador de Justicia,* while several lesser writings, including the *Minḥat qena'ot* (Zealous Offering), are extant in Hebrew MSS. All of these works are still unpublished. Their contents have become known mainly through the extensive quotations in A. de Spina's *Fortalitium fidei;* Loeb's "Polémistes," *REJ,* XVIII, 52–63; and particularly the aforementioned analytical essays by Baer, "Abner von Burgos," *KA,* X, 20–37; "Minḥat qena'ot by Alphonso," *Tarbiz,* XI, 188–206; and "The Kabbalistic Doctrine in the Christological Teachings of Abner of Burgos" (Hebrew), *ibid.,* XXVII, 278–89. Abner also engaged in an extensive polemical correspondence with the young Jewish mathematician Joseph Shalom concerning the meaning and import of the messianic prophecies in the book of Daniel, and particularly the identification of the "fourth monarchy" with Rome. This issue had considerable bearing on the justification of the respective Jewish and Christian messianic expectations. Abner's three epistles have recently been published from a Parma MS (which had once been in the possession of Leon de Modena) by Judah Rosenthal. See his "From 'Sefer Alfonso,'" *Neuman Jub. Vol.,* Hebrew section, pp. 588–621; his "The Second Epistle of Abner of Burgos," *Weiss Jub. Vol.,* Hebrew section, pp. 483–510; and his "The Third Letter of Abner of Burgos," *Studies in Bibliography and Booklore,* V, Hebrew section, pp. 42–51. See also *infra,* n. 11; and the list of Abner's other apologetic writings in H. Graetz's *Geschichte,* 4th ed., VII, 451 f. Note 7.

(2) Pablo de Santa Maria (Solomon ha-Levi), often called Paul of Burgos. *Scrutin-*

*ium scripturarum* (title derived from "Search the Scriptures" of John 5:39), the first part of which bears the telling title *Dialogus Pauli et Sauli contra Judaeos.* See the older but still useful study by H. Tallin, *Des Paulus Burgensis Schriftbeweis gegen die Juden;* and *infra,* n. 20.

(3) Alphonso (Alonso) de Cartagena. *Defensorium unitatis christianae,* ed. with an introduction and notes by Manuel Alonso. See also the biographical study of both these authors by L. Serrano, *Los Conversos D. Pablo de Santa María y D. Alfonso de Cartagena, gobernantes, diplomaticos y escritores.*

(4) F. Cantera Burgos, *Alvar García de Santa María y su familia de conversos: Historia de la judería de Burgos y de sus conversos más egregios.*

(5) Alphonso de Zamora. *Ḥokhmat Elohim* (Libro de la Sabiduria de Dios, or God's Wisdom), now available in the Spanish trans. entitled *El Manuscrito apologetico de Alfonso de Zamora,* with notes by F. Pérez Castro.

(6) Victor von Carben. *Liber aureum ac novum . . . in quo omnes Judaeorum errores manifestantur . . . declarantur etiam mores . . . ac tandem ex Veteri tantum Testamento convincuntur.*

(7) Petrus Columna Galatinus. *Opus . . . de arcanis catholicae ueritatis, contra obstinatissimam Judaeorum . . . perfidiam,* Ortona, 1518, with the comments thereon by E. d'Alançon in his "Galatin, Pierre," *Dictionnaire de théologie catholique,* VI, 1052–54; A. Berthier in *AFP,* VI, 284 f.; and, particularly, A. Kleinhans in "De vita et operibus Petri Galatini," *Antonianum,* I, 145–79, 327–56. (D'Alançon and Kleinhans deny Galatinus' Jewish origin.)

(8) Johannes Pfefferkorn, a contemporary of Zamora, Von Carben, and Galatinus, may be mentioned here in passing. Although his *Judenspiegel* appeared in 1507, or slightly before some of the other apologetic works, it provoked Johannes Reuchlin's reply in 1511 which marked a turning point in the entire Judeo-Christian dialogue. For the first time a distinguished Christian scholar took up the cudgel in defense of the Talmud, and thus gave rise to a famous controversy in which both the emperor and the pope became involved. This controversy will be treated more fully in Chap. LVII.

Many older writings continued to circulate. Petrus Alphonsi in particular was frequently copied, with or without acknowledgment. His *Dialogus* was also translated for popular usage. See esp. J. Ainaud de Lasarte, "Una Versión catalana desconocida de los *Dialogi* de Pedro Alfonso," *Sefarad,* III, 35–76. Another literary curiosity of great popular appeal was a tract attributed to one Samuel Maroccanus (Marochianus), going under various titles, such as *De adventu Messiae quem Judaei temere expectant Liber,* most readily available in *PL,* CXLIX, 335–68. Purportedly written in Arabic by a Moroccan convert (possibly a confused reminiscence of Samuel b. 'Abbas ibn Yaḥya), it became known only in the Latin trans. allegedly made *ca.* 1339 by the Spanish Dominican, Alphonso Bonhomo. See the detailed title page in J. W. Helm's ed., Prague [1718]. On the translator, see R. Ricard's twin essays, "Sur Fr. Alfonso Bonhome. Notes bibliographiques," *BH,* LX, 500–504; and "La Patrie de Fr. Alfonso Bonhome," *ibid.,* LXII, 331–32. The popularity of this pamphlet is clearly attested by the numerous reprints at the very beginning of printing. The Jewish Theological Seminary of America alone possesses no less than seven different incunabula dating between 1479 and 1498.

7. In their chronological order the following Jewish apologists and apologias of the later Middle Ages are particularly significant:

(1) Jacob b. Reuben, probably a Spaniard living in Franco-English Gascony, whose *Milḥamot ha-Shem* (Wars of the Lord) originated from numerous discussions he had had with a friendly Catholic priest (ca. 1170). Fully described and quoted in a few interesting excerpts in 1888–89 by A. Neubauer (in his "Jewish Controversy and the 'Pugio Fidei,'" *Expositor*, VII, 91–95); and Loeb (in "Polémistes chrétiens et juifs," *REJ*, XVIII, 46–52), it was but recently published in full by J. Rosenthal. It was quite popular in the Middle Ages and greatly influenced the later Jewish apologists. Its pioneering critique of the New Testament, Jerome, and Augustine, to which Jacob b. Reuben devoted a special section (xi) of his treatise, would particularly deserve further monographic treatment.

(2) Meir b. Simon of Narbonne, *Milḥemet miṣvah* (War in Fulfillment of a Commandment) which arose out of a (perhaps fictitious) disputation in Narbonne in 1245. He has become known only through a few published excerpts from a Parma MS. See esp. A. Neubauer, "Rapport sur une mission scientifique dans le midi de France," *Archives des missions scientifiques*, 3rd ser. XVI, 556 f.; H. Gross, "Meir b. Simon und seine Schrift Milchemet Mizwa," *MGWJ*, XXX, 295–305, 444–52, 554–69; in the English trans. by S. Stein in "A Disputation on Moneylending between Jews and Gentiles in Meir b. Simon's Milḥemeth Miṣwah (Narbonne, 13th Cent.)," *JJS*, X, 45–61; and *supra*, Vol. IV, p. 224. Stein's promised full publication of Meir's text (p. 61), has not yet appeared.

(3) Jacob b. Elijah of Valencia, who entered the ranks against his cousin Pablo Christiani in an *Iggeret* (Epistle), ed. by J. Kobak in his *Jeschurun*, Hebrew part, VI, 1–34. See J. Mann, "Une Source de l'histoire juive au XIIIᵉ siècle: La Lettre polémique de Jacob b. Elie à Pablo Christiani," *REJ*, LXXXII, 363–77.

(4) Nathan Official and his son Joseph called the Zealous, see *supra*, Chap. XXXVIII, n. 28; and E. Urbach's "Etudes," *REJ*, C, 49 ff.

(5) *Sefer Niṣṣaḥon* (Book of Disputation), a thirteenth-century anonymous work, called *ha-yashan* (the Old) in contradistinction to Lipmann-Mühlhausen's work listed *infra*, item 13, was first published with a Latin trans. by J. C. Wagenseil in his *Tela ignea*, II, 1–260.

(6) Solomon b. Moses de' Rossi, *'Edut Adonai ne'emanah* (The Testimony of the Lord is Lasting), ed. by J. Rosenthal in his "Debates with Churchmen" (Hebrew), *Sura*, III, 257–74 (a fuller edition still is in preparation). Although the Introduction to this work had been published from an inferior Vienna MS by N. Brüll in the *Bet ha-Midrash*, ed. by I. H. Weiss, II, 143 ff., Rosenthal did not republish that part of the text but only the other excerpts preserved in the mutually complementary Munich and New York MSS. On their late thirteenth-century author see H. Vogelstein and P. Rieger, *Geschichte der Juden in Rom*, I, 269 f.

(7) Moses b. Solomon of Salerno, whose calm but trenchant *Ṭa'anot* (Objections) to Christian teachings were published from a Breslau MS with a German translation and an extensive introduction by S. Simon in his dissertation, *Mose ben Salomo von Salerno*.

(8) Isaac b. Joseph Pollegar, *Iggeret ha-ḥarufot* (Epistle on Blasphemies) and *Sefer 'Ezer ha-dat* (The Support of Faith), both containing replies to Abner of Burgos. The former work is known only through Abner's polemic, while the *'Ezer* is available in print, ed. by G. S. Belasco.

(9) Moses Kohen of Tordesillas, *'Ezer ha-dat* (Aid to Faith) written in 1374–75 after a disputation. Excerpts were published by Neubauer in *The Fifty-Third*

*Chapter of Isaiah,* I, 108–21 (Hebrew); II, x f., 115–28 (English); and by Loeb in his "Polémistes chrétiens et juifs," *REJ,* XVIII, 226 ff. See also *supra,* Chap. XXXVIII, n. 28.

(10) Shem Ṭob b. Isaac Shapruṭ, *Eben boḥan* (Touchstone), written in 1380–85 and closely following in the footsteps of Jacob b. Reuben. Extant in several MSS, it was briefly analyzed and illustrated by several excerpts in Hebrew and in French and English translations, respectively, by Loeb in *REJ,* XVIII, 219–26, and Neubauer in *The Fifty-Third Chapter of Isaiah,* I, 88–94; II, ix f., 92–98. See also A. Marx's aforementioned data in *Freidus Mem. Vol.,* pp. 265 ff.; *supra,* Chap. XXXVIII, n. 28. But the entire text remains unpublished.

(11) Joshua b. Joseph ha-Lorqi, *Iggeret* (Epistle to Paul of Burgos), first ed. by E. Aschkenazi in his *Dibre ḥakhamim* (Words of the Wise: a Collection of Eleven Tracts), pp. 41–46, and reedited from three MSS with a German translation and notes by L. Landau.

(12) Profiat Duran (Isaac b. Moses, called Efodi from his work *Ma'aseh Efod*), *Kelimat ha-goyim* (The Shame of Gentiles), written in 1397 and ed. from a Vienna and ten other MSS with notes and a postscript by Z. A. Posnanski in *Ha-Zofeh,* III, 99–113, 143–80; IV, 37–48, 81–96, 115–32. (On the closely related anonymous tract, an excerpt of which was published by A. Marmorstein, followed by A. Porges's and D. Camerini's corrections in *REJ,* LXVI–LXVII, see *supra,* Vol. V, p. 340 n. 38.) See also his satirical letter *Al tehi ka-abotekha* (Be Not Like Your Fathers), first published by A. Geiger in his *Melo Chofnajim* [ḥofnayim; A Fistful]; *Biographie Joseph Salomo del Medigo's,* Hebrew section, pp. 42–49; with a German trans. in Geiger's "Priphot Duran's Schreiben zu einem Abtrünnigen," *Wissenschaftliche Zeitschrift für jüdische Theologie,* IV, 451–58.

(13) Yom Ṭob Lipmann-Mühlhausen, *Sefer ha-Niṣṣaḥon* (Book of Disputation), referring to a disputation with a convert Peter in 1399. It was written before 1406 and first edited by T. Hackspann in his *Liber Nizzachon Rabbi Lipmanni.* The author evidently borrowed both the title and some ideas from the older *Sefer Niṣṣa-ḥon* mentioned here in Item 5. An accompanying poem *Zikhron Sefer Niṣṣaḥon* was republished soon thereafter with a Latin trans. entitled *Carmen memoriale libri Nizzachon,* and a sharp critique (*confutatio*) by Wagenseil in his *Tela ignea,* I, 105–17, 118–40 (633). It is now available in a well-annotated English translation in O. S. Rankin's *Jewish Religious Polemic,* pp. 49 ff. The authorship of this poem, long attributed to Lipmann-Mühlhausen himself, has been clearly demonstrated as belonging to the otherwise unknown Italian Hebrew poet, Meshullam b. Uri of Modena. See I. Davidson, "The Author of the Poem *Zikhron Sefer Niṣṣaḥon,*" *JQR,* XVIII, 257–65. Such polemical poems were no rarity in either the Latin or the Hebrew poetry of the Middle Ages. See *infra,* n. 8. See also the careful analysis of the pertinent problems in J. Kaufmann's Hebrew biographical study of *R. Yom Ṭob Lipmann-Mühlhausen;* and the independent summary by B. Bernstein, "Der Sieg des Rabbi Jomtov-Lippman Mühlhausen," in *Jewish Studies in Memory of Michael Guttmann,* I, 201–20.

(14) Simon b. Ṣemaḥ Duran, *Qeshet u-Magen* (Bow and Shield), a polemical tract against Christianity and Islam, originally a chapter in his *Magen Abot* (The Shield of Fathers, a commentary on the tractate *Abot*), written in 1423 and first published in the anonymous collection of apologias, *Milḥemet Ḥobah* (Obligatory War). Later the section dealing with Islam was reedited from MSS with a German translation by

M. Steinschneider under the title *Islam und Judenthum*. See also Jakob Guttmann, "Die Stellung des Simon ben Zemach Duran in der Geschichte der jüdischen Religionsphilosophie," *MGWJ*, LII, 641–72; LIII, 46–79, 199–228.

(15) Solomon b. Simon Duran, the latter's son, *Milḥemet Miṣvah* (War in Fulfillment of a Commandment, a reply to Geronimo de Santa Fé), written in 1437 and first published as an appendix to his father's *Qeshet u-Magen*.

(16) David Nasi of Candia, *Sefer Hoda'at ba'al din* (The Party's Confession), written *ca.* 1435 for Bishop Francesco Bentivoglio and adducing Christian "testimonies" against Christian doctrines.

(17) Joseph ibn Shem Ṭob, *Sefeqot 'al ma'aseh Yeshu* (Doubts about the Life of Jesus) extant only in a Paris MS; see Loeb, *La Controverse religieuse*, p. 50. Joseph also translated Crescas' apologetic "Tractate" into Hebrew (see *infra*, n. 8) and wrote a commentary on Profiat Duran's *Al tehi ka-abotekha*.

(18) Ḥayyim b. Yehudah ibn Musa, *Magen ve-romaḥ* (Shield and Spear), written in 1456 and largely devoted to a refutation of Nicholas de Lyra's anti-Jewish arguments. See D. Kaufmann, "A Letter by R. Ḥayyim ibn Musa to His Son Yehudah, ed. with Notes and a Biographical Sketch of the Author" (Hebrew), *Beth Talmud*, II, 110–25.

(19) Elijah Ḥayyim b. Benjamin of Genezzano, *Viqquaḥ* (Disputation). This is allegedly a report of a three-day disputation which the author had conducted with a friendly Franciscan monk, Francesco di Aquapendente in Orvieto under papal suzerainty. It is edited by J. Rosenthal in "A Judeo-Chistian Debate of the Fifteenth Century" (Hebrew), *Sura*, I, 156–77. Accepting a suggestion by Umberto Cassuto, who placed Elijah Ḥayyim in the late fifteenth century, Rosenthal dates that disputation and its subsequent record some time between 1472 and 1489. In any case, it clearly betrays the new liberal spirit of the Renaissance.

(20) Abraham b. Mordecai Farissol (Perizol), *Magen Abraham* (Shield of Abraham) or *Viqqu'aḥ ha-dat* (Religious Disputation), written in 1503–1504. Stimulated by a debate with two monks at the court of Ercole I d'Este in Ferrara, Abraham was greatly indebted to Duran's critique of both Christianity and Islam in *Qeshet u-magen*. Although available in several MSS and frequently discussed, this work still remains unpublished. See M. Steinschneider, "Die italienische Literatur der Juden," *MGWJ*, XLII, 421. This apologia, as well as the other works by this scientist and Bible commentator, clearly betrays the intellectual atmosphere of the Renaissance age. See also the other Jewish apologias mentioned by Loeb in *La Controverse religieuse*, p. 50 n. 4.

(21) Less well datable is such an anonymous tract, addressed to an imaginary Christian polemist and ed. by A. Berliner under the title, *Sefer Nestor ha-Komer* (Book of the Priest Nestor).

Like their Christian counterparts (*supra*, n. 4), Jewish copyists often collected several apologetic tracts for ready reference in a single volume or even in part of a volume. One such Hebrew MS, written in a Spanish hand of the fifteenth century and entitled *Lequṭot* (Miscellany), includes a number of less familiar treatises or excerpts. See A. Berliner's brief description of the Munich MS in his *Pletath Soferim, Beiträge zur jüdischen Schriftauslegung im Mittelalter*, pp. 31 ff. Some of these have since become more fully known through the aforementioned essays by Zadok Kahn and others. (See *supra*, item 4.) Several other such collections are listed by A. Marx in the *Freidus Mem. Vol.*, pp. 148 ff. Of course, for an opposite purpose, namely to document Jewish hostility toward Christians, J. C. Wagenseil published in 1681 his frequently cited collection, *Tela ignea Satanae*. Most of the tracts here mentioned are more conveniently assembled, though often in an uncritical as well as abbreviated form, in J. D. Eisenstein's *Oẓar Wikuḥim*.

Not only do most editions of apologetic writings, when such exist, leave much to be desired, but their analytical treatment in the context of their time is left almost entirely to general historians. We do not even possess any good general survey of late medieval and early modern Jewish apologetic literature apart from the brief essays by Loeb. This is the more surprising as the bibliographical groundwork was laid some two centuries ago by G. B. de Rossi in his *Bibliotheca judaica antichristiana;* and by J. C. Wolf in his *Bibliotheca hebraea*, II, 993 ff., listing both Christian polemics against Jews and reciprocal Jewish apologias. The latter are characteristically headed by the title of "Syllabus of Jewish writers who have dared to attack the Christian faith" (pp. 1048 ff.). On the other hand, I. Ziegler's *Religiöse Disputationen im Mittelalter* is little more than a popular sketch. Slightly more searching is S. Bäck, "Die Apologeten vom 14. bis Ende des 18. Jahrhunderts," in J. Winter and A. Wünsche, *Die Jüdische Literatur seit Abschluss des Kanons*, III, 653–719, which includes a number of representative excerpts in German translation. Of considerable interest is the collection of excerpts pertaining to the messianic controversy, culled from books and manuscripts by A. Posnanski in his *Schiloh: Ein Beitrag zur Geschichte der Messiaslehre*, Vol. I (reviewing the various interpretations of Gen. 49:10), supplemented by his list of such works published by D. Simonsen in "Eine Sammlung polemischer und apologetischer Literatur," *Festschrift für Aron Freimann*, pp. 114–20. See also such monographs as H. Friedenwald's "Apologetic Works of Jewish Physicians," *JQR*, XXXII, 227–55, 407–426 (dealing with the early modern period). A full and up-to-date bibliography entitled "Anti-Christian Polemic from Its Beginnings to the End of the Eighteenth Century" (Hebrew) was compiled by J. Rosenthal and published in *Aresheth*, II, 130–79; with "Supplements," *ibid.*, III, 433–39; IV. But much remains to be done before this significant phase of Judeo-Christian relations, however unpleasant and at times unsavory on both sides, will be satisfactorily elucidated.

8. See A. Marx, "A List of Poems on the Articles of the Creed," *JQR*, IX, 305–336; and the additional texts published by him in *Freidus Mem. Vol.*, pp. 275 ff. App. 4. This genre was not at all uncommon in medieval and early modern Hebrew poetry. See the fairly extensive list in the Index to I. Davidson's *Oṣar ha-shirah ve-ha-piyyuṭ* (Thesaurus of Medieval Hebrew Poetry), IV, 497 Nos. 19 and 21; and his earlier analytical study, *Parody in Jewish Literature*. Poems as a weapon in ideological and partisan struggles were even more common in medieval Latin writings. See esp. H. Walther, *Das Streitgedicht in der lateinischen Literatur des Mittelalters*. Ḥisdai b. Yehudah Crescas' *Tratado* (the full title is unknown; it is called by De Rossi, *Bibliotheca*, pp. 24 f. No. 28, 39 ff. No. 60: *Tractatus de articulis religionis*), was apparently rather freely translated into Hebrew by Joseph ibn Shem Ṭob in 1451 under the title, *Biṭṭul 'iqqere dat ha-Noṣrim* (Refutation of the Principles of the Christian Faith). Only the Hebrew version has appeared in print, first in Salonica (1860), and then ed. by E. Deinard. It is fully excerpted in J. D. Eisenstein's *Oẓar Wikuḥim*, pp. 288–310. The numerous parallels between this tract and Profiat Duran's *Kelimat* have long been recognized. On Moses Kohen of Tordesillas, Joseph Albo, and Ibn Verga see *supra*, Chap. XXXVIII, nn. 28 and 42.

9. Raymond Martini, *Pugio fidei*, ed. by J. B. Carpzov, together with De Voisin's earlier notes thereto. The passages quoted in the text are from Martini's Intro. and Chaps. ii, xiii.8; see also A. L. Williams's *Adversus Judaeos*, pp. 248 ff. No contemporary or early successor speaks of Martini's Jewish origin. However, Peter Nigri, a fifteenth-century Dominican, and Paul of Burgos refer to him as a former rabbi who, according to Nigri, was converted at the age of forty. See J. C. Wolf, *Bibliotheca hebraea*, III, 900; Paul of Burgos, *Scrutinium*, i, dist. 8, cap. 15, 1475 ed., fol. M 56 ("Raimundus Rabbi tuus in suo pugione"). Neither Nigri nor Paul of Burgos has any particular interest in emphasizing Martini's former Judaism. Nor is attendance at Peñaforte's college proof of Martini's prior unfamiliarity with Hebrew; he may have gone there principally to study Arabic and to familiarize himself with missionary techniques. F. Cavallera's assumption that, because Martini's earlier *Explanatio symboli apostolorum* written in 1258 contained no references to Jewish sources, he must have acquired his Hebraic knowledge in the subsequent twenty years, is not only an *argumentum a silentio*, but it is also controverted by Martini's appointment in 1264 to the commission in charge of censoring Hebrew books. He actually seems to have been the commission's leading expert, which he could not possibly have become in the intervening six years alone. Nor do his translations of rabbinic texts, many of them quite complex even if almost exclusively aggadic in nature, appear to be the work of a relative tyro. See F. Cavallera's *"L'Explanatio symboli* de Raymond Martin O.P. (1258),"* Studia mediaevalia* in honor of Raymond Joseph Martin, p. 201 n. 1; and *supra*, Vol. V, p. 357 n. 8. Nor is S. Lieberman's suggestion (in *Shkiin* [*Sheqi'in*]: *a Few Words on Some Jewish Legends*, esp. pp. 43 ff.) that Martini used several assistants, Jewish or converted, borne out by documentary evidence. In fact, the occasional misunderstandings of rabbinic texts and lapses in their translation would more likely be made by a man who had neglected his rabbinic studies for thirty or more years than by assistants who would have been competent in the field.

In "La Polémique contre les Juifs et le Pugio fidei de R. Martini," *Mélanges Charles Moeller*, I, 519–26, J. Nicks incorrectly suggests that the *Pugio* was little used before 1687, except by Petrus Columna Galatinus (1518) and Porcheto de Salvatici (1520). As a matter of fact, Porcheto wrote his tract in 1303, possibly serving as the main direct source for Galatinus, and he was but one of many successors inspired by Martini, even if they never mentioned his name. See Porcheto's *Victoria adversus impios Hebraeos*, and Galatinus' *De arcanis catholicae veritatis*, with the comments thereon by E. d'Alançon in the *Dictionnaire de théologie catholique*, VI, 1052–54; and by A. Kleinhans in *Antonianum*, I, 145–79, 327–56, both denying Galatinus' conscious plagiarism of the *Pugio*. Certainly most Spanish controversialists used the vast materials accumulated by the learned thirteenth-century Dominican. See also F. Secret, "Notes pour une histoire du Pugio fidei à la Renaissance," *Sefarad*, XX, 401–407. On the other hand, J. M. de Garganta has quite rightly postulated the priority of certain arguments in Thomas Aquinas' *Summa contra gentiles*. See his intro. to the new ed. of that work, with a Spanish trans. directed by J. M. Pla Castellano, I. Brief and mutually complementary summaries of the *Pugio*, all sympathetic to the author, are offered by C. Werner in *Der heilige Thomas von Aquino*, new ed., I, 655–61; M. Menéndez y Pelayo in his *Historia de los heterodoxos españoles*, 2d ed. rev. and annotated by A. Bonilla y San Martin *et al.*, III, 250–55 (in his *Obras completas*, Edición nacional, ed. by M. Artigas *et al.*, XXXVI, 318–22, mainly analyzing Martini's critique of the philosophers; in which, as

Menéndez points out, Maimonides served him in very good stead); and A. L. Williams, *Adversus Judaeos*, pp. 248 ff.

10. Don Isaac Abravanel's *Yeshu'ot meshiḥo* (The Salvation of His Anointed), fols. 5a, 36b f., etc. The accusation of forgeries was taken up by S. M. Schiller-Szinessy in "The *Pugio Fidei*," *Journal of Philology*, XVI, 130–52; and it found a most able and informed exponent in F. Y. Baer. See his "The Forged Midrashim of Raymond Martini and Their Place in the Religious Controversy during the Middle Ages" (Hebrew), *Studies in Memory of Asher Gulak and Samuel Klein*, pp. 28–48. Baer effectively utilized the subsequent debates at Tortosa and his own aforementioned analytical studies of that disputation. See *supra*, Chap. XXXVIII, n. 40. Martini's veracity was, on the other hand, strongly defended by A. Neubauer in his "Jewish Controversy," *Expositor*, VII, 81–105, 179–97; A. Epstein in his "Bereschit-rabbati. . . . Dessen Verhältnis zu Rabba-Rabbati, Moses ha-Darschan und Pugio fidei," *MWJ*, XV, esp. pp. 85 ff.; S. Lieberman in his *Shkiin* (*Sheqi'in*), pp. 43 ff. (a list of rabbinic authorities cited in the *Pugio* shows that Martini not only used older talmudic sources but also quoted some forty times so recent an author as David Qimḥi); and his "Raymund Martini and His Alleged Forgeries," *HJ*, V, 87–102. See also Williams, *Adversus Judaeos*, pp. 248 ff.; A. Díaz Macho's analysis of these opposing points of view in his "Acerca de los midrašim falsificados de Raimundo Martini," *Sefarad*, IX, 165–96; and *supra*, Vol. VI, p. 410 n. 24.

11. Arnaldo de Vilanova, *Allocutio super Tetragrammaton*, Intro., ed. by J. Carreras y Artau in *Sefarad*, IX, 80; Paul de Santa María, *Scrutinium scripturarum*, end. The story of Abner of Burgos (Alphonso de Valladolid) has long been known from references to him and his work in Paul's *Scrutinium* and Alphonso de Spina's *Fortalitium fidei*. Several of Abner's writings, too, have been preserved in large manuscripts at the Bibliothèque Nationale in Paris and in the Rossi collection in Parma. Baer, the most searching student of that remarkable personality, reiteratedly intimated that he expected to publish at least considerable parts of Abner's *Moreh ṣedeq* (Teacher of Righteousness) and *Minḥat qena'ot* (Zealous Offering). However, thus far this expectation has not been fulfilled and we are limited to Baer's analytical essays in *KA*, X, 20–37; and *Tarbiz*, XI (see *supra*, n. 6); the comprehensive summary in his *Toledot*, 2d ed., pp. 192 ff., 514 ff. (in the English trans., *A History of the Jews in Christian Spain*, I, 327 ff., 446 f.); and his more recent "The Kabbalistic Doctrine in the Christological Teaching of Abner of Burgos" (Hebrew), *Tarbiz*, XXVII, 278–89 (citing another lengthy excerpt in Hebrew). See also Abner's "Epistles," ed. by J. Rosenthal and cited *supra*, n. 6 item 1. Abner's conversion has sometimes been connected with the miracle tale reported by De Spina, according to which two Jewish messianic pretenders appeared in Ávila and Ayllón in 1295 and were stopped by the sudden appearance of crosses on the white garments of the assembled Jewish congregation. But it is generally agreed that Abner proceeded to the baptismal font a quarter of a century later, perhaps as late as 1330. He became known as Alphonso de Valladolid. Like Donin he revealed great familiarity with antitalmudic trends in Judaism; in fact, he contended that even in his day there were many Jewish sects. But he was a far more penetrating student of Jewish mystic lore, out of which he culled certain passages which had, or could be invested with, christological significance. When he finally decided to make the fateful transition, he tried to persuade his former coreligionists to follow his example. On the connections

between certain kabbalistic and Christian teachings see *infra*, n. 15 and Chap. LVII.

12. Alphonso de Spina's *Fortalitium fidei*, iii.7, cited by H. Graetz in his *Geschichte*, 4th ed., VII, 451. King Alphonso XI's prohibition of the so-called *Birkat ha-minim* (the antiheretical benediction) is also alluded to by the contemporary Hebrew poet, Samuel b. Joseph ibn Sason, in his collection *Abne Shoham* (Onyx Stones). See the excerpts, cited by Baer in his "Fragments of Fourteenth-Century Castilian Poems" (Hebrew), *Minḥah le-David* (Offering to David: the David Yellin Jubilee Volume), pp. 197–204, esp. 199 f.; and H. Schirmann, *Ha-Shirah ha-'ibrit bi-Sefarad u-bi-Provence* (Hebrew Poetry in Spain and the Provence), II, 524 ff. See also Baer's *Toledot*, 2d ed., p. 213; and his *History of the Jews in Christian Spain*, I, 357.

13. Joseph Albo's *Sefer ha-'Iqqarim*, iii.25, ed by Husik, III, 217 ff. There is no way of telling whether this Christian debater was but a straw man set up for easy demolition. Albo may well have known some such Christian objectors to the Old Testament along Marcionite-Catharist lines. In general, however, even Albo's moderate defense of Judaism aroused the opposition of Christian polemists, and in the following century a Cluniac monk, Gilbert Génébrard, translated the relevant chapter of the *Sefer ha-'Iqqarim* into Latin and published it, together with his reply, under the title *R. Josephi Albonis, R. Davidis Kimchi et alii cujusdam Hebraei anonymi argumenta quibus nonnullos fidei christianae articulos oppugnant*. The questions put to Albo reflected the newer approaches of the scholastic Bible exegesis, which had gone far beyond the purely allegorical interpretations of the High Middle Ages. That they colored much Jewish thinking will become clearer in the context of the Jewish philosophy and Bible exegesis of the period. On the parallels between Albo's chapter and Simon b. Ṣemaḥ Duran's apologia, see Jakob Guttmann's brief observation in "Die Stellung des Simon . . . Duran," *MGWJ*, LIII, 224 n. 3.

14. Profiat Duran, *Al tehi ka-abotekha*, ed. by Geiger in *Melo ḥofnayim*, pp. 42 ff.; idem, *Kelimat ha-goyim*, ed. by A. Posnanski in *Ha-Zofeh*, III, 143, both also in Eisenstein's *Oẓar Wikuḥim*, pp. 95 ff., 264 f.

15. Raymond Lull's (or Pietro Mainardi's?) *De auditu kabbalistico* in his *Opera*, 1598 ed., pp. 44–116; Arnaldo de Vilanova, *Allocutio super Tetragrammaton* in *Sefarad*, IX, 80 ff.; the observations by J. Carreras y Artau in "Arnaldo de Vilanova," *ibid.*, VII, 49 ff., and by Baer in "The Kabbalistic Doctrine in the Christological Teaching of Abner of Burgos," *Tarbiz*, XXVII, 278 ff.; Giovanni Pico della Mirandola, *Conclusiones DCCCC quas olim Romae disputandas exhibuit*, in his *Opera omnia*, Basel, 1572–73 ed., I, 105, No. 9; and his *Apologia*, i, *ibid.*, pp. 123 f. On Pico's attitude to Jews and Judaism and his kabbalistic studies see *infra*, Chap. LVII. See also J. M. Millás Vallicrosa, "Algunas relaciones entre la doctrina luliana y la cabala," *Sefarad*, XVIII, 241–55. Solomon ibn Verga, too, presents a pro-Jewish statesman, Thomas, telling the king, "I have seen three great [Jewish] scholars from Germany and studied some kabbalistic books under them. From these it became evident to me that Trinity is really Unity." See *Shebeṭ Yehudah*, vii, ed. by Wiener, pp. 17 (Hebrew), 33 (German); ed. by Shohet, p. 37. These christological elements in the Kabbalah, both genuine and spurious, will be more fully elucidated

in later chapters. For the time being see J. L. Blau, *The Christian Interpretation of the Cabalah in the Renaissance* (among other matters "categorically" denying Lull's authorship of *De auditu;* pp. 117 f.); and G. G. Scholem, "Zur Geschichte der Anfänge der christlichen Kabbala," *Essays Presented to Leo Baeck,* pp. 158–93; also the literature mentioned by F. Secret in "Les Dominicains et la kabbale chrétienne à la Renaissance," *AFP,* XXVII, 319–36; and in "Les Debuts du kabbalisme chrétien en Espagne et son histoire à la Renaissance," *Sefarad,* XVII, 36–48.

16. Isaac Pollegar, *'Ezer ha-dat,* Intro., ed. by Belasco, p. 2. It may be noted that the author found it necessary to conceal some of his innermost thoughts behind a cloak of "a poem and riddle." He did it not out of fear of Christian reprisals, but rather in anticipation that many orthodox Jews might misunderstand his interpretations and see them as widely differing from their own. These internal Jewish conflicts will emerge more clearly from our treatment in later volumes.

17. Profiat Duran, *Al tehi ka-abotekha,* ed. by Geiger in *Melo hofnayim,* pp. 42 ff.; in Eisenstein's *Ozar Wikuhim,* pp. 95 ff. In this popular satire Duran avoided many theological subtleties which had long become the mainstay of apologetic argumentation on both sides. But he effectively quoted the Christian sources themselves. He could have added many details, such as had been adduced by Jacob b. Reuben and his predecessors as well as successors and which had also long become familiar to such Christian Hebraists as Nicholas de Lyra. See esp. J. Rosenthal's notes on his ed. of Jacob b. Reuben's *Milhamot ha-Shem.*

18. Hisdai Crescas' unpublished *Tratado,* in Joseph ibn Shem Tob's Hebrew trans., *Bittul 'iqqere dat ha-Nosrim* (Refutation of the Principles of the Christian Faith), i, ed. by E. Deinard; Eisenstein, *Ozar,* p. 289; Moses b. Solomon of Salerno, *Ta'anot,* fol. 246b in S. Simon's aforementioned dissertation, *Mose ben Salomo,* pp. v (Hebrew), 58 f. (German); Abner of Burgos, *Minhat qena'ot,* cited from a Parma MS in Baer's *Toledot,* pp. 197 ff.; and his *History,* I, 337 ff. See also Simon's nuanced analysis of the arguments presented by Moses b. Solomon's Christian interlocutors and the related teachings of Augustine and Thomas Aquinas (pp. 40 ff.). The reaction against the rigid antianthropomorphism of the Jewish thinkers under Islam had gathered momentum in the Christian West soon after Maimonides' death. But Abner's seems to have been the first attempt to link this Orthodox opposition with the Christian doctrine of Incarnation. See *supra,* Vols. V, pp. 90, 106 f., etc.; VIII, pp. 99 ff., 329 nn. 61–63.

19. Joachim of Floris, *Adversus Judaeos,* ed. by A. Frugoni, p. 23, based on the ancient equation of the Word-Logos with the Son of God (see also *ibid.,* p. 29); Abner of Burgos, *Teshubot,* cited from the Parma MS in Baer's *Toledot,* 2d ed., pp. 200 f.; idem, *A History,* I, 344 ff. See also idem, "The Kabbalistic Doctrine in the Christological Teaching of Abner of Burgos" (Hebrew), *Tarbiz,* XXVII, 278–89. In his implied praise of the mystic book, *She'ur qomah* (Measure of the [Divine] Stature), from which he quoted the approving statements of R. Ishmael and R. 'Aqiba, Abner ran counter to the majority opinion held among "enlightened" Jews ever since the days of the geonim. More remarkably, it escaped his attention that that grossly anthropomorphic book had been used as a major illustration of Jewish "superstitions" censured half a millennium before by Archbishop Agobard of Lyons,

a far more representative ecclesiastical critic of Judaism. See *supra*, Vol. VIII, pp. 286 n. 28, 329 n. 61. These few samples of the theological-philosophic arguments must suffice here. As the theological controversies in question also deeply colored some philosophic teachings by Crescas and other Jewish thinkers in Christian lands, they will be discussed more fully in a later chapter.

20. Raymond Lull, *Llibre de Contemplació*, cclxxxvii, in the English trans. by E. A. Peers, entitled *The Art of Contemplation* (with intro.; also Peers's biography, *Raymond Lull*, pp. 66 ff.); Paul of Burgos' reply to Joshua ha-Lorqi, ed. by A. Geiger in his "Epistle to Ignaz Blumenfeld" (Hebrew) in *Oẓar Nechmad*, II, 5 f. Paul developed his views more fully in his *Scrutinium scripturarum*. The early popularity of the *Scrutinium*, which Paul completed in 1432, is attested to by the six editions published in the years 1469–78 in such diverse localities as Rome, Strasbourg, Mantua, and Mayence. In the first section of that treatise devoted to a fictitious dialogue between Saul the Jew and Paul the Catholic, the author presented the Jewish arguments not unfairly. As a former rabbi and an ardently patriotic Jew he certainly was fully familiar with them. (See, for instance, his letter and poem, addressed from London to Don Meir Alguades and published by I. Abrahams in his "Paul of Burgos in London," *JQR*, [o.s.] XII, 255–63; F. Cantera, "Šelomó ha-Leví, rehén en Inglaterra en 1389," *Homenaje a Millás Vallicrosa*, I, 301–307.) On the other hand, once he became a leading churchman and statesman Paul could not indulge in many personal deviations from accepted theological doctrine. These problems had deeply preoccupied Christian thinkers for centuries, and a variety of comprehensive analyses of the Trinitarian dogma and all its derivatives was available to students. Whatever differences may have existed among Christian teachers, particularly of the sectarian wings, they all agreed on these fundamentals of their faith. As Francisco Suárez was to observe more than a century after Paul, "that the promised Messiah had already come no person can deny who glories in the name of Christian, however heretical. In this respect, more than any other, the Christian faith is differentiated from the Jews' infidelity." See his *Commentary* on the *Tertia Pars Summae Theologicae* by Thomas Aquinas, Disput. i, Intro. in his *Opera omnia*, ed. by C. Berton, XVII, 5. See also the brief summary of Paul's *Scrutinium* in Williams's *Adversus Judaeos*, pp. 267 ff.; and, more generally, L. Serrano's biography of Paul in *Los Conversos*, esp. pp. 109 ff.

21. Ḥisdai Crescas, *Or Adonai* (The Light of the Lord), 81a f.; Joseph Albo, *Sefer ha-'Iqqarim*, I, ii-iv, ed. by Husik, I, esp. pp. 55, 61, 64 ff.; Profiat Duran, *Kelimat ha-goyim*, x, ed. by Posnanski in *Ha-Zofeh*, IV, 88 f. (Eisentein, *Oẓar*, p. 284) and many other writers. See also J. Sarachek, *The Doctrine of the Messiah in Medieval Jewish Literature*; and *supra*, Vols. V, pp. 159 ff., 363 ff.; VIII, pp. 125 ff., 341 ff. The ramified Jewish messianic speculations and movements of that period will be more fully analyzed in a later chapter.

22. Jacob b. Reuben, *Milḥamot ha-Shem*, ed. by J. Rosenthal, pp. 141 ff.; Profiat Duran, *Kelimat ha-goyim*, i, ed. by Posnanski in *Ha-Zofeh*, III, 102 (Eisenstein, *Oẓar*, p. 261); Simon Duran, *Qeshet u-magen*, ed. by Steinschneider, pp. 33 f. (Hebrew), 44 f. (German). Profiat's interpretation of the term "Marrano" is not shared by modern scholars. Alternative explanations are discussed *infra*, Chap. LVI. Apart from its theological arguments, Profiat's critique of the use and interpretation

of Old Testament passages in the New is of considerable historical interest. He devoted to this reexamination an entire chapter (ten) of his *Kelimat*.

23. Ḥisdai Crescas, *Biṭṭul*, xiv, xviii, ed. by E. Deinard (Eisenstein, *Oẓar*, pp. 304, 307). Another Crescas pupil, Joseph Albo, attacked the New Testament by stressing certain historical deficiencies in its record. In his reply to the aforementioned strictures of his Christian interlocutor who glorified the New above the Old Testament, Albo pointed out that the transfer of the weekly holiday from Saturday to Sunday had been an illegitimate later innovation. (He dated it fully five hundred years after Jesus.) Not only did it run counter to the Old Testament commandment, borne out by the miracle of manna which did not descend on Saturdays, but it also controverted the wishes of Jesus and his disciples, who had observed the Jewish Sabbath. See Albo's *Sefer ha-'Iqqarim*, iii.25, ed. by Husik, III, 241 f.; and *supra*, n. 13. Needless to say, the Jewish apologists greatly oversimplified the evolution of the observance from Saturday to Sunday, on which see, for instance, P. Cotton's dissertation, *From Sabbath to Sunday: a Study in Early Christianity;* and R. Johanan's statement cited *supra*, Vol. II, pp. 134, 380 n. 6. Curiously, Profiat felt obliged to apologize before his teacher, Crescas, for spending so much time and effort criticizing the New Testament, "for I know for certain that it will bring joy and pride in their portion to the heirs of the true faith, whose chief you, the glory of the rabbinate, are today." See Profiat's *Kelimat ha-goyim*, Intro. and x.2, ed. by Posnanski in *Ha-Zofeh*, III, 102; IV, 48 (Eisenstein, *Oẓar*, pp. 261, 282).

24. John Duns Scotus, *Ordinatio*, Prol., Part ii in his *Opera omnia*, Vatican, 1950 ed., I, 72; Samuel Maroccanus, *Tractatus indicans errorem Judaeorum*, iii, Prague ed., pp. 10 ff. (under the title *De adventu Messiae . . . liber* in *PL* CXLIX, 339 f.).

25. Abner of Burgos (Alphonso de Valladolid), *Mostrador de Justicia*, quoted from the Paris MS by Loeb in "Polémistes chrétiens et juifs," *REJ*, XVIII, 52 ff.; and by Baer in "Abner von Burgos," *KA*, X, 20 ff. Here Baer points to both the Karaite antecedents and contemporary reformatory trends in Spanish Jewry. On the controversial *Kol Sakhal*, see E. Rivkin, *Leon da Modena and the Kol Sakhal* (reprinted from *JQR*, XXXVIII–XLI). Even Isaac Pollegar, Abner's sharp opponent, had to acknowledge that Abner "was a skillful person and familiar with the ways of religion and also philosophy." See his *'Ezer ha-dat*, i.7, ed. by G. S. Belasco, p. 25. For this reason it seems doubly unlikely that it was Abner who masqueraded under the name of Alphonso Bonhomo and translated (or invented) Samuel Maroccanus' tract or epistle. This suggestion by Moritz Steinschneider has rightly been rejected by scholars, among them A. L. Williams in his *Adversus Judaeos*, pp. 228 ff.

26. Joshua ha-Lorqi, "Iggeret" (Epistle to Paul of Burgos), ii.7, ed. by Landau, pp. 12 (Hebrew), 37 f. (German); Einstein, *Oẓar*, p. 101; Lipmann-Mühlhausen, *Sefer ha-Niṣṣaḥon*, Amsterdam, 1711 ed., p. 118.

27. Alphonso de Spina, *Fortalitium fidei*, iii.12, 6, Lyons, 1511 ed., fol. ccxxxvib; Paul of Burgos, *Scrutinium scripturarum*, ii. dist. 6, cap. 10, Mantua, 1475 ed., fols. L 1b ff. See also Williams, *Adversus Judaeos*, pp. 275, 280; and *supra*, Vol. V, pp. 146 f., 357 f. n. 8. True to his general philosophy of history, Joachim of Floris believed that the final cycle of human history had already begun and that the days of the long-

lasting Jewish Exile were drawing to a close. He calculated that it took forty years from Cyrus, and seventy from the Jews' deportation to Babylonia, until their return to the Holy Land and the rebuilding of the Temple. "This indicates that forty generations after the Lord's incarnation, or some seventy generations after David, the entry of the multitude of the nations ought to be consummated and, with it, all of Israel will be saved." See his *Tractatus super quatuor Evangelia,* ed. by E. Buonaiuti, p. 82. So convinced was Joachim of the correctness of his calculations that he introduced his very anti-Jewish polemic by stating, "I feel that the time is at hand to take pity on them [the Jews], the time of their consolation and conversion." See his *Adversus Judaeos,* pp. 3, 85, 95. These computations were largely based, as we recall, on the rabbinic division of history into three epochs of two thousand years, which was so often cited by Christian apologists to prove that the birth of Jesus came in the final, "messianic," cycle. See *supra,* n. 5. Some Jewish writers replied that these assertions did not square even with the Christian chronology. Citing Eusebius and other Christian authors, Ḥayyim ibn Musa showed that they differed as to whether Jesus had come in the year 5000 or 5528 of the era of Creation. In the latter case, "there remained only 494 [406] years for the days of their Messiah." Moreover some rabbinic teachings controverted the original computation, and allowed fully seven thousand years for the messianic era. See his *Magen ve-romaḥ,* cited from a Breslau MS by D. Kaufmann in *Beth Talmud,* II, 114 f. See also *supra,* Vols. V, pp. 119 f., 344 n. 48; VIII, pp. 206 f., 378 f. n. 73.

28. Samuel Maroccanus, cited *supra,* n. 24; Paul of Burgos, *Scrutinium,* ii. dist. 6, cap. 1 and 14, Mantua, 1475 ed., fols. J 5 ff. and L 7 ff., well summarized by A. L. Williams in his *Adversus Judaeos,* pp. 273 ff.; Abner of Burgos, *Mostrador de Justicia,* Intro., cited from the Paris Spanish MS by Loeb in "Polémistes chrétiens," *REJ,* XVIII, 54 f.; idem, *Minḥat qena'ot,* cited from another Paris MS by Baer in his *Toledot,* 2d ed., p. 209; *A History,* I, 352. See also *infra,* n. 32.

29. Albo, *Sefer ha-'Iqqarim,* iii.25, ed. by Husik, III, 228; Nathan b. Meshullam, cited from a Munich MS by A. Berliner in his *Pletath Soferim,* Hebrew section, p. 34 No. 20. Albo's rationale of Jewish powerlessness, of which Yehudah Halevi had been a most eloquent champion, was intimately linked to the doctrine of the chosen people and the ancient controversy between the two faiths as to which was now the true Israel. Characteristically, we rarely hear echoes of Halevi's related contention that even the early Christians had revered their saints and martyrs far above their statesmen and conquerors, thereby admitting the superiority of spiritual values. See *supra,* Vols. V, pp. 101, 336 n. 37; VIII, pp. 123 ff., 340 ff.; and more fully, my "Yehudah Halevi: an Answer to an Historic Challenge," *JSS,* III, 243–72. Evidently, in the crucible of the power struggles of the late Middle Ages the former great veneration of passive martyrs and saints had been greatly tempered in comparison with that given the successful activist leaders of both Church and state. The Halevian argument now made little impression on the predominantly power-conscious readers of apologetic tracts.

30. Alphonso de Spina, *Fortalitium fidei,* iii and v, Lyons, 1511 ed., fols., cviiic–cixc, ccxiic–ccxixd, ccxlvc ff. (Book V is entitled *De bello demonum.*) De Spina devoted a special section in his Book iii dealing with *De bello Judaeorum* to a discussion of seventeen forms of "Jewish cruelties" toward Christians (fols. clxxxiiid–

cxcvib), repeating all sorts of accusations concerning Jewish slaughter of Christian children, hanging of Christians crowned with thorns, poisoning of wells, and so forth. Characteristically, however, as A. L. Williams points out in *Adversus Judaeos*, p. 278 n. 4, he did not specifically stress ritual murders in connection with the Passover celebration.

31. De Spina's *Fortalitium,* fol. ccxxxvab with reference to the views of Duns Scotus, cited *supra,* Chap. XXXVII, n. 15. In the preceding 11th "consideration" of Book iii, Alphonso reviewed the existing laws (*De Judaeorum obligatione ex iure canonico et civili ac ordinatione regia*), emphasizing their discriminatory and segregationist features (fols. ccxxiiid–ccxxxiiid). See also Baer's succinct analysis in his *Toledot,* 2d ed., pp. 385 ff., 545 n. 79 (includes a warning against confusing De Spina with his namesake, a Dominican inquisitor of Barcelona). The evolution of anti-Jewish medieval folklore will be analyzed *infra,* Chap. XLIX.

32. Abner, *Mostrador de Justicia,* last chapter, extensively cited by Baer in his *Toledot,* 2d ed., pp. 206 ff. (largely omitted in the English version). This chapter, devoted to a detailed critique of the Maimonidean Code, bears many similarities with the attacks on Rabbanite law by Karaites, as well as pre-Reform antinomian writers. See esp. Baer's note, *ibid.,* pp. 515 f. n. 38; and his essay, "Abner von Burgos," in *KA,* X. The former contains also a succinct refutation of Abner's willful misconstructions of both letter and intent of Jewish law. The problem of the extent to which, if at all, Abner used the writings by Karaite critics such as Salmon or Hadassi, can be solved only after his works are published and submitted to a minute comparison with Karaite letters. Although repressed in Spain long before, Karaite ideas could well have persisted under the surface to the fourteenth century and after. On the other hand, a talmudically trained propagandist could independently reach similar critical conclusions. In any case, Abner was in the peculiar position of arguing against Jewish law without opposing any accepted doctrines of the Catholic Church, which of course had been of little concern to the Palestinian Karaite assailants of the Talmud. For this reason a more detailed examination of the similarities and dissimilarities between the Karaite works, the "enlightened" antinomian arguments, and the dogmatically restricted critique by Abner, should yield interesting results for the history and psychology of religious polemics.

33. Moses b. Joshua Narboni (Vidal Blascom), *Ha-Ma'amar bi-Beḥirah* (Treatise on Free Will), ed. by E. Aschkenazi in *Dibre ḥakhamim* (Words of the Wise: a collection of manuscript sources), pp. 37, 40 f., with the comments thereon by S. Munk in his *Mélanges de philosophie juive et arabe,* p. 502 n. 1; and by H. Graetz in the still very informative Note 13 of his *Geschichte,* VII, 450. The majority of Spanish Jews may not have shared Narboni's insistence upon man's full freedom of choice and his general Averroist orientation. Yet they doubtless shared his objections to Abner's fatalistic doctrine, as well as to the renegade's unbridled attacks on Jewish tradition.

34. Ibn Verga, *Shebeṭ Yehudah,* vii, ed. by Wiener, pp. 14, 24 (Hebrew), 26, 47 (German); ed. by Shohet, pp. 34, 45. This lengthy dialogue between the king and Thomas, in many ways the most interesting section of the whole book, goes over many of the controversial issues which agitated the minds of Jews and Christians in

Spain shortly before the expulsion. Although writing several decades later, the apologist caught the spirit of the main fifteenth-century debates. Of course, by portraying a moderate Christian rather than an extremist of the type of Ferrant Martinez, Vicente Ferrer, or De Spina, Ibn Verga failed to reproduce the more heated arguments of the rabid Jew-baiters of both the intellectual and the popular variety. Since the *Shebeṭ Yehudah* covers much ground of both factual history and imaginary debate, it will engage our attention in various other connections. See also Baer, *Untersuchungen über Quellen und Komposition des Shebet Jehuda,* esp. pp. 61 ff.

35. Ibn Verga, *Shebeṭ Yehudah,* lxiii, ed. by Wiener, pp. 95 (Hebrew), 195 (German); ed. by Shohet, p. 127, etc.; K. Eubel, "Weitere Urkunden," *Römische Quartalschrift,* XVII, 186; the excerpts from anonymous Jewish apologetic works in E. Urbach's "Etudes," *REJ,* C, 66, 70 f. Another altercation on the subject of confession, in which Nathan Official tried to explain to the "pope" an apparent contradiction between Ps. 32:1 and Prov. 28:13, is recorded in an excerpt from "Le Livre de Joseph le Zélateur," cited by Z. Kahn in *REJ,* III, 24 f. (Hebrew and French). In the censure of his coreligionists Ibn Verga had "Thomas" quaintly explain the Jewish prohibition of pork, fat, and blood by the effect of these foods on the increase of sexual appetite. "The Jews, prone to fornication, as the Creator testified [by addressing them], 'Wherefore, O harlot, hear the word of the Lord!' [Ezek. 16:35], had to be warned and prevented from consuming foods increasing lust. But the Christians, because of their self-control and perfection, adapt everything to their character, just as honey turns the bitterness of an orange peel into sweetness." See *Shebeṭ Yehudah,* ed. by Wiener, pp. 16 (Hebrew), 29 f. (German); ed. by Shohet, p. 36.

More typical of the Jewish apologias was Ḥayyim ibn Musa's reply to Nicholas de Lyra's stress on the numerous evil deeds of the ancient Israelites recorded in Scripture, which allegedly illustrated the perennial misbehavior of Jews. In his answer Ibn Musa pointed to the record of Christian immoralities which, in his opinion, overshadowed anything mentioned in connection with the ancient Jews. In one case a powerful lord humiliated an underling by forcing him to don a horse's bridle, eat straw, and hold two candles while the lord cohabited with the victim's wife. According to another story, a priest committed adultery with one of his married parishioners in front of a crucifix, whereupon the campanile of the church fell off the building of itself and settled some hundred ells away. "No such abomination is recorded in any prophecy of the entire Scripture!" See Ibn Musa's *Magen ve-romaḥ,* cited from the Breslau MS by D. Kaufmann in *Beth Talmud,* II, 114; and on similar earlier altercations, *supra,* Vol. V, pp. 133 f., 351 nn. 66–67. Controversies over the comparative superiority in the ethical behavior of Christians and Jews naturally ranged over so vast a field of human relations that they will necessarily crop up in various contexts of our forthcoming presentation. See esp. *infra,* Chap. XLIX.

36. Ibn Verga, *Shebeṭ Yehudah,* vii, ed. by Wiener, pp. 12 (Hebrew), 22 f. (German); ed. by Shohet, p. 32. On the popular preachers see *infra,* n. 37; *supra,* Chap. XXXVIII, n. 43; and such monographs as L. Luszczki, "La Predicazione del B. Matteo d'Agrigento a Barcellona e Valenza," *AFH,* XLIX, 255–351.

37. Meir b. Simon, *Milḥemet miṣvah* (Obligatory War), cited from a Parma MS by A. Neubauer and reproduced *supra* Vols. IV, pp. 224, 352 n. 94; V, pp. 128, 348

n. 59; H. Gross's biographical sketch, "Meir ben Simon und seine Schrift Milchemet Mizwa," *MGWJ*, XXX, 295–305, 444–52, 554–69; S. Stein's trans. and observations in "A Disputation on Moneylending," *JJS*, X, 45 ff.; Jacob b. Elija's *Iggeret*, ed. by Kobak in *Jeschurun*, VI, Hebrew section, pp. 16 f., with the comments thereon by J. Mann in "Une Source de l'histoire," *REJ*, LXXXII, 376 f.

38. On the Italian preachers see, for instance, D. Pacetti, "Le Prediche autografe di S. Giacomo della Marca (1393–1476) con un saggio delle medesime," *AFH*, XXXV, 296–327, esp. p. 324 No. 101; A. Ghinato, "Apostolato religioso e sociale di S. Giacomo della Marca in Terni," *AFH*, XLIX, 106–42, 352–90; and G. Tiraboschi, *Storia della letteratura italiana*, Milan, 1822–24 ed., IX, 1670. The popularity of Bernardino de' Busti's *Rosarium sermonum praedicabilium* is attested by the still extant numerous copies of editions printed in Venice, 1498, Hagenau, 1500, Lyons, 1502, etc. See also *supra*, Chap. XXXVII, n. 61.

39. Ḥayyim b. Yehudah ibn Musa, *Magen ve-romaḥ*, ed. by D. Kaufmann in *Beth Talmud*, II, 110–25. See also Loeb's observation in "Polémistes chrétiens," *REJ*, XVIII, 230 f. Ibn Musa's puzzling reference to *Paulina* by Samuel [Solomon] ha-Levi, or Paul of Burgos, was doubtless aimed at the latter's *Dialogus Pauli et Sauli contra Judaeos*, the first part of his *Scrutinium*, published in Rome, *ca.* 1469; but probably circulating in manuscript form ever since 1432. See *supra*, n. 20. Writing in 1456, Ibn Musa pays particular attention to the problem of authoritative sources. He repudiates even the Aggadah as often reproducing historically worthless fantasies. It is small wonder then that Ibn Musa, just as Yom Ṭob Lipmann-Mühlhausen did half a century before him, concentrated on commenting on Old Testament verses which had long been under dispute. He thus intended to invalidate the widely accepted Christian exegesis of Nicholas de Lyra's *Postilla*. On another occasion, it may be noted, it was Abner's turn to deny the authority of Josephus. See his first epistle in his controversy with Joseph Shalom, ed. by J. Rosenthal in *Neuman Jub. Vol.*, pp. 591 f. The new appreciation of historical arguments came to the fore even more strongly in the *Shebeṭ Yehudah* by Ibn Verga. Here we have an avowed mixture of apologetics and history, where historic fact and religious argumentation are often indistinguishably blended. As such Ibn Verga's work constitutes a part of the new Jewish historiography which will be analyzed in a later chapter.

40. Martini, *Pugio fidei*, Preface, in Carpzov's ed. p. 20; O. Gierke, *Das deutsche Genossenschaftsrecht*, esp. Vol. III; idem, *Political Theories of the Middle Age*, trans. with an Intro. by F. W. Maitland. See also, from another angle, K. W. Deutsch's suggestive essay, "Anti-Semitic Ideas in the Middle Ages: International Civilizations in Expansion and Conflict," *Journal of the History of Ideas*, VI, 239–51.

# CHAPTER XL: SERF OF THE CHAMBER

1. Augustine, *Civitas dei*, iv.34; *Sermones*, 374, 2; *Enarrationes in Psalmos*, 40:14, 56:9, 136:18; *Locutiones in Heptaeuchum*, i.73, all in *Opera Omnia, PL*, XXXIV, 567; XXXVI, 463, 666; XXXVII, 1771 f., XXXIX, 1666 f.; XLI, 140; and other sources cited *supra*, Vol. II, pp. 168 f., 298 f., 395 n. 2; Seventeenth Toledan Council, canon 8, in Mansi's *Sacrorum Conciliorum collectio*, XII, 102 ff. (only summarized in Hefele, *Histoire des Conciles*, III, Part 1, p. 587; and in the English trans. by W. R. Clark, V, 247 f.). Characteristically, however, the Toledan canon was not played up in the *Decretum Gratiani*, although other decisions of the Toledan councils were extensively cited by this twelfth-century codifier. See *supra*, Vols. II, pp. 168 f., 395 n. 52; III, pp. 42 f.; IV, pp. 17 ff., 241 f. nn. 18–19. Certainly, neither Gratian nor the other compilers of the *Corpus* wished by emphasizing "perpetual" serfdom to convey the idea that Jews were personally unfree. On this connotation of "perpetuity" at least in some medieval writings, see K. Pivec, "Servus und Servitium in den frühmittelalterlichen Salzburger Quellen," *Festgabe dargebracht Harold Steinacker*, pp. 55–66, esp. p. 65.

2. See the sources cited *supra*, Vols. III, pp. 27 ff., 242 ff.; IV, pp. 6 ff., 17, 235 n. 2, 240 f. n. 17. The struggle between Papacy and Empire and, more generally, the expansion of the papal power and aspirations have been debated for many decades. Contemporary scholars have evinced particular interest in the rationales advanced by medieval statesmen, theologians, and jurists, and their impact on the entire political life and thinking of medieval Europe. Apart from the numerous older treatments, well summarized by R. W. Carlyle and A. J. Carlyle in *A History of Mediaeval Political Theory in the West*, esp. Vol. V, see the recent studies by W. Ullmann, *Medieval Papalism: the Political Theories of the Medieval Canonists*, and *The Growth of Papal Government in the Middle Ages;* and by E. H. Kantorowicz, *The King's Two Bodies: a Study in Mediaeval Political Theology*. Of considerable interest also are the excerpts from contemporary sources and the introductions thereto in E. Lewis, *Medieval Political Ideas*, esp. Vol. II.

3. Innocent III's bull, *Sicut Judaeis*, of September 15, 1199, and his letter to the Archbishop of Sens and the Bishop of Paris of July 15, 1205 in his *Epistolae*, ii.302, viii.121 in *PL*, CCXIV, 864 f.; CCXV, 694 f.; or in Grayzel, *The Church and the Jews in the XIIIth Century*, pp. 92 ff. No. 5, 114 ff. No. 18. On Innocent's general attitude to Jews and Judaism see *supra*, Vol. IV, pp. 10, 16 f., 240 n. 16; Chap. XXXVII, nn. 7, 8, 12, 18; and the extensive literature cited there. See also H. Tillmann's biography of *Papst Innocenz III;* and *infra*, n. 4.

4. Innocent III's address to the Consistory at the reception of Philip of Swabia's delegation (end of 1199 or beginning of 1200) reproduced in F. Kempf's ed. of *Regestum Innocentii III papae super negotio Romani imperii*, pp. 48 f.; Gregory IX's and Innocent IV's bulls cited *supra*, Chap. XXXVII. The use of biblical quotations in support of any political argument was of course no novelty at that

time. In this particular matter see M. Hackelsperger's dissertation, *Bibel und mittelalterlicher Rechtsgedanke. Studien und Beiträge zum Gebrauch der Bibel im Streit zwischen Kaisertum und Papstum zur Zeit der Salier*. Curiously, despite the efforts of generations, not all the bulls of those important popes have thus far been published. See, for instance, F. Kempf's "Zu den Originalregistern Innocenz' III. Eine kritische Auseinandersetzung mit Friedrich Bock," *Quellen und Forschungen aus italienischen Archiven und Bibliotheken*, XXXVI, 86–137; L. Santifaller's review of the *Neuere Editionen mittelalterlicher Königs- und Papsturkunden*; and the publications listed *supra*, Chap. XXXVII, nn. 12 and 18.

Apart from new documentary finds, the attitude of the popes, particularly of the successors of Innocent III, toward the Jews, would bear further investigation. On the impact of their teachings on the development of Jewish serfdom, see my essay, "'Plenitude of Apostolic Powers' and Medieval 'Jewish Serfdom'" (Hebrew), *Baer Jub. Vol.*, pp. 102–24 (with an English summary *ibid.*, p. xi). See also, more generally, F. Kempf, *Papstum und Kaisertum bei Innocenz III*, which includes a careful analysis of Innocent's guiding principle that "principaliter et finaliter negotium imperii ad sedem apostolicam pertinet" (pp. 57 ff.); and A. Hof, "'Plenitudo potestatis' und 'Imitatio imperii' zur Zeit Innocenz' III," *ZKG*, LXVI, 39–71. This papal extremism had long been prepared by the teachings of both theologians and canonists. See esp. P. A. van den Baar's dissertation, *Die Kirchliche Lehre der Translatio Imperii Romani bis zur Mitte des 13. Jahrhunderts*; A. M. Stickler's "Imperator vicarius papae. Die Lehren der französich-deutschen Dekretistenschule des 12. und beginnenden 13. Jahrhunderts über die Beziehungen zwischen Papst und Kaiser," *MIOG*, LXII, 165–212 (largely based on medieval manuscripts); his bibliographical survey of the earlier writings in his "Sacerdozio e Regno nelle nuove ricerche attorno ai secoli XII e XIII nei Decretisti e Decretalisti fino alle decretali di Gregorio IX" in F. Kempf, ed., *Sacerdozio e Regno da Gregorio VII a Bonifacio VIII*, pp. 1–26; and other essays in that volume.

5. See *supra*, Vol. IV, pp. 48 ff., 260 ff. nn. 62–68, esp. n. 66. The main exponent of the nexus between the Teuton "law of aliens" and medieval Jewish status has been J. E. Scherer in *Die Rechtsverhältnisse der Juden in den deutsch-österreichischen Ländern*, pp. 3 ff., 62 ff. To be sure, he could not prove this nexus in the minds of the Carolingian rulers, their early successors, or the contemporary jurists or theologians. Nevertheless with the populace at large increasingly viewing the Jews as a body of aliens, some contemporaries may thus have explained the extraordinary position of their Jewish neighbors and particularly their need for royal protection and special taxes. However, this consideration, if it ever was voiced in authoritative circles, was neither responsible for the origin of the peculiar Jewish status nor did it ever significantly influence the legal and political destinies of medieval Jewry, which were shaped by other, more fundamental factors. Yet, this semiconscious element need not, for this reason, be dismissed out of hand, as is sometimes done by Scherer's opponents. See also, more generally, H. Thieme, "Die Rechtsstellung der Fremden in Deutschland vom 11. bis zum 18. Jahrhundert," *Recueils* of the Société Jean Bodin, X, 201–216; and J. Gilissen, *ibid.*, pp. 231–331 (on Belgium).

6. Henry IV's Epistle of March 27, 1076; and Bishop Rüdiger-Huozmann's letter to the priests of Lombardy in L. Wieland, ed., *Constitutiones et acta publica imperatorum et regum*, I, 110 f. No. 62, 117 f. No. 69 (also *ibid.*, pp. 111 ff. No. 63). See

also the sharp antipapal declaration of twenty-six bishops, including Huozmann, of Jan. 24, 1176, in C. Erdmann and N. Fickermann, eds., *Briefsammlungen der Zeit Heinrichs IV*, pp. 46 ff. No. 20. The decrees issued by bishop and emperor in 1084–90 have long been known, and are readily accessible in the excerpts of J. Aronius, *Regesten*, pp. 69 ff. Nos. 168, 170–71. We must bear in mind, however, that these documents are preserved only in later copies. In particular, the important privilege for Worms Jewry is extant only in its confirmation by Frederick I in 1157, and it is quite possible that the crucial phrase concerning the imperial Chamber was inserted by Barbarossa in the light of the intervening evolution. But there is no compelling reason for denying the invention of that phrase by Henry IV. See the 1952–53 edition by D. von Gladiss of *Die Urkunden Heinrichs IV*, esp. pp. 543 ff. Nos. 411–12. On the extensive discussions concerning these important texts see the literature cited *supra*, Vol. IV, pp. 67 ff., 117 f., 272 f. nn. 86 ff., 299 n. 38.

7. Aronius, *Regesten*, pp. 123 No. 280, 139 ff. No. 314a; E. Täubler, "Urkundliche Beiträge zur Geschichte der Juden in Deutschland im Mittelalter," *Mitteilungen des Gesamtarchivs der deutschen Juden*, IV, 31–62, 186; V, 127–48, esp. IV, 32 ff., 44 f. Although it is possible that the rhetorical introduction to the Ratisbon privilege (cited more fully *supra*, Vol. IV, p. 72) may have been found in the document underlying the confirmation, its style does bear the imprint of Frederick's personality. See *supra*, Vol. IV, p. 274 n. 92. In all these matters the impact of the struggle with the Papacy must be fully borne in mind. See esp. the more recent biographies of the two protagonists by R. Wahl, *Kaiser Friedrich Barbarossa*, 3d ed.; and M. Pacaut, *Alexandre III, étude sur la conception du pouvoir pontifical dans sa pensée et son oeuvre;* and, from another angle, W. Herold's unpublished dissertation, *Die Canones des 3. Lateran-Konzils (1179)*. Nor was the example of the Byzantine Empire with its "caesaropapism" and the far-reaching claim of the Eastern Roman emperors to world supremacy lost on the Hohenstaufen dynasts. See esp. the collected essays by W. Ohnsorge in his *Abendland und Byzanz*.

8. The conflict between Frederick II and Popes Gregory IX and Innocent IV has often been treated. The ideological controversies, too, about the respective ranges of authority have been analyzed in the volumes mentioned *supra*, nn. 2 and 4, to which one might add E. Kantorowicz's *Kaiser Friedrich der Zweite*, esp. pp. 244 ff., 317 ff., 378 ff., 503; together with the *Ergänzungsband* thereto, esp. pp. 111 f., 151, 169 f. (also in the English translation entitled *Frederick the Second, 1194–1250*); and, on Frederick's opponents, J. Felton, *Papst Gregor IX;* and F. Podesta, *Papa Innocenzo IV*. As pointed out in my aforementioned essay in the *Baer Jub. Vol.*, these ideological disputes had considerable bearing on Jews. But little attention has been paid to this aspect even in Kantorowicz's comprehensive biographical work or in the additional observations thereon by A. Stern in his "Kaiser Friedrich II. der Hohenstaufe und die Juden," with an "Ergänzung" by R. Straus, *ZGJD*, II, 68–77. Incidentally, even the emperor's expedition to the Holy Land, where he regained Jerusalem through successful negotiations with the Muslims, was dictated by purely political motives. We have no reason to doubt the veracity of the report by the Muslim envoy, Faḥr ad-Din Yusuf, that Frederick had been quite skeptical about Jerusalem's importance. In this conversation the emperor also supposedly gave vent to his antipapal feelings and contrasted the Muslim choice of relatives of Mohammed to serve as their caliphs with the Christian world's spiritual submission to men

from a "garbage heap." See H. L. Gottschalk, "Die Aulad Šaiḫ aš-šuyuḫ (Banu Hamawiya)," *Wiener Zeitschrift für die Kunde des Morgenlandes,* LIII, 68.

9. Jordanus' accusation cited in Girardus de Fracheto's biographical sketch in his *Vitae fratrum ordinis praedicatorum,* iii.42, 2, ed. by B. M. Reichert, p. 137; Gregory IX's anathema of Frederick II in 1239 reproduced in Raynaldus, *Annales ecclesiastici,* II, 209 ff., esp. pp. 218 f. Nos. xxvi–xxviii; B. Lagumina and G. Lagumina, *Codice diplomatico dei Giudei di Sicilia,* I, 17 ff. Nos. xix-xx (titulus xxvii), 26 ff. No. xxx; Sibṭ ibn al-Jauzi, cited by H. L. Gottschalk in "Der Untergang der Hohenstaufen," *Wiener Zeitschrift für die Kunde des Morgenlandes,* LIII, 269 (also showing the Muslim contemporaries' exaggerated notions of papal power); and *supra,* Vol. V, pp. 103, 336 f. n. 29. The extremes to which both parties were prepared to go are well illustrated by some of Frederick's letters recently made known by H. M. Schaller in "Eine kuriale Briefsammlung des 13. Jahrhunderts mit unbekannten Briefen Friedrichs II (Trier, Stadtbibliothek, Cod. 859/1097)," *DAGM,* XVIII, 171–213, esp. pp. 194 ff. Nos. v-vii, 202 f. No. viii. That the use of the phrase *servi camerae* did not betray any anti-Jewish animus is evident from the entire tenor of this legislation. In fact, Eduard Winkelmann, an eminent student of Frederick II's Sicilian policies, suggested that these measures had been initiated by leading Jews themselves, particularly those of Trani, with whom the emperor was in constant communication. Frederick may also have been influenced by some of the Jewish scholars whom he had attracted to his court in Naples. See E. Winkelmann, *Kaiser Friedrich II,* II, 283; and, more generally, R. Straus, *Die Juden im Königreich Sizilien unter Normannen und Staufern,* esp. pp. 19 ff. But apart from his absolutist proclivities and his attempt to build a unified and centralized state, Frederick was doubtless motivated, particularly also in the Jewish area, by his wish to wrest total control over his Jewish subjects from the Church organs, both local and Roman. It is worth noting that the term *camera,* of which the Sicilian Jews were declared to be serfs, carried broader connotations and was used at times as the equivalent of the *curia,* or the royal court as a whole. See W. E. Heupel, *Der sizilische Grosshof unter Kaiser Friedrich II. Eine verwaltungsgeschichtliche Studie,* pp. 110 ff.

10. Aronius, *Regesten,* pp. 216 ff. Nos. 496–97, 220 ff. Nos. 509–10 and 518, 239 ff. Nos. 556 and 565–68; Grayzel, *The Church,* pp. 218 f. No. 81, 224 ff. Nos. 86–88, 260 f. No. 111, 262 ff. Nos. 113–14, 268 ff. No. 116, 274 f. No. 118. Frederick II's use of the traditional canonical terminology in his Vienna charter of 1237 was by no means a departure from his antipapal line, but rather an effort to make it doubly clear that he was the divinely appointed defender of the Church. It was wholly in accord with his reiterated attempts to preserve for the imperial Crown of Germany and the royal authority of Sicily the exclusive jurisdiction over heretics. His pertinent constitution of Melfi so deeply aroused Gregory IX that he called the emperor "a persecutor of the Church and a destroyer of public liberty." See the pope's letter, dated July 5, 1231 and reprinted in the *Epistolae saeculi XIII,* ed. by C. Rodenberg, I, 357 f. No. 443. See also the summaries in Gregory's *Registres,* ed. by Auvray, I, 430 Nos. 676–78. On Frederick II's memorable intervention against the Blood Accusation see more fully *infra,* Chap. XLIX.

The Vienna Jewish privilege of 1238 was fated, as we shall see, to initiate a most significant new chain of legal evolution all over east-central Europe, just as the preceding decree in favor of the city formed but a link in a long chain of legal enactments affecting its status. See R. Geyer, "Die mittelalterlichen Stadtrechte Wiens," *MIOG*, LVIII, 589–613, which shows, among other matters, that the exclusion of Jews from public office, emphasized by Frederick II in 1237 and repeated in 1247, was not inserted into his similar decrees in favor of the cities of Korneuburg and Krems (p. 610). See also *infra*, n. 17.

11. Gregory IX's letter to the German Church of March 4, 1233 in his *Registres*, ed. by Auvray, I, 658 No. 1159; Innocent IV's letters to the bishop of Marseilles of August 11, 1246, and the archbishop of Vienne of July 23, 1253, in his *Registres*, ed. by E. Berger, I, 317 No. 2128; III, 314 No. 6981 (the 1246 letter is also reproduced in C. Rodenberg's ed. of *Epistulae saeculi XIII*, II, 175 f. No. 236); his letter to the dean of Würzburg of Sept. 25, 1253 summarized in Potthast's *Regesta pontificum*, II, 1246 No. 15143; Aronius, *Regesten*, pp. 202 f. No. 460, 253 f. No. 583; Grayzel, *The Church*, pp. 198 ff. No. 69, 258 ff. No. 109, 292 f. No. 131, 294 ff. No. 133; and *supra*, Chap. XXXVII. Understandably, contemporaries, followed by many historians, failed to comprehend these apparent vagaries in the pro- and anti-Jewish statements by various popes. They readily attributed, therefore, every favorable action to Jewish bribery. Without completely discounting the impact of the generally substantial Jewish contributions to the papal Treasury and of the probable *douceurs* secretly extended by Jewish spokesmen to highly placed personalities at the Roman *curia*, one must always look also for the more fundamental adjustments of the long-range ecclesiastical *Realpolitik* to changing constellations of power.

12. Knowledge of Josephus was quite widespread in the Middle Ages. Less directly available was Hegesippus, but he, too, was not completely overlooked in medieval historiography, which was nurtured directly or indirectly on his folkloristic data. See esp. V. Usani, "Nuovi contributi alla storia delle fortune dell'Egesippo nel medioevo" in *Corona quernea. Festgabe Karl Strecker*, pp. 29–40. We have seen that via Latin literature these ancient tales penetrated even Hebrew letters, particularly Yosephon. On the other hand, medieval scholars as well as chancery officials did not hesitate, whenever the occasion arose, to invent alleged historical facts or even to forge documents in their support. See, for one example, the recent study by H. Goetting, "Papsturkundenfälschungen für die Abteien Werden und Helmstadt," *MIOG*, LXII, 425–46, showing that two papal bulls of 1182 and 1356, respectively, exempting two abbeys from the jurisdiction of the archbishops of Cologne, were outright forgeries. If Goetting is right, these forgers had successfully misled not only medieval jurists, but also critical modern scholars until 1954. See also *supra*, Vol. VI, pp. 188 ff., 417 ff.; and Chap. XXXVII, n. 5.

13. Eike von Repgow, *Sachsenspiegel, Landrecht*, iii.7, 3, ed. by C. G. Homeyer, under the title, *Des Sachsenspiegels erster Teil oder das Sächsische Landrecht*, pp. 306 f.; ed. by K. A. Eckhardt under the title, *Sachsenspiegel Land- und Lehnrecht*, 2nd ed., pp. 112 f., well summarized in Aronius, *Regesten*, pp. 200 f. No. 458; Eike's *Sächsische Weltchronik*, ed. by L. Weiland, pp. 100 ff. See also the analytical studies by K. Zeumer, "Die Sächsische Weltkronik: Ein Werk Eikes von Repgow," *Festschrift für Heinrich Brunner*, pp. 143 f.; H. Ballschmiede, "Die Sächsische Weltkronik," *Niederdeutsches Jahrbuch*, XL, 81–140; and *infra*, n. 14. See also K. A. Eckhardt, "Eine unbekannte Handschrift sächsischer Rechtsbücher," *DAGM*, XIV, 500–504, although the few examples quoted in this brief summary do not indicate any variants in the passages relating to Jews.

14. *Des Schwabenspiegels Landrechtsbuch,* ccxiv.3 and 6, ed. by H. G. Gengler, 2nd ed., pp. 174 f.; summarized in Aronius, *Regesten,* pp. 327 ff. No. 771; Ottokar von Horneck, *Österreichische Reimchronik,* vv. 91239–775, esp. 91276–78, ed. by J. Saemüller, II, 1186 ff. These legal and historical sources have been most carefully reanalyzed by G. Kisch in *The Jews in Medieval Germany,* esp. pp. 34 ff., 153 ff., and the notes thereto. Regrettably, the text of the important Swabian lawbook is not completely dependable. While it is preserved in a multitude of manuscripts, their frequently conflicting versions have created much confusion in scholarly circles. Century-long efforts to prepare a critical text are only now promising to reach a more satisfactory solution. See H. Lentze, "Die Schwabenspiegelausgabe der Öster-reichischen Akademie der Wissenschaften und der Monumenta Germaniae His-torica," *Anzeiger* of the Österreichische Akademie der Wissenschaften, Philos.-hist. Klasse, XCII, 394–404. Substantively, too, the origin of the Josephus legend reported in the German law books is still rather obscure. It has been traced back to somewhat older German writings and even connected with the well-known talmudic legend about R. Johanan b. Zakkai's negotiations with Vespasian in Giṭṭin 56b. See H. Levy, "Josephus the Physician: a Mediaeval Legend of the Destruction of Jerusalem," *Journal of the Warburg Institute,* I, 221–42; and G. Kisch, "A Talmudic Legend as the Source for the Josephus Passage in the Sachsenspiegel," *HJ,* I, 105–18. However, neither explanation is quite satisfactory and, unless one assumes that the additional parts of this story had been invented by partisans of imperial overlord-ship perhaps in the days of Frederick Barbarossa, one would have to postulate some intervening thirteenth-century sources, since lost.

15. A. Werminghoff, *Die Verpfändungen der mittel- und niederrheinischen Reichsstädte während des 13. und 14. Jahrhunderts;* "Notitia de precariis civitatum et villarum (1241)" in J. Schwalm, ed., *Constitutiones et acta publica imperatorum et regum,* III, *MGH,* Leges, Sectio IV, 3, pp. 1 ff.; I. Rösel, "Die Reichssteuern der deutschen Judengemeinden von ihren Anfängen bis zur Mitte des 14. Jahrhunderts," *MGWJ,* LIII, 679–708; LIV, 55–69, 206–23, 333–47, 462–73 (also reprint); and *infra,* Chap. LIV. Frederick's own retreat is analyzed in E. Klingenhöfer's revised Marburg dissertation, *Die Reichsgesetze von 1220, 1231–32 und 1235; supra,* Vol. IV, pp. 22, 243 n. 22; and *infra,* Chap. XLVII. We shall presently see that even in Frederick's lifetime his son, Conrad IV, continued to give away or mortgage some Jewish communities and even individuals. See *infra,* n. 19. Significantly, this type of im-perial property was not considered sufficiently important or universally accepted to require in each case the German princes' consent for its alienation to other masters. With or without consent, however, such alienation proceeded apace. See, for in-stance, K. Frey, *Die Schicksale des königlichen Gutes unter den letzten Staufern seit König Philipp.*

16. See R. Geyer's aforementioned analysis of the parallel imperial and ducal legislation for the city of Vienna in *MIOG,* LVIII, 589–613. Four decades later these diverse, even conflicting, origins were often overlooked and the Habsburg rulers readily combined documents stemming from either source. The confirmation by Rudolph in 1286 included two such diverse sections. The two important charters of 1238 and 1244 are fully reproduced and annotated by J. E. Scherer in *Die Rechts-verhältnisse,* pp. 135 ff., 173 ff. According to Scherer (p. 131 n. 2), the imperial decrees for Wiener Neustadt of 1237 and 1247 are but spurious copies of the

emperor's privileges for the city of Vienna. See also the numerous writings relating to the history of the Jews in medieval Austria, mentioned *infra*, Chap. XLI, nn. 2 and 4.

17. Přemysl Ottakar II's decree is reproduced in both the Latin original and a German translation in G. Bondy and F. Dworský, eds., *Zur Geschichte der Juden in Böhmen, Mähren und Schlesien von 906 bis 1620*, I, 17 ff. No. 24, where the extant later medieval manuscripts are briefly reviewed. This decree was reaffirmed by the king in 1268, with special reference to the Jews of the relatively young city of Brünn (Brno) in Moravia (*ibid.*, pp. 31 f. No. 27). Moreover, Ottakar also confirmed the pro-Jewish bulls of Innocent IV, mentioned *supra*, n. 11 (*ibid.*, pp. 23 ff. No. 25). The literature on Bohemian and Moravian Jewry is likewise quite extensive. See esp. A. Stein's popular summary, *Die Geschichte der Juden in Böhmen;* B. Bretholz's far more detailed *Geschichte der Juden in Mähren im Mittelalter*, Vol. I (to 1350); and other publications listed *infra*, Chap. XLI, nn. 7–8, 10 and 12. The medieval legal evolution in Hungary and Poland will be analyzed *infra*, Chap. XLII.

18. Aronius, *Regesten*, pp. 249 No. 585, 260 No. 616, 268 No. 637, 284 f. Nos. 682 and 686; and *infra*, Chap. XLIII, n. 65. Aronius slightly mistranslates the passage from the *Annales Wormatienses* by speaking of Richard's confirmation of their rights in Worms as "den christlichen Bürgern und den Juden," whereas the Latin text *civibus christianis et iudeis* is better rendered by "Christian and Jewish burghers." See *infra*, nn. 52–53; and Chap. XLVII. That the Worms Jews still were a politically potent factor may also be seen from William's 1255 letter to the municipal authorities and the burghers of that city, in which he pledged himself to preserve intact and even to amplify the existing privileges so that "not only you, the Christians . . . but also the Jews will rejoice in having submitted to Our regime." (Aronius, p. 259 No. 613.) See also, more generally, A. Kober, "Die deutschen Kaiser und die Wormser Juden," *ZGJD*, V, 134–51. The treaty of 1256 is reproduced in *MGH, Constitutiones*, ed. by L. Wieland, II, 611 ff. No. 444; and summarized in Aronius's *Regesten*, p. 291 No. 706. On the older treaties, see *supra*, Vol. IV, pp. 70, 72, 274 f. nn. 90, 93; and J. Gernhuber's analysis of *Die Landfriedensbewegung in Deutschland bis zum Mainzer Reichslandfrieden von 1235*, esp. pp. 95 ff., 133 ff.; with G. Kisch's review thereof in the *Tijdschrift voor Rechtsgeschiedenis*, XXI, 359–65. On the continued weakening of imperial control see also the other examples cited by O. Stobbe in *Die Juden in Deutschland*, pp. 19 ff. Similar earlier developments in France are analyzed by H. Hoffmann, with special reference to the *Gottesfriede und Treuga Dei*.

19. Aronius, *Regesten*, pp. 230 f. No. 534, 249 No. 583; Meir b. Baruch, *Resp.*, Berlin, 1891–92 ed., pp. 20 No. 150, 286 f. No. 348; Lwów, 1860 ed., fol. 35b No. 381. Conrad's mortgage of the city of Rothenburg along with the Jews underscored the fact that this was merely the transfer of a *regalium*, or a specific source of revenue, without in any way affecting the freedom of the persons concerned. It so happened that soon thereafter Rothenburg, through its rabbi Meir b. Baruch, was to occupy a focal position in German Jewry. On the emperor's much-discussed retention of that rabbi's corpse for some fourteen years as security for Jewish tax arrears, see *infra*, Chap. LIV. See also H. Breslau, "Zur Geschichte der Juden in Rothenburg an der Tauber," *ZGJD*, [o.s.] III, 301–36; IV, 1–17.

20. Wiener, *Regesten*, pp. 9 ff. Nos. 51, 54, 57, 60, 62, 64, 74–75; *supra*, Chap. XXXVII, n. 7; G. Bondy and F. Dworský, *Zur Geschichte der Juden in Böhmen*, I, 32 ff. No. 27; F. S. Kurz, *Oesterreich unter den Königen Ottakar und Albrecht I*, II, 185 f. App. ix; J. P. Schunck, *Codex diplomaticus [Moguntinus] exhibens chartas historiam medii aevi illustrantes*, pp. 122 ff.; Scherer, *Rechtsverhältnisse*, pp. 78 f., 339 f.; *supra*, n. 16. As Scherer points out, Rudolph, who made a special effort to disavow the legislation of Přemysl Ottakar II, the legitimacy of whose rule he altogether denied, had to fall back on the decree of Duke Frederick II. But he lent it the validity of a Roman imperial law. Yet he did take over from Ottakar's formulation the article (28) relating to Jewish festivals, during which pawns placed with Jewish lenders were not to be redeemed. As German king he also regulated some local affairs in Moravia. Thus, in two decrees of 1278 he proclaimed the principle that the Jews of Brünn and Olmütz (Olomouc) should pay the same taxes as their fellow citizens. Bondy and Dworský, I, 38 Nos. 33–34. See also J. F. Böhmer, ed., *Regesta imperii*, VI (*Die Regesten des Kaiserreichs unter Rudolf, Adolf, Albrecht, Heinrich VII, 1273–1313*), rev. ed. by O. Redlich and V. Samanek, I, 395 No. 1799b, 444 ff. Nos. 2047, 2048 and 2053–54, 468 No. 2153b, 475 No. 2185; O. Redlich, *Rudolf von Habsburg: Das Deutsche Reich nach dem Untergange des alten Kaisertums*, esp. pp. 498 ff.

21. J. P. Schunck, ed., *Codex diplomaticus [Moguntinus]*, pp. 122 f. No. ii. At the same time the emperor ordered the Jewish communities to cooperate with his officials (*ibid.*, pp. 124 f. No. iii). The reason for the Jewish mass flight from the Rhinelands in 1282–83 is not indicated in the source, Schunck suggesting that it had been stimulated by the appearance of a false messiah in Syria. However, H. Graetz has rightly questioned this connection, since we have no other evidence for such a messianic movement at that time. See his *Geschichte*, VII, 422 f. Note ix. It is far more likely that this commotion originated from a local disturbance followed by the archbishop's condemnation of Mayence Jewry in 1282, allegedly confirmed by Emperor Rudolph at a convention of princes in that city in 1283. See Abbot Johannes von Tritheim's *Annales Hirsaugienses*, II, 44 f. At that time Rudolph had ordered that "everything on Jewish property removed [during the disturbance] be delivered to the hands of the procurator of the royal Treasury" under the sanction of capital punishment and prosecution for the crime of *lèse-majesté*. The emperor had allegedly distributed all that revenue among the poor, giving nothing even to the Church, because "the Jewish possessions had been acquired through usury." Rumors of these proceedings, perhaps even more than the original riot in Mayence, may have inspired fears in the neighboring communities and induced many Jews to abandon their property and leave the country. See K. A. Schaab, *Diplomatische Geschichte der Juden in Mainz*, pp. 50 ff. Though extensively reporting both events, Schaab does not perceive the nexus between them. On Graetz's hypothesis that the imprisonment of Meir b. Baruch was the result of the emperor's suspicions aroused by that earlier commotion, see *infra*, Chap. LIV.

22. Wiener, *Regesten*, pp. 14 ff. Nos. 88, 92, 95, 106, 108, 109 and 121; J. F. Böhmer, *Regesta imperii*, VI, Part 2, pp. 22 f. No. 40, 27 No. 56, 81 f. No. 230, 94 f. No. 277, 120 f. No. 365, 276 No. 798, 299 f. No. 857, 352 No. 986; Schaab, *Diplomatische Geschichte*, pp. 62 ff.; and Scherer, *Rechtsverhältnisse*, pp. 345 ff. Adolph's gift to the archbishop of Mayence was increased, in 1297, by the assignment of 300

marks annually from the Jewish revenue in Frankfort as an indemnity for his severe losses during the war. See Wiener, p. 16 No. 101. The curious dichotomy between Albert I's sharp condemnation of the Rindfleisch massacres and the penalties he imposed upon the various cities on the one hand, and the far milder treatment of the community of Korneuburg in Austria by his son Rudolph on the other hand, was not necessarily the result of personal differences between father and son or even of the general contrast between an emperor's behavior in the Reich and that of rulers in their hereditary possessions. It may in part be accounted for by local Korneuburg conditions. We shall see that Duke Rudolph himself proceeded quite severely against the city of St. Pölten. See *infra*, Chap. XLI, n. 2. In all such cases, humanitarian interests were doubtless subordinated to the interests of state and the political ambitions of rulers. On the Rindfleisch massacres and the accusations of the desecration of hosts, see *infra*, Chaps. XLIX and L.

23. Wiener, *Regesten*, pp. 20 ff. Nos. 128–31, 136, 138–42 and 144–46. It was in his capacity as imperial overlord that Henry issued the permits to individual barons to admit Jews. When he allowed his relative, Frederick von Schleiden, to take Jews into his castle, he emphasized that this was done to improve the latter's fief in the empire (1309). Neither here nor even in his outspoken grant to the bishop of Eichstädt did he really relinquish his ultimate imperial authority over all Jews. See Wiener, pp. 21 f. Nos. 135–36.

24. The anonymous "Vita Ludovici Quarti imperatoris, 1312–1347" in J. F. Böhmer's ed. of *Fontes rerum germanicarum*, I, 156; Wiener, *Regesten*, pp. 44 f. Nos. 136–37; and *infra*, Chaps. XLI, n. 13; and XLVI. On Frederick the Handsome, see Wiener, pp. 47 f.; Scherer, *Rechtsverhältnisse*, pp. 356 ff. Because of the protracted war between the two opposing monarchs, Frederick rewarded some of his partisans with the proceeds of Jewish taxes in the area under his authority. For instance, in 1320 he indemnified the bishop of Salzburg for his war losses by assigning him 800 marks from the Jewish revenue in Vienna—which did not imply, however, Frederick's renunciation of all controls over the Jews of Salzburg, as suggested by A. Altmann in his *Geschichte der Juden in Stadt und Land Salzburg*, pp. 64 f., 201.

25. Wiener, *Regesten*, pp. 25 ff., 50 Nos. 136–37; A. Bierbach, ed., *Urkundenbuch der Stadt Halle*, II, 384 No. 642a. In 1322, Louis mortgaged to King John of Bohemia the city and district of Eger (Cheb) together with a number of fortresses, cloisters, and Jews, in recognition of John's war services and of the substantial payment of 20,000 marks. John proceeded immediately to reassure the Eger burghers that their rights would be maintained and added, "We also do you the favor of making the Jews of Eger serve Us together with the city," which evidently meant that, in addition to whatever Jewish taxes they paid, the Jews would also contribute their proportionate share to the city's payments to the Treasury. Yet two years later Louis, as duke of Bavaria, allowed an Eger Jew to settle in the city of Nabburg, promising the new arrival that he would enjoy the same rights as the Jews of Nuremberg. There is no evidence that he had first ascertained whether that individual had met all his obligations to either the municipality or the Jewish community of Eger. See Bondy and Dworský, *Zur Geschichte*, I, 46 Nos. 53-55; *infra*, Chap. XLI, n. 13; and, more generally, F. von Weech's Munich dissertation, *König Ludwig*

*der Bayer und König Johann von Böhmen.* On the Armleder disturbances, see *infra,* Chap. L.

26. J. F. Böhmer, *Regesta imperii,* VIII (*Die Regesten des Kaiserreichs unter Kaiser Karl IV, 1346–1378*), ed. by A. Huber, pp. 42 No. 464, 62 No. 751, etc., and Huber's *Erstes Ergänzungsheft* thereto in the numerous passages listed in the Index, p. 819 *s.v.* Juden; Wiener, *Regesten,* pp. 126 f., 223 ff.; Bondy and Dworský, *Zur Geschichte,* I, 56 ff. Nos. 94–98, 113; A. Stein, *Die Geschichte der Juden in Böhmen,* pp. 13 ff., 22 ff.; and, more generally, E. Werunsky's comprehensive, though incomplete, *Geschichte Kaiser Karls IV und seiner Zeit,* esp. II, 239 ff.; and G. Groveland Walsh, *The Emperor Charles IV, 1316–1378: a Study in Holy Roman Imperialism.* Despite his efforts to establish, with the aid of Trostlin and Samuel, a more efficient system of tax collections from Jews (see the text of the decree dated September 9, 1348 published by M. Stern in his *König Ruprecht von der Pfalz in seinen Beziehungen zu den Juden,* pp. xxvii ff.), Charles was extremely lavish in giving away his Jewish revenue. Curiously, on the same day Charles issued another lengthy document transferring all imperial "Bussen und Besserungen" to Archbishop Baldwin (published in full, *ibid.,* pp. xxxvi ff.). He also freely canceled debts owed to Jews; for example, by the Burgraves John and Albert of Nuremberg, and Bishop Markwart of Augsburg (1347). At the same time, he did not reduce any taxes due from Nuremberg Jewry but, within a few days, he insisted that it deliver 200 pounds heller to the burghers for the purchase of lumber for the castle. See Wiener, *Regesten,* pp. 31 No. 209, 126 f. Nos. 175, 177 and 183.

27. Böhmer and Huber, *Regesta imperii,* VIII, 71 Nos. 868–69; Wiener, *Regesten,* pp. 127 ff., 224 ff. The privilege in favor of Eger is cited by Stein (in his *Geschichte,* pp. 28 ff.), together with a German translation, from the Latin original in Eger's municipal archives. It must be borne in mind, however, that even while providing in his Golden Bull that "all the princes electors should be free to have Jews and to collect the revenue from customs" (K. Zeumer, ed., *Die Goldene Bulle Kaiser Karls IV,* Art. ix), the emperor clearly indicated by the very juxtaposition of these revenues that he had a purely fiscal renunciation in mind. This was essentially also the tenor of his earlier decree in favor of the city of Worms in 1348, in which he transferred to the burghers "the Jews and the Jewry of Worms with its body and property and all its revenue and all the rights . . . which We and Our ancestors in the Empire . . . have hitherto exercised upon the Jews and Jewry of Worms or might exercise in the future." See G. Wolf, *Zur Geschichte der Juden in Worms,* p. 34 (here the date is 1349); Stobbe, *Die Juden,* pp. 22 f. On the Golden Bull, see also the text, ed. in Latin with a German trans. by K. Müller; and the extensive literature listed by H. Planitz and T. Buyker, eds., in their *Bibliographie zur deutschen Rechtsgeschichte,* pp. 442 ff. Charles IV's unusual liberality largely stemmed from his sense of helplessness in protecting Jews against the popular onslaughts, which also explains his curious anticipatory pardon concerning Jews who "yet might be slain." Clearly, like the rest of the German economy, the Treasury suffered severely from the aftereffects of the great pestilence. It tried to recover some of its losses from the one group in the population which could least afford it—the few Jewish survivors. See E. Kelter, "Das deutsche Wirtschaftsleben des 14. und 15. Jahrhunderts im Schatten der Pestepidemien," *Jahrbücher für Nationalökonomie,* CLXV, 161–208. In any case, the complicated relationships between Charles IV and

the Jews during that portentous period shortly before, during, and after the Black Death would deserve monographic treatment. See *infra*, Chaps. XLIX and L.

28. A. F. Glafey, ed., *Anecdotorum S.R.I. historiam ac ius publicum illustrantium collectio*, p. 494 No. 372; F. Kürschner's observations on "Die Urkunden Herzog Rudolfs IV von Oesterreich (1358–1365). Ein Beitrag zur speciellen Diplomatik," *Archiv für österreichische Geschichte*, XLIX, 1–88; Wiener's *Regesten*, p. 225 Nos. 59–61; and Scherer's *Rechtsverhältnisse*, p. 376. The promise not to admit one another's Jews did not necessarily imply the obligation to "extradite" unlawful entrants. In this respect the Austro-Bohemian treaties were somewhat milder than their French prototypes. That Charles IV was not animated here by any antagonism toward Jews is evidenced by his decree, issued but four days later, in which he confirmed the customary rights of Austrian Jews. See Glafey, pp. 501 f.

29. See the documents reproduced by P. von Stetten in his *Geschichte der Heil. Röm. Reichs-Freyen Stadt Augspurg*, I, 127 ff.; and by K. Hegel *et al.* in their ed. of *Die Chroniken der deutschen Städte von 14. bis ins 16. Jahrhundert*, I (Nuremberg), 111 ff.; IV (Augsburg), 166 ff.; and other sources summarized in Wiener's *Regesten*, pp. 152 ff. Nos. 337–38, 357–58. See also the anonymous *Geschichte der Juden in der Reichsstadt Augsburg*, written for the pacification of fellow citizens of Augsburg who were disturbed by the prospect of the resettlement of Jews in the city, esp. pp. 15 f. These radical measures and the ill effects they had on the entire German economy are analyzed by A. Süssmann in *Die Judenschuldentilgungen unter König Wenzel*. See also T. Lindner, *Geschichte des deutschen Reiches unter König Wenzel*, esp. I, 271 ff.; II, 63, 108 ff.; and *infra*, Chap. LIII.

30. Wiener, *Regesten*, pp. 151 ff. Nos. 333–36, 339, 354 and 370. Wenceslaus' lavishness in southwestern Germany was not duplicated in his own Bohemian kingdom; he expected to obtain greater returns there by forcing the debtors to pay his Jewish "serfs" in full. In the very year of 1385 (May 5), he ordered the royal cities of Bohemia to handle Jewish claims "with due justice" and in accordance with the usages of the kingdom. That this circular was not inspired by pure ethics may be seen from his earlier order to the Bohemian judiciary quietly to imprison all Jews in their districts on March 3 at 2 A.M. and to seize all their possessions. A similar command was issued four years later (April 19, 1389) by the deputy treasurer, Sigmund Huler. These Draconian measures were, of course, intended only to extort from the Jews as high a ransom as possible. Otherwise, Wenceslaus was perfectly amenable not only to renew the old Jewish privileges of Přemysl Ottakar II but also to grant, in 1389, full tax exemption to all inhabitants of Eger, in return for a lump sum payment by burghers and Jews of 1,000 schock of Prague groschen. Two years later he even more pointedly ordered that the Jews of Eger, "his serfs of the Chamber," who formed a community (*ein Ding*) with the other burghers, be fully protected and aided in the collection of their loans. See Bondy and Dworský, *Zur Geschichte*, I, 80 ff. Nos. 161–63, 172–74 and 177–79. See also, *infra*, Chap. XLI, n. 9; and the king's 1391 decree of protection for several West-German Jewries, *infra*, n. 47.

31. David b. Solomon Gans, *Ṣemaḥ David* (The Scion of David; a World Chronicle), Part II, Prague, 1592 ed., fol. 93a; Frankfort, 1692 ed., II, 52a. See the fully

documented study by M. Stern, *König Ruprecht von der Pfalz in seinen Beziehungen zu den Juden*. On the expulsion of the Jews from the Palatinate in 1390 and Rupert's role therein see also L. Löwenstein, *Geschichte der Juden in der Kurpfalz*, pp. 15 ff., 19 ff.; and *infra*, Chap. XLI, n. 9. Löwenstein's efforts to place the blame for the expulsion exclusively on the shoulders of Rupert's father, Count-Palatine Rupert II, are plausibly controverted by Stern, pp. xii f. The value of Rupert's privileges, including his two renewals of Wenceslaus' pledge not to cancel Jewish debts, is underestimated by Stern, however. See the text of his privilege for the Jews of Mayence, dated Jan. 9, 1401, in J. Chmel's ed. of *Regesta chronologico-diplomatica Ruperti regis Romanorum*, p. 192 No. 5; and the summaries, *ibid.*, pp. 6 Nos. 95–98, 28 No. 537, 55 No. 981; and other such renewals in Wiener's *Regesten*, pp. 54 ff. Nos. 6–9, 14 and 28; M. Stern, *König Ruprecht*, pp. xv ff.

32. Stern, *König Ruprecht, passim*. In his general condemnation of Rupert, Stern is in sharp contrast to the praise showered upon the emperor by earlier Jewish historians, beginning with David Gans in 1592. True, Gans may not have been fully informed about the medieval developments, and he frequently followed his Christian sources. But he must have heard enough about what happened to his Jewish compatriots in the preceding century to evaluate Rupert by comparison with other monarchs of his age. On the work of this eminent historian and scientist, see our analysis of the Jewish historiography of that period in a later chapter.

33. Wiener, *Regesten*, pp. 175 ff. Nos. 487, 511 and 516, 243 No. 188; Bondy and Dworský, *Zur Geschichte*, I, 95 f. Nos. 210–11; Gans, *Ṣemaḥ David*, Prague, 1592 ed., fol. 94b (Frankfort, 1692 ed., II, fol. 63a). On the various attempts to buttress the collection of imperial taxes and fines through the aid of Jewish spiritual leaders, see M. Stern's carefully documented study, "Der Wormser Reichsrabbiner Anselm," *ZGJD*, V, 157–68, which also supplies some new documentation for Anselm's predecessors. See also W. Altmann, *Die Urkunden Kaiser Siegmunds (1410–1437)* in the numerous entries listed in the Index, *s.v.* Juden; D. Kerler, "Zur Geschichte der Besteuerung der Juden durch Kaiser Sigmund und König Albrecht II," *ZGJD*, [o.s.] III, 1–13, 107–29; M. Ginsburger, "Zur Geschichte der Juden in der Schweiz unter Kaiser Sigismund (1411–1437)," *ZGJD*, IV, 77–82; and, more generally, the older but still highly informative biographical study by J. Aschbach, *Geschichte Kaiser Sigmunds*. Of interest also are the numerous monographs relating to the Councils of Constance and Basel; and on the international background, F. Schoenstedt, "König Siegmund und die Westmächte 1414–1415," *Die Welt als Geschichte*, XIV, 149–64. On Sigismund's relations with Italian Jewry see *infra*, Chap. XLVI.

34. Wiener, *Regesten*, pp. 177 f. No. 497; W. Altmann, *Die Urkunden*, I, 42 f. No. 721. On the other protective provisions of the important decree of April 4, 1416, see *infra*, Chap. XLVII. Independently, Sigismund also acted as king in his hereditary possessions of Hungary, Bohemia, and the adjacent lands. Here, too, as we shall see, he yielded to local pressures, as when in 1419, at the very beginning of his reign in Bohemia after Wenceslaus' death, he had to accede to certain demands of the Bohemian Estates adversely affecting Jewish moneylenders. See Bondy and Dworský, p. 94 No. 205. Later he allowed the city of Eger to expel the Jews in 1430 and to readmit them in 1434, while he opened to them the new township of Neu-Pilsen. See also *infra*, Chap. XLI, n. 10.

35. Wiener, *Regesten,* pp. 194 ff. Nos. 589, 591, 593–94 and 596–97, 244 ff. Nos. 204, 206, 210 and 214; S. Stein, *Geschichte der Juden in Schweinfurt,* pp. 32 f. Albert did not limit his exactions to German Jews; he also authorized an official to collect, "according to old custom," one-third of all Jewish property in his Italian possessions. But there is no evidence that this attempt was in any way successful. Wiener, p. 246 No. 216. (In "Zur Geschichte," *ZGJD,* [o.s.] III, Kerler ignores that phase of imperial taxation.) See also other data made available in H. Koller's ed. of *Das Register König Albrechts II (1438–39).* On Albert's much longer regime in Austria (as Albert V), during which time Jews were expelled from Vienna in 1421, see *infra,* Chap. XLI, n. 4. Not surprisingly, a contemporary Austrian chronicler wrote an "epitaph" after Albert's death in 1439, in which he extolled the duke's burning of the Jews *(Jussi Judaeos ante cremare meos)* along with his defense against the Turks and his struggle against the Hussites. See *Anonymi Mellicensis breve chronicon Austriae,* in H. Pez's ed. of *Scriptores rerum Austriacarum veteres ac genuini,* II, 462; Scherer, *Rechtsverhältnisse,* p. 419.

36. Wiener, *Regesten,* pp. 82 ff. Nos. 32, 34 and 36–37, 246 No. 214; Scherer, *Rechtsverhältnisse,* pp. 422 ff.; Albert Achilles' statement in P. E. Spiess, *Archivalische Nebenarbeiten und Nachrichten,* I, 127 f. See also his earlier statement cited *infra,* Chap. XLVII. The two extant receipts dated in 1441 (?) and 1453 for the payment of the coronation tax by a Nuremberg Jew, which Hugo Barbeck considered identical, preferring the latter date, were more likely independent receipts for the two coronation taxes. See his *Geschichte der Juden in Nürnberg und Fürth,* p. 16.

37. Wiener, *Regesten,* pp. 78 ff., 247 ff.; Scherer, *Rechtsverhältnisse,* pp. 422 ff. On the summons of the Jewish representatives in 1434, 1453, 1470, as well as under Frederick's successor in 1510, see the documents published by Kerler and H. Bresslau in *ZGJD,* [o.s.] III, 123 ff., 315 ff.; and by M. Stern in "Die Versammlung zu Worms im Jahre 1510," *ibid.,* pp. 248 ff. The support given by the city of Frankfort (as well as other municipalities) to the Jewish resisters was in line with its action at the earlier gathering of Jewish representatives, convoked for similar purposes by Albert II at the Diet of Nuremberg in 1438. At that time the Frankfort council specifically instructed its envoy to the Diet to seek as substantial a reduction as possible in the assessment of its Jewry. See the text in J. Janssen's ed. of *Frankfurts Reichscorrespondenz nebst andern verwandten Aktenstücken von 1376–1519,* I, 468 No. 835.

Four years later it was Nuremberg's turn to resist the encroachments of Frederick's officials in assessing the coronation tax upon the local Jewish community. The royal collectors had first demanded the huge total of 20,000 florins. When, at the insistence of the municipal elders, this amount was halved and yet the Jews continued to resist, the royal treasurer ordered the imprisonment of the entire community, "young and old," and the seizure of all their property. Only after another intervention by the municipality was an agreement reached that the Jews be freed after taking an oath that "they would not remove their bodies and possessions [to another locality] without the consent and the will of the Council." Needless to say, such interventions were not entirely disinterested. By advancing 1,000 florins due from her Jews, the city of Mühlhausen not only secured the promise that no further imperial taxes would be exacted from that Jewry for five years, but she was also given free rein to tax it for her own benefit. See K. Hegel, ed., *Die Chroniken der deutschen Städte,* III (Nuremberg), 374 f.; Wiener, pp. 81 ff. Nos. 23, 36; and other data cited by Stobbe in *Die Juden,* pp. 18 f., 60 f., 204 f. n. 19. See also I. Kracauer, *Geschichte der Juden in Frankfurt,* I, 180 ff., 225 ff.

38. Nicholas V's bull of 1451 and Frederick's decree of June 22, 1470 are reproduced by Scherer in his *Rechtsverhältnisse,* pp. 436 ff. See his notes thereon, pp. 425 n. 1, 431 n. 1; his general analysis of Frederick's Jewish policies, *ibid.,* pp. 422 ff.; and *infra,* Chap. XLI, nn. 5–6. See also I. Kracauer, "L'Affaire des Juifs d'Endingen de 1470: Pretendu meurtre des Chrétiens par des Juifs," *REJ,* XVI, 244; and H. Strack, *The Jew and Human Sacrifice,* English translation from the 8th German edition, pp. 260 ff. (pointing out that Frederick's decree was also confirmed by several later emperors from 1544 to 1665).

39. Frederick's authorization for Count Ulrich of Württemberg of July 20, 1465, reproduced in Wiener's *Regesten,* pp. 101 f. App. vi; the Bavarian chronicle cited by J. J. Schudt in his *Jüdische Merckwürdigkeiten,* IV, 232; Matthias Döring, *Continuatio chronici Theodorici Engelhusii,* ed. by J. B. Mencken in his *Scriptores rerum Germanicarum,* III, 10; and *supra,* Chap. XXXVII, n. 38. On Frederick's Austrian policies see *infra,* Chap. XLI, nn. 5–6. It is truly remarkable how effectively the emperor resisted the various pressures on the part of the Austrian Estates and such influential leaders as the historian, diplomat, and preacher, Thomas Ebendorfer de Haselbach. Among Ebendorfer's numerous writings is a tract, *De Judaeorum et Christianorum communione et conuersatione ac constitionum super hac re innouatione,* in which he espoused a fifteen-point program of discrimination against Jews, all supported by extensive quotations from older sources. This rare incunabulum was consulted by me at the National Library in Vienna. Other anti-Jewish tracts by Ebendorfer, still extant in part in autograph manuscripts, are listed by A. Lhotsky in his *Thomas Ebendorfer: ein österreichischer Geschichtsschreiber, Theologe und Diplomat des 15. Jahrhunderts,* pp. 73 No. 36, 90 Nos. 172–74. See also *infra,* Chap. XLI, n. 5; and, more generally, A. Bachmann, *Deutsche Reichsgeschichte im Zeitalter Friedrichs III und Maximilians I* (covers only the period of 1461–86); F. Tremel, "Studien zur Wirtschaftspolitik Friedrichs III. 1435–1453," *Carinthia,* I, 549–80.

40. Joseph ha-Kohen, '*Emeq ha-bakha* (Valley of Tears: a chronicle), ed. by M. Letteris, p. 92; in Wiener's German trans., p. 73; M. Stern in *ZGJD,* [o.s.] III, 248 ff.; I. Kracauer, *Geschichte der Juden in Frankfurt,* I, 180 ff.; S. Stern, *Josel von Rosheim;* A. Würfel, *Historische Nachrichten von der Judengemeinde . . . Nürnberg,* pp. 149 ff.; H. Barbeck, *Geschichte der Juden in Nürnberg,* pp. 31 ff.; Wiener, *Regesten,* pp. 208 ff. Nos. 690 and 692–98. According to E. Mummenhoff, the brief of the Nuremberg lawyers of 1496, mentioned in the protocols of the City Council, is no longer extant. See "Die Juden in Nürnberg bis zu ihrer Austreibung im Jahre 1499" (1908), reprinted in his *Gesammelte Aufsätze und Vorträge,* I, 301–34, esp. p. 328. Although Maximilian had to consent to the expulsion of the Jews from Styria, he simultaneously instructed the officials of other localities (Marcheck, Eisenstadt) to admit the Styrian exiles. See Scherer, *Rechtsverhältnisse,* pp. 441 ff., 492 ff.; F. Ilwof, "Kaiser Maximilian I und die Vertreibung der Juden aus Steiermark," *Forschungen zur deutschen Geschichte,* X, 654–55; and *infra,* Chap. XLI, n. 6. See also W. Winker's biography of *Kaiser Maximilian I. zwischen Wirklichkeit und Traum;* and on the changing evaluation of his personality and achievements, H. Wiesflecker,

"Das Bild Maximilians I in der deutschen Geschichtsschreibung," *Österreich in Geschichte und Literatur*, I, 142–55.

41. Aronius, *Regesten*, pp. 245 No. 574, 327 ff. No. 771; V. F. von Gudenus, *Codex diplomaticus exhibens anectoda [sic] res Moguntiaca . . . illustrantia*, I, 514 f. No. ccccxxxiii; II, 254 No. ccii, 277 ff. No. ccxxv; *Des Schwabenspiegels Landrechtsbuch*, ed. by Gengler, 2d ed., p. 93 Art. cv, 2; Wiener, *Regesten*, pp. 12 ff. Nos. 72, 74–75, 77, 88, 92 and 109, 28 No. 26; J. F. Böhmer, *Regesta imperii*, VI, ed. by O. Redlich, I, 395 No. 1799b; J. P. Schunck, *Codex diplomaticus*, pp. 121 ff. Nos. i-iii, 215 No. xc; and particularly K. A. Schaab's older but well-documented *Diplomatische Geschichte der Juden zu Mainz und dessen Umgebung, passim*. Albert's decree of 1299 doubtless referred to estates left by victims of the Rindfleisch massacres; it merely confirmed an earlier royal judgment. See also E. Vogt *et al.*, eds., *Regesten der Erzbischöfe von Mainz von 1289–1396*, Section I, Vol. I, Part 1, pp. 99 f. No. 566. On other editions of the *Schwabenspiegel* and its author's strong canonical biases, see G. Kisch, *The Jews in Medieval Germany*, esp. pp. 39 ff.; and *supra*, n. 14. See also S. Salfeld's analysis, "Zur Geschichte des Judenschutzes in Kurmainz," *Philippson Festschrift*, pp. 135–67. Schaab (pp. 51 ff.) quotes some rather dubious contemporary reports about a Blood Accusation of 1282–83, which led to anti-Jewish riots in Mayence and its vicinity and the emperor's condemnation of some alleged Jewish culprits; this despite his confirmation, eight years earlier, of the two papal bulls controverting that accusation. A number of Mayence martyrs of 1283 are indeed recorded in *Das Martyrologium des Nürnberger Memorbuches*, ed. by S. Salfeld, p. 144 f. In his essay in *Philippson Festschrift*, p. 140, Salfeld also mentions other attacks on Mayence Jewry in the years 1281–86, the first attested by a tombstone inscription, published by him. On other Mayence inscriptions, see the publications listed *infra*, n. 52. The constitutional status of the Mayence archbishop during any *interregnum* is analyzed in W. Wendehorst's dissertation, *Das Reichsvikariat nach der Goldenen Bulle* (typescript).

42. Schaab, *Diplomatische Geschichte*, pp. 93 ff.; E. Vogt *et al.*, eds., *Regesten der Erzbischöfe von Mainz*, II section (ed. by F. Wigener), Vol. I, Part 1, p. 101 No. 400; L. Rothschild, *Die Judengemeinden zu Mainz, Speyer und Worms von 1349–1438*, pp. 76 ff., 84 ff.; A. Süssmann, *Das Erfurter Judenbuch (1357–1407)* (reprinted from *MGDJ*, V, 1–126), esp. pp. 21 ff.; A. Jaraczewsky, *Die Geschichte der Juden in Erfurt*, pp. 27 ff., 83 ff. No. vii; S. Neufeld, *Die Juden im thüringisch-sächsischen Gebiet während des Mittelalters* (the second part dealing with the period after 1348 had previously appeared in the *Thüringisch-sächsische Zeitschrift für Geschichte*, IX, 6–16; XII, 66–87; XV, 158–78). On Erfurt and Frankfort see *infra*, Chap. XLI, nn. 26 ff. The story of Mayence Jewry after the Black Death has been carefully reexamined by J. S. Menczel in his *Beiträge zur Geschichte der Juden von Mainz im XV. Jahrhundert*. The origin of the curious Jewish "dice toll" has often been attributed to a misreading of the Gospel story concerning the Roman soldiers' casting lots over Jesus' garments (Matthew 27:35). True, as pointed out by Schaab a century ago, the text of the Vulgate merely spoke of casting lots (*sortem mittentes*) without mentioning dice. However, the medieval mind was prone to identify ancient happenings with contemporary customs, especially if such identification could serve the combined purposes of lowering the dignity of the Jew and creating new revenue. On

this toll see I. Rivkind, "Dice Tax in Connection with the Tax of Disgrace" (Hebrew), *Zion*, I, 37–48; and *infra*, Chap. LIV.

43. Mansi, *Collectio*, XXXII, 131; *supra*, Chap. XXXVII, n. 32; Menczel, *Beiträge*, *passim*. On the background, see A. Gerlich's observations, "Zur Kirchenpolitik des Erzbischofs Johann II und des Domkapitels von Mainz, 1409–17," *Zeitschrift für Geschichte des Oberrheins*, CV, 334–44. Menczel also analyzes the often moot and contradictory sources relating to the expulsion of the Jews in 1438 and their readmission in 1445 (pp. 42 ff.), and summarizes at length the documents relating to the controversy between the archbishop and the municipality in the years 1441–1449 (pp. 110 ff.). The tiny size of the reconstituted Jewish communities in the entire archdiocese under Diethrich's reign may be noted from the relatively small number of families to whom he granted letters of protection. The largest number came from Bingen, where 20 families received such letters. More than a dozen other communities are listed with only 1 to 9 families who received letters valid from one to ten years. In addition, the archbishop also extended some protection to transient Jews. See Menczel, pp. 27 f.

44. L. Ennen and G. Eckertz, *Quellen zur Geschichte der Stadt Köln*, II, 321 f. No. 308 (from the original in the Municipal Archives), 543 No. 495; A. Kober, "Die Kölner Juden von den ältesten Zeiten bis zur Schwelle unseres Jahrhunderts" in Z. Asaria (Helfgott), ed., *Die Juden in Köln von den ältesten Zeiten bis zur Gegenwart*, pp. 34–70, esp. pp. 34 f. The ancient Jewish community of Cologne was undoubtedly victimized during the destruction of the city by the Franks in 456. Whatever reconstruction may have taken place subsequently was largely nullified by the destructive conquest by the Normans in 881. *Ibid.*, p. 36. Nevertheless, there is a good chance that some underground survivals maintained a certain continuity from Roman days in Jewish life as they did in many phases of the city's general evolution. See K. Corsten, "Das Fortleben der Antike im mittelalterlichen Köln," *Jahrbuch des Kölnischen Geschichtsvereins*, XXXIII, 85–98.

The provisions in favor of Jewish judicial autonomy were doubtless inserted on Jewish initiative. An incident which had occurred in Cologne in the days of R. Eliezer b. Joel ha-Levi was later often cited as a legal precedent. A newly elected cantor was invited by the bishop who, to enhance his new position, formally conferred the office upon him. Exclaiming, "It is against my law to secure from you the investiture for the service of our Lord," the cantor resigned. Quoted by Meir b. Baruch in his *Resp.*, Prague, 1608 ed., No. 137 (also in the new impression revised by M. A. Bloch, Budapest, 1895, fol. 22a); Mordecai b. Hillel ha-Kohen, *Sefer Mordecai* on Baba Qamma, No. 107. See I. A. Agus's summary in his *Rabbi Meir of Rothenburg*, II, 491 f. No. 534. It has plausibly been suggested, however, that this incident had happened to R. Eliezer himself upon his election to the rabbinic office in Cologne (*ca.* 1199). See A. Aptowitzer, *Mabo le-Sefer Rabiah* (Introduction to the Book Rabiah by R. Eliezer b. Joel ha-Levi), pp. 16, 220 f.; and other sources cited in my *Jewish Community*, III, 135 f. n. 53.

45. L. Ennen and G. Eckertz, *Quellen zur Geschichte der Stadt Köln*, IV, 82 No. 95, 93 f. Nos. 106–107, 106 ff. Nos. 121–23, 111 f. Nos. 126–27, 181 Nos. 166–67, 249 f. No. 231, 264 ff. No. 251, etc.; L. Korth, "Das Urkundenarchiv der Stadt Köln bis 1396," *Mitteilungen aus dem Stadtarchiv von Köln*, ed. by K. Höhlbaum, I–II, esp.

II, Part 5, pp. 45 f. No. 1033, 60 No. 1173, 77 Nos. 1315–16; O. Doppelfeld, "Die Ausgrabungen im Kölner Judenviertel" in Z. Asaria, *Die Juden in Köln*, pp. 71–145, esp. p. 74; Kober's essay in that volume, pp. 43 f.; and those listed below. The Jewish real estate transactions of the period are fully reviewed by R. Hoeniger and M. Stern in *Das Judenschreinsbuch der Laurenzpfarre zu Köln*.

The gradual transfer of the episcopal authority over Jews to the municipality cannot be completely reconstructed from the extant sources. As late as 1258 Archbishop Conrad insisted that "the burghers have no claim whatsoever [*nihil.....  pertinet*] on his Jews." Yet from the following year on, the city obviously collected taxes from Jews with no archepiscopal objections. See the data analyzed by R. Köbner in *Die Anfänge des Gemeinwesens der Stadt Köln. Zur Entstehung und ältesten Geschichte des deutschen Städtewesens*, pp. 444 ff.; and F. Kreutzkampf's dissertation, *Die Territorialpolitik des Kölner Erzbischofs Heinrich von Virneburg, 1306–1322*, pp. 51 ff., 66 f. Of special interest is K. Bauer's *Judenrecht in Köln bis zum Jahre 1424*.

It may be noted that among the eminent patricians of the Rhenish city was a family called Jude or Judaeus. Very likely its ancestors were of Jewish descent, which it did not try to hide. In the war between the city and the archbishop of 1252, one Daniel Judaeus so distinguished himself that his bravery was recognized even by the hostile archbishop. See the romanticized description in the anonymous *Reimchronik*, ed. by E. von Groote, pp. 121 f.; Godefrit Hagen's *Reimchronik der Stadt Cöln aus dem dreizehnten Jahrhundert*, ed. by E. von Groote with notes and glossary, pp. 168 ff. vv. 4933 ff.; Ennen and Eckertz, II, 401 No. 386, 432 No. 415, 437 No. 418, 612 f. (a brief obituary); III, *passim* (see Index, p. 565 *s.v.* Jude, von). Occasionally the official record stresses that Daniel or one of his relatives was called [*dictus*] "Judaeus." The use of that name, or its equivalents, by many Western Christian families (for the most part of Jewish descent) has long been observed. See the instances quoted by Stobbe in *Die Juden*, pp. 268 f. n. 156. For that reason the Astrugius Judaeus who, after disregarding an ecclesiastical excommunication for more than a year, was forced to submit by Charles I's threat to confiscate his property, need not even have been a convert. See A. de Boüard, *Actes et lettres de Charles I, roi de Sicile*, p. 190 No. 689; and Willy Cohn's observations thereon in *MGWJ*, LXXIV, 433 f. n. 1. See also such stray items as J. F. Böhmer, *Regesta imperii*, VI, rev. ed. by O. Redlich and V. Samanek, pp. 444 No. 2049 (mentioning a "knight Daniel named Jude" under Rudolph I); K. Hegel, *Die Chroniken der deutschen Städte*, XVII (Mayence), pp. 6, 21, 357 (on Helfrich Jude of 1239 and Peder or Peter Jude of 1332); R. Wackernagel and R. Thommen, eds., *Urkunden-buch der Stadt Basel*, VIII, 502 No. 659 (relating to Leutpriester Johann Jud of the church of St. Peter in 1482); and *infra*, Chap. XLVI. One must exercise caution, therefore, in identifying as Jews without further proof persons thus designated in the sources.

Like that of Mayence Jewry, the history of the Jews of Cologne has engaged the attention of many scholars, particularly since the publication a century ago of E. Weyden's *Geschichte der Juden in Köln a. Rh. von den Römerzeiten bis auf die Gegenwart;* and of C. Brisch's *Geschichte der Juden in Cöln und Umgebung aus ältester Zeit bis auf die Gegenwart*, esp. I, 73 ff., 103 ff. Cologne has been fortunate in having preserved many archival materials relating to medieval Jews and particularly to their real estate transactions. Apart from R. Höniger and M. Stern see A. Kober, *Grundbuch des Kölner Judenviertels 1135–1425.* Kober, who had published his dissertation, *Studien zur mittelalterlichen Geschichte der Juden in Köln a. Rhein* as early as 1903, also wrote a comprehensive if semipopular history of the Jews of that city (*Cologne*, in the Jewish Communities Series). See also his "Vier Generationen einer jüdischen Familie am Rhein um 1400," *Festschrift . . . Jacob Freimann*, pp. 106–18; his "Notizen über jüdische Altertümer im Kölner Raum," *Jahrbuch des Kölnischen Geschichtsvereins*, XXVIII, 64–66 (describing recently recovered Jewish tombstones of 1156 and 1306 and a fragment of a fourteen-century Talmud MS); and his "Zwei Kölner hebräische Grabsteine des 14. Jahrhunderts," *ibid.*, XXXI–XXXII, 108–10, 359 (on two additional tombstones dated 1302 and 1323). These publications bring the total of known medieval Cologne Jewish tombstones up to 65. See Kober's more general review of "Jewish Monuments of the Middle Ages in Germany," *PAAJR*, XIV, 149–220; XV, 1–91; and that by E. L. Rapp and O. Böcher, "Die Mittelalterlichen hebräischen Epitaphien des Rheingebiets," *Mainzer Zeitschrift*, LVI–LVII, 155–82. See also *infra*, n. 52. Of considerable interest also are the general documentary collections by T. J. Lacomblet, *Urkundenbuch für die Geschichte des Niederrheins oder des Erzbistums Cöln;* L. Ennen and G. Eckertz's aforementioned ed. of *Quellen zur Geschichte der Stadt Köln;* and the comprehensive publication, begun in 1954 by F. W. von Oediger, *Die Regesten der Erzbischöfe von Köln im Mittelalter*.

46. Ennen and Eckertz, *Quellen zur Geschichte der Stadt Köln*, V, 1 ff. No. 1, etc.; Brisch, *Geschichte der Juden in Cöln*, II, *passim;* Kober, *Cologne*, pp. 43 ff., 118 ff. On the weavers' revolution of 1370 and the restoration of the patrician controls two years later, see esp. C. Hegel, *Verfassungsgeschichte von Cöln im Mittelalter* (reprinted from his ed. of *Die Chroniken der deutschen Städte*, pp. clix f., clxxxvi f.).

47. C. Brisch, *Geschichte der Juden in Cöln*, II, 7 ff., 13 f., 32 ff.; Menaḥem Ṣiyyon b. Meir, *Ṣiyyon meʿon ḥishqi* (Zion, Dwelling of My Delight), in the publications listed by I. Davidson in his *Oṣar ha-shirah* (Thesaurus of Mediaeval Hebrew Poetry), III, 322 f. No. 312; Sigismund's confirmation of the archbishop's rights dated November 8, 1414 in W. Altmann's ed. of *Die Urkunden Kaiser Sigmunds*, I, 76 No. 1279; Kober, *Cologne*, pp. 130 ff., 362 ff. n. 42. The interesting documents concerning the controversy between the archbishop and the city are in part reproduced by T. J. Lacomblet in his ed. of *Urkundenbuch für die Geschichte des Niederrheins*, IV, 176 ff. Much detailed information is also included in K. Höhlbaum's ed. of *Mitteilungen aus dem Stadtarchiv von Köln*, III–VI. Among other matters it presents a summary of Wenceslaus' decree of April 22, 1391 addressed to the cities of Cologne, Mayence, Worms, Spires, Frankfort, and others, which took the Jews under the protection of their imperial overlord (Part 9, p. 64 No. 4353); and Cologne's justification for the expulsion of the Jews in its communication addressed to Sigismund on August 28, 1431 (V, Part 15, p. 62). See E. L. Ehrlich, *Geschichte der Juden in Deutschland*, pp. 42 f. On this stormy period of the electorate's history (1414–63), see also G. Droege, *Verfassung und Wirtschaft in Kurköln unter Dietrich von Moers*.

48. Kober, *Cologne*, pp. 138, 141 ff. The story of these expulsions will be analyzed *infra*, Chap. L.

49. H. Beyer *et al.*, eds., *Urkundenbuch zur Geschichte der jetzt die preussischen Regierungsbezirke Coblenz und Trier bildenden mittelrheinischen Territorien*, p.

400; Stobbe, *Die Juden,* p. 209 n. 29; Aronius, *Regesten,* pp. 247 f. No. 581; Wiener, *Regesten,* pp. 21 No. 131, 82 No. 28, 87 No. 63, 101 f. App. vi; K. Lamprecht, *Deutsches Wirtschaftsleben im Mittelalter: Untersuchungen über die Entwicklung der materiellen Kultur des platten Landes. Auf Grund der Quellen zunächst des Mosellandes,* I, 1449 ff., 1472 ff.; the documents, *ibid.,* Vol. III, esp. pp. 419 ff. No. 291, and the numerous other entries listed in the Index to that volume, pp. 556 f.; and, more generally, G. Liebe's well-documented study of "Die rechtlichen und wirtschaftlichen Zustände der Juden im Erzstift Trier," *Westdeutsche Zeitschrift für Geschichte und Kunst,* XII, 311–74. The interesting thirteenth-century decree cited in the text is dated by Beyer and Stobbe at *ca.* 1220, and is placed, more uncertainly, by Aronius in the middle of the century (*ca.* 1250). However, Liebe (following von Schoop) puts it more precisely in the years 1215–19 (p. 323). Nor were the imperial claims wholly overlooked. See their reassertion in 1242–44 in the document cited by Liebe, pp. 321 f. On the periods antedating 1200, see *supra,* Vols. II, p. 406 n. 42; IV, pp. 92, 105 f., 283 n. 2, 293 n. 21, 310 n. 68.

50. J. N. von Hontheim, *Historia Trevirensis diplomatica et pragmatica,* II, 227 f. No. dccxvi, 608 ff. No. dccccxxiii; H. Haupt, "Zur Geschichte der Juden im Erzstift Trier," *Westdeutsche Zeitschrift für Geschichte,* XIII, 143–49; F. Haubrich's more popular survey, *Die Juden in Trier;* and J. May, "Die Steuern und Abgaben der Juden im Erzstift Trier," *ZGJD,* VII, 156–79 (giving detailed information particularly for the early modern period). Despite the small size of their community, Jews emigrating from Treves played a considerable role in their new places of settlement. This is particularly true of the family named Treves (under several variations), members of which were to occupy important rabbinic posts in Italy and elsewhere.

51. Meir b. Baruch, *Resp.,* Prague, 1608 ed., fol. 97a No. 950 (Budapest, 1895 ed., fol. 136a); the English summary thereof by I. A. Agus in his *R. Meir of Rothenburg,* II, 407 No. 413; A. Epstein, "Der Wormser Judenrath," *MGWJ,* XLVI, 157–70. See also my *Jewish Community,* II, 35 ff.; III, 113 n. 29; M. Freudenthal, "Die Eigenart der Wormser Gemeinde in ihrer geschichtlichen Wiederkehr," *ZGJD,* V, 100–114 (offering data mainly from the early modern period).

52. See the documentation supplied by A. Hilgard, ed., *Urkunden zur Geschichte der Stadt Speyer,* esp. pp. 284 f. No. 354, 387 ff. Nos. 435, 447, 449–50, 458–59 and 461–63, 441 Nos. 496–97; and H. Boos, *Geschichte der rheinischen Städtekultur . . . mit besonderer Berücksichtigung der Stadt Worms,* 2d ed., esp. II, 126 ff.; idem, *Quellen zur Geschichte der Stadt Worms,* esp. II, 193, 285; III, 90, 93 f. (from an anonymous Worms chronicle), etc. There are also a number of extant monumental vestiges of these and other Rhenish communities. The light they throw on the general life of the medieval and modern Jewries of that region is reviewed by A. Kober and E. Moses in their *Aus der Geschichte der Juden im Rheinland; Jüdische Kult- und Kunstdenkmäler;* and by the former also in his aforementioned essay in *PAAJR,* XIV-XV, as well as by E. L. Rapp and O. Böcher in "Die Ältesten hebräischen Inschriften Mitteleuropas in Mainz, Worms und Speyer," *Jahrbuch* of the Vereinigung "Freunde der Universität Mainz," VIII, 1–48, and their study cited *supra,* n. 45. Many of these surviving vestiges, including documents and other manuscripts, were displayed at the noteworthy exhibition in the Cologne City Museum between October 15, 1963 and February 15, 1964. See its comprehensive

*Katalog* included in K. Schilling's ed. of *Monumenta Judaica. 2000 Jahre Geschichte und Kultur der Juden am Rhein.* See also Kober's "Die deutschen Kaiser und die Wormser Juden," *ZGJD,* V, 134–51; G. Kisch, "Die Rechtsstellung der Wormser Juden im Mittelalter," *ibid.,* pp. 122–33 (reproduced with slight changes in his *Forschungen zur Rechts- und Sozialgeschichte der Juden in Deutschland während des Mittelalters,* pp. 93–106); other essays included in that volume of the *Zeitschrift* issued on the nine-hundredth anniversary of the Worms community; and E. L. Rapp's more recent "Beiträge zur Geschichte der Juden Speyers im Mittelalter," *Mitteilungen* of the Historischer Verein der Pfalz, LVIII, 150 ff. The Rhenish cities, it may be noted, also played an important role in various treaties designed to maintain peace within Germany, treaties which had been one of the mainstays of Jewish life in the Empire ever since 1103. See T. Schwarz's juridical dissertation, *Die Teilnahme der Stadt Speyer an den Landfriedenseinigungen im späteren Mittelalter* (typescript).

53. See the data, supplied especially from the archives of the Foreign Ministry in Vienna by G. Wolf in his *Zur Geschichte der Juden in Worms und des deutschen Städtewesens* (particularly interesting in its extensive documentation of the imperial interventions and trials after 1561; pp. 11 ff., 44 ff. Apps. v–xxiii); L. Rothschild's aforementioned dissertation, *Die Judengemeinden zu Mainz, Speyer und Worms von 1349–1438;* and that by E. Carlebach, *Die Rechtlichen und sozialen Verhältnisse der jüdischen Gemeinden: Speyer, Worms und Mainz von ihren Anfängen bis zur Mitte des 14. Jahrhunderts.* On the peasants' rebellion of 1432 and its relation to Jews, see *Reichstagsakten,* ed. by the Historical Commission of the Bavarian Akademie der Wissenschaften, X, 230, Nos. 137 and 140. See also the other literature cited *supra,* n. 52; and *infra,* Chap. XLVII.

54. Aronius, *Regesten,* pp. 204 No. 466 (more fully in J. A. L. Huillard-Bréholles, *Historia diplomatica Friderici Secundi,* IV, Part 2, pp. 698 f.), 240 No. 563, 253 f. Nos. 592–93, 282 No. 675, 291 f. Nos. 707 and 709; Grayzel, *The Church,* pp. 292 ff. No. 132; S. Salfeld, ed., *Das Martyrologium,* pp. 43 ff. (Hebrew), 192 ff. (German); W. Engel, ed., *Urkundenregesten zur Geschichte der Städte des Hochstifts Würzburg (1172–1413),* p. 30 No. 46; H. Hoffmann, "Die Würzburger Judenverfolgung von 1349," *Mainfränkisches Jahrbuch,* V, 91–114. At the beginning of the century, it may be noted, Bishop Otto von Lobdeburg (1207–1223) employed a Jewish mintmaster; a coin, still extant, bears the imprint of its minter, Yeḥiel, in Hebrew letters. See *Monumenta Judaica,* ed. by K. Schilling, *Katalog,* B 171. While there is little positive evidence for the presence of Jews in Würzburg before the twelfth century, the fact that their quarter was situated in the very heart of town, would point, as elsewhere, toward their belonging to the oldest settlers. Curiously, in his attempt to free the Franciscans from the ecclesiastical tithe on their property, Gregory IX addressed himself to the bishop of Würzburg, as well as the archbishops of Cologne and Magdeburg in 1231, asking that the monks not be treated by the secular clergy on a par with Jews. See Aronius, pp. 198 ff. Nos. 450 (with the note thereon) and 455; W. Engel, ed., *Urkundenregesten zur Geschichte der kirchlichen Verwaltung des Bistums Würzburg im hohen und späten Mittelalter;* and *supra,* Vol. IV, p. 239 n. 11. On the close relationships on the one hand between the Würzburg bishopric and the Papacy, and on the city's struggle for independence on the other, see Engel's analysis, "Die Stadt Würzburg und die Kurie. Aus dem mittelalterlichen Verfassungs-

kampf einer deutschen Bischofsstadt," *ZRG*, Kanonistiche Abt., LXVIII, 303–59. See also the literature listed in the next note.

55. See L. Heffner, *Die Juden in Franken;* F. X. Himmelstein, "Die Juden in Franken," *Archiv* of the Historischer Verein von Unterfranken und Aschaffenburg, XII; Wiener, *Regesten*, esp. pp. 197 ff. Nos. 614, 616, 621–25 and 630; H. Epstein, "Ein Beitrag zur Geschichte der Juden im ehemaligen Herzogtum Ostfranken," *MGWJ*, XXIX, 193–204, 258–67, 452–72, 496–513; H. von Hessberg, "Zur politischen Geschichte der Stadt Würzburg im 14. Jahrhundert," *Mainfränkische Jahrbücher*, VIII, 96–106; and, particularly, M. Szulwas's dissertation, *Die Juden in Würzburg während des Mittelalters*. On the Süsslein affair and the early career of Levy Colner, see the documents in M. Stern's *König Ruprecht von der Pfalz*, pp. 33 ff. Nos. 43, 47–48 and 50–54. The vicissitudes of the Jewish community under Gottfried IV are described in telling detail by A. Zuckerman in his "'It Can't Happen Here!' An Episode in the Failure to Achieve Territorial Unification of Franconian Jewry in the Mid-Fifteenth Century," *Baron Jub. Vol.*, pp. 443–58. See also, the biographical sketches by A. Amrhein, "Gottfried IV. Schenk von Limpurg, Bischof von Würzburg und Herzog zu Franken 1442–1455," *Archiv* of the Historischer Verein von Unterfranken, L, 1–150; and by S. Zeissner, *Rudolf II von Scherenberg, Fürstbischof von Würzburg, 1466–1495*, 2d ed.; *infra*, n. 56.

56. Aronius, *Regesten*, pp. 64 ff. No. 152, 94 No. 204, 131 No. 307; Benjamin of Tudela, *Massa'ot* (Travels), ed. by M. N. Adler, pp. 72 (Hebrew), 80 (English); Frederick von Hohenlohe, *Rechtsbuch, 1348*, ed. with a commentary by C. Höfler, pp. 5, 18; S. Haenle, *Geschichte der Juden im ehemaligen Fürstentum Ansbach*, pp. 207 f. No. iiia; H. Epstein in *MGWJ*, XXIX, 452 ff.; and *supra*, n. 55. The available data have been carefully reviewed by A. Eckstein in his *Geschichte der Juden im ehemaligen Fürstbistum Bamberg*, which also summarizes various documents and the text of the privilege of 1400; see Appendices, pp. 297 ff. See also the more recent edition, by E. von Guttenberg, of *Die Regesten der Bischöfe und des Domkapitels von Bamberg*. In one interesting summary Eckstein tells about a protracted litigation which arose from a deed of indebtedness signed by Bishop Anton von Rotenhan in 1445 to a local Jew, Meyer. Long after the expulsion of 1478, this claim was ineffectually pursued by the noble family Lobkowitz, to which the deed had been assigned, and was dragged from court to court until it finally reached the king. In 1538, when the documentation ceases, Ferdinand I and his advisers were still pondering over it, with the ultimate outcome remaining unknown. See Eckstein, pp. 298 ff. App. ii.

57. Aronius, *Regesten*, p. 25 No. 69, 29 f. No. 80, 303 ff. No. 725; the Salzburg *Stadtrecht*, reproduced by F. V. Zillner in his *Geschichte der Stadt Salzburg*, II, 697. The prayer, *Pro perfidis Judaeis*, was discussed *supra*, Vol. V, pp. 351 f. n. 68. On the various places called *Judendorf* and their meaning, see the list in *Germania Judaica*, ed. by M. Brann *et al.*, I, 136 f.; Scherer, *Rechtsverhältnisse*, pp. 115 ff.; and A. Kober, *Grundbuch des Kölner Judenviertels*, p. 13.

The history of the Jews in the bishopric of Salzburg has received considerable attention from scholars, perhaps disproportionate to the general importance and size of the population. But one can learn a good deal from it about the history of all German Jewry, since much of it concerns relatively small communities like Mühldorf,

Hallein, Friesach (Carinthia), and Pettau. Such tiny settlements existed all over the Empire, but not all of them left as many records. See the data assembled by Scherer in his *Rechtsverhältnisse*, pp. 543 ff. (here the two pledges of the Jewish exiles of 1498 are fully reproduced, pp. 565 ff.); E. Baumgarten, *Die Juden in Steiermark, eine historische Skizze* (includes much material for Salzburg as well); and most fully by A. Altmann, *Geschichte der Juden in Stadt und Land Salzburg.*

58. *Supra*, Vol. IV, pp. 120 f.; Benjamin of Tudela, *Massa'ot, loc. cit. (supra*, n. 56); J. Euting, "Ueber die älteren hebräischen Steine im Elsass," *Festschrift* of the Protestantisches Gymnasium in Strasbourg, 1888, I, 227–54, esp. pp. 233 f. No. 1; the Second Strasbourg City Statute, Art. lvii, in the *Urkundenbuch der Stadt Strassburg,* Vol. I, ed. by W. Wiegand, p. 481 No. 617; Aronius, *Regesten*, pp. 158 No. 357, 196 Nos. 444–45, 256 f. Nos. 598–601, 280 Nos. 672–73, 284 No. 681; and other data assembled by M. Ginsburger in "La Première communauté israélite de Strasbourg," *Publications* of the University of Strasbourg, Faculté de Lettres, CIV; C. T. Weiss, *Geschichte und rechtliche Stellung der Juden im Fürstbistum Strassburg;* A. Glaser, *Geschichte der Juden in Strassburg.* Much interesting material is also included in the more general histories of the Jews in Alsace, such as E. Scheid, *Histoire des Juifs d'Alsace* (with a large documentary appendix, pp. 320–424); M. Ephraim, "Histoire des Juifs d'Alsace et particulièrement de Strasbourg depuis le milieu du XIIIᵉ siècle jusqu'à la fin du XIVᵉ siècle," *REJ*, LXXVII, 127–65; LXXVIII, 35–84 (with an extensive bibliography); and J. Rochette, *Histoire des Juifs d'Alsace des origines à la Révolution.* See also such general monographs as H. Dubled's "Aspects de la vie économique de Strasbourg au XIIIᵉ et XIVᵉ siècles," *Archives d'église d'Alsace,* XXII, 23–56. An interesting local controversy of 1229 had wider repercussions. A Jewish convert, whose wife refused to join him at the baptismal font, wished to take their son with him. The matter was brought before the diocesan synod and finally submitted by the bishop to Pope Gregory IX. Not surprisingly, the pope decided in favor of the father, since if the child were to remain with his mother "she may easily mislead him into the error of infidelity." See Grayzel, *The Church*, pp. 180 ff. No. 59. It should be noted that, although Strasbourg never revoked its prohibition of Jewish settlement until it was forced to do so by the royal government of France late in the eighteenth century, the municipality often extended short-term hospitality to individual Jews, particularly during warlike disturbances. This happened, in particular, during the stormy year of the Peasant War of 1525. See *infra*, Chaps. LVIII–LIX. On the noteworthy local developments during the great crisis of the Black Death, which allegedly destroyed 16,000 lives in the city of Strasbourg alone, and the interurban correspondence concerning the alleged Jewish responsibility for it, see *infra*, Chaps. XLIX and L.

59. I. Loeb, "Les Juifs de Strasbourg depuis 1349 jusqu'à la Révolution," *Annuaire* of the Société des Études Juives, II, 137–98; C. T. Weiss, *Geschichte und rechtliche Stellung*, pp. 121 f. No. 1; A. Glaser, *Geschichte der Juden in Strassburg,* p. 9; J. Rochette, *Histoire des Juifs d'Alsace*, esp. pp. 34 f., reporting the origin of the horn ritual in Strasbourg, on the basis of the report by the chronicler, Bernhard Herzog, and the petition of the Society of Friends of the Constitution in 1790 asking for its discontinuation. The absence of the Jews from the city is illustrated by the census of 1444, on which see P. Dollinger, "Le Premier recensement et le chiffre de population de Strasbourg en 1444," *Revue d'Alsace*, XCIV, 112–24.

60. Aronius, *Regesten*, pp. 55 ff. Nos. 129 and 133–34, 61 No. 143, 93 No. 201, 110 f. Nos. 240–41, 144 No. 319, 281 No. 674; and the data assembled by M. Güdemann in his *Zur Geschichte der Juden in Magdeburg* (reprinted from *MGWJ*, XIV); E. Forchhammer, "Beiträge zur Geschichte der deutschen Juden mit besonderer Beziehung auf Magdeburg und die benachbarte Gegend," *Geschichtsblätter für Stadt und Land Magdeburg*, XLVI, 119–78, 328–408; S. Neufeld, *Die halleschen Juden im Mittelalter;* G. Kisch, "Die Anfänge der jüdischen Gemeinde zu Halle," *Jahrbuch* of the Historische Kommission für die Provinz Sachsen, Sachsen und Anhalt, IV, 132 ff.; *supra*, Vol. IV, pp. 65 f., 184 f., 271 n. 84, 330 n. 44. As pointed out by Georg Caro, Magdeburg Jewry could not have been considered very valuable imperial property if Otto IV, in his struggle with the archbishop who was a partisan of the Hohenstaufen dynasty, destroyed all houses lying outside the city walls including the Judendorf, which here evidently meant merely a Jewish quarter. See Caro's *Sozial- und Wirtschaftsgeschichte der Juden*, I, 418.

As elsewhere, any sign of friendliness shown by an archbishop to Jews was viewed as having been prompted by purely mercenary motives. When in 1207 the returning Archbishop Albert was publicly welcomed by the Jews, he kissed the scroll of law presented to him. This gesture, so different from the customary rejection of the Torah by popes and emperors, called forth the chronicler's comment that "many believed for this reason that he [the archbishop] was led to the approval of that sect and to balkiness toward the Gospel of peace." See Aronius, p. 165 No. 372.

61. See the sources cited in the publications listed in the previous note, esp. that by S. Neufeld, the documentary appendix of which includes four letters of protection issued by the archbishops in favor of individual Jews in the years 1440–74 (pp. 95 ff.). At any rate, in 1443 Frederick III considered the revenue of the Magdeburg Jews sufficiently important to place them under a ban and to order Elector Frederick II of Brandenburg "to attack their persons and property" until they paid up their due to the imperial Treasury. See A. F. Riedel, ed., *Codex diplomaticus brandenburgensis*, 2d ser. IV, 287 No. 1650.

From the Ottonian age Magdeburg served as a gateway for German trade and political influence in east-central Europe. Its impact was felt even more strongly during the German colonization of the eastern Slavonic lands. The so-called Magdeburg law served as the principal legal system among these German colonists, who often used the Magdeburg supreme court as their court of appeal. Understandably, this situation could not remain without influence on the development of East-European Jewry as well. In adumbration of these developments, in 1261 Duke Barnim I of Pomerania provided that the Jews of Stettin and vicinity "should in all respects be subject to the laws observed by the Jews residing in the city of Magdeburg." See *Pommersches Urkundenbuch*, published by the Staatsarchiv of Stettin, (ed. by A. Prümers *et al.*), II, 86 No. 708; *infra*, Chap. XLII, n. 52. See also M. Balaban's brief survey of "Der Gang der jüdischen Kulturelemente vom Rhein bis an die Weichsel und den Dniepr (XI–XVII. Jahrhundert)," *La Pologne au VIIe Congrès International des sciences historiques*, III, 191–216; and, more generally, W. Kuhn, *Geschichte der deutschen Ostsiedlung in der Neuzeit*.

62. Aronius, *Regesten*, pp. 271 f. No. 646; Mansi, *Collectio*, XXIII, 1000; XXXII, 131; Hefele, *Histoire des conciles*, VI, Part 1, pp. 92 f.; Kober, *Cologne*, pp. 54 f.; Schaab, *Diplomatische Geschichte*, p. 64 n. 2; and *supra*, n. 45. Some bishoprics,

other than those treated in our text, played a considerable role in Jewish history. This is particularly true of such cities as Augsburg and Ratisbon. In the latter case the city gradually freed itself from episcopal control to such an extent that the destinies of its Jewry must more properly be treated within the framework of its municipal evolution. See *infra,* Chap. XLI. In regard to Augsburg we need refer only to the large materials accumulated and analyzed ever since Paul von Stetten's comprehensive eighteenth-century work, *Geschichte der Heil. Röm. Reichs-Freyen Stadt Augspurg.* See esp. F. L. Steinthal, *Geschichte der Augsburger Juden im Mittelalter;* and R. Straus, *Regensburg and Augsburg* (Jewish Communities Series). Many lesser bishoprics have also had considerable significance for Jewish history. See, for example, the extensive *Urkundenbuch des Hochstifts Halberstadt und seiner Bischöfe,* ed. by G. Schmidt; H. Kraft, "Die Rechtliche, wirtschaftliche und soziale Lage der Juden im Hochstift Paderborn," *Westfälische Zeitschrift,* XCIV, Part 2, pp. 101–204. Many others will be mentioned in appropriate contexts. But despite numerous variations in detail, which could be observed also in the great centers of Jewish life under the rule of bishops treated in this chapter, they reveal so many basic similarities that they allow for certain generalizations suggested here.

# CHAPTER XLI: VICTIM OF FEUDAL ANARCHY

1. A mere glance at the dense Jewish settlements recorded along the Rhine alone will give an inkling of the vast dispersion of these communities; most of them of very small size. See the chart in K. Schilling's ed. of *Monumenta Judaica*, Katalog, to B 62. A more detailed analysis of some larger settlements is given in *Germania Judaica*, ed. by M. Brann *et al.*

2. Rudolph I's confirmations of the privileges of the cities of Tulln in 1276, Art. 23, and of Laa in 1277, Art. 4, in G. Winter, *Urkundliche Beiträge zur Rechtsgeschichte ober- und niederösterreichischer Städte, Märkte und Dörfer*, pp. 25 ff. Nos. 10 and 23; his Vienna privilege of 1278, Art. 3, in both Latin and German published by J. A. Tomaschek in *Die Rechte und Freiheiten der Stadt Wien*, I, 52, 58 (Nos. xvi–xvii); P. Ludewig, *Reliquiae manuscriptorum omnis aevi*, IV, 272 f. No. xv; Scherer, *Rechtsverhältnisse*, pp. 339 ff., 345 ff., 356 ff. Scherer also points out that even during those years public opinion, at least in so far as it was represented by the literati, was far more antagonistic to Jews. In his satirical poems written in 1292, one Seyfried Helbling sharply ridiculed them, while an unnamed jurist (possibly the city clerk, Eberhard of Wiener Neustadt) tried to secure Rudolph's approval for his private compilation (probably completed in 1276–78), the so-called "Wiener Neustadt city statute," which included several unauthorized restrictions of Jewish rights. See the text, ed. by G. Winter, "Das Wiener Neustädter Stadtrecht des XIII. Jahrhunderts," *Archiv für österreichische Geschichte*, LX, 160 ff. However, this work was never approved by Rudolph and probably exerted no influence. After a careful examination, particularly of MS 352 in the Vienna National Library, Rudolph Geyer has shown that while the city of Vienna had succeeded in acquiring most favorable imperial and ducal charters, the prohibition against employing Jews in public office is found only in the original privilege of 1237 (renewed in 1247, again by Rudolph in 1278, and by Albert in 1296), but it does not occur in some other texts nor did it apparently apply to such other cities as Korneuburg or Krems. See Geyer, "Die mittelalterlichen Stadtrechte Wiens," *MIOG*, LVIII, 589–613, esp. pp. 594, 610. Records of the various justices of the Jews in Vienna are still extant. See the list of occupants of this office from 1295 to 1420, compiled by Tomaschek, II, 295–97; and by I. Schwarz in *Das Wiener Ghetto, seine Häuser und seine Bewohner*, pp. 10 f. n. 16, with some corrections by A. Goldmann in the essay (pp. 14 f.) cited *infra*, n. 4. On the earlier period, see the comprehensive *Urkundenbuch zur Geschichte der Babenberger in Österreich*, ed. by O. von Mitis *et al.*

3. The pro-Jewish provisions included in the peace treaty between the Habsburgs and Louis the Bavarian in 1330, and the emperor's subsequent privilege for the Austrian dukes freely to admit Jews (1331), are cited from F. F. Schrötter, *Abhandlungen aus dem österreichischen Staatsrechte*, I, 162 f.; IV, 247; and other sources by Scherer in his *Rechtsverhältnisse*, p. 362 n. 1. On Benedict XII's bull, *Ex zelo fidei* (reproduced in O. Raynaldus, *Annales ecclesiastici*, VI, 124 ff. *ad* 1338, Nos. xviii–xx) and other Avignonese popes, see *supra*, Chap. XXXVII; and *infra*, Chap. XLVI. The

Hebrew declaration of the Viennese elders of June 19, 1338 was originally published by G. Wolf in his "Actenstücke zur Geschichte der Juden," *Hebräische Bibliographie,* III, 17 f., 31; and in his *Studien zur Jubelfeier der Wiener Universität im Jahre 1865,* p. 170. The excerpt quoted in the text is given in a variant of the English translation in M. Grunwald's *Vienna,* p. 21. See also Wiener, *Regesten,* pp. 221 f. No. 32; and other sources cited by Scherer, pp. 365 ff. On the size of the Vienna community we possess the testimony of Conrad von Megenberg, a Ratisbon teacher who had left Vienna in 1341. In ridiculing the alleged Jewish role in the spread of the Black Death, Megenberg declared that "there were more Jews in Vienna than, as far as I know, in any other German city." See his *Buch der Natur,* written in 1349 and reed. by F. Pfeiffer, p. 112; and in H. Schulz's trans. into modern German, p. 91. See *infra,* Chap. XLIX; and on the expulsion from Hungary, *infra,* Chap. XLII, n. 26.

4. See *supra,* Chap. XL, n. 16; and the extensive documentation in Scherer's *Rechtsverhältnisse,* pp. 374 ff. On the governmental reprisals for the confiscation of Jewish property left behind by the Styrian and Carinthian refugees and the related problem of the rights of Austrian Jewry to own real estate, see the data presented by O. H. Stowasser, "Zur Frage der Besitzfähigkeit der Juden in Österreich während des Mittelalters," *Mitteilungen* of the Verein für Geschichte der Stadt Wien, IV, 23–27; and O. Brunner, "Das Archiv des Landmarschalls Ulrich von Dachsberg mit einem Exkurs zur Geschichte der Juden in Wien," *ibid.,* VII, 66 ff., 68 n. 30, 88 f. App. ii. See also A. Diringer's dissertation, *Die Judenpolitik in der Ostmark bis 1420* (typescript; kindly placed at my disposal by the authorities of the Vienna University Library), pp. 26, 37 f. Important data have been assembled particularly in the *Quellen und Forschungen zur Geschichte der Juden in Deutsch-Österreich* published by the Historische Kommission of the Israelitische Kultusgemeinde in Vienna, the following being particularly relevant for the medieval period: A. Goldmann, ed., *Das Judenbuch der Scheffstrasse zu Wien (1389–1420)* (Vol. I of the series), supplemented by his "Das Verschollene Wiener Judenbuch (1372–1420)," in Vol. XI, pp. 1–14; I. Schwarz, ed., *Das Wiener Ghetto* (Vol. II); R. Geyer and L. Sailer, eds., *Urkunden aus Wiener Grundbüchern zur Geschichte der Wiener Juden im Mittelalter,* with an intro. by O. H. Stowasser (Vol. X). Of interest also are the more general histories of the community by I. Schwarz, "Geschichte der Juden in Wien bis zum Jahre 1625," in *Geschichte der Stadt Wien,* published by the Wiener Altertumsverein; H. Tietze, *Die Juden Wiens. Geschichte—Wirtschaft—Kultur;* and M. Grunwald, *Vienna.* On the second largest Austrian community as well as the entire province of Lower Austria, see the monographs by M. Pollack, *Die Juden in Wiener Neustadt;* L. Moses, *Die Juden in Niederösterreich (mit besonderer Berücksichtigung des XVII. Jahrhunderts);* and W. Messing, "Beiträge zur Geschichte der Juden in Wien und Niederösterreich im 16. Jahrhundert," *Jahrbuch* of the Verein für Geschichte der Stadt Wien, I, 11–49. Less rewarding is Moses's somewhat cantankerous survey of "Jüdische Geschichtsforschung in Österreich," *ZGJT,* III, 166–71.

5. Scherer, *Rechtsverhältnisse,* pp. 317 ff., 336, 422 ff., 455 ff.; Paul II's bull, *Sedis apostolicae copiosa benignitas* of May 31, 1469, in J. Chmel's *Materialien zur österreichischen Geschichte,* II, 306 No. ccxlvii. On the humanist Pope Paul II and his general attitude toward the Jews, see *infra,* Chap. XLVI. Regrettably, many Austrian developments in the mid-fifteenth century are related to us principally by the chronicler Thomas Ebendorfer von Haselbach (died 1464) who, in the case of

Jews, was more of "the malevolent theologian," as he was styled by his opponent Johannes Cuspinianus, than a calm rapporteur. Ebendorfer's influence seemed doubly dangerous since his *Austrian Chronicle* enjoyed the sponsorship of Frederick III; in some respects this work, forming part of a larger *History of the Roman Kings*, was written on Frederick's prompting. Upon its speedy completion, to be sure, the king was far from pleased with its vast size, haphazard order, and the author's moralistic tone. But he and his contemporaries seem to have accepted Ebendorfer's historical narrative as wholly factual. Ebendorfer's compendium, though extant in several sixteenth-century copies, has never been published in full. In its truncated form, however, as published in Hieronymus Pez's ed. of *Scriptores rerum Austriacarum*, II, it enjoyed quite a vogue among contemporaries and still more among modern historians. See A. Lhotsky, "Studien zur Ausgabe der österreichischen Chronik des Thomas Ebendorfer," Parts I–II, *DAGM*, VI, 188–245; Part III, *MIOG*, LVII, 193–230, esp. p. 201. Ebendorfer's anti-Jewish bias came to the fore even more strongly in several polemical treatises. In his *Mendacia et calumniae Judaeorum impiorum* he combated particularly the *Toledot Yeshu* which, with his smattering of Hebrew, he tried to translate into German. His *De Judaeo relapso sive Consilium super lapsu cuiusdam baptizati olim Judaei*, written in the form of a responsum to an inquiry by Bishop Ulrich III of Passau, sharply condemned such relapses, although he did not advocate execution of the transgressors. In this respect he was milder than most canonists. See Scherer, p. 433; *supra*, Chap. XL, n. 39; *infra*, Chap. L; and A. Lhotsky's aforementioned biographical study, *Thomas Ebendorfer*, esp. pp. 56 f., 90 Nos. 172–74 (two autographs).

6. The vicissitudes of Styrian and Carinthian Jewry during the late Middle Ages are told in full and illuminating detail by Scherer in his *Rechtsverhältnisse*, pp. 455 ff. Regrettably, much of our information is derived from such overtly biased accounts as Valentin Preuenhueber's *Annales Styrenses* (see, for instance, pp. 58, 83 f.). But considerable firsthand evidence from archival sources has since been assembled in the numerous monographs pertaining to certain phases of that history. Apart from the older summary by H. Grave, "Zur Geschichte der Juden in Steiermark," *Wertheimers Jahrbuch für Israeliten*, n.s. V, 1–21; see esp. E. Baumgarten, *Die Juden in Steiermark;* A. Rosenberg, *Beiträge zur Geschichte der Juden in Steiermark;* D. Herzog, *Urkunden und Regesten zur Geschichte der Juden in der Steiermark (1475–1585)*, esp. pp. xix n. 50, xxvi; his "Jüdische Grabsteine und Urkunden aus der Steiermark," *MGWJ*, LXXV, 30–47; LXXX, 58–79, 118–21; and his aforementioned "Kleine Beiträge," *ZGJT*, III–V. The antecedents and effects of the expulsions of 1496–1515 will be more fully described *infra*, Chap. L.

7. Bondy and Dworský, *Zur Geschichte*, esp. pp. 43 ff. Nos. 47, 57, 61, 64, 70, 74, 75, 91, 126, etc.; Wiener, *Regesten*, pp. 48 f. Nos. 166, 170–71 and 174; Stein, *Geschichte der Juden in Böhmen*, pp. 10 ff., 22 ff.; *supra*, Chap. XL, nn. 11 and 17. On Ibrahim ibn Ya'qub, see *supra*, Vols. III, 217 f., 338 n. 57; VI, 221 f., 434 f. n. 87. See also I. Hrbek, "A New Arabic Source on East-Central Europe" (Czech), *Československa Ethnografie*, II, 151–75 (analyzing the report by the twelfth-century author, Abu Hamid al–Andalusi). An attempted legislation concerning Jewish taxes and the disposal of their foreclosed property was included in the original codification of the so-called *Majestas Carolina*, submitted to the Diet in April 1348, but it was revoked seven years later. See Bondy and Dworský, pp. 58 ff. Nos. 101, 124. But

the provision that Jews should not dispose of hereditary estates acquired by foreclosure without royal permission, lest royal property thus be alienated, offers a remarkable counterpart to the suspicions voiced by the English barons a century earlier that the king acquired control over much of the nobles' property via Jewish foreclosures. See *infra*, Chap. XLIII, n. 61. The Crown's intrinsic insecurity in extending to its Jewish "serfs" effective protection explains, in part, Charles IV's lukewarm behavior during the upheaval of 1349–50 in his hereditary possessions; for instance, his pardon for the assassins of Eger. Bondy and Dworský, p. 62 No. 116. On the other hand, the burghers of Breslau were promised support in their prosecution of the pogromists. The city followed up that promise by pledging itself to grant protection even to Jewish newcomers. See, in general, the detailed analysis of all existing data by M. Brann in his *Geschichte der Juden in Schlesien*, esp. his excursus on the "Schlesische Juden-Privilegien" in the Appendix to Part I. See also T. Goerlitz, "Eine bisher unbekannte Urkunde von 1301 über die Breslauer Juden," *Beiträge zur Geschichte . . . Breslau*, n.s. III, 107–14.

We have treated Silesia here as part of the Bohemian kingdom, and indirectly also as part of the Holy Roman Empire, regardless of the ethnic composition of its population, which, as in Bohemia proper, was still overwhelmingly Slavonic. Politically the province now came under the rule of the Bohemian kings, who, however, inherited much of its chaotic legal structure from the former Polish duchies. On the extended controversies between the Polish and German scholars regarding Silesia's ethnic character, see, for instance, the literature analyzed by Z. Kaczmarczyk in "The Problem of Silesia's Germanization in the Light of Recent Researches" (Polish), *Przegląd zachodni*, III, 931–43. See also the comprehensive history of Breslau (Wrocław) to 1807 in W. Długoborski *et al.*, *Dzieje Wrocławia do roku 1807* (The History of Breslau to 1807; with an extensive English summary, pp. 899–916).

Considerable information is also available on the Jews of Moravia who for the most part lived under the Bohemian Crown. We are fortunate in possessing an excellent source collection, as well as analytical history, of the medieval period by B. Bretholz in his *Quellen zur Geschichte der Juden in Mähren vom XI. bis zum XV. Jahrhundert (1067–1411)*; and his *Geschichte* mentioned, together with an earlier study by C. d'Elvert, *supra*, Chap. XL, n. 17. See also *infra*, n. 12. Of interest also are the various essays, ed. by H. Gold in *Die Juden und Judengemeinden Mährens in Vergangenheit und Gegenwart. Ein Sammelwerk;* and such monographs as F. Čáda, "The Origin of the Jewish Community of Brno," *Festschrift Guido Kisch*, pp. 261–68.

8. Bondy and Dworský, *Zur Geschichte*, p. 57 No. 98; Wiener, *Regesten*, p. 223 Nos. 43–44; A. Stein, *Geschichte der Juden in Böhmen*, pp. 39 ff. In contrast to the provincial histories of the Moravian and Silesian Jewries, the main Jewish concentration in Bohemia has never been the subject of a comprehensive analysis. Stein's *Geschichte* and even the various essays included in H. Gold's ed. of *Die Juden und Judengemeinden Böhmens in Vergangenheit und Gegenwart*, are far from adequate. One must constantly refer, therefore, to Bondy and Dworský's collection of excerpts and summaries in their *Zur Geschichte*, although its incompleteness has rightly been stressed by J. Bergl on the example of the "Judaica in the Archives of the Ministry of Interior in Prague" (Czech), *Sborník archivu* of the Ministry of Interior of the Czechoslovak Republic, VI, 12 f. Much information is of course available in such general collections of sources as E. F. Rössler, ed., *Deutsche Rechtsdenkmäler aus*

*Böhmen und Mähren;* and the more recent *Regesta diplomatica nec non epistolaria Bohemiae et Moraviae,* ed. by B. Mendl and M. Linhartová. Of considerable value is *Die Jüdischen Denkmäler in der Tschechoslowakei,* published by the *Denkmal-Kommission* of the Supreme Council of the Union of Jewish Communities in Bohemia, Moravia and Silesia.

Even the local history of Prague Jewry, which from the standpoint of antiquity, size, and interterritorial influence, was one of the most important communities of Ashkenazic Jewry, still awaits its competent historian. For the time being the essays collected by S. Steinherz in *Die Juden in Prag,* may serve as a substitute. Not that there were lacking monographic researches for more than a century. See O. Muneles and M. Bohatec, *Bibliographical Survey of Jewish Prague,* the usefulness of which is somewhat impaired by its arrangement in the chronological order of the publications without a subject index. See also H. Volavková's art historical contributions, *The Synagogue Treasures of Bohemia and Moravia;* and *The Pinkas Synagogue;* O. Muneles and M. Vilimková, *Starý židovsky hřbitov v Praze* (The Old Jewish Cemetery in Prague, reproducing inscriptions from 1439 to 1588). On the Jews in the borderland of Lower Lusatia, which during the Middle Ages and the early modern period belonged for the most part to Bohemia, see R. Lehmann, "Zur Geschichte der Juden in der Niederlausitz bis zur Mitte des 19. Jahrhunderts," *Niederlausitzer Mitteilungen,* XXXIV, 1–46. Other studies are listed in the review article by B. Brilling, "Neues Schrifttum zur Geschichte der Juden in der Tschechoslowakei," *Zeitschrift für Ostforschung,* VI, 572–82.

9. Bondy and Dworský, *Zur Geschichte, passim;* A. Blaschka, "Die Jüdische Gemeinde zu Ausgang des Mittelalters," in *Die Juden in Prag,* ed. by S. Steinherz, pp. 58–80; V. V. Tomek, *Déjepis města Prahy* (A History of the City of Prague), III, 339 ff.; J. Kaufmann, *Yom Ṭob Lipmann-Mühlhausen, ba'al ha-niṣṣaḥon,* pp. 19 ff.; B. Bernstein, "Der 'Sieg' des R. Jomtov-Lippman Mühlhausen," *Jewish Studies in Memory of Michael Guttmann,* I, 201–220; *supra,* Chap. XL, n. 31. There is considerable confusion in regard to the dates of the disturbances in Prague. Basing themselves upon the printed editions of Lipmann-Mühlhausen's *Sefer Niṣṣaḥon,* L. Zunz and H. Graetz assumed that, in addition to the persecution of 1389, there was another in 1399. On the other hand, finding that a MS of that work read "149," that is 1389, Kaufmann denied altogether the second attack. However, he could not controvert the debate with Pesaḥ-Peter and its sombre finale in the execution of the seventy-seven martyrs on August 22, 1400. The connection, if any, between these events and the deposing of King Wenceslaus from the German throne on the very day of that execution is not clear from the record. Most likely it was only the general weakening of royal authority even in Bohemia which encouraged the Jew-baiters to proceed with their persecution of the Jewish leaders. See also E. Schwartz, "Zur Geschichte der Juden von Prag unter König Wenzel IV," *JGJCR,* V, 429–37. Apart from questioning the Prague locale of the persecution of 1399–1400 (in view of the total silence of Czech sources), Schwartz offers merely a German translation of the pertinent passage in Lipmann-Mühlhausen's *Sefer Niṣṣaḥon.*

10. Bondy and Dworský, *Zur Geschichte,* I, 132 ff. Nos. 243–55; W. Haage, *Olmütz und die Juden;* C. d'Elvert, *Zur Geschichte der Juden in Mähren und Österreichisch-Schlesien,* pp. 101 ff. (citing the text of the 1454 decree of expulsion from Olmütz); L. Oelsner, "Schlesische Urkunden zur Geschichte der Juden im Mittelalter," *Archiv für*

*Kunde österreichischer Geschichts-Quellen*, XXXI, 57–144, esp. p. 143 No. 39; M. Brann, *Geschichte der Juden in Schlesien*, Part 4, pp. 115 ff., 129 ff., App. pp. lxxi ff. No. V (includes the reprint of an anonymous narrative, *De expulsione Judaeorum*). In the Moravian city of Iglau (Jihlava), all ten-year-old Jewish loans were invalidated in 1411. This relatively mild restriction was followed fifteen years later by total expulsion and the disposal of all Jewish houses and the synagogue, allegedly because the Jews had favored the Taborite rebels. That such expulsions were not necessarily fully carried out, however, is demonstrated by Iglau itself, where a garden in Jewish possession and a house in the Jewish quarter are recorded in 1462–63. See C. D'Elvert, *Geschichte und Beschreibung der (königlichen Kreis- und) Bergstadt Iglau in Mähren*, pp. 53 ff.

The financial dependence of the princes on Jewish loans is well illustrated by several Silesian documents. In 1347 Boiko II had to mortgage the city of Schweidnitz to the Jew Canan in Breslau for 1013 marks; a year later he similarly gave the town of Löwenberg (Lwówek-Śląski) as security to a Jew, Isaac of Schweidnitz, for the relatively small loan of 175 marks. One can gauge, therefore, the extent of the indebtedness of Boleslas II of Liegnitz, who owed a Schweidnitz Jew alone the huge amount of 8,000 marks. See the data presented by Oelsner in *Archiv*, XXXI, 89 f., 128 f. No. 30, 139 ff. No. 37; Brann, *Geschichte*, p. 38; and G. Helmrich's Nazi-inspired *Geschichte der Juden in Liegnitz*, p. 14. On the social background of these radical transformations, see R. R. Betts's succinct remarks, "The Social Revolution in Bohemia and Moravia in the Later Middle Ages," *Past and Present*, II, 24–31 (with reference to recent Czech publications, particularly by F. Graus). These studies and, generally, the role of Jews in the Hussite movement and the effects on them of the protracted Hussite wars will be more fully analyzed, *infra*, Chaps. L and LVIII. Suffice it to mention here that the revolutionary assembly which met at Čáslav in 1421 adopted no anti-Jewish resolutions. See F. G. Heymann, "The National Assembly of Čáslav," *Medievalia et humanistica*, VIII, 32–55.

11. J. C. Čelakovský, "Contributions to the History of the Jews in the Jagiellon Era" (Czech), *Časopis Musea Kralovství Českého*, LXXII, 385–454, largely summarized by A. Stein in *Die Geschichte der Juden in Böhmen*, pp. 30 ff.; Bondy and Dworský, *Zur Geschichte*, I, 146 ff. See also the documents assembled by A. Bachmann in his ed. of *Urkunden und Aktenstücke zur österreichischen Geschichte im Zeitalter Kaiser Friedrichs III und König Georgs von Böhmen (1440–1471)*. Needless to say, Jews suffered, along with the rest of the population, from pestilences and other elementary catastrophes. A particularly severe contagion in 1473 allegedly victimized three-quarters of the Prague inhabitants. Among Jews, too, five of the seven communal elders died of the pestilence and subsequently the local synagogues could rarely muster more than twenty adult men. See Stein, p. 21. Remarkably, however, this time no one seems to have accused the Jews of direct responsibility for that contamination. On the lists of Jewish moneylenders in Prague in 1497–1500, see Bondy and Dworský, pp. 173 ff. Nos. 292, 294–95, 297 and 299; and A. Blaschka's analysis of "Die Judenschulden im Register des Prager Burggrafenamtes 1497–1500," *JGJČR*, II, 97–119. At the same time Jews were allowed to own houses, in and outside the Jewish quarter, in many Bohemian cities. Apart from Kolin, we possess such records from Komotau (Chomatov); see R. Wenisch, "Juden als Hausbesitzer in Komotau vor der Ausweisung (1468–1526)," *ZGJT*, I, 91–98. See also *infra*, Chaps. L and LIV.

12. I. Herrmann *et al.*, *Das Prager Ghetto*, esp. p. 29; J. Lippert, "Die Stellung der Juden in Böhmen vor und nach der Epoche des Husitenkrieges," *Mittheilungen* of the Verein für Geschichte der Deutschen in Böhmen, V, 133–44, esp. pp. 139 ff., 142 f.; and A. Engel, "Die Ausweisung der Juden aus den königlichen Städten Mährens und ihre Folgen," *JGJCR*, II, 50–96. See also, from another angle, W. Weizsäcker, "Aus der Geschichte des Judenrechts in Böhmen und Mähren," *Zeitschrift für osteuropäisches Recht*, VI, 457–67. On the intellectual activities in the Prague community, see A. Horowitz, "Die Rabbiner und jüdischen Gelehrten Prags im XV. Jahrhundert," *ZGJT*, I, 229–42 (offering ten biographical sketches, including those of Abigdor b. Isaac Kara, Yom Ṭob Lipmann-Mühlhausen, and Jacob Pollak). See also, from another angle, G. Kisch, *Die Prager Universität und die Juden 1348–1848*, mainly of interest for the modern period.

13. See *supra*, Vol. IV, pp. 65 f., 271 n. 84; Aronius, *Regesten*, pp. 162 No. 365, 191 No. 432, 237 No. 549, 262 f. Nos. 623 and 626; Wiener, *Regesten*, esp. p. 121 Nos. 135–36; and, more generally, the older but still very useful works by J. C. von Aretin, *Geschichte der Juden in Baiern;* and by S. Tausig under the same title. See also E. M. Fuchs's data *Ueber die ersten Niederlassungen der Juden in Mittelfranken*, reviewing the story of the individual communities, large and small. On Louis the Bavarian's controversial reign, see F. Bock's "Bemerkungen zur Beurteilung Kaiser Ludwigs IV in der neueren Literatur," *Zeitschrift für bayerische Landesgeschichte*, XXIII, 115–27.

14. See the careful examination of the available data in L. Löwenstein's *Geschichte der Juden in der Pfalz*, pp. 1 ff., with the documentary appendix, pp. 282 ff.; M. Weinberg, *Geschichte der Juden in der Oberpfalz*, Parts III–IV; M. Stern's *König Ruprecht von der Pfalz;* and *supra*, Chap. XL, n. 31. The remarkable privilege of November 1, 1367 in favor of Jewish lepers is reproduced by A. Koch *et al.* in their *Regesten der Pfalzgrafen am Rhein, 1214–1508*, I, 222 No. 3743. Leprosy was a far more common disease in the Middle Ages than it has been in recent decades. According to J. J. Walsh, after the Crusades it became "almost as much of a folk disease as tuberculosis came to be towards the end of the nineteenth century." See his *The History of Nursing*, p. 39. Jews may have been less frequently afflicted by this dreaded disease than their neighbors. It has even been suggested that their ancestors in ancient Palestine had been totally immune from it until the Hellenistic age. See A. Bloom, *La Lèpre dans l'ancienne Egypte et chez les anciens Hébreux*. Were the contagion among medieval Jews as widespread as among their Christian contemporaries, we doubtless would read much more about it in the contemporary rabbinic and medical sources. Nevertheless those who suffered from that disease, generally subject to isolation, must have been doubly miserable if they were Jews. See E. Wickersheimer, "Lèpre et Juifs au moyen âge," *Janus Archives internationales pour l'histoire de la médécine*, XXXVI, 43–48 (publishing the text of deliberations of the municipality of Bourg in 1462); and *infra*, Chap. XLIX.

15. Wiener, *Regesten*, pp. 140 ff. Nos. 279, 298, 308, 317, 363, 389, 468, 473, 496, 499, 505 and 626; Stern, *König Ruprecht von der Pfalz*, pp. xii ff.; Von Aretin, *Geschichte der Juden in Baiern*, pp. 31 ff. (all largely following the eighteenth-century chronicler, A. F. Oefele, in his *Rerum boicarum scriptores*, I; see the numerous entries in its Index, *s.v. Judaeorum*). Most importantly, Bavarian Jewish

history was affected by the developments in some of its major cities, such as Nuremberg, Ratisbon, Augsburg, Bamberg, Ulm, and Würzburg in which the dukes at best shared control with either a bishop or a city council or both. On the role played by Josel of Rosheim in 1551, see the text published in Von Aretin's *Geschichte*, pp. 52 ff.; S. Stern in her *Josel von Rosheim*, pp. 204 ff., 265 n. 47; and *infra*, Chap. LIX. Of importance also are the regional histories of areas which were frequently connected with the constantly changing Bavarian spheres of influence, such as S. Haenle, *Geschichte der Juden im ehemaligen Fürstentum Ansbach;* A. Eckstein's *Geschichte der Juden im Markgrafentum Bayreuth;* F. X. Himmelstein, "Die Juden in Franken. Ein Beitrag zur Kirchen- und Rechtsgeschichte Frankens," *Archiv* of the Historischer Verein von Unterfranken, XII, 125–88; and somewhat more remotely, K. Hoppstädter's Nazi-oriented *Der Jude in der Geschichte des Saarlandes.*

16. See A. Lévy, "Notes sur l'histoire des Juifs en Saxe," *REJ*, XXV, 217–34; XXVI, 257–67; idem, *Geschichte der Juden in Sachsen;* S. Neufeld, *Die Juden im thüringisch-säschsischen Gebiet während des Mittelalters;* idem, "Jüdische Gelehrte in Sachsen-Thüringen während des Mittelalters," *MGWJ*, LXIX, 283–95 (listing some eighty scholars); the rather colored description by J. G. Hartenstein, *Die Juden in der Geschichte Leipzigs;* B. H. Auerbach, *Geschichte der israelitischen Gemeinde Halberstadt;* A. Human, "Geschichte der Juden im Herzogtum S. Meiningen-Hildburghausen," *Schriften* of the Verein für Sachsen-Meiningische Geschichte und Landeskunde, XXX, 3–157 (offers only a few scattered data on the 14th–16th centuries); the equally dispersed records pertaining to the origial Guelf areas of Hanover, Brunswick, and vicinity, assembled by M. Wiener in the intro. to his "Zur Geschichte der Juden in der Residenzstadt Hannover," *Jahrbuch für die Geschichte der Juden,* I, 167–216; L. Donath, *Geschichte der Juden in Mecklenburg von den ältesten Zeiten (1266) bis auf die Gegenwart (1874).* As Donath points out, Rostock had much less of a recorded Jewish history than Wismar. Rostock shared its relative aloofness with many Hanseatic cities, whether or not they were members of the Hanseatic League. See also some of the general literature listed in M. Jahn's *Bibliographie zur Vor- und Frühgeschichte Mitteldeutschlands.*

Of considerable importance for Jewish history also are the areas which were later included in the states of Württemberg and Baden. Their history has not yet been fully examined, since the governmental archives alone seem to contain more than 2,000 fascicles of pertinent documents. On the Middle Ages see, for instance, the *Württemberger Regesten,* ed. by the State Archives, Stuttgart, I, 237 Nos. 6408–20. A fairly complete listing of the *Jüdische Gotteshäuser und Friedhöfe in Württemberg* was published by the Oberrat of the Jewish communities in Württemberg in 1932. See also W. Grube's "Quellen zur Geschichte der Judenfrage in Württemberg," *Zeitschrift für württembergische Landesgeschichte,* II, 117–54, esp. pp. 119, 149.

17. A. F. Riedel, ed., *Codex diplomaticus brandenburgensis,* 1st ser. I, 62 f. No. 38, 64 No. 44; IX, 20 f. No. 28, 33 No. 48; XV, 44 f. No. 57; XXIII, 6 No. 6; P. Voigt and E. Fidicin, eds., *Urkundenbuch zur Berlinischen Chronik, 1232–1550,* p. 21; and other sources cited by A. Ackermann in his *Geschichte der Juden in Brandenburg a. H.;* L. Davidsohn in his succinct and well-documented *Beiträge zur Sozial- und Wirtschaftsgeschichte der Berliner Juden vor der Emanzipation* (more fully in type-script); and W. Heise, *Die Juden in der Mark Brandenburg bis zum Jahre 1571.* The

text of the 1344 privilege (Riedel, XXIV, 35, No. lxiv) was subjected to careful scrutiny by G. Sello in his "Markgraf Ludwig des Aelteren Neumärkisches Juden-privileg vom 9. September 1344," *Der Bär*, V, 21 ff. See also *infra*, n. 18; and, more generally, the still important compilation of 1790 by J. B. König, *Annalen der Juden in den preussischen Staaten, besonders in der Mark Brandenburg;* and, of more local interest, J. Landsberger, "Zur Geschichte der Juden in der Mark Brandenburg, insbesonders in der Stadt Stendal, um die Mitte des 15. Jahrhunderts," *MGWJ*, XXXI, 34–39; E. Wolbe's more popularly written *Geschichte der Juden in Berlin und in der Mark Brandenburg;* and other publications listed in the *Bibliographie zur Geschichte der Mark Brandenburg und der Stadt Berlin, 1941–1956*, recently published by the Institut für Geschichte of the Deutsche Akademie der Wissenschaften. In connection with the Beelitz accusation L. Davidsohn (p. 17) cites similar cases in Priegnitz in 1287 and other Brandenburg localities. Nor was miscarriage of justice against individual Jews altogether rare. This is the more remarkable as the fourteenth-century judicial record book of Stendal reveals a noteworthy effort to treat Jews on a par with Christians in criminal prosecutions as well as in civil litigations. See J. F. Behrend, ed., *Ein Stendaler Urteilsbuch aus dem vierzehnten Jahrhundert als Beitrag zur Kentniss des Magdeburger Rechts*, esp. pp. 49 ff. No. x, 112 f. No. xxvii. In 1336 the city of Berlin-Cölln became embroiled in a controversy with Duke Rudolph of Saxony because it imprisoned a Jew Schmolke (Samuel) who persistently claimed that the city owed him money. The duke relented and declared the city free of debt against the payment of 80 marks to him, rather than the creditor. See the document reproduced by Voigt and Fidicin, p. 70. On the early beginnings of Brandenburg Jewry, see the theories discussed by L. Davidsohn, p. 10. See also the documents summarized by K. Kletke, cited *infra*, n. 18.

18. S. Salfeld, *Das Martyrologium*, pp. 77 f. No. ii, 81 ff. No. v end (Hebrew), 247, 270, 287 f. (German); Riedel, *Codex diplomaticus*, 1st ser. II, 149 ff. Nos. 13–18; III, 381 f. No. 75; XV, 139 ff. No. 185; XVI, 252 ff. No. 695 (with the editor's note thereon); XIX, 223 No. 84; 2d ser. VI, 87 f. No. 2301; 3d ser. I, 177 f. No. 110, 240 ff. No. 149; II, 245 ff. No. 196; and other sources cited by Ackermann, Davidsohn, and Heise (see n. 17). Albert Achilles' extreme definition of the Jewish serfdom of the imperial Chamber is cited *supra*, Chap. XL, n. 36; and *infra*, Chap. XLVII. See also S. Stern, *Der Preussische Staat und die Juden*, I, 6 ff.; and K. Kletke, *Regesta historiae neomarchicae. Die Urkunden zur Geschichte der Neumark und des Landes Sternberg in Auszügen*, I, 155, 190 f. The gradual resettlement of the Jews after 1350 is discussed by H. Lichtenstein in his "Zur Wiederaufnahme der Juden in die brandenburgischen Städte nach dem Schwarzen Tode," *ZGJD*, V, 59–63; and in E. Littmann's more comprehensive Cologne dissertation, *Studien zur Wiederaufnahme der Juden durch die deutschen Städte nach dem schwarzen Tode*.

19. U. Grotefend, *Geschichte und rechtliche Stellung der Juden in Pommern von den Anfängen bis zum Tode Friedrich des Grossen*, pp. 39 ff., 84, 114 f. (reproduces text of Bogislav X's decree of 1481). The *cause célèbre* of 1510, for which we possess an interesting Jewish eye-witness testimony (in the brief Hebrew notes, "The Memory of Days," ed. from a Maharil MS by J. H. Wagner in *MWJ*, XVII, Hebrew section [*Oṣar toḇ*], pp. 42–43, with Wagner's comments thereon reproduced in A. Berliner's remarks, "Zur hebräischen Abteilung," *ibid.*, German section, pp. 326–27), has been fully analyzed by F. Holtze in *Das Strafverfahren gegen*

*die märkischen Juden im Jahre 1510;* by D. Kaufmann in "Die Märtyrer des Berliner Autodafés von 1510," *MWJ,* XVIII, 48–53; and almost at the same time by G. Sello in "Der Hostienschändungsprozess vom Jahre 1510 vor dem Berliner Schöffengericht," *Forschungen zur brandenburgischen und preussischen Geschichte,* IV, 121–35. On the Frankfort Diet's dealings with Jews, and Melanchthon's testimony of 1539, see *infra,* Chaps. XLIX and LVIII.

20. H. Planitz, *Die Deutsche Stadt im Mittelalter. Von der Römerzeit bis zu den Zunftkämpfen,* esp. pp. 200 ff.; L. Wallach, "Die Judenansiedlung der Staufer in Deutschland," *MGWJ,* LXXIX, 241–46; *Pommersches Urkundenbuch,* ed. by R. Prümmers *et al.* and published by the Staatsarchiv of Stettin, III, No. 1491 (decree of 1289, promising that Jews would not be allowed to settle in Greifswald *absque consensu et voluntate ipsius consulum civitatis*); Grotefend, *Geschichte,* pp. 31 ff., 50 f.; J. F. Böhmer, *Regesta imperii,* VIII, ed. and revised by A. Huber, p. 42 No. 464 (excerpt from Charles IV's privilege for the Jews of Nuremberg of Nov. 30, 1347). Of course, repudiation of Jewish settlement need not have been permanent. In fact, in 1264 Greifswald itself had obtained from Duke Barnim I a privilege granting the city many liberties and stating bluntly that "the most perfidious Jews [*perfidissimos Judeos*] should for ever be excluded from settlement." *Pommersches Urkundenbuch,* II, No. 757; Grotefend, *Geschichte,* p. 28. Evidently, after a quarter century the burghers themselves had reconsidered.

Of the vast literature relating to constitutional developments and internal class struggles in medieval German cities, we need but mention the mutually complementary essays by P. Dollinger, "Les Villes allemands au moyen âge. Les groupements sociaux," *Recueils* of the Société Jean Bodin, VII, 371–401; J. Schneider, "Les Villes allemandes au moyen âge. Les institutions économiques," *ibid.,* pp. 551–76; E. Maschke, "Verfassung und soziale Kräfte in der deutschen Stadt des späteren Mittelalters, vornehmlich in Oberdeutschland," *VSW,* XLVI, 289–349, 433–76, and their numerous bibliographical references. In regard to Jews in smaller cities, see the more or less typical developments described by A. Riemer in "Die Juden in niedersächsischen Städten des Mittelalters," *Zeitschrift* of the Historischer Verein für Niedersachsen, V, 303–64; VI, 1–57, esp. pp. 36 ff. For information on many localities we are dependent, however, primarily on juridical sources stating what was expected to be done rather than what actually happened. On the other hand, the few references to Jews in city chronicles must be critically examined because of their authors' likely anti-Jewish bias and their specific dependence on the wishes of the municipal authorities. See J. B. Menke, "Geschichtsschreibung und Politik in deutschen Städten des Mittelalters," *Jahrbuch des Kölnischen Geschichtsvereins,* XXXIII, 1–84; XXXIV–XXXV, 85–194 (originally diss. Münster, 1957); and H. Schmidt, *Die Deutschen Städtechroniken als Spiegel des bürgerlichen Selbstverständnisses im Spätmittelalter.*

21. The Mayence chronicle in K. Hegel, ed., *Die Chroniken der deutschen Städte,* XVII (Mayence), 175; Ḥayyim b. Isaac Or Zaru'a, *Resp.,* fol. 33c No. 110. See J. S. Menczel, *Beiträge zur Geschichte der Juden von Mainz im XV. Jahrhundert,* pp. 36 f.; and *supra,* Vol. IV, pp. 100 f., 289 f. n. 13.

22. On the thirteenth-century transfers of royal authority to the cities see, in particular, the data assembled by H. Fischer in *Die Verfassungsrechtliche Stellung*

*der Juden in den deutschen Städten während des dreizehnten Jahrhunderts.* Notwithstanding certain juristic reservations advanced by G. Kisch in his review of that volume, reprinted in his *Forschungen zur Rechts- und Sozialgeschichte der Juden in Deutschland während des Mittelalters,* pp. 257 ff., Fischer offers the most complete and authoritative analysis of extant sources. One wished that similar studies of equally crucial transformations were available for the later centuries. See, for instance, Fischer's complementary study of "Die Judenprivilegien des Goslarer Rates im 14. Jahrhundert," *ZRG,* Germanistische Abteilung, LVI, 89–149; analyzing 27 extant documents of 1312–40, in part published in G. Bode and I. Hölscher's ed. of the *Urkundenbuch der Stadt Goslar,* esp. Vol. III. At the time when Goslar like many other cities achieved more independence, the growing penetration of canon and Roman law into local legislation naturally also affected the Jewish status; it accounts in part for the gradual changes observed by Fischer. See K. Frölich, "Zum Goslarer Urkundenwesen in 14. Jahrhundert" in *Festschrift Edmund E. Stengel* [ed. by E. Kunz], pp. 40–55.

23. A. Erler, *Bürgerrecht und Steuerpflicht im mittelalterlichen Städtewesen, mit besonderer Untersuchung des Steuereides,* esp. p. 19; with the modifications suggested by Fischer in *Die Verfassungsrechtliche Stellung,* pp. 119 ff. and exemplified by the thirteenth-century documentation in Strasbourg and Augsburg, *ibid.,* pp. 201 ff., 205 f. After settling in a city a Jew did not have to wait a year and a day to achieve "freedom," as was required from a peasant serf, simply because he had never really been unfree. For the same reason the difference between "Stadtluft" and "Königsluft," as drawn by H. Strahm (in his "Mittelalterliche Stadtfreiheit," *Schweizer Beiträge zur allgemeinen Geschichte,* V, 77–113), hardly ever applied to him. See also H. Mitteis, "Ueber den Rechtsgrund des Satzes 'Stadtluft macht frei'," *Festschrift Edmund E. Stengel,* pp. 342–58; and *supra,* Vol. IV, p. 274 n. 91.

24. K. Hegel, ed., *Die Chroniken der deutschen Städte,* I (Nuremberg), 25 f., 113 ff.; Stobbe, *Die Juden in Deutschland,* pp. 57, 134 f., 224 n. 65, 252 n. 127; J. S. Menczel, *Beiträge,* p. 36 (a payment of 12 gulden by Joselin of Mayence is mentioned in the Frankfort municipal account book for 1367; see I. Kracauer, *Urkundenbuch,* I, 227); H. J. Zimmels, *Beiträge zur Geschichte der Juden in Deutschland im 13. Jahrhundert insbesondere auf Grund der Gutachten des R. Meir Rothenburg,* p. 2 (discussing the earlier biographical studies of R. Meir by S. Back and J. Wellesz). On the domestic objectives of the urban leagues, see esp. K. Czok, "Städtebünde und Zunftkämpfe in ihren Beziehungen während des 14. und 15. Jahrhunderts," *Wissenschaftliche Zeitschrift der . . . Universität Leipzig,* Ges. Reihe, VI, 517–42 (with special reference to the Oberlausitz); and, more fully, in his 1957 Leipzig diss. (typescript). The Swabian treaty of 1385, it may be noted, with its numerous extraordinary provisions, related to many important Jewish communities, including Augsburg, Nuremberg, and Ulm. The Jews' "burghers' rights" in Worms and elsewhere and their equivocal meaning will be more fully discussed *infra,* Chap. XLVII.

25. See Azriel b. Yeḥiel's (?) *Haggahot Mordecai* (Mordecai Glosses) on Qiddushin, No. 561, in the Vilna Talmud and Alfasi ed., fol. 5a. According to U. Grotefend (in his *Geschichte,* p. 52) Jews were forbidden to settle in Pomeranian villages. If true, this seems to have been an exception, Grotefend himself admitting that many Jews lived from peddling which doubtless presupposed at least their tempo-

rary residence in rural districts. On the relations of such outlying Jewish homesteads to the main communities, see my remarks in *The Jewish Community*, I, 281 ff., III, 65 ff. (largely based upon early modern sources). These suggestions are made here with considerable diffidence, because the extant sources are almost totally silent with respect to rural Jews in medieval Europe. However, considering how little is known about the large masses of the Christian peasantry, unless they are mentioned in some chance document preserved in urban archives or reported by ecclesiastical chroniclers, this lack of pertinent Jewish information is not at all surprising.

26. H. Planitz, *Die Deutsche Stadt in Mittelalter*, pp. 131, 396; *Annales Erphorden-ses ad* 1241, ed. by G. H. Pertz in *MGH*, Scriptores, XVI, 34; Matthew Paris, *Chronica majora*, ed. by Luard, IV, 131 f.; J. F. Böhmer, *Regesta imperii, 1246–1313*, Reichssachen, p. 357 No. 88; Aronius, *Regesten*, pp. 226 ff. Nos. 529 and 531, 291 No. 706; and other documents reproduced by I. Kracauer in his *Urkundenbuch zur Geschichte der Juden in Frankfurt am Main von 1150–1400*, I; and his "Die Politische Geschichte der Frankfurter Juden bis zum Jahre 1349," *Beilage zum Programm des Philanthropins*, Ostern, 1911, pp. 1–46. Kracauer again reviewed the developments up to 1349 briefly, and discussed the subsequent evolution in greater detail and with fuller documentation, in his *Geschichte der Juden in Frankfurt a. M.*, Vol. I. He also collaborated with A. Freimann in a succinct summary in the English volume, *Frankfort*, translated by B. S. Levin for the "Jewish Community Series." On the sudden outbreaks in 1241 see H. Grotefend, "Die Frankfurter Judenschlacht von 1241," *Mitteilungen* of the Verein für Geschichte und Altertumskunde in Frankfurt a. M., VI, 60–66; M. Horovitz, *Frankfurter Rabbinen*, p. v (German), App. pp. 45 f. (Hebrew); H. Bresslau, "Juden und Mongolen 1241," *ZGJD*, [o.s.] I, 99–102; II, 382–83; and *infra*, Chaps. XLII and L.

27. See the documents in J. F. Böhmer and F. Lau, eds., *Codex diplomaticus Moenofrancofurtanus*, I, 510; II, 310 No. 415, 460 No. 610; Wiener, *Regesten*, pp. 35 ff. Nos. 81, 112, 113, 118, 153 and 156; Kracauer, *Urkundenbuch*, p. 37 No. 108; his *Geschichte*, I, 26 ff. On the city's unusual intervention in behalf of the Jews who still were under clear imperial authority, see the various suggestions discussed by Kracauer in "Die Politische Geschichte," p. 15 n. 3. It appears that while Louis held his memorable diet in the city of Frankfort in 1338, in which he took up the cudgel against the Papacy's pretensions to interfere in German elections, he was also approached by the local Jews whom he always favored more than any other community in the Empire. It is small wonder, then, that despite his endless fiscal demands Jews mourned his passing very deeply, at least if we are to believe the contemporary chronicler, Mathias von Neuenburg in his *Chronica* according to the version of the Vienna MS ed. by A. Hofmeister, 2d ed., pp. 425 ff. See Kracauer, "Die Politische Geschichte," pp. 26 ff.; and, on the author of the *Yalqut, supra*, Vol. VI, pp. 161 f., 404 n. 11. The death of Eliezer b. Joel in Frankfort, and even his residence there at any time, are somewhat doubtful. He is only recorded there as a visitor arranging for the redemption of some Jewish captives. See A. (V.) Aptowitzer in his *Mabo le-Sefer Rabiah* (Introduction to the Book Rabiah by R. Eliezer b. Joel ha-Levi), p. 14.

28. Kracauer, *Urkundenbuch*, esp. pp. 50 ff. No. 141 (1349), 69 No. 174 (1360), 95 No. 234 (1372); idem, "Die Politische Geschichte," pp. 43 f. (reproducing Charles IV's deed of mortgage of 1349); idem, *Geschichte der Juden in Frankfurt a. M.*, I,

41 ff., 135 ff. The Black Death massacre had made such an impression in Frankfort
that some persons began dating particular events *anno Judenschlacht.* According to
G. L. Kriegk, Jews returned in 1356–57. See his *Frankfurter Bürgerzwiste und
Zustände im Mittelalter,* pp. 425 f., 545 f. n. 231. This suggestion, which would place
that return closer to those to Erfurt, Nuremberg (see *infra,* nn. 33 and 37), Rothenburg, and Augsburg (1353–55), was effectively controverted, however, by J. Gold-
schmidt in "Die Rückkehr der Juden nach Frankfurt am Main im Jahre 1360,"
*ZGJD,* [o.s.] II, 154–71; and Kracauer in his *Geschichte,* p. 47 n. 5. In any case, the
1390 cancellation of debts showed how deeply indebted the various classes of the
population had been to the Frankfort returnees. Among the debtors appeared 7
churchmen, led by Archbishop Conrad of Mayence himself who owed 1,000 guilders;
63 nobles, including Duke Rupert the Elder of the Palatinate; a number of peasants
in the environs of Frankfort; and particularly burghers from many cities as far away
as Worms and Augsburg. See the texts reproduced in Kracauer's *Urkundenbuch,* esp.
pp. 162 ff. No. 403, rearranged according to the names of creditors in his *Geschichte,*
I, 412 ff. App. i. See also *ibid.,* pp. 61 ff.; and A. Süssmann, *Die Judenschuldentilgungen,* pp. 128 ff.

29. See the analysis of the extant Frankfort *Stättigkeiten* in Kracauer's *Geschichte,*
I, 445 ff. App. vi. This extraordinary mobility of Frankfort Jewry well mirrors
the general instability of Jewish life under divided sovereignties, aggravated by
the unceasing internal conflicts in the city. Not only was Frankfort affected by the
perennial drive of the industrial guilds, those sworn enemies of Jews, to displace the
patrician control over the city council, but the city was often drawn into similar
struggles in the electoral capital of Mayence. See J. Fischer, "Frankfurt und die
Bürgerunruhen in Mainz," *Beiträge zur Geschichte der Stadt Mainz,* XV; and W.
Becht, *Die Entwicklung der alten Zunft im 14. und 15. Jahrhundert dargestellt an
den Frankfurter Zunft- und Gesellenurkunden, 1355–1525.* Mobility also accounted
in a large measure for the fitful changes in the size of the Jewish population (see
note 30), whose smallness was long ago noted by G. L. Kriegk in his *Frankfurter
Bürgerzwiste,* p. 426; and, following him, by O. Stobbe in *Die Juden,* p. 231 n. 88. See
also K. Bücher's older but still authoritative study of *Die Bevölkerung von Frankfurt
am Main im 14. und 15. Jahrhundert,* Vol. I, esp. pp. 526–601.

30. G. Florian and A. A. von Lersner, *Der Welt-berühmten Freyen Reichs- Wahl-
und Handels-Stadt Frankfurt am Mayn Chronica,* I, 263 f.; Kracauer, *Geschichte,
passim.* From time to time the council also had to protect its Jews against assaults by
powerful debtors, some of whom had been disappointed by Wenceslaus' and
Rupert's pledges not to cancel further debts owed to Jews. Occasionally a noble took
matters into his own hands. For instance, one Ludwig von Waldeck, engaged in a
controversy with a Frankfort Jew, Hirsch, over a house claimed by Von Waldeck as
his property, issued in 1449 a "letter of feud" *(Fehdebrief)* not only against Hirsch
but against all Frankfort Jews. This threat was reinforced by similar hostile declarations of Waldeck's noble friends. The matter was settled judicially, as suggested by
Hirsch, but only after the city council had propitiated the feuding nobles with
substantial *douceurs.* Needless to say, the Jews recompensed the council for its
outlays. Kracauer, *Geschichte,* I, 188 f. On the Frankfort ghetto, whose location may
be seen on the city map reproduced (from Püschel) by H. Planitz in *Die Deutsche
Stadt,* p. 240, and the Reuchlin-Pfefferkorn controversy in so far as it affected that

community, see *supra*, Chap. XXXVII, n. 38; and *infra*, Chap. LVII. See also, more generally, K. Nahrgang's topographical study of *Die Frankfurter Alstadt.*

31. Aronius, *Regesten*, pp. 105 No. 227, 158 No. 355, 171 No. 384, 225 No. 527, 298 No. 717, 321 No. 761; E. Mummenhof and J. Scherer, *Denkmäler der deutschen Poesie und Prosa*, 2d ed., p. 240 (see *supra*, Chap. XXXVII, nn. 45–46); L. Zunz, *Die Ritus des synagogalen Gottesdienstes*, p. 127 (the fast day of Sivan 25); and other data assembled by A. Jaraczewsky in *Die Geschichte der Juden in Erfurt;* and by A. Kroner in his "Geschichte der Juden in Erfurt," *Festschrift zur Einweihung der Synagoge in Erfurt*. The Erfurt Municipal Archive possessed an earlier MS by B. Hartung, *Beiträge zu einer Geschichte der Juden in Erfurt* which was utilized by A. Süssmann in his work (cited *infra*, n. 33, p. 79 n. 7), but its nature is not otherwise described. Interesting additional material is to be found in S. Neufeld, *Die Juden im thüringisch-sächsischen Gebiet, passim;* and in several other studies relating to the neighboring Jewish communities in the archbishopric of Magdeburg and the Saxon principalities, mentioned *supra*, Chap. XL, nn. 60–61. See also H. Stern, *Geschichte der Juden in Nordhausen*. The remarkable epigraphic sources for early Erfurt Jewry long ago attracted the attention of scholars. As early as 1799, J. J. Bellermann devoted to them a special study, *De inscriptionibus hebraicis Erfordiae repertis*. His frequent misreadings have since been corrected by Jaraczewsky and Kroner.

32. *Chronica S. Petri Erfordensis*, ed. by O. Holder-Egger in *MGH*, Scriptores, XXX, Part 1, pp. 435, 442; the German version thereof in the Thuringian continuation of the *Sächsiche Weltchronik*, ed. by L. Weiland, in *MGH*, Deutsche Chroniken, II, 309, 312; Jaraczewsky, *Die Geschichte der Juden in Erfurt*, pp. 17 ff. Intellectually, too, leaders of the community of Erfurt must have played a sufficiently important role in the thirteenth century to be cited among the rabbinic authorities who decided that Jewish newcomers to a locality must share in its established communal taxes, rather than make independent arrangements with its rulers. Obviously this was a vital decision for the preservation of communal discipline. See Meir b. Baruch, *Resp.*, Lwów, 1860 ed., fol. 6a No. 108, and other sources cited by I. A. Agus in his *Rabbi Meir of Rothenburg*, II, 505 No. 551.

33. Wiener, *Regesten*, pp. 133 No. 229, 138 No. 260, 247 f. Nos. 222, 229 and 231; *Deutsche Reichstagsakten*, published by the Historische Kommission of the Bavarian Academy of Science, XI, 298 f., 313 No. 171; D. Kerler, "Zur Geschichte der Besteuerung der Juden," *ZGJD*, [o.s.] III, 123 ff., 127 ff.; Jaraczewsky, *Geschichte*, pp. 47 f. (translation of Sigismund's decree of 1417), 58 f., 86 ff. To the earlier data assembled by Jaraczewsky and Kroner were added those included in the *Liber Judeorum*, apparently so called in the early fifteenth century when it seems to have been put together from loose earlier entries. This MS was reproduced by A. Süssmann in *Das Erfurter Judenbuch (1357–1407)*.

34. See Jaraczewsky, *passim*. The richness and diversity of Jewish communal life in Erfurt in the first half century after its reconstruction is well illustrated by its three synagogues, a bathhouse, a dancing house (*domus tripudialis;* this was in fact a general-purpose communal building resembling a modern Jewish center), as well as a bakery, a women's school (*Frouwinschule*), and public toilets. There also existed, of course, a cemetery. Not mentioned in the *Judenbuch*, but evidenced from other

sources, was a Jewish hospital. See the entries listed by Süssmann in *Das Erfurter Judenbuch*, pp. 18 f.; and, on the legislation concerning Jewish clothing, his observations, p. 70 n. 1. See also Jaraczewsky, *Geschichte*, pp. 70 ff.; Neufeld, *Die Juden im thüringish-sächsischen Gebiet*, I, 27 f. These communal institutions, as well as a rabbinical assembly which took place in Erfurt in 1391, and the question of Jewish books left behind by the exiles of 1458, which by Frederick III's order of 1483 were to be sold at a low price to a Jew, Levi (Wiener, *Regesten*, p. 251 No. 244), will be more fully discussed in later chapters.

35. Sigmund Meisterlin, *Nieronbergensis chronica*, iii. 14–15, ed. by K. Hegel and D. Kerler in *Die Chroniken der deutschen Städte*, III, 146 ff.; and Hegel's comments on "Der Aufstand zu Nürnberg im Jahr 1348," *ibid.*, pp. 317 ff. (see *supra*, Vol. IV, pp. 117, 299 n. 37); S. Salfeld, *Das Martyrologium*, pp. 61 ff. (Hebrew), 219 ff. (German; with the bibliographical note, pp. 229 f.); and the more general surveys by Stobbe in *Die Juden in Deutschland*, pp. 49 ff.; H. Barbeck in his *Geschichte der Juden in Nürnberg und Fürth*; E. Mummenhof in "Die Juden in Nürnberg bis zu ihrer Austreibung im Jahre 1499" (1908), and "Die Juden in Nürnberg bis zu ihrer Vertreibung im Jahre 1499 in topographischer und kulturhistorischer Beziehung" (1908), reprinted in his *Gesammelte Aufsätze und Vorträge*, I, 301–34 and 335–66. See also S. Schwarzfuchs, "Mordecai ben Hillel et le judaïsme allemand," *REJ*, CXII, 43–52. Many of these data are derived from sources assembled as far back as 1755 by the Nuremberg pastor, Andreas Würfel, who published at that time his *Historische Nachrichten von der Judengemeinde, welche ehehin in der Reichsstadt Nürnberg angericht gewesen aber Ao. 1499 ausgeschaffet worden*, esp. pp. 129 ff. Nos. vii-xv. See also the additional source material summarized in the *Nürnberger Urkundenbuch*, whose publication by the city council of Nuremberg has been under way since 1951; and, from another angle, J. Podro's sharp condemnation of *Nuremberg: the Unholy City*.

36. Wiener, *Regesten*, pp. 40 No. 110, 127 No. 188; *Urkundenbuch der Stadt Nürnberg*, p. 445 No. 761; A. F. Oefele, *Rerum boicarum scriptores*, I, 743 (decree of 1333). The substantial size of the Nuremberg community is evidenced not only by the numerous victims of the massacres of 1298 and 1349, but also by the amounts collected from Jews by the imperial and other officials. As pointed out by Stobbe (p. 53), Jews were told in 1347 to set aside a sum of 1,000 pounds heller annually for the burgrave and another 200 pounds for the city to help defray the cost of lumber for the royal castle. These amounts, but a part of the Jewish contribution, contrasted with the total of 2,000 pounds paid by the city to the imperial Treasury. These payments were made before the inflationary forces greatly reduced the value of silver coins in relation to gold and when a pound groschen still was valued at about a gold florin. Nonetheless the city tried to stem the further growth of the Jewish community and the Jews' acquisition of houses from Christians. See H. Barbeck, *Geschichte der Juden in Nürnberg und Fürth* pp. 2 f.; and, on the impact on the Jews of the growing inflation and of the political ascendency of the artisan guilds, *infra*, Chaps. LI and LIII.

37. Wiener, *Regesten*, pp. 53 f. No. 4, 131 ff. Nos. 214, 216, 237, 258, 315 and 385; the fuller texts in Würfel, *Historische Nachrichten*, pp. 134 No. xv; *Singularia Norimbergensia*, p. 372; and M. Stern, *König Ruprecht von der Pfalz*, pp. 1 ff. No. 3, with

Stern's comments thereon, pp. xiv f. On the internal changes in Nuremberg's municipal administration, see E. Reicke, *Geschichte der Reichsstadt Nürnberg*, pp. 220 ff.; P.
Sander, *Die Reichsstädtische Haushaltung Nürnbergs*, pp. 48 ff.; and D. Kerler in
*ZGJD*, [o.s.] III, 123 ff., 127 ff. Because of the size and wealth of the Nuremberg
community, the cancellations of debts in 1385 and 1390 yielded the city a net profit
of some 60,000 and 2,400 florins, respectively. See K. Hegel's remarks in his ed. of *Die
Chroniken der deutschen Städte*, I (Nuremberg), 25 f., 121 ff., 128. Many years later
Nuremberg still insisted on its "rights" to collect on the loans of the unfortunate
Jewish creditors. It appears that a Jewish widow and her sons failed to deliver their
writs of indebtedness and later succeeded in bringing them to Italian Treviso. Somewhat brazenly, they tried to collect these debts in 1409. The city reacted strongly,
suing the Jewish family before the imperial court for damages amounting to 2,000
gold marks. It easily won its case, and secured from Rupert an imperial ban on the
creditors and the right to seize their Nuremberg properties up to the full yield of
2,000 marks. See the texts reproduced by M. Stern, pp. 59 ff. Nos. 72–75: and A.
Süssman, *Die Judenschuldentilgungen*, pp. 121 ff.

38. Würfel, *Historische Nachrichten*, esp. pp. 83 ff., 96, 148 ff. Nos. xxxviii-xlii;
Wiener, *Regesten*, pp. 79 No. 9, 87 No. 58, 190 ff. Nos. 556, 566, 677 and 694–701.
Sigismund's liberal law of 1416 was further amplified by his *Freibrief* of 1421, which
was to be in force for ten years. See Wiener, pp. 177 f. No. 497, 184 f. No. 530. The
new municipal code of 1479–84 included a lengthy and degrading formula of the
Jewish oath, which was repeated in the new editions of 1488, 1499, and even 1503,
although the Jews had interveningly been expelled from the city. The oath was first
deleted in the new impression of 1522, the other anti-Jewish articles in that of
1564. This was not sheer conservatism, for a few Jews received temporary residence
permits during the sixteenth century. Thus the humanistic preacher, Andreas
Osiander, persuaded the city council in 1529 to allow a Jew from neighboring
Schnaittach to reside in the city and to teach him Hebrew. Otherwise, most
sixteenth-century records refer only to Jews who had come to Nuremberg to accept
baptism. See Barbeck, *Geschichte*, pp. 24 ff. (citing the text of the Jewish oath), 38 f.
"Die Ausweisung der Juden von Nürnberg im Jahre 1499" is described by H. C. B.
Briegleb in *Jeschurun*, ed. by J. Kobak, VI, 1–27 (includes a somewhat revised text
of Maximilian I's decree of expulsion of July 21, 1498, pp. 12 ff., compared with
Würfel, pp. 152 ff. No. xlii). See also *infra*, Chap. L.

39. See *supra*, Vol. IV, pp. 67, 71 f., 100, 175 f., 272 n. 86, 274 n. 92, 325 f. n. 31;
Aronius, *Regesten*, pp. 57 No. 135 (981), 64 No. 150 (1006–28), 166 No. 374 (1207), 180
No. 403 (1216), 197 f. No. 448 (1230), 201 f. No. 459 (1233), 237 No. 549 (1244), 248 f.
No. 582 (1251); Benjamin, *Massa'ot*, *loc. cit.* (*supra*, Chap. XL, n. 56); Wiener,
*Regesten*, pp. 4 No. 19, 8 No. 40, 110 n. 45; M. Stern, "Aus der älteren Geschichte
der Juden in Regensburg," *ZGJD*, [o.s.] I, 383–86; A. Schmetzer, "Die Regensburger
Judenstadt," *ibid.*, [n.s.] III, 18–39; and other sources discussed by S. Bromberger in
his Berlin dissertation *Die Juden in Regensburg bis zur Mitte des 14. Jahrhunderts*.
Interest in the history of Ratisbon Jewry has been kept alive for the last century and
a half by the rich materials included in C. T. Gemeiner's comprehensive work,
*Reichsstadt Regensburgische Chronik*, and first analyzed in 1837 by J. K. von Train
in "Die Wichtigsten Thatsachen aus der Geschichte der Juden in Regensburg von
ihrer Ansiedlung bis zu ihrer Vertreibung," *Zeitschrift für die historische Theologie*,

ed. by Illgen, VII, Part 3, pp. 39–138. True, the pre-Christian origin of the community allegedly reaching back to 300 B.C.E. has long been relegated into the limbo of legend. But no medieval Jew or Christian ever expressed doubts regarding this claim, which the Jews were prepared to defend even in their formal petition of 1476 to Frederick III. The Jewish pleaders invoked the testimony of a letter allegedly sent to Ratisbon Jewry from Jerusalem, announcing the birth of Jesus. See Von Aretin, *Geschichte der Juden in Baiern*, pp. 6 f. This testimony appeared the less doubtful as even the more sober Western historians of the time often accepted similar fanciful legends and genealogies at their face value. See *supra*, Vol. VI, pp. 437 f. n. 92.

40. *Regensburger Urkundenbuch*, ed. by J. Widemann *et al.*, esp. I, 76 f. No. 148, 92 ff. Nos. 177 (the Vienna original of this document is illustrated by a "wide-rimmed hat with a hanging cord; on its point a bird; on both sides a half-moon and star, [also] a Hebrew legend") and 178, 323 No. 583, 533 No. 982, 552 No. 1003, 671 ff. No. 1250; II, 73 No. 179; Eberhard Archdiaconus, *Annales Ratisponenses, ad* 1298, ed. by P. Jaffe in *MGH*, Scriptores, XVII, 597; Wiener, *Regesten*, esp. pp. 117 ff. Nos. 92, 95, 132, 195, 291, 325, 345–49, 407–408, 479, 534–35 and 652–58; and other data analyzed by H. Fischer in *Die Verfassungsrechtliche Stellung*, esp. pp. 164 ff. Notes 1–3; and Bromberger, *Die Juden in Regensburg*, *passim*. The remarkable Jewish seal of 1297 is reproduced and interpreted in A. Altmann's *Geschichte der Juden in Salzburg*, pp. 54 ff., 266. Jews and their revenues were at times considered so valuable to the city that for instance in 1374 the council foiled an attempt of some Jews to leave; they had to promise that they would remain for at least twelve more years and renounce all contrary privileges of outside princes. This remarkable agreement was reinforced by the signatures of the Jewish communal elders, the two justices of the Jews, and the bishop. In 1384, before the expiration of that term, Gnendl, one of the richest Ratisbon bankers, tried to move elsewhere but was prevented from doing so by the city. He and his son, Chalman, were made to promise that they would continue living and paying taxes in Ratisbon for the following four years. See Gemeiner, *Reichsstadt Regensburgische Chronik*, II, 168, 174, 213 (Wiener, pp. 139 No. 270, 149 No. 322).

41. Meir b. Baruch, *Resp.*, Prague, 1608 ed., fol. 96abc No. 946 (Budapest, 1895 ed., fol. 134d No. 946). On the frequency of such marital discords, see also *ibid.*, fols. 31ab No. 228, 36bc No. 261, 49d f. Nos. 442–43 (Budapest ed. fols. 33a No. 228, 40d f. No. 261, 62c ff. Nos. 442–43). The internal evolution of the Jewish community and its intellectual eminence are briefly described by A. Freimann in "Regensburg," *Germania Judaica*, I, 285–305 (also in the second instalment of his "Vorarbeiten" thereto in *MGWJ*, LIII, 589–615). On the Ratisbon synagogue and its foundation by Yehudah he-Ḥasid (the Pious), see Moses b. Isaac ha-Levi Menz, *Resp.*, Lwów 1850 ed., fol. 70a No. lxxvi; R. Krautheimer, *Mittelalterliche Synagogen*, pp. 179, 270 n. 167 (doubting Menz's attribution but conceding the completion of the synagogue in 1227, some ten years after Yehudah's death); *supra*, Vols. VI, pp. 222 ff.; VIII, pp. 42 ff. Jewish security was doubtless enhanced also by Ratisbon's relatively stable regime in the hands of a few patrician families and by the decline in the political, if not the spiritual, influence of the clergy. Even more than elsewhere members of the same wealthy families occupied important posts in Ratisbon's municipal administration generation after generation; some of them for two centuries and longer. On the other hand, while preachers of the rank of Berthold of Ratisbon (died in 1272)

exerted great influence upon the public (see *supra*, Chap. XXXVIII, n. 1), politically the power of the bishop constantly declined and the clergy's contributions to the political life of the city became ever more circumscribed. See Planitz, *Die Deutsche Stadt*, pp. 270 f.; F. Morrés's Berlin dissertation, *Ratsverfassung und Patriziat in Regensburg bis 1400;* and more fully in the 1935 *Verhandlungen* of the Historischer Verein für Regensburg und Oberpfalz; and T. Liegel's Munich dissertation, *Reichs-stadt Regensburg und Klerus im Kampf um ihre Rechte* (typescript). See also the studies listed in note 42.

42. Gemeiner, *Reichsstadt Regenburgische Chronik*, III, 567 ff., 589 ff., 602 ff. (esp. No. 1215), 616 ff., 640 ff., 649 ff.; IV, 33 ff., 354 ff., etc.; Wiener, *Regesten*, p. 208 No. 690. Peter Schwartz (Nigri), who repeatedly preached to the Jews in Hebrew, doubtless advanced the same arguments as those he employed in his polemical works, *Tractatus contra Judaeos;* and *Stern des Messias*, published in Esslingen in 1475 and 1477. In the same vein he also wrote his *Erklärung der Psalmen nach dem Urtext*. The important blood libel of 1476, the ensuing trial, and negotiations with Frederick III, are analyzed with full documentation by M. Stern in *Der Regens-burger Judenprozess 1476–1480* (revised from his previous article under the same title in *JJLG*, XVIII, 363–86; XX, 157–79). See also his "Aus Regensburg. Urkund-liche Mitteilungen," *JJLG*, XXIII, 1–123; and the literature relating to Bavaria listed *supra*, n. 13.

43. Matthias Döring, cited *supra*, Chap. XL, n. 39. The story of the Ratisbon community during the last century has become relatively well known through the extensive materials extant in the local archives, which have been fully utilized by R. Straus in *Die Judengemeinde Regensburg im ausgehenden Mittelalter, auf Grund der Quellen kritisch untersucht und neu dargestellt*. Its documentary appendix of 464 pages, in print in the 1930s, was suppressed by the Nazis. But a new edition was reconstructed from a few surviving copies; it was revised and published in 1960 by the Historical Commission of the Bavarian Academy of Science under the title, *Urkunden und Aktenstücke zur Geschichte der Juden in Regensburg 1453–1738*. Straus's original material was interveningly used, however, for an antisemitic presentation of the struggle between the city and the Jews during the seven decades preceding the expulsion, by W. Grau in his *Antisemitismus im späten Mittelalter. Das Ende der Regensburger Judengemeinde 1450–1519*, 2d ed. On the antecedents of this volume, see esp. Straus's "Foreword" to his English volume, *Regensburg and Augsburg*, trans. from the German by F. N. Gerson, p. x. By contrasting the history of the Jews in Ratisbon with that of Augsburg (and, to a lesser extent, of Munich) this briefer English version succeeds in underscoring certain peculiarities of each. See also Straus's necessarily far more restrained reply to Grau in his "Antisemitismus im Mittelalter. Ein Wort pro domo," *ZGJD*, VI, 17–24. On the aftermath of the expulsion from Ratisbon and Charles V's ultimate forgiveness in 1521 of the city's arbitrary act, see Straus's *Urkunden*, pp. 404 ff. Nos. 1096–97, 417 No. 1113.

Not surprisingly, during the 1930s many other Nazi historians, too, evinced con-siderable interest in the history of Jews in Germany. Apart from such exponents of a general revaluation of the Jewish past as G. Kittel and W. Grau (see *supra*, Vol. II, p. 406 n. 42) there were numerous writers on local history. Most of these mono-graphs reveal a strong Nazi bias and always have to be used with caution. Neverthe-less some may be consulted with profit, particularly on account of data, partly archival, supplied by them for the first time. Apart from the studies mentioned here in various other contexts, the following arranged in alphabetical order of their authors appear to be more or less relevant: W. Auener, "Die Juden im mittelalter-lichen Mühlhausen," *Mühlhäuser Geschichtsblätter*, XXXVI–XXXVII, 73–109; E. Gebele, *Die Juden in Schwaben* (reprinted from *Schwabenland*, V, 45–116); M. Krieg, "Die Juden in der Stadt Minden bis zum Stadtreglement von 1723," *Zeitschrift für vaterländische Geschichte und Altertumskunde Westfalens*, XCIII, Pt. 2, pp. 113–96; G. Krusemarck, *Die Juden in Heilbronn*; G. A. Löning, "Juden im mittelalterlichen Bremen und Oldenburg," *Zeitschrift der Savigny–Stiftung für Rechtsgeschichte*, Germanistische Abteilung, LVIII, 257–74; M. Schütz, *Eine Reichsstadt wehrt sich. Rothenburg ob der Tauber im Kampf gegen das Judentum*. On the other hand, such studies as F. Debus, *Kaiser, Erzbischof und Juden. Eine Zusammenstellung von Tatsachen aus der Geschichte der Stadt Frankfurt am Main*, are pure Nazi propaganda and of interest merely as documentation for the operation of the Nazi mind. Many other examples have been assembled by M. Weinreich in his *Hitler's Professors*.

Many earlier and far more objective writings (up to 1930) have been reviewed in the bibliographical surveys by A. Kober, "Die Geschichte der deutschen Juden in der historischen Forschung der letzten 35 Jahre," *ZGJD*, I, 13–23; and Z. (H.) Lichtenstein, "Recent Literature on the History of the Jews in Germany (a Review)" (Hebrew), *Tarbiz*, II, 218–34. See also A. Freimann, *Katalog der Judaica und Hebraica, Stadtbibliothek Frankfurt a. M.*, Vol. I (listing the Judaica available in 1931 at the Municipal Library in Frankfort; the second volume which was to record the Hebraica was never published). Remarkably, despite, or perhaps because of, this plethora of monographic information there has not yet appeared a comprehensive, well-documented history of German Jewry. I. Elbogen, *Geschichte der Juden in Deutschland;* and M. Lowenthal, *The Jews of Germany. A Story of Sixteen Centuries*, were primarily intended for broader popular audiences. It is to be hoped, however, that the Leo Baeck Institute, whose *Yearbook* and other publications have recently contributed much to the knowledge of the modern history of German Jewry, may stimulate also some such comprehensive works relating to the Middle Ages. In the meantime it plans to publish a continuation of the *Germania Judaica*, the first volume of which in two parts, edited by M. Brann *et al.*, and published in 1917–34, has long served as a reference work for the history of the various German Jewish communities up to 1238.

44. A. F. Riedel, *Codex diplomaticus brandenburgensis*, 1st ser., XXIV, 32 ff., Nos. xlviii and lxiv; Heise, *Die Juden in . . . Brandenburg*, pp. 66 ff. (see *supra*, n. 17); *Das Rechtsbuch nach Distinctionen nebst einem Eisenachischen Rechtsbuch*, iii.17, 2, ed. by F. Ortloff, p. 168; *Reichspolizeiordnungen* of 1548 and 1577, discussed *infra*, Chap. LIX. On the correct version of the passage in the *Rechtsbuch nach Distinctionen*, see G. Kisch, *The Jews in Medieval Germany*, pp. 195, 457 n. 73. See also Aronius, *Regesten*, pp. 292 ff. No. 711. Typical of the innumerable enactments of German princes concerning their Jewish subjects is the text of a 1539 decree given in an English translation by E. Voss in "An Edict of Philip, by the Grace of God Landgrave of Hessia, Count of Catzenelenbogen, Dietz, Ziegenhain and Nidda—How and in Which Form the Jews From Now On Shall Be Tolerated and Treated in Our Principality and Our Countries and Dominions," *Transactions* of the Wisconsin Academy of Sciences, XXVI, 161–66.